SUZUKA

2

Kouji Seo

TRANSLATED AND ADAPTED BY
David Ury

LETTERED BY
Janice Chiang

DEL
REY

BALLANTINE BOOKS · NEW YORK

Suzuka volume 2 is a work of fiction. Names, characters, places, and incidents are the products of the author's imagination or are used fictitiously. Any resemblance to actual events, locales, or persons, living or dead, is entirely coincidental.

A Del Rey Trade Paperback Original

Published in the United States by Del Rey Books,
an imprint of The Random House Publishing Group,
a division of Random House, Inc., New York.

Publication rights arranged through Kodansha Ltd.

First published in Japan in 2004 by Kodansha Ltd., Tokyo

ISBN-10: 0-345-48632-3
ISBN-13: 978-0-345-48632-5

Printed in the United States of America

www.delreymanga.com

9 8 7 6 5 4 3 2 1

Translator/adaptor: David Ury
Lettering: Janice Chiang

Contents

A Note from the Author

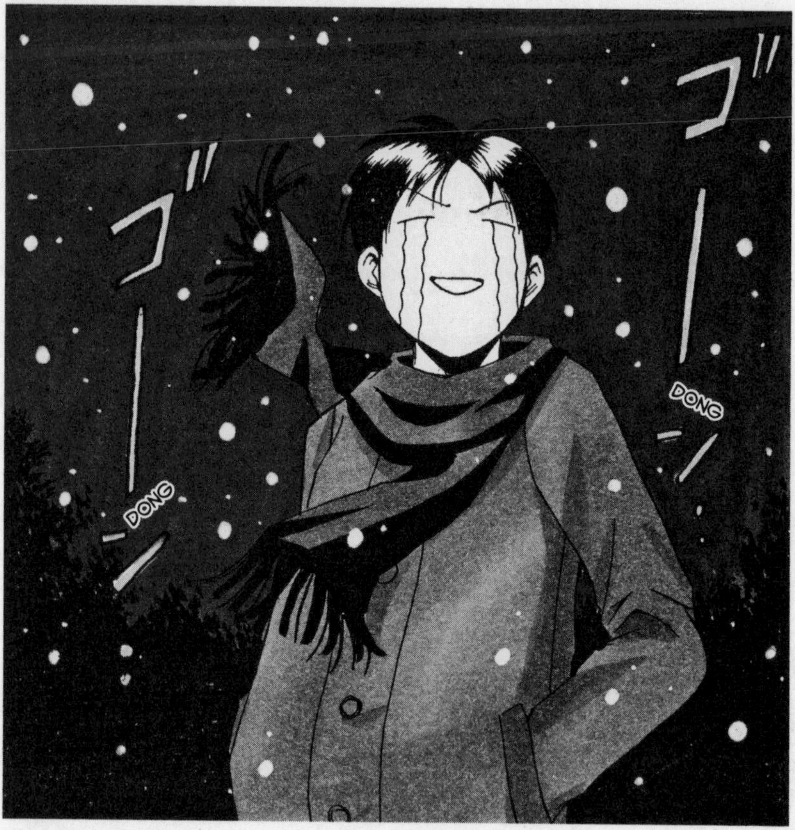
DONG
DONG

Pretty much everybody alive has suffered from heartbreak at least once or twice. I once confessed my love to a girl on New Year's Eve, only to be turned down on the spot. The next thing I knew they were ringing the New Year's bell...and it suddenly started snowing. My body and heart both went stone cold. It was the worst New Year's ever! Well, looking back, it doesn't seem so bad.

Honorifics Explained

Throughout the Del Rey Manga books, you will find Japanese honorifics left intact in the translations. For those not familiar with how the Japanese use honorifics and, more important, how they differ from American honorifics, we present this brief overview.

Politeness has always been a critical facet of Japanese culture. Ever since the feudal era, when Japan was a highly stratified society, use of honorifics—which can be defined as polite speech that indicates relationship or status—has played an essential role in the Japanese language. When addressing someone in Japanese, an honorific usually takes the form of a suffix attached to one's name (example: "Asuna-san"), is used as a title at the end of one's name, or appears in place of the name itself (example: "Negi-sensei," or simply "Sensei!").

Honorifics can be expressions of respect or endearment. In the context of manga and anime, honorifics give insight into the nature of the relationship between characters. Many translations into English leave out these important honorifics and therefore distort the "feel" of the original Japanese. Because Japanese honorifics contain nuances that English honorifics lack, it is our policy at Del Rey not to translate them. Here, instead, is a guide to some of the honorifics you may encounter in Del Rey Manga.

-san: This is the most common honorific and is equivalent to Mr., Miss, Ms., or Mrs. It is the all-purpose honorific and can be used in any situation where politeness is required.

-sama: This is one level higher than "-san." It is used to confer great respect.

-dono: This comes from the word "tono," which means "lord." It is an even higher level than "-sama" and confers utmost respect.

-kun: This suffix is used at the end of boys' names to express familiarity or endearment. It is also sometimes used by men among friends, or when addressing someone younger or of a lower station.

-chan: This is used to express endearment, mostly toward girls. It is also used for little boys, pets, and even among lovers. It gives a sense of childish cuteness.

Bozu: This is an informal way to refer to a boy, similar to the English terms "kid" and "squirt."

Sempai/
Senpai: This title suggests that the addressee is one's senior in a group or organization. It is most often used in a school setting, where underclassmen refer to their upperclassmen as "sempai." It can also be used in the workplace, such as when a newer employee addresses an employee who has seniority in the company.

Kohai: This is the opposite of "sempai" and is used toward underclassmen in school or newcomers in the workplace. It connotes that the addressee is of a lower station.

Sensei: Literally meaning "one who has come before," this title is used for teachers, doctors, or masters of any profession or art.

[blank]: This is usually forgotten in these lists, but it's perhaps the most significant difference between Japanese and English. The lack of honorific means that the speaker has permission to address the person in a very intimate way. Usually, only family, spouses, or very close friends have this kind of permission. Known as *yobisute,* it can be gratifying when someone who has earned the intimacy starts to call one by one's name without an honorific. But when that intimacy hasn't been earned, it can be very insulting.

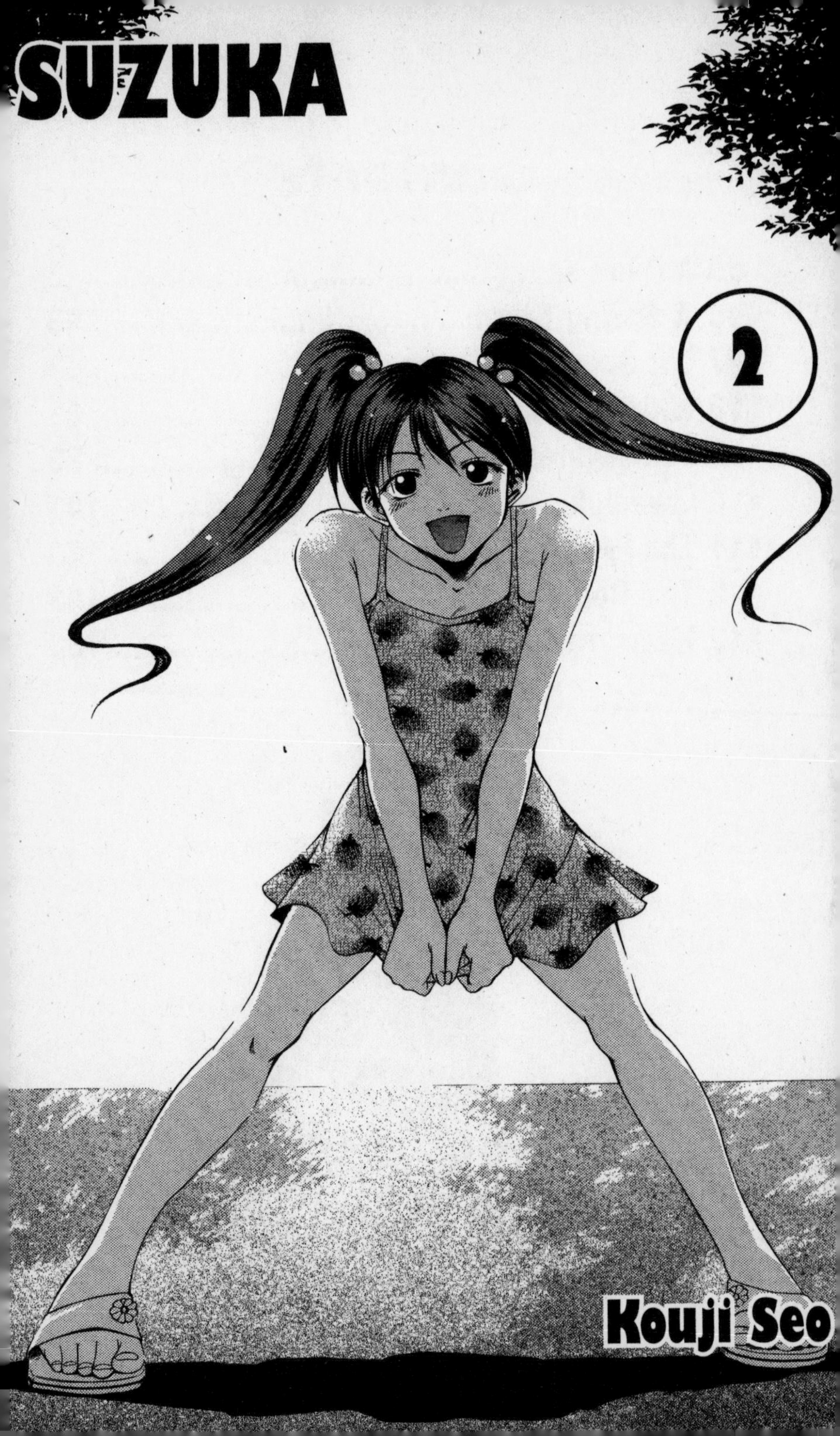
SUZUKA
2
Kouji Seo

Contents

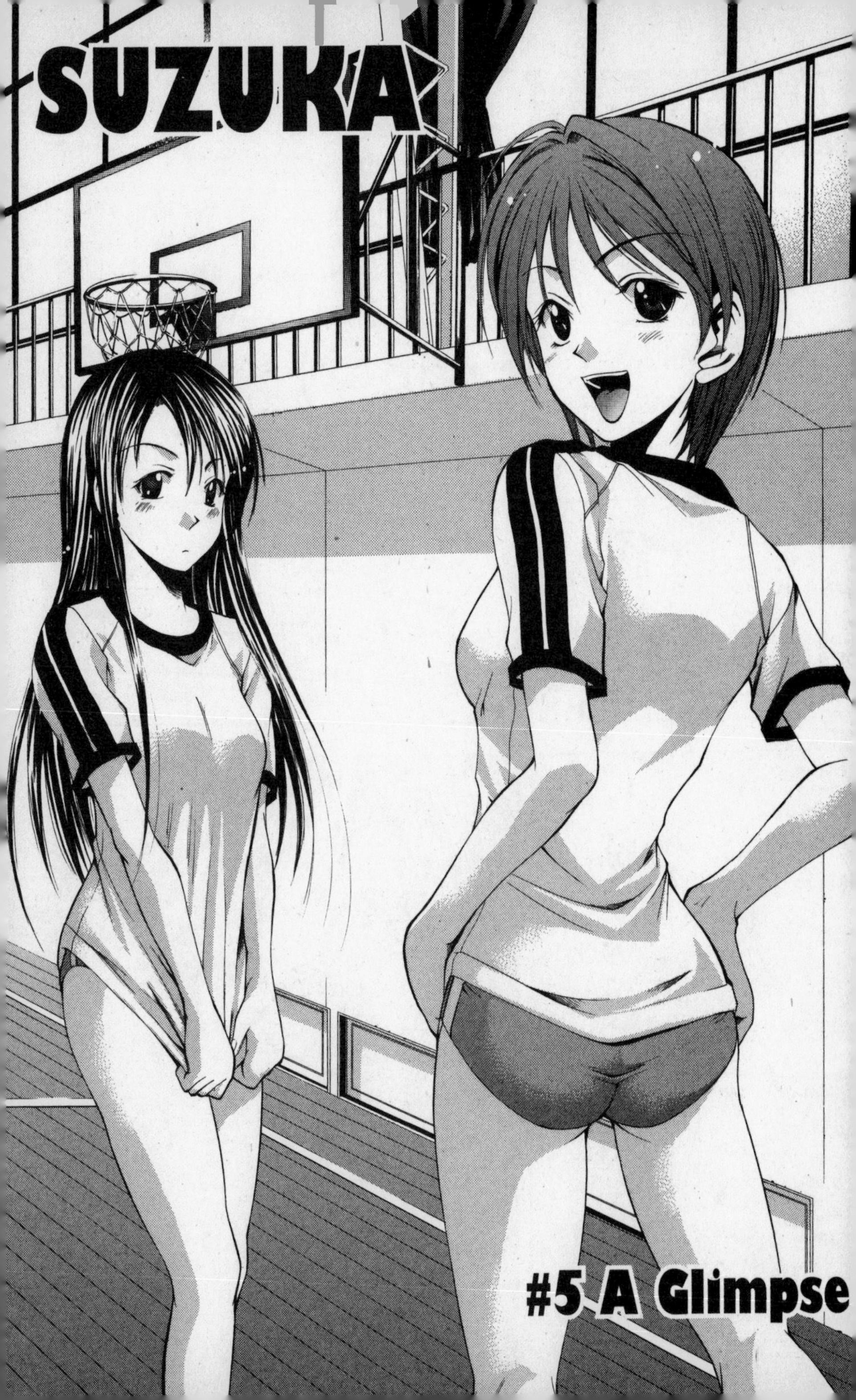
SUZUKA
#5 A Glimpse

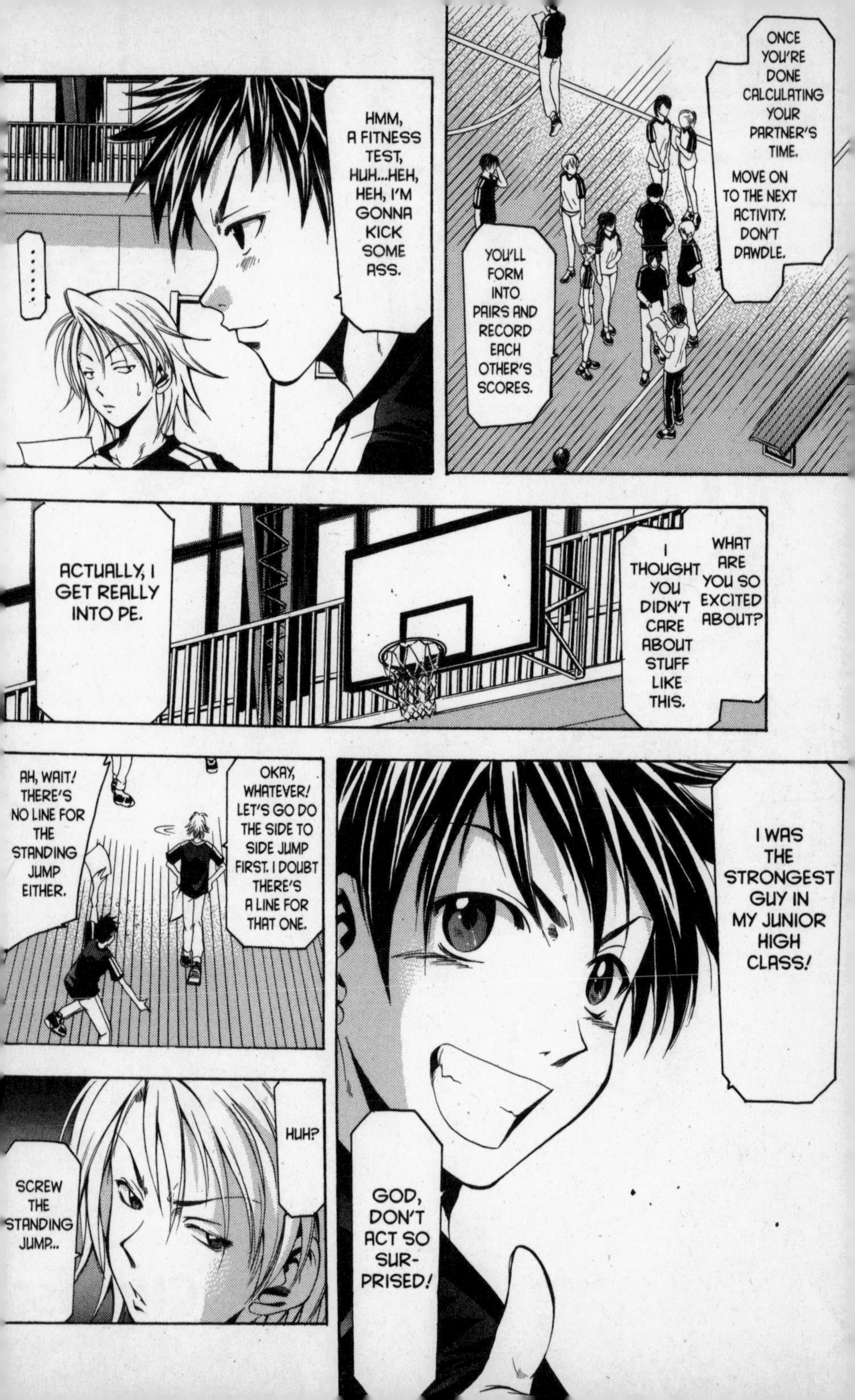
ONCE YOU'RE DONE CALCULATING YOUR PARTNER'S TIME.
MOVE ON TO THE NEXT ACTIVITY. DON'T DAWDLE.
YOU'LL FORM INTO PAIRS AND RECORD EACH OTHER'S SCORES.
HMM, A FITNESS TEST, HUH...HEH, HEH, I'M GONNA KICK SOME ASS.
......
WHAT ARE YOU SO EXCITED ABOUT?
I THOUGHT YOU DIDN'T CARE ABOUT STUFF LIKE THIS.
ACTUALLY, I GET REALLY INTO PE.
I WAS THE STRONGEST GUY IN MY JUNIOR HIGH CLASS!
GOD, DON'T ACT SO SUR-PRISED!
OKAY, WHATEVER! LET'S GO DO THE SIDE TO SIDE JUMP FIRST. I DOUBT THERE'S A LINE FOR THAT ONE.
AH, WAIT! THERE'S NO LINE FOR THE STANDING JUMP EITHER.
HUH?
SCREW THE STANDING JUMP...

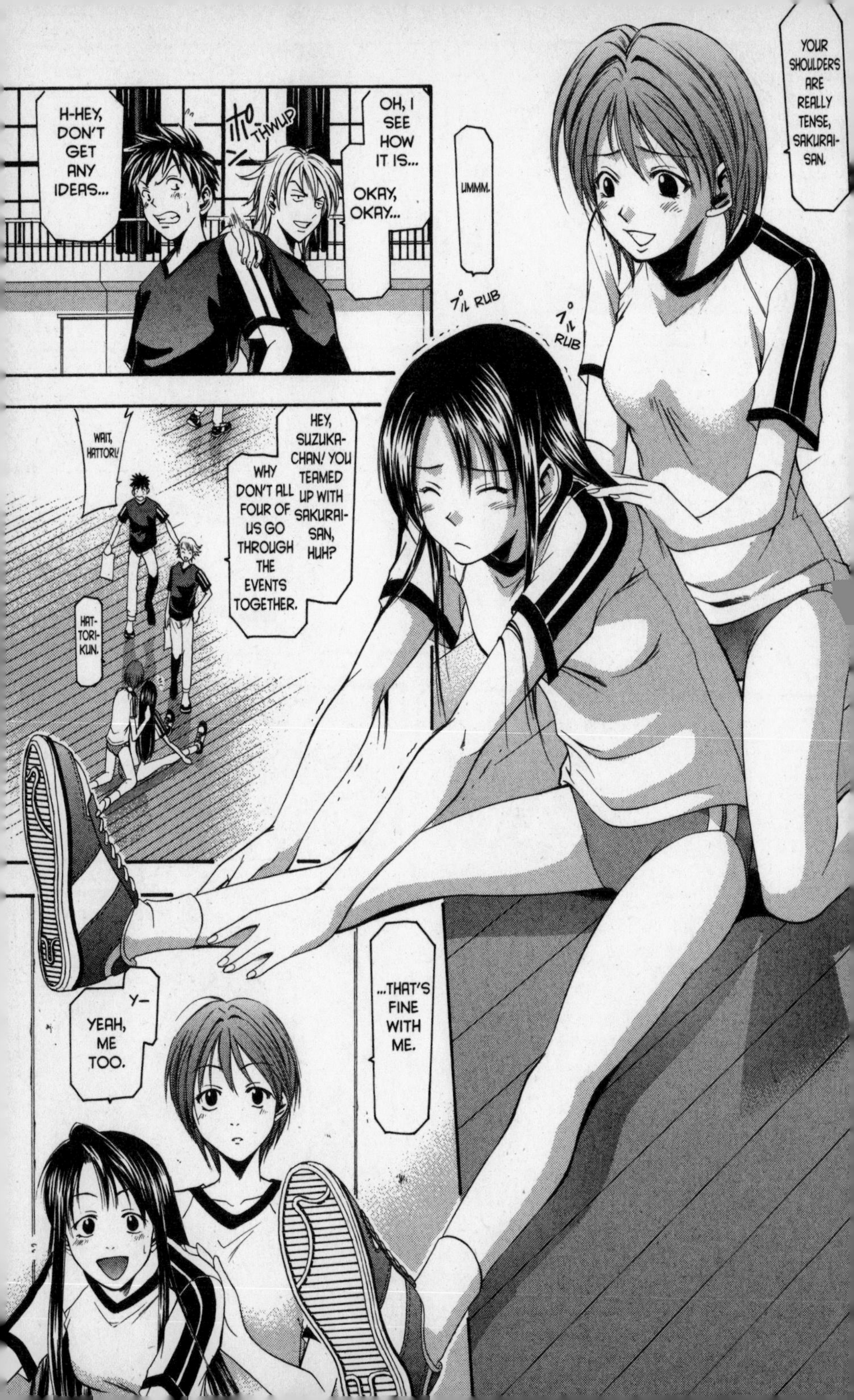
YOUR SHOULDERS ARE REALLY TENSE, SAKURAI-SAN.
UMMM.
RUB
RUB
OH, I SEE HOW IT IS... OKAY, OKAY...
THWUP
H-HEY, DON'T GET ANY IDEAS...
HEY, SUZUKA-CHAN! YOU TEAMED UP WITH SAKURAI-SAN, HUH?
WHY DON'T ALL FOUR OF US GO THROUGH THE EVENTS TOGETHER.
WAIT, HATTORI!
HATTORI-KUN.
...THAT'S FINE WITH ME.
Y— YEAH, ME TOO.

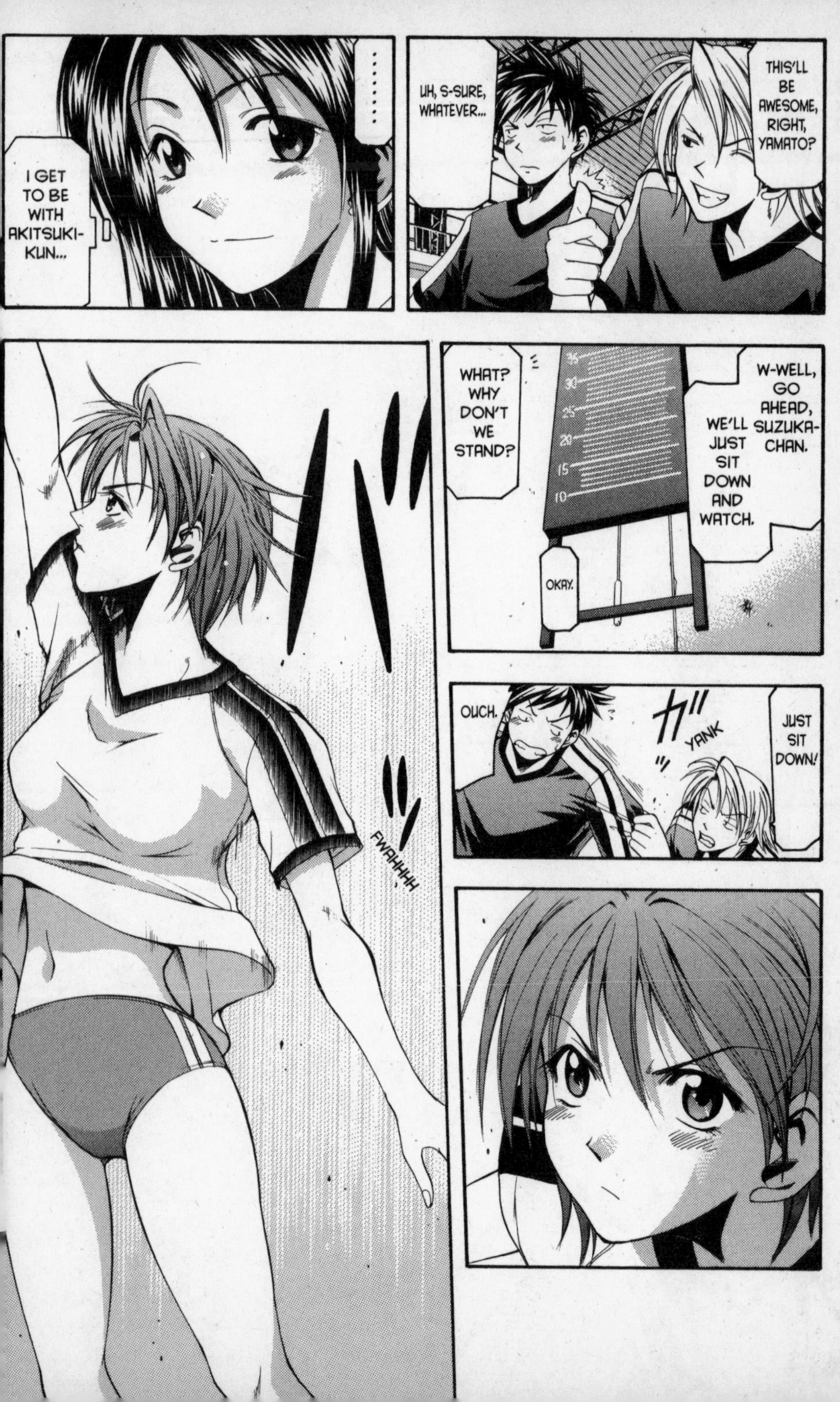
THIS'LL BE AWESOME, RIGHT, YAMATO?
UH, S-SURE, WHATEVER...
......
I GET TO BE WITH AKITSUKI-KUN...
W-WELL, GO AHEAD, SUZUKA-CHAN.
WE'LL JUST SIT DOWN AND WATCH.
WHAT? WHY DON'T WE STAND?
OKAY.
JUST SIT DOWN!
ガ
YANK
OUCH.
FWAHHHH

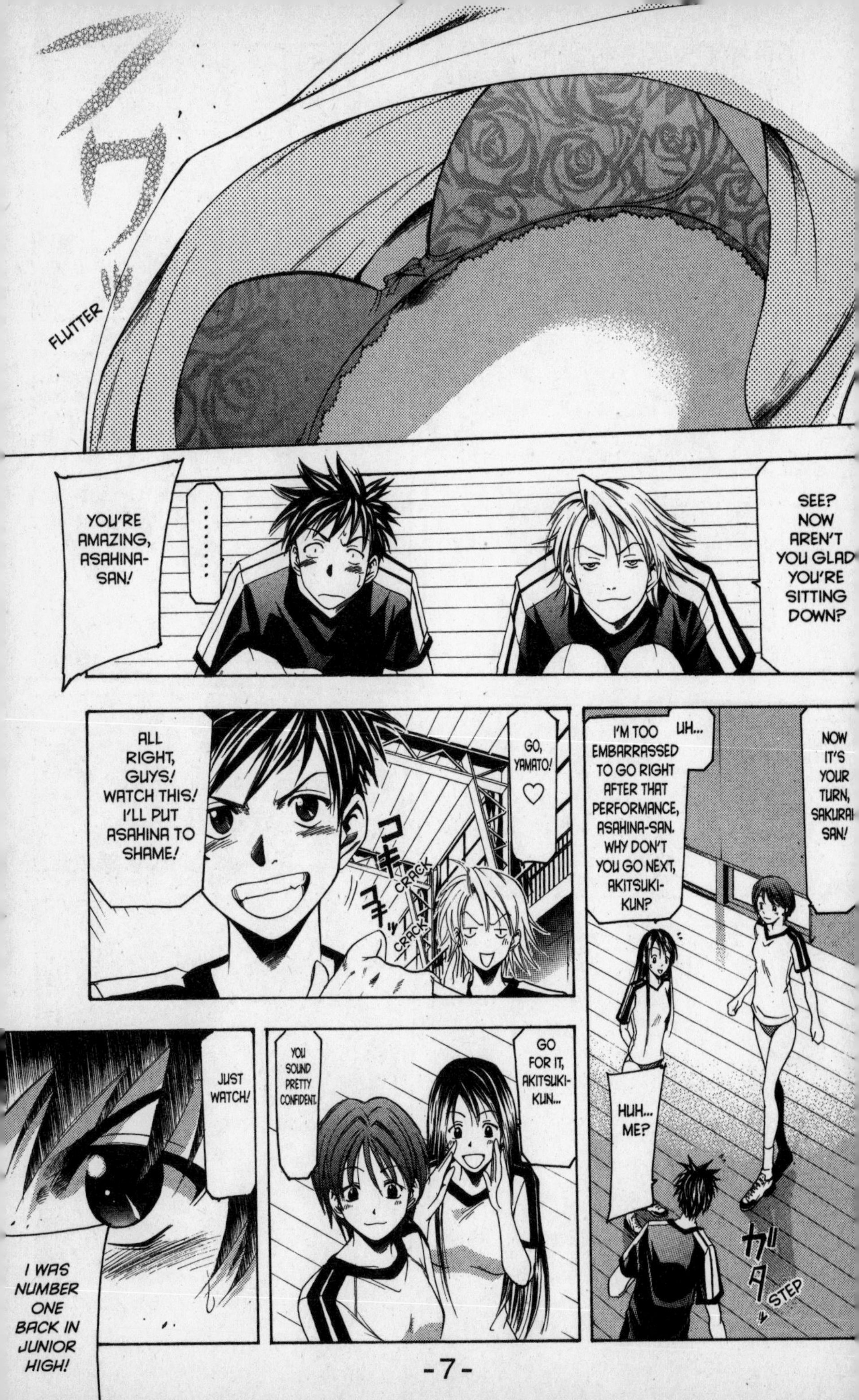
FLUTTER
SEE? NOW AREN'T YOU GLAD YOU'RE SITTING DOWN?
......
YOU'RE AMAZING, ASAHINA-SAN!
NOW IT'S YOUR TURN, SAKURAI-SAN!
UH...
I'M TOO EMBARRASSED TO GO RIGHT AFTER THAT PERFORMANCE, ASAHINA-SAN. WHY DON'T YOU GO NEXT, AKITSUKI-KUN?
HUH... ME?
STEP
GO, YAMATO! ♡
CRACK
CRACK
ALL RIGHT, GUYS! WATCH THIS! I'LL PUT ASAHINA TO SHAME!
GO FOR IT, AKITSUKI-KUN...
YOU SOUND PRETTY CONFIDENT.
JUST WATCH!
I WAS NUMBER ONE BACK IN JUNIOR HIGH!

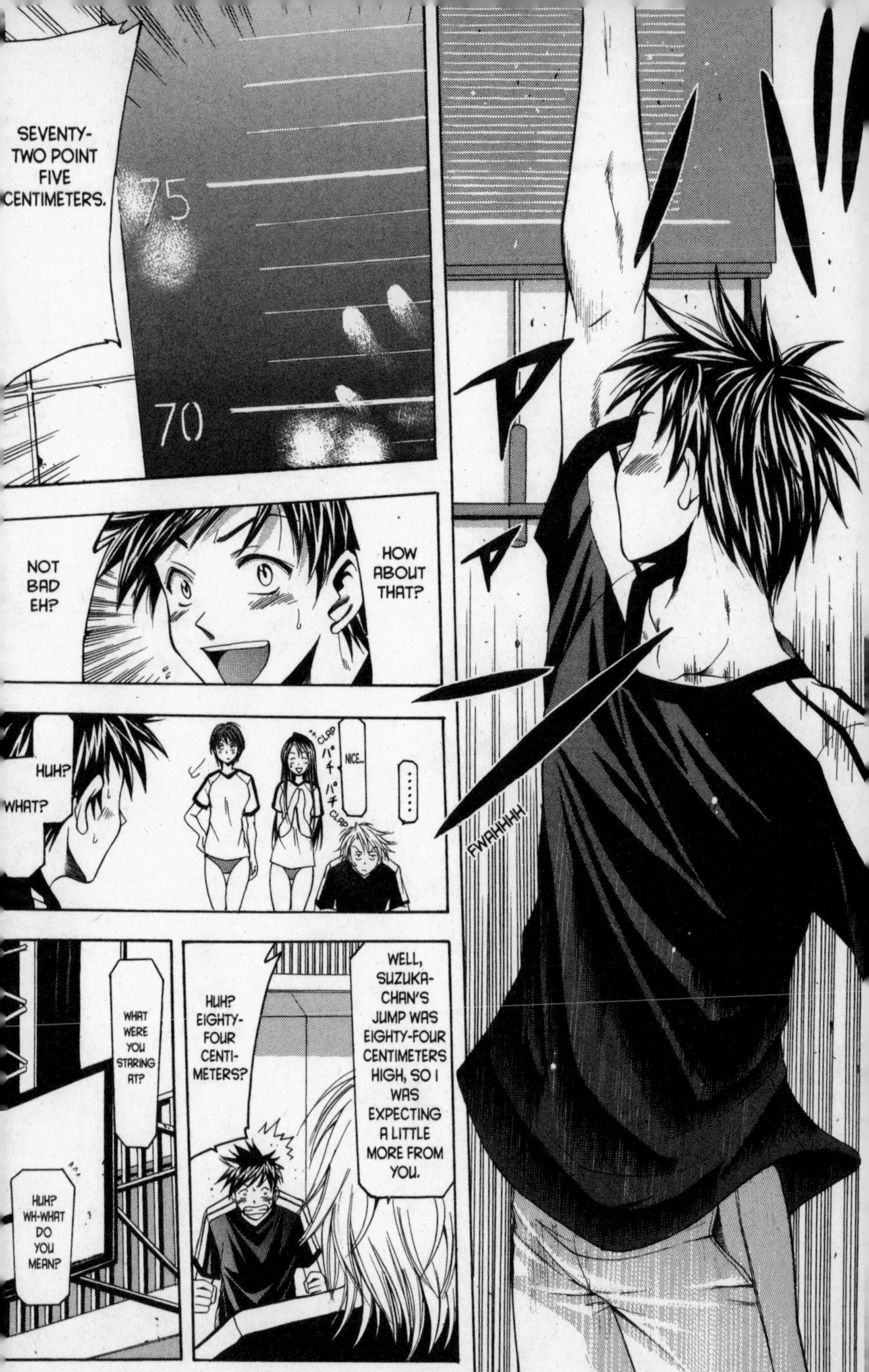
FWAHHHH
75
70
SEVENTY-TWO POINT FIVE CENTIMETERS.
HOW ABOUT THAT?
NOT BAD EH?
CLAP パチ パチ CLAP
NICE...
......
HUH?
WHAT?
WELL, SUZUKA-CHAN'S JUMP WAS EIGHTY-FOUR CENTIMETERS HIGH, SO I WAS EXPECTING A LITTLE MORE FROM YOU.
HUH? EIGHTY-FOUR CENTI-METERS?
WHAT WERE YOU STARING AT?
HUH? WH-WHAT DO YOU MEAN?

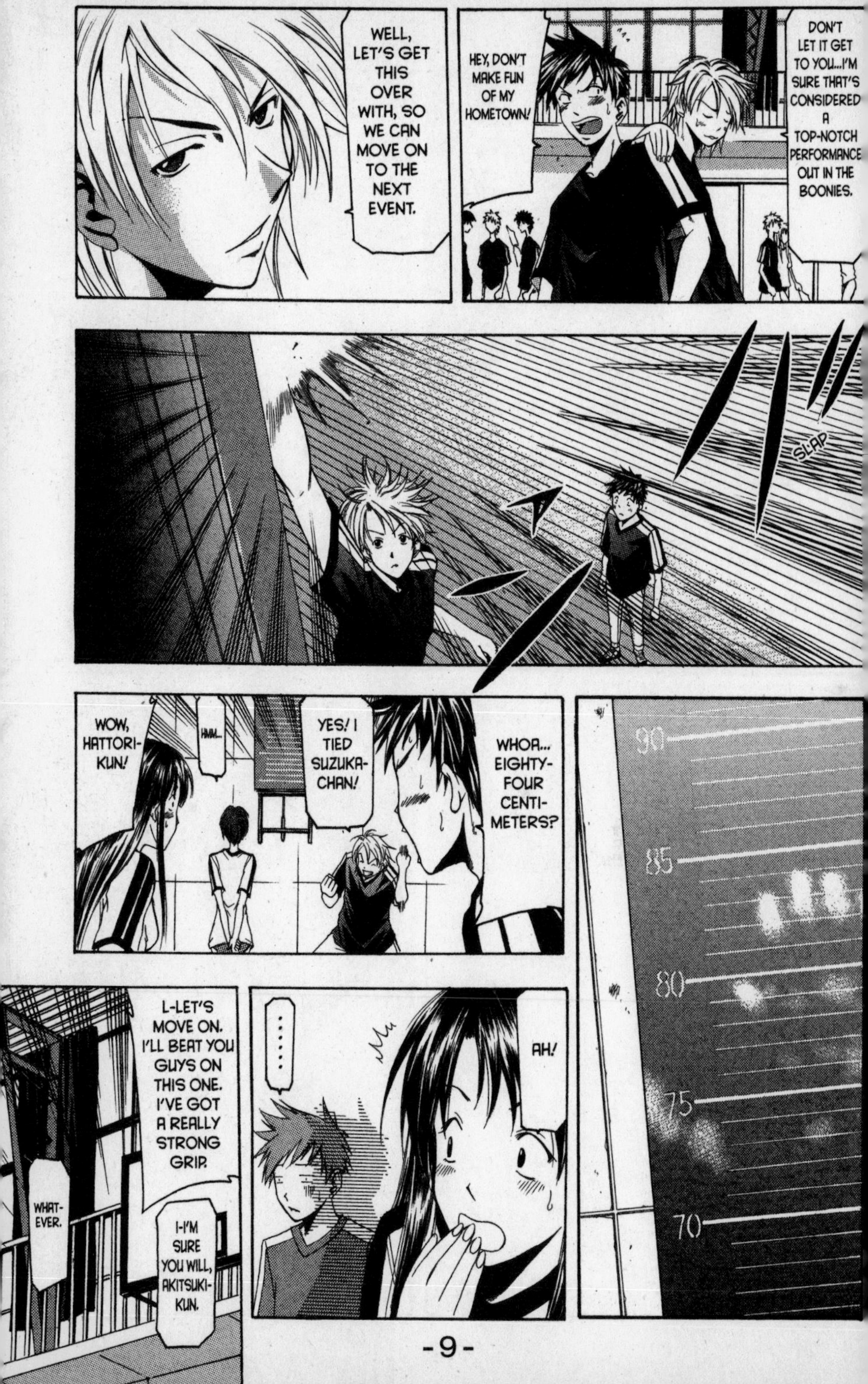
DON'T LET IT GET TO YOU...I'M SURE THAT'S CONSIDERED A TOP-NOTCH PERFORMANCE OUT IN THE BOONIES.
HEY, DON'T MAKE FUN OF MY HOMETOWN!
WELL, LET'S GET THIS OVER WITH, SO WE CAN MOVE ON TO THE NEXT EVENT.
SLAP
90
85
80
75
70
WHOA... EIGHTY-FOUR CENTI-METERS?
YES! I TIED SUZUKA-CHAN!
HMM...
WOW, HATTORI-KUN!
AH!
......
L-LET'S MOVE ON. I'LL BEAT YOU GUYS ON THIS ONE. I'VE GOT A REALLY STRONG GRIP.
WHAT-EVER.
I-I'M SURE YOU WILL, AKITSUKI-KUN.

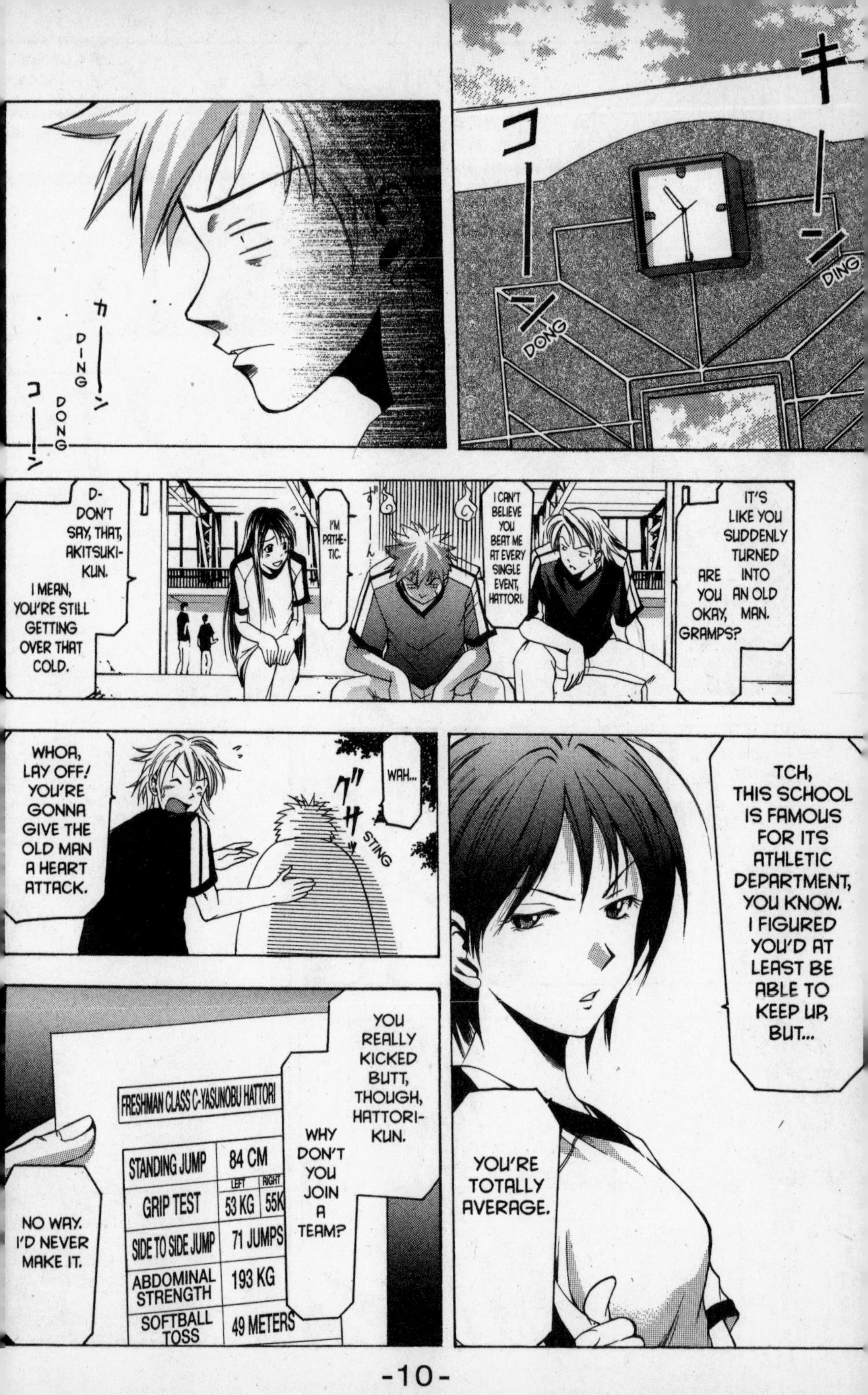
キーン
DING
コーン
DONG
カーン
DING
コーン
DONG
IT'S LIKE YOU SUDDENLY TURNED INTO AN OLD MAN.
ARE YOU OKAY, GRAMPS?
I CAN'T BELIEVE YOU BEAT ME AT EVERY SINGLE EVENT, HATTORI.
I'M PATHETIC.
ずーん
D-DON'T SAY, THAT, AKITSUKI-KUN.
I MEAN, YOU'RE STILL GETTING OVER THAT COLD.
TCH, THIS SCHOOL IS FAMOUS FOR ITS ATHLETIC DEPARTMENT, YOU KNOW. I FIGURED YOU'D AT LEAST BE ABLE TO KEEP UP, BUT...
YOU'RE TOTALLY AVERAGE.
WAH...
グサ
STING
WHOA, LAY OFF! YOU'RE GONNA GIVE THE OLD MAN A HEART ATTACK.
YOU REALLY KICKED BUTT, THOUGH, HATTORI-KUN.
WHY DON'T YOU JOIN A TEAM?
FRESHMAN CLASS C-YASUNOBU HATTORI
STANDING JUMP 84 CM
GRIP TEST LEFT 53 KG RIGHT 55K
SIDE TO SIDE JUMP 71 JUMPS
ABDOMINAL STRENGTH 193 KG
SOFTBALL TOSS 49 METERS
NO WAY. I'D NEVER MAKE IT.

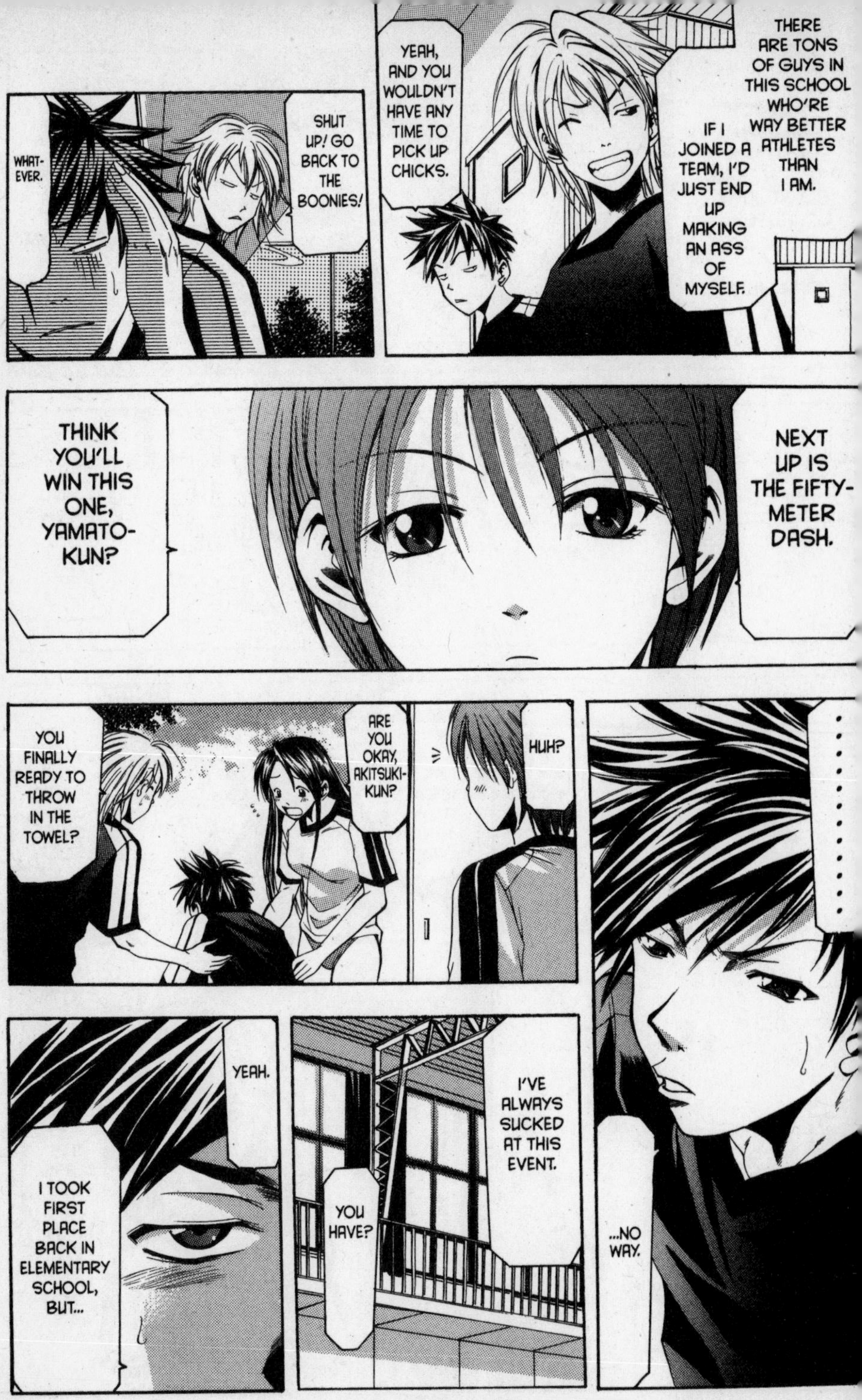
THERE ARE TONS OF GUYS IN THIS SCHOOL WHO'RE WAY BETTER ATHLETES THAN I AM.
IF I JOINED A TEAM, I'D JUST END UP MAKING AN ASS OF MYSELF.
YEAH, AND YOU WOULDN'T HAVE ANY TIME TO PICK UP CHICKS.
SHUT UP! GO BACK TO THE BOONIES!
WHAT-EVER.
NEXT UP IS THE FIFTY-METER DASH.
THINK YOU'LL WIN THIS ONE, YAMATO-KUN?
......
...NO WAY.
HUH?
ARE YOU OKAY, AKITSUKI-KUN?
YOU FINALLY READY TO THROW IN THE TOWEL?
I'VE ALWAYS SUCKED AT THIS EVENT.
YOU HAVE?
YEAH.
I TOOK FIRST PLACE BACK IN ELEMENTARY SCHOOL, BUT...

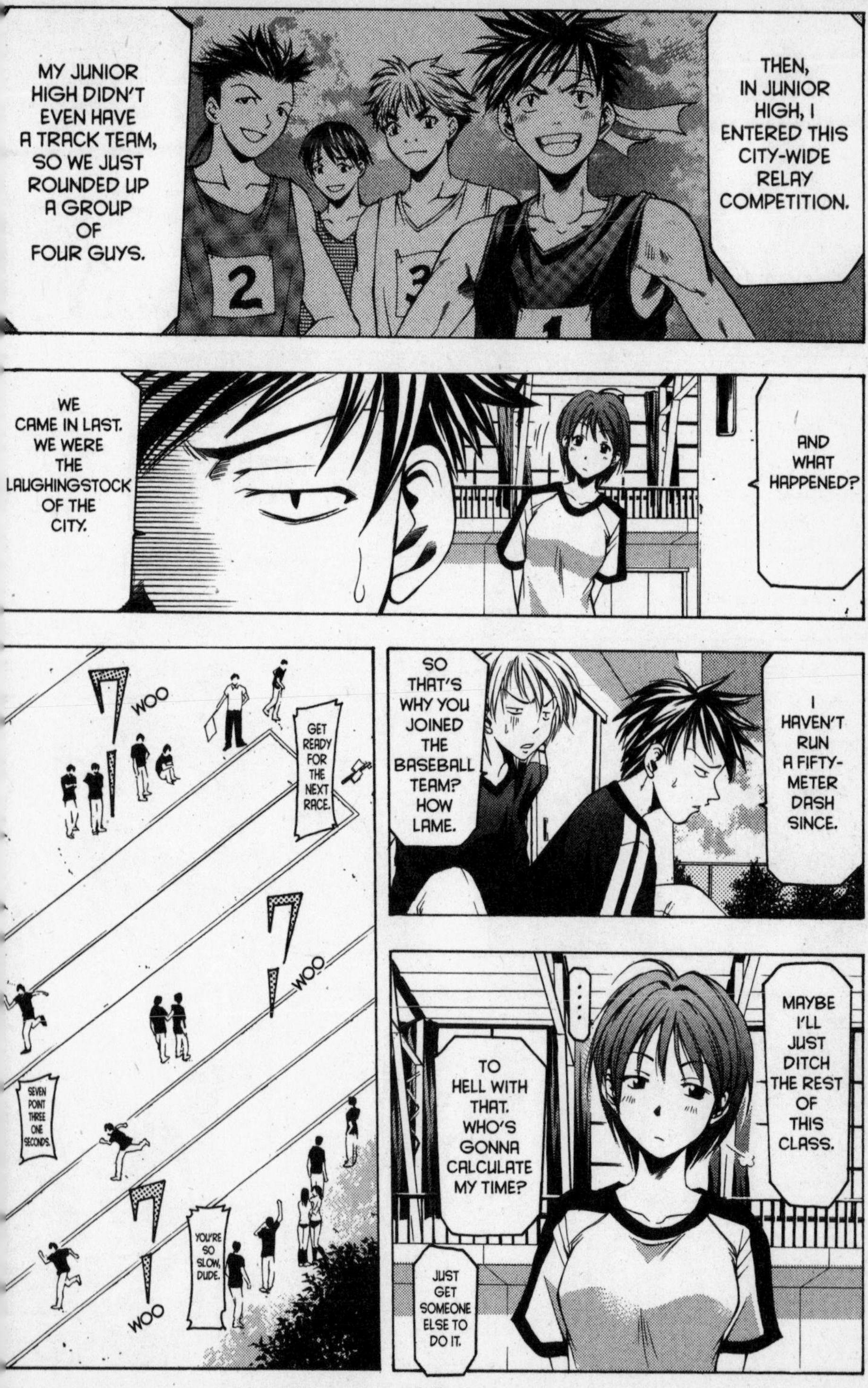
THEN, IN JUNIOR HIGH, I ENTERED THIS CITY-WIDE RELAY COMPETITION.
MY JUNIOR HIGH DIDN'T EVEN HAVE A TRACK TEAM, SO WE JUST ROUNDED UP A GROUP OF FOUR GUYS.
AND WHAT HAPPENED?
WE CAME IN LAST. WE WERE THE LAUGHINGSTOCK OF THE CITY.
I HAVEN'T RUN A FIFTY-METER DASH SINCE.
SO THAT'S WHY YOU JOINED THE BASEBALL TEAM? HOW LAME.
MAYBE I'LL JUST DITCH THE REST OF THIS CLASS.
....
TO HELL WITH THAT. WHO'S GONNA CALCULATE MY TIME?
JUST GET SOMEONE ELSE TO DO IT.
WOO
GET READY FOR THE NEXT RACE.
WOO
SEVEN POINT THREE ONE SECONDS.
YOU'RE SO SLOW, DUDE.
WOO

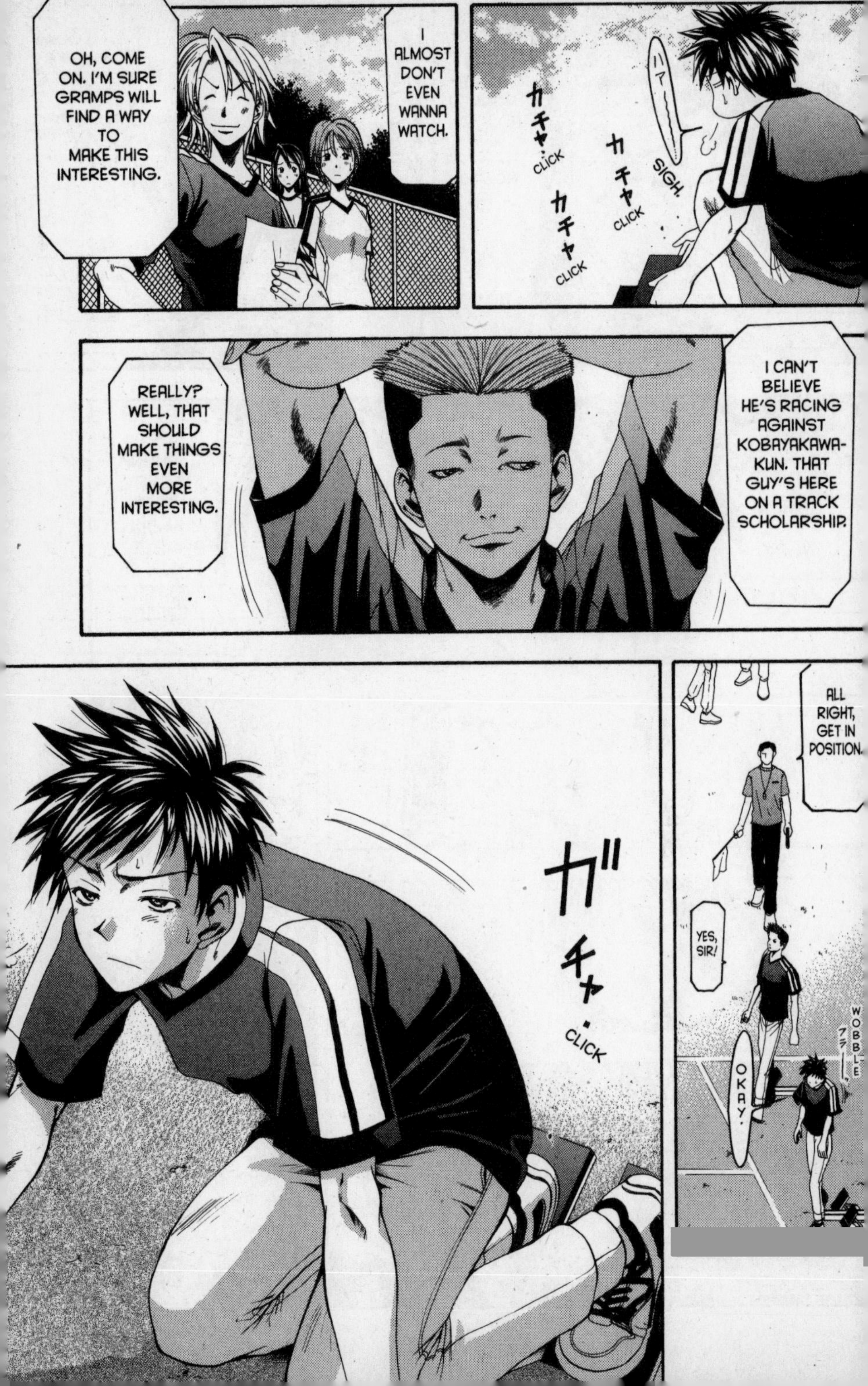
ハァー
SIGH.
カチャ
CLICK
カチャ
CLICK
カチャ
CLICK
I ALMOST DON'T EVEN WANNA WATCH.
OH, COME ON. I'M SURE GRAMPS WILL FIND A WAY TO MAKE THIS INTERESTING.
I CAN'T BELIEVE HE'S RACING AGAINST KOBAYAKAWA-KUN. THAT GUY'S HERE ON A TRACK SCHOLARSHIP.
REALLY? WELL, THAT SHOULD MAKE THINGS EVEN MORE INTERESTING.
ALL RIGHT, GET IN POSITION.
YES, SIR!
OKAY.
フラー
WOBBLE
ガチャ
CLICK

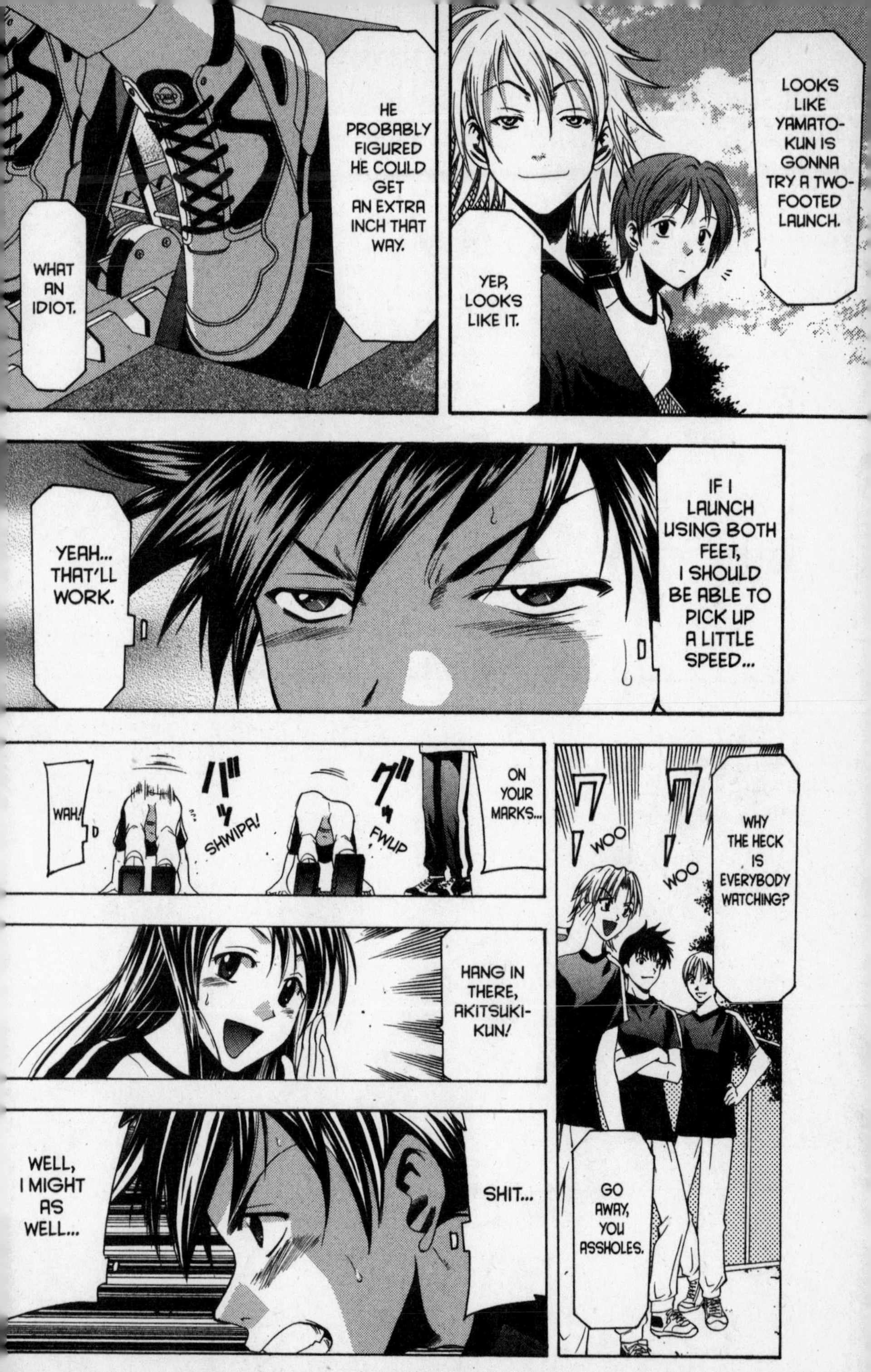
LOOKS LIKE YAMATO-KUN IS GONNA TRY A TWO-FOOTED LAUNCH.
YEP, LOOKS LIKE IT.
HE PROBABLY FIGURED HE COULD GET AN EXTRA INCH THAT WAY.
WHAT AN IDIOT.
IF I LAUNCH USING BOTH FEET, I SHOULD BE ABLE TO PICK UP A LITTLE SPEED...
YEAH... THAT'LL WORK.
WHY THE HECK IS EVERYBODY WATCHING?
WOO
WOO
GO AWAY, YOU ASSHOLES.
ON YOUR MARKS...
FWUP
SHWIPA!
WAH!
HANG IN THERE, AKITSUKI-KUN!
SHIT...
WELL, I MIGHT AS WELL...

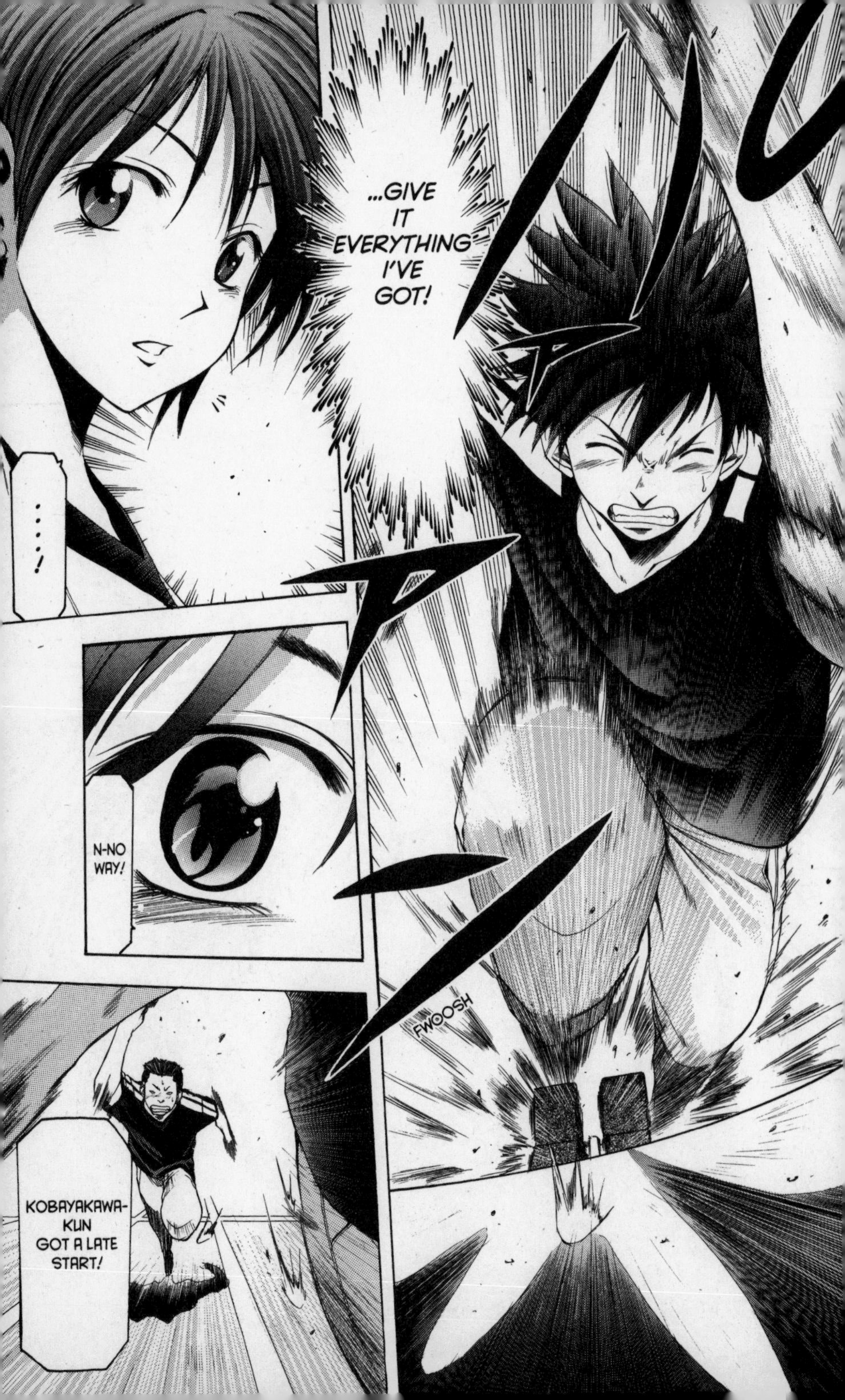
...GIVE IT EVERYTHING I'VE GOT!
FWOOSH
.....!
N-NO WAY!
KOBAYAKAWA-KUN GOT A LATE START!

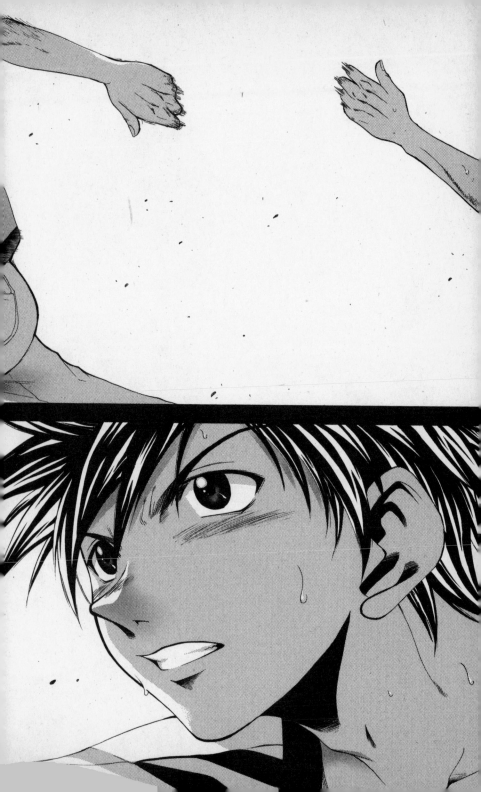

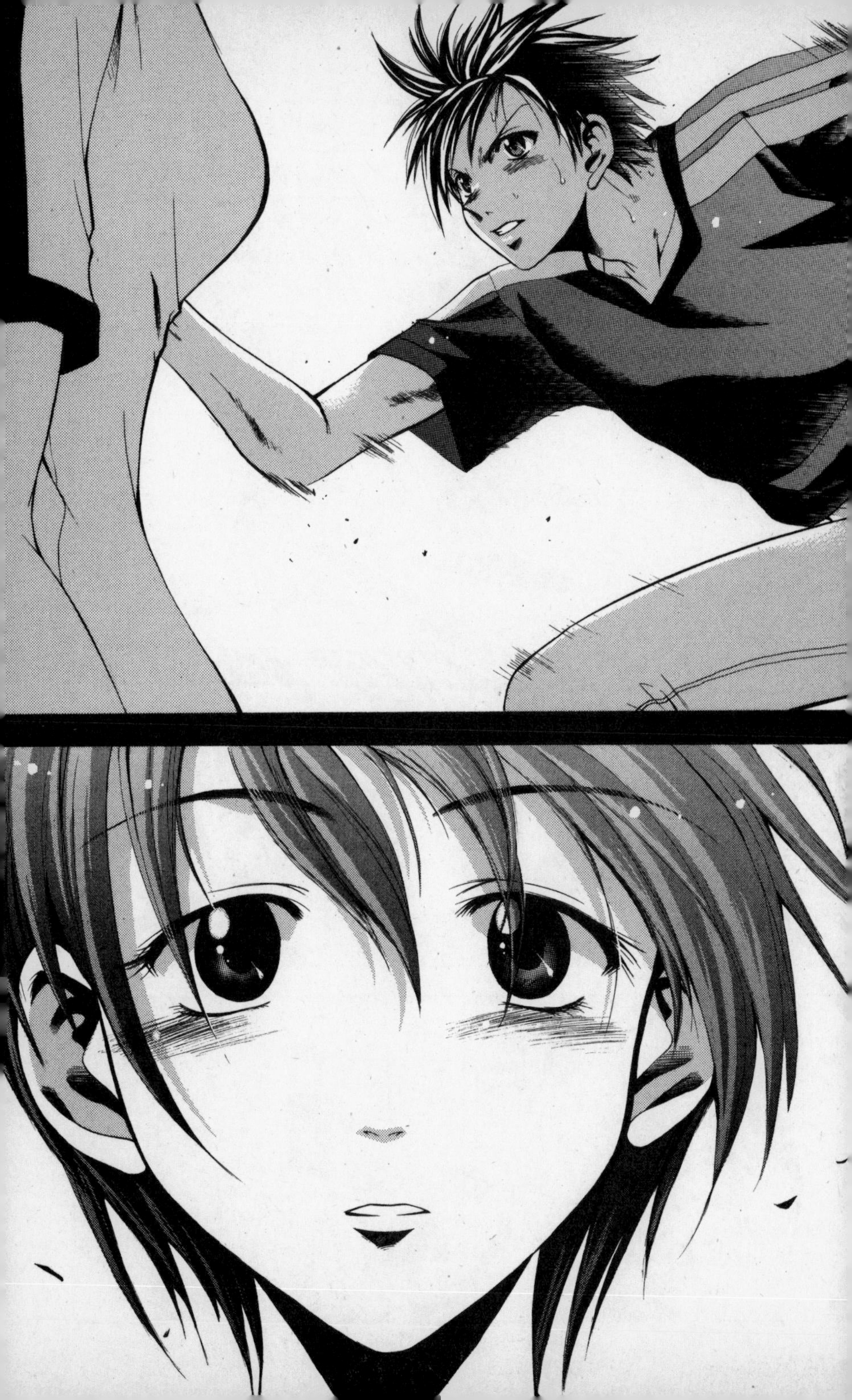

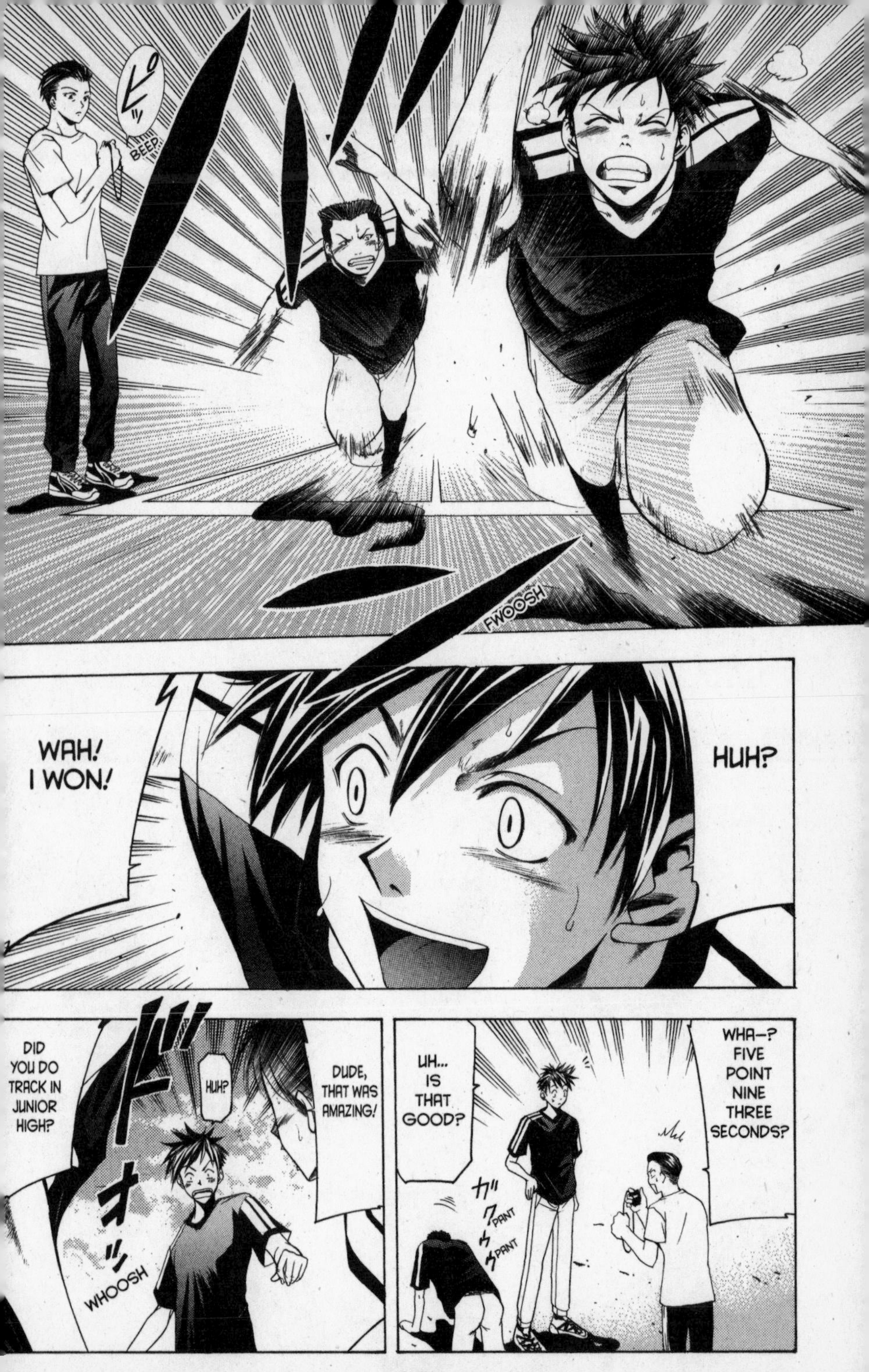
BEEP
FWOOSH
HUH?
WAH! I WON!
WHA-? FIVE POINT NINE THREE SECONDS?
PANT
PANT
UH... IS THAT GOOD?
DUDE, THAT WAS AMAZING!
HUH?
DID YOU DO TRACK IN JUNIOR HIGH?
WHOOSH

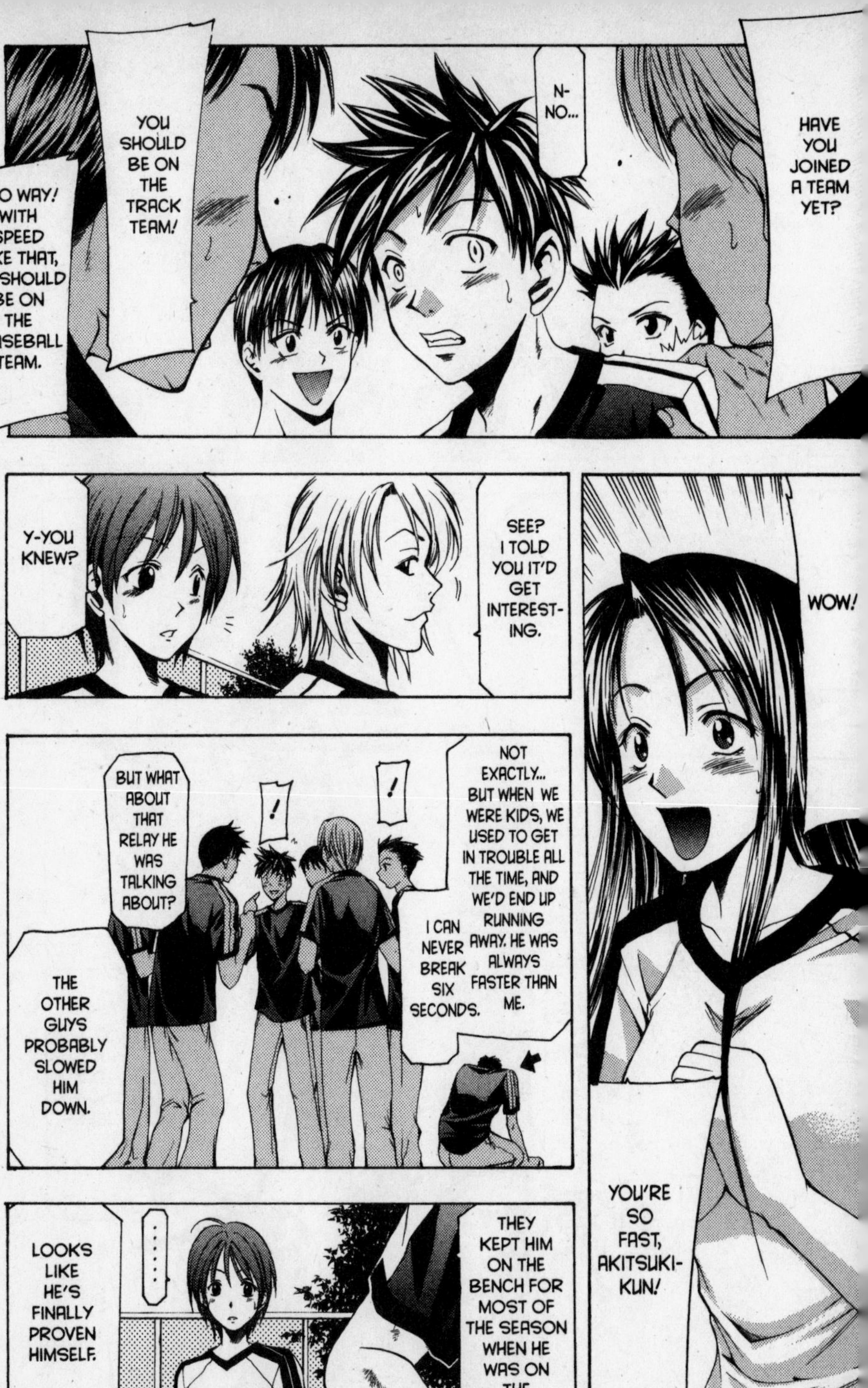
HAVE YOU JOINED A TEAM YET?
N-NO...
YOU SHOULD BE ON THE TRACK TEAM!
NO WAY! WITH SPEED LIKE THAT, HE SHOULD BE ON THE BASEBALL TEAM.
WOW!
YOU'RE SO FAST, AKITSUKI-KUN!
SEE? I TOLD YOU IT'D GET INTERESTING.
Y-YOU KNEW?
NOT EXACTLY... BUT WHEN WE WERE KIDS, WE USED TO GET IN TROUBLE ALL THE TIME, AND WE'D END UP RUNNING AWAY. HE WAS ALWAYS FASTER THAN ME.
I CAN NEVER BREAK SIX SECONDS.
!
!
BUT WHAT ABOUT THAT RELAY HE WAS TALKING ABOUT?
THE OTHER GUYS PROBABLY SLOWED HIM DOWN.
THEY KEPT HIM ON THE BENCH FOR MOST OF THE SEASON WHEN HE WAS ON THE BASEBALL TEAM.
....
LOOKS LIKE HE'S FINALLY PROVEN HIMSELF.

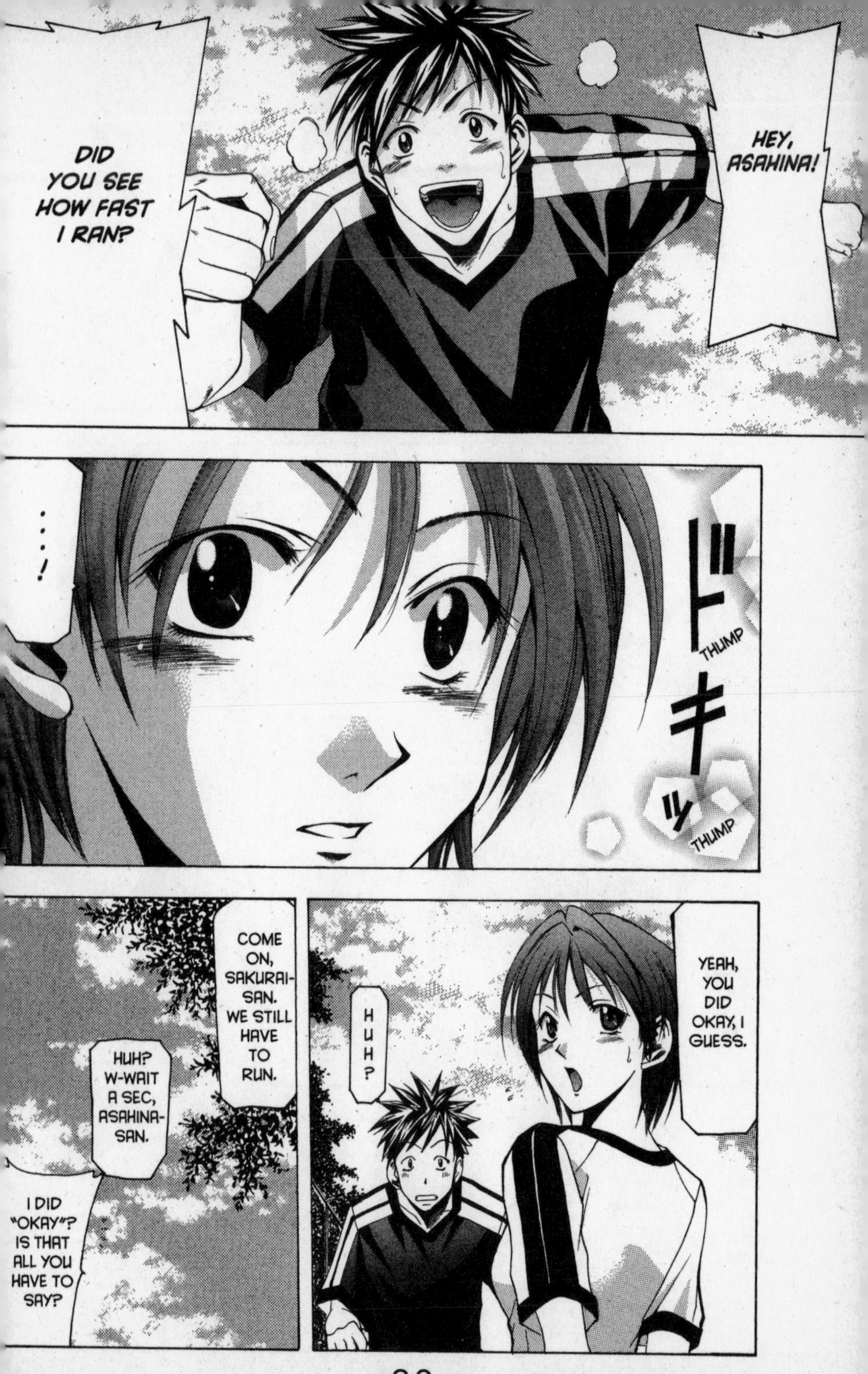
HEY, ASAHINA!
DID YOU SEE HOW FAST I RAN?
ドキッ
THUMP THUMP
...!
YEAH, YOU DID OKAY, I GUESS.
HUH?
COME ON, SAKURAI-SAN. WE STILL HAVE TO RUN.
HUH? W-WAIT A SEC, ASAHINA-SAN.
I DID "OKAY"? IS THAT ALL YOU HAVE TO SAY?

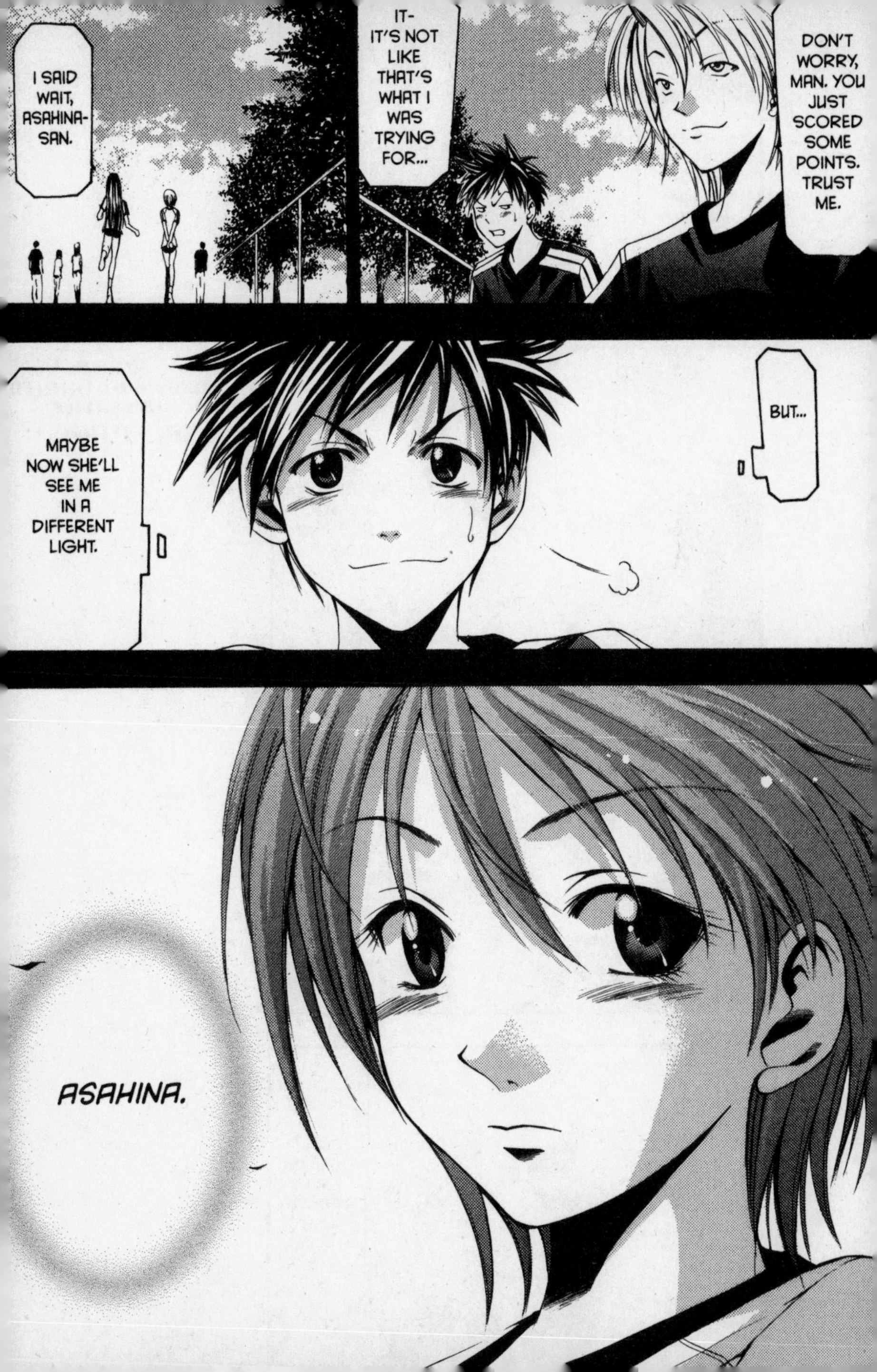
DON'T WORRY, MAN. YOU JUST SCORED SOME POINTS. TRUST ME.
IT- IT'S NOT LIKE THAT'S WHAT I WAS TRYING FOR...
I SAID WAIT, ASAHINA-SAN.
BUT...
MAYBE NOW SHE'LL SEE ME IN A DIFFERENT LIGHT.
ASAHINA.

SUZUKA FOUR-PANEL THEATER NUMBER FIVE

THE OPTIMIST

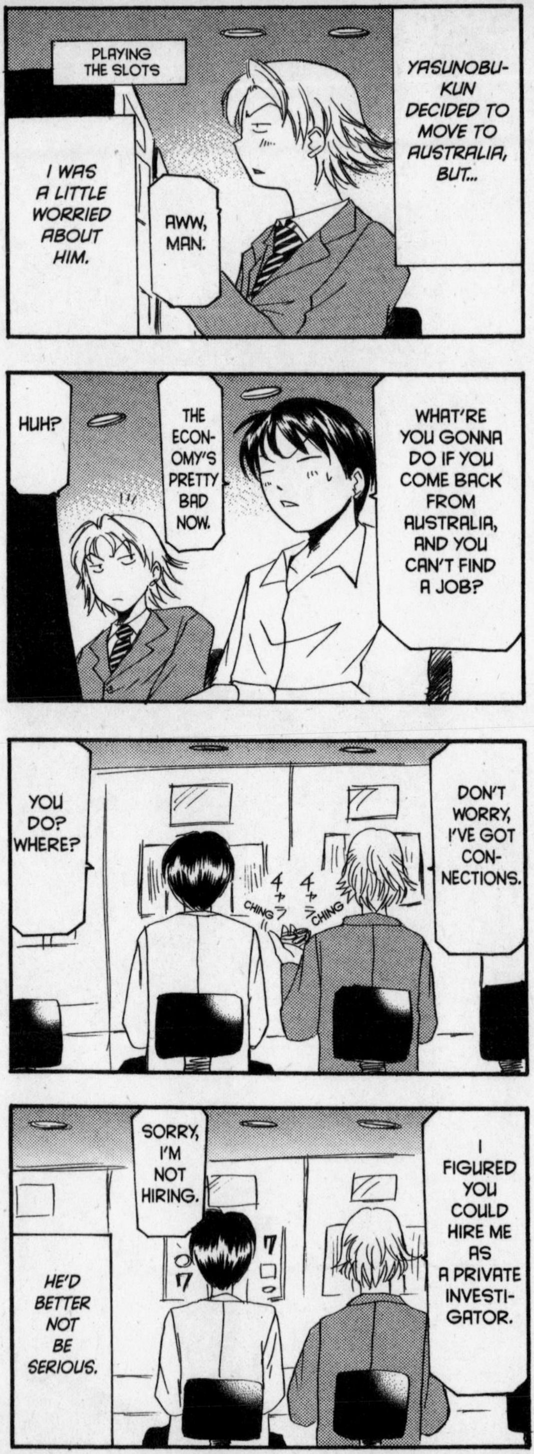
YASUNOBU-KUN DECIDED TO MOVE TO AUSTRALIA, BUT...
PLAYING THE SLOTS
AWW, MAN.
I WAS A LITTLE WORRIED ABOUT HIM.
WHAT'RE YOU GONNA DO IF YOU COME BACK FROM AUSTRALIA, AND YOU CAN'T FIND A JOB?
THE ECONOMY'S PRETTY BAD NOW.
HUH?
DON'T WORRY, I'VE GOT CONNECTIONS.
CHING
CHING
YOU DO? WHERE?
I FIGURED YOU COULD HIRE ME AS A PRIVATE INVESTIGATOR.
SORRY, I'M NOT HIRING.
HE'D BETTER NOT BE SERIOUS.

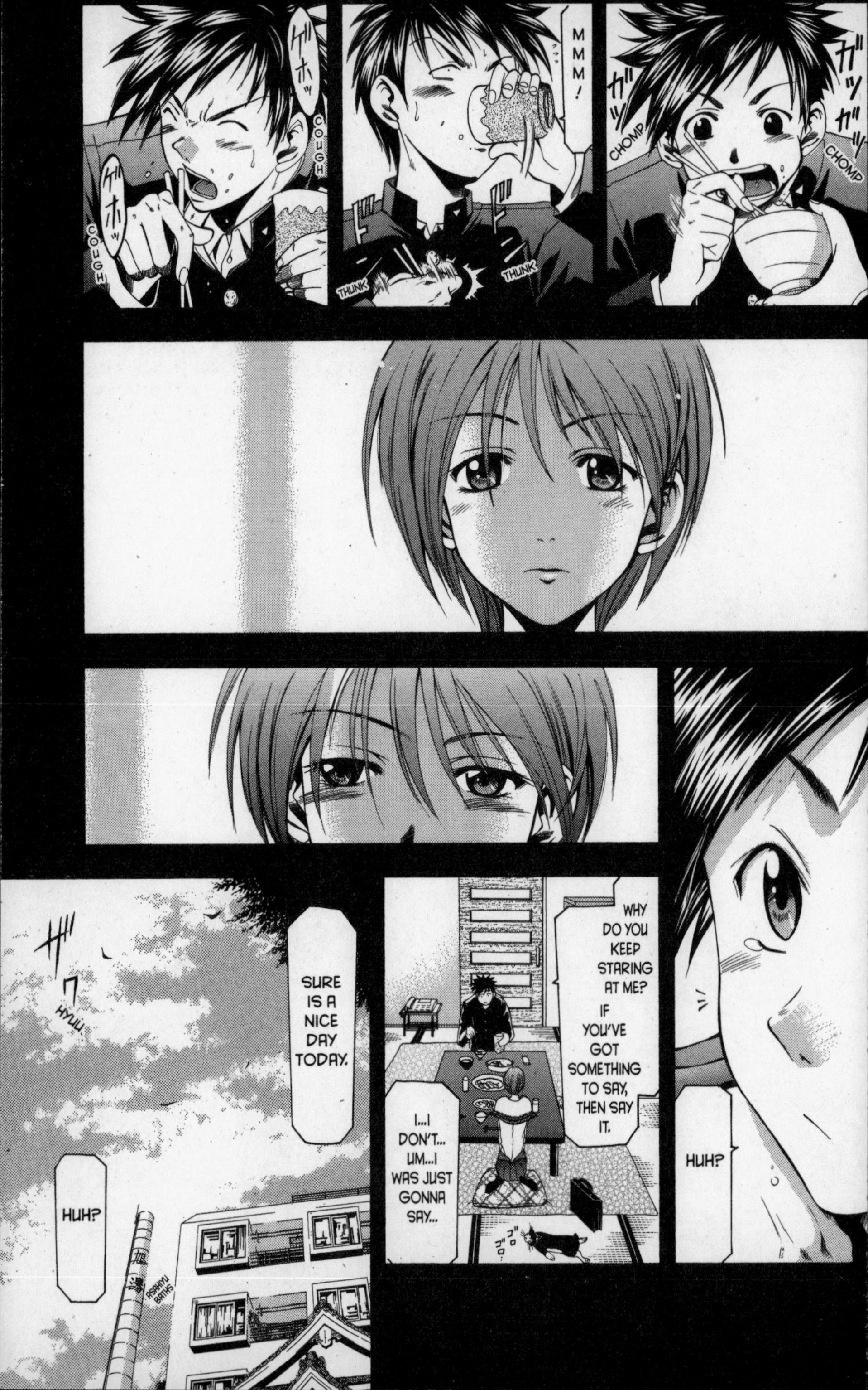

ガツ
ガツ
CHOMP
CHOMP
MMM!
THUNK
THUNK
ゲホッ
ゲホッ
COUGH
COUGH
HUH?
WHY DO YOU KEEP STARING AT ME?
IF YOU'VE GOT SOMETHING TO SAY, THEN SAY IT.
I...I DON'T... UM...I WAS JUST GONNA SAY...
ゴロ ゴロ
SURE IS A NICE DAY TODAY.
HYUU
HUH?
ASAHIYU BATHS

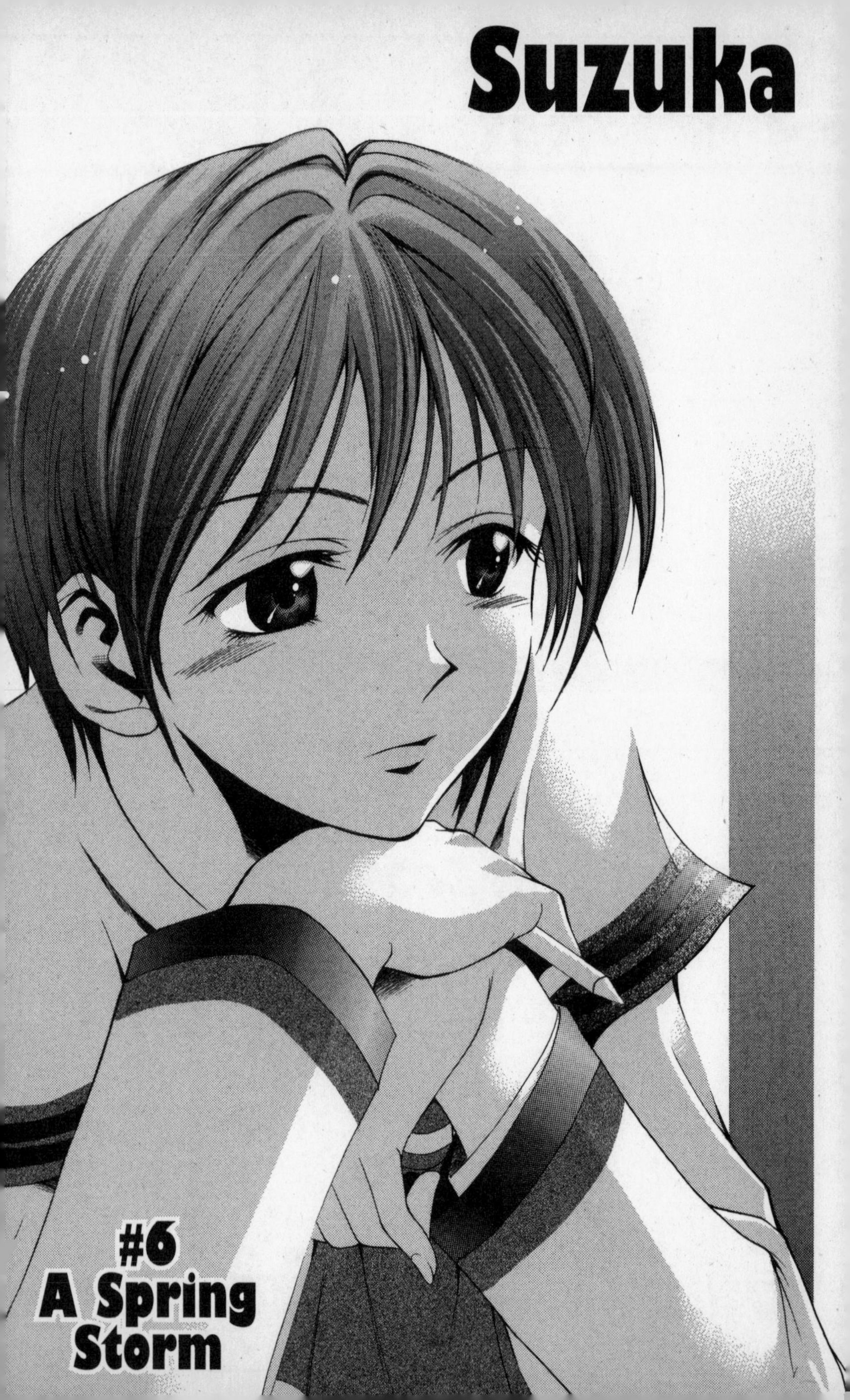
Suzuka
#6
A Spring
Storm

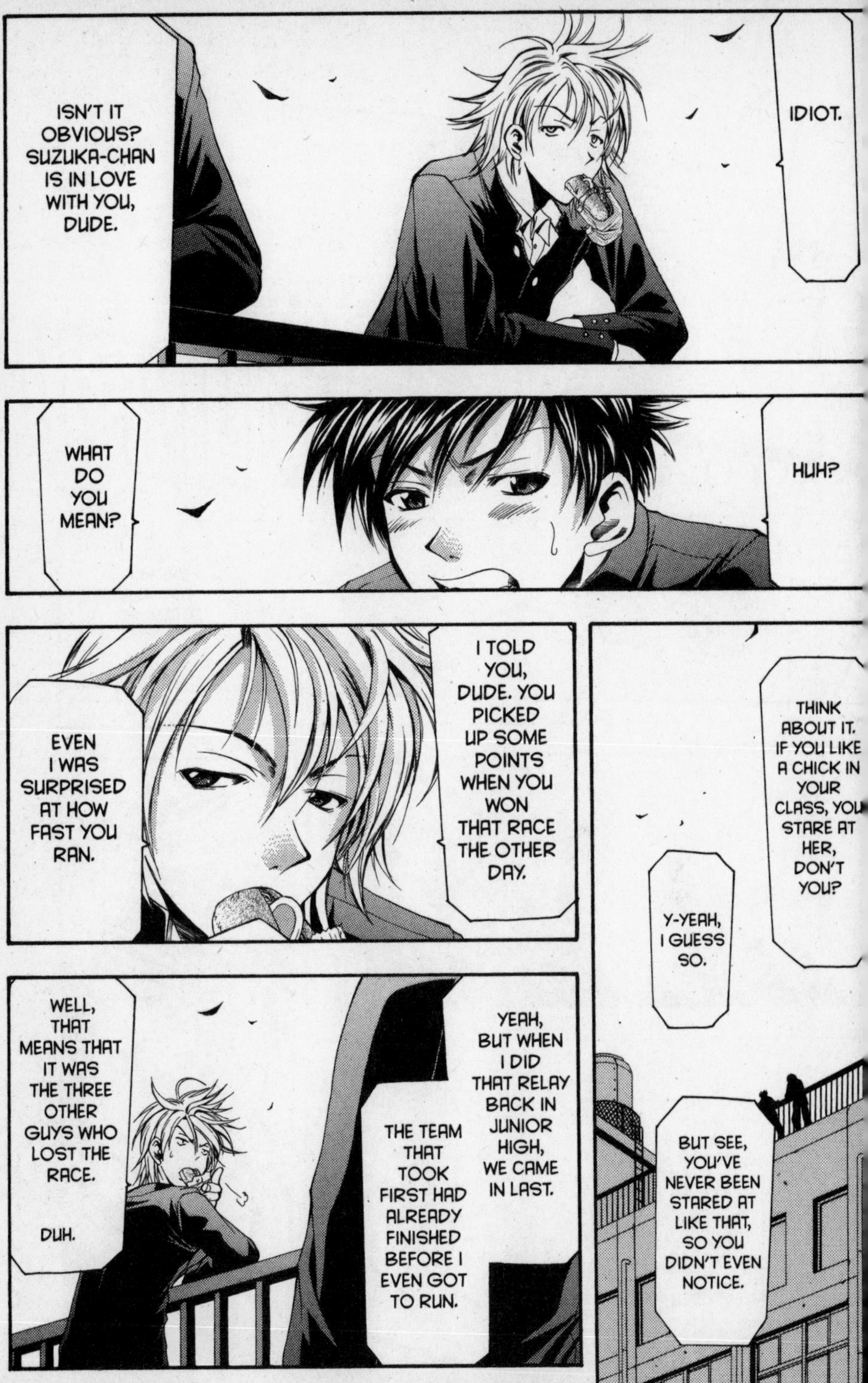
IDIOT.
ISN'T IT OBVIOUS? SUZUKA-CHAN IS IN LOVE WITH YOU, DUDE.
HUH?
WHAT DO YOU MEAN?
THINK ABOUT IT. IF YOU LIKE A CHICK IN YOUR CLASS, YOU STARE AT HER, DON'T YOU?
Y-YEAH, I GUESS SO.
BUT SEE, YOU'VE NEVER BEEN STARED AT LIKE THAT, SO YOU DIDN'T EVEN NOTICE.
I TOLD YOU, DUDE. YOU PICKED UP SOME POINTS WHEN YOU WON THAT RACE THE OTHER DAY.
EVEN I WAS SURPRISED AT HOW FAST YOU RAN.
YEAH, BUT WHEN I DID THAT RELAY BACK IN JUNIOR HIGH, WE CAME IN LAST.
THE TEAM THAT TOOK FIRST HAD ALREADY FINISHED BEFORE I EVEN GOT TO RUN.
WELL, THAT MEANS THAT IT WAS THE THREE OTHER GUYS WHO LOST THE RACE.
DUH.

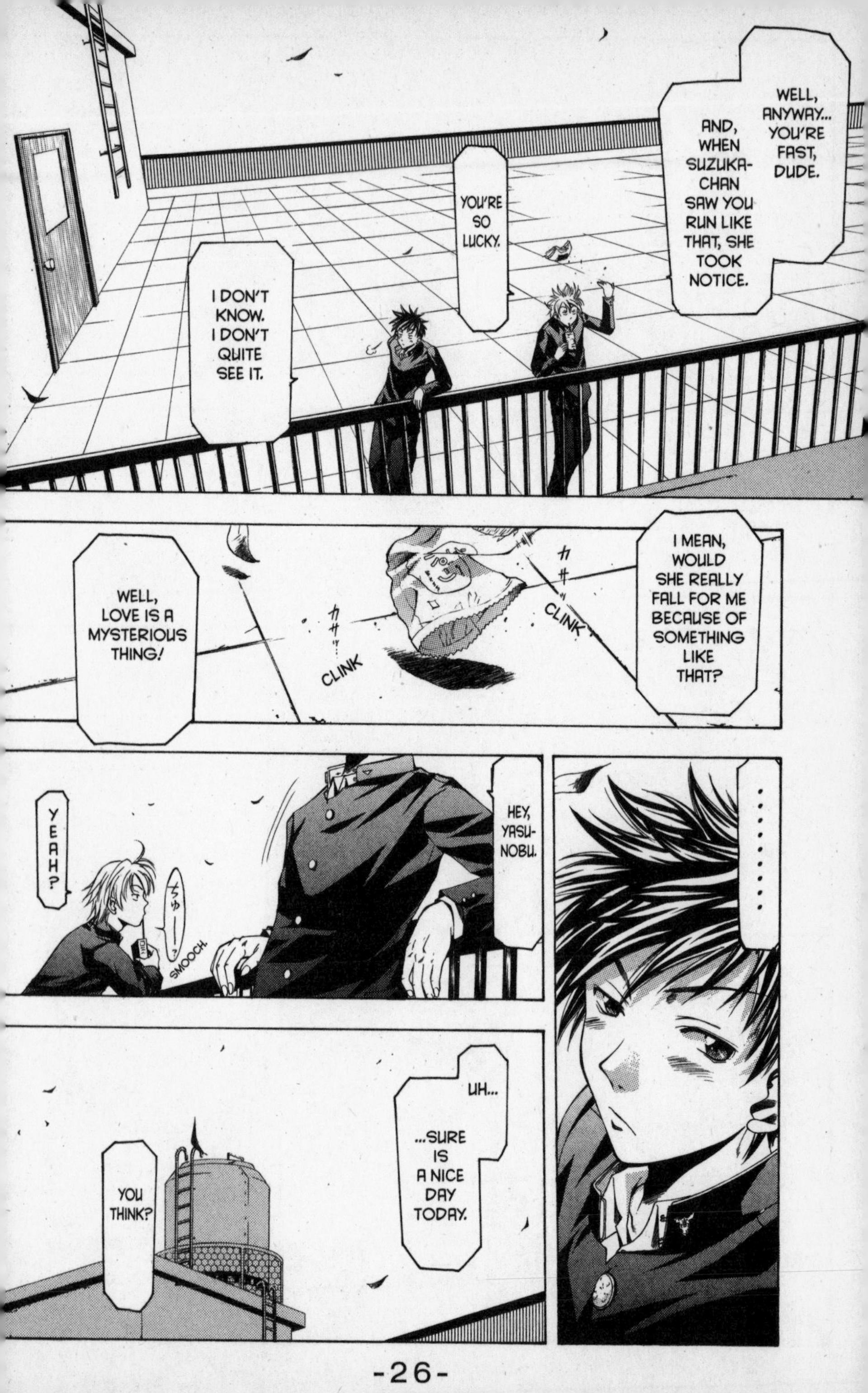
WELL, ANYWAY... YOU'RE FAST, DUDE.
AND, WHEN SUZUKA-CHAN SAW YOU RUN LIKE THAT, SHE TOOK NOTICE.
YOU'RE SO LUCKY.
I DON'T KNOW. I DON'T QUITE SEE IT.
I MEAN, WOULD SHE REALLY FALL FOR ME BECAUSE OF SOMETHING LIKE THAT?
CLINK
CLINK
WELL, LOVE IS A MYSTERIOUS THING!
......
HEY, YASU-NOBU.
SMOOCH.
YEAH?
UH...
...SURE IS A NICE DAY TODAY.
YOU THINK?

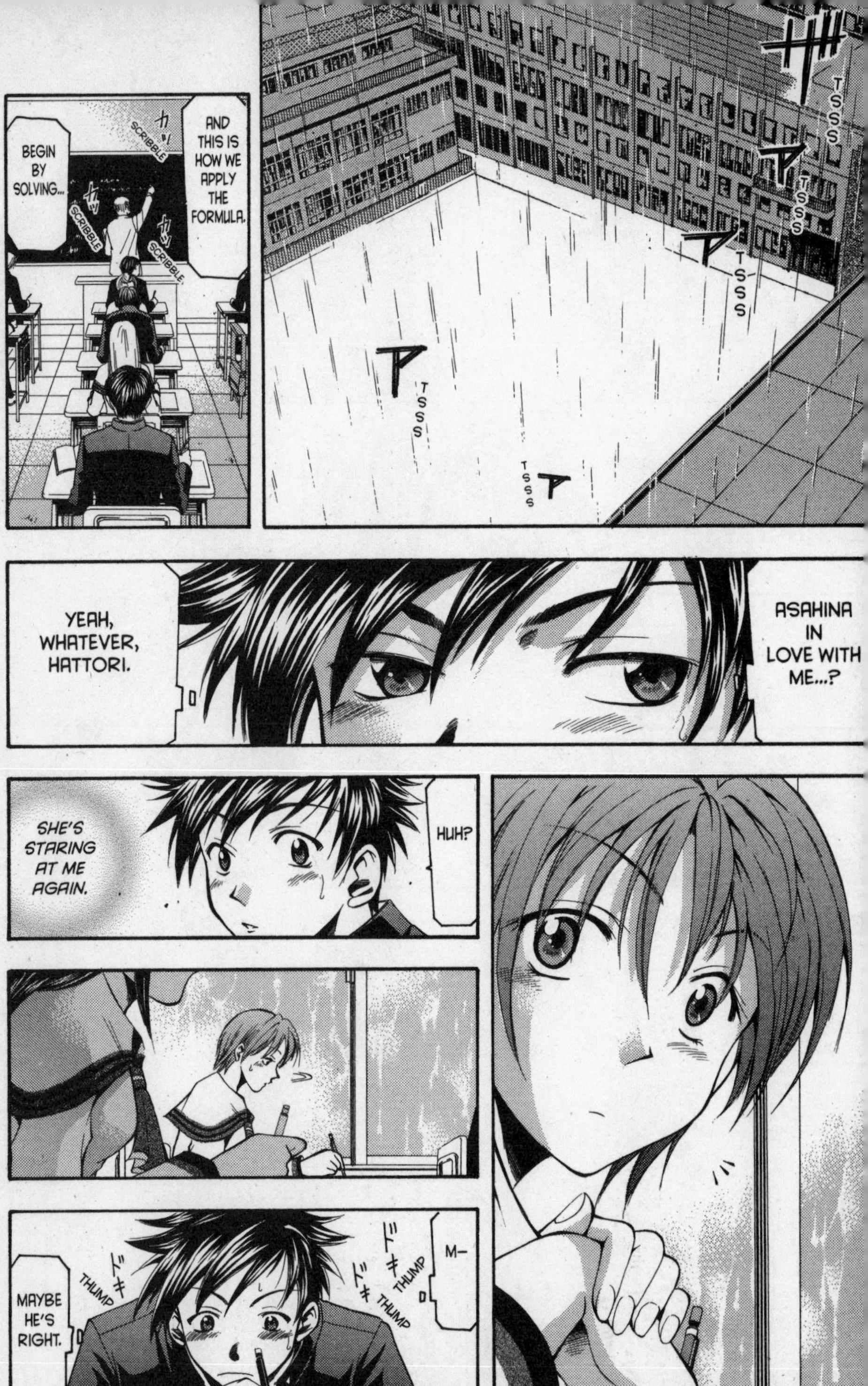
TSSS
TSSS
TSSS
TSSS
TSSS
AND THIS IS HOW WE APPLY THE FORMULA.
SCRIBBLE
SCRIBBLE
SCRIBBLE
BEGIN BY SOLVING...
ASAHINA IN LOVE WITH ME...?
YEAH, WHATEVER, HATTORI.
HUH?
SHE'S STARING AT ME AGAIN.
M—
THUMP
THUMP
THUMP
MAYBE HE'S RIGHT.

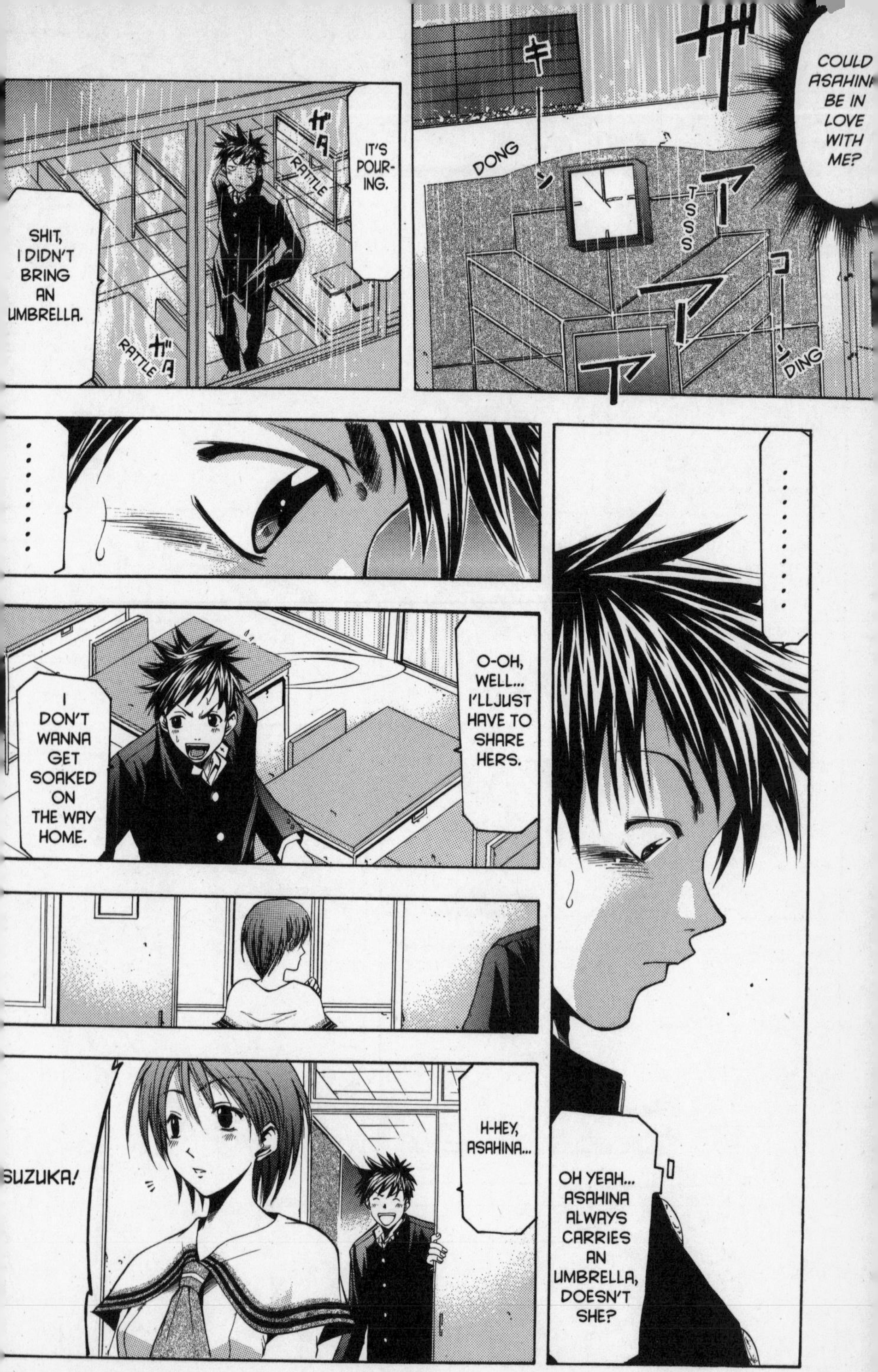
COULD ASAHINA BE IN LOVE WITH ME?
DONG
TSSS
DING
IT'S POURING.
RATTLE
SHIT, I DIDN'T BRING AN UMBRELLA.
RATTLE
......
OH YEAH... ASAHINA ALWAYS CARRIES AN UMBRELLA, DOESN'T SHE?
......
O-OH, WELL... I'LLJUST HAVE TO SHARE HERS.
I DON'T WANNA GET SOAKED ON THE WAY HOME.
H-HEY, ASAHINA...
SUZUKA!

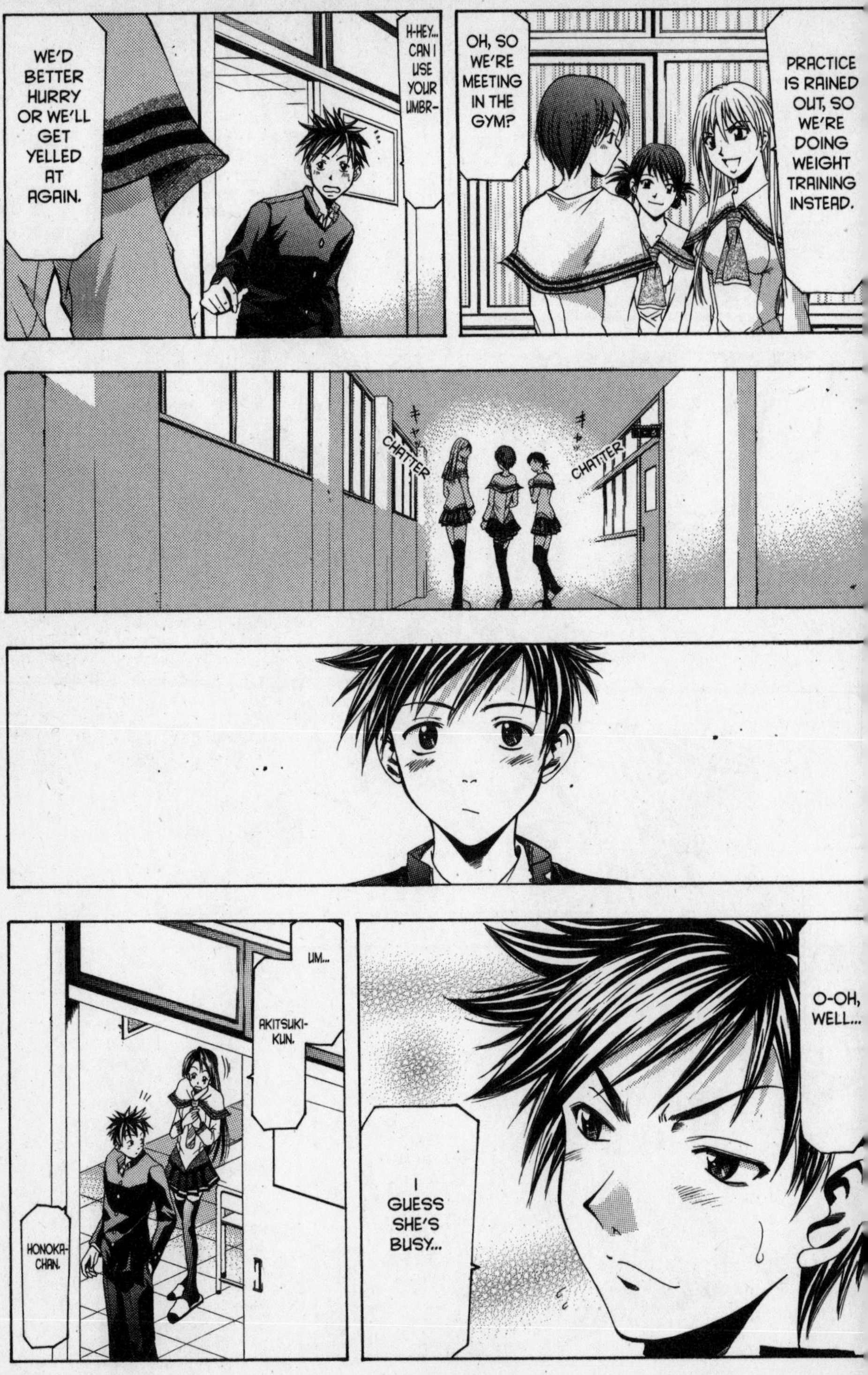
PRACTICE IS RAINED OUT, SO WE'RE DOING WEIGHT TRAINING INSTEAD.
OH, SO WE'RE MEETING IN THE GYM?
H-HEY... CAN I USE YOUR UMBR-
WE'D BETTER HURRY OR WE'LL GET YELLED AT AGAIN.
CHATTER
CHATTER
O-OH, WELL...
I GUESS SHE'S BUSY...
UM...
AKITSUKI-KUN.
HONOKA-CHAN.

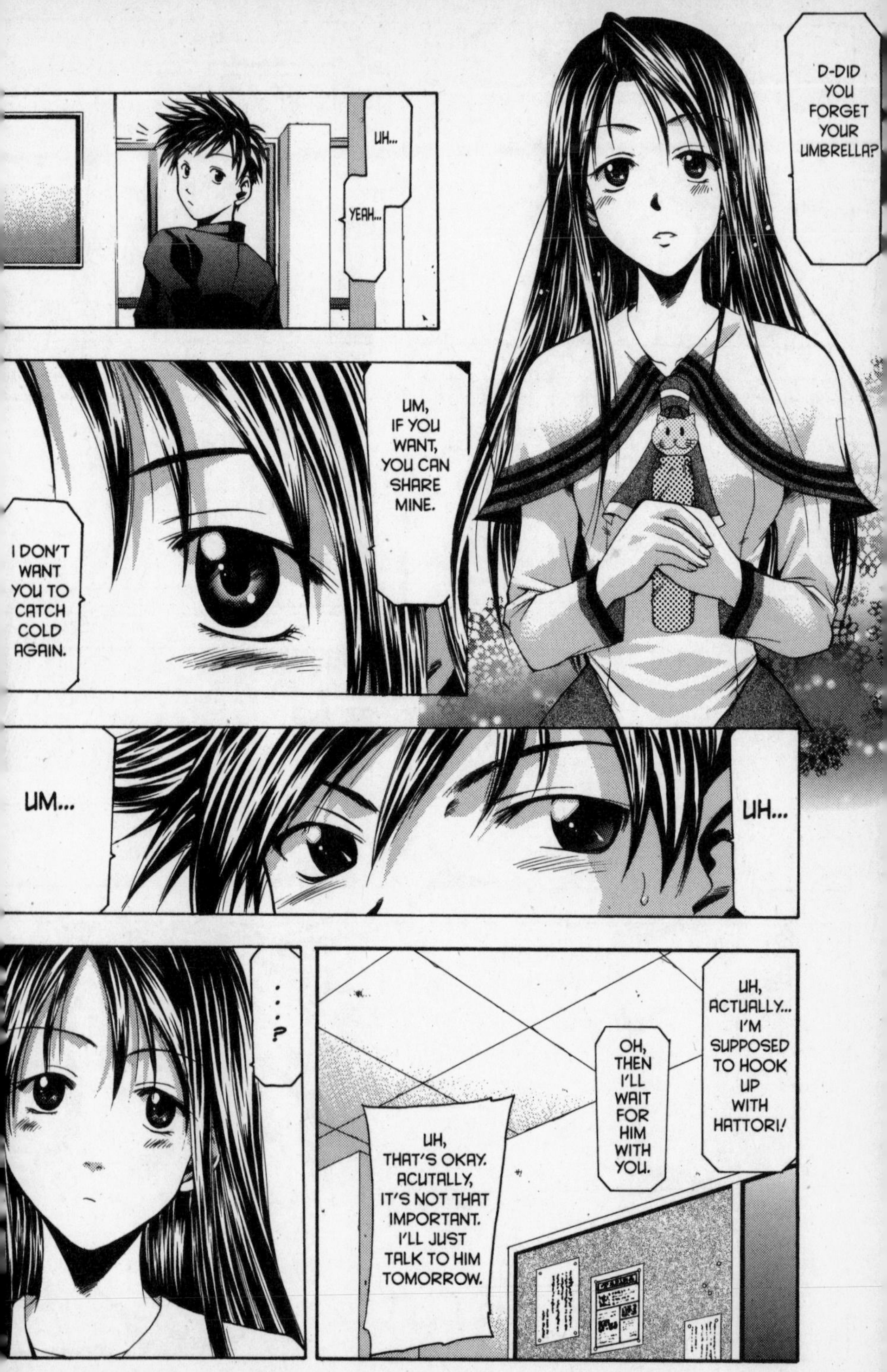
D-DID YOU FORGET YOUR UMBRELLA?
UH...
YEAH...
UM, IF YOU WANT, YOU CAN SHARE MINE.
I DON'T WANT YOU TO CATCH COLD AGAIN.
UH...
UM...
UH, ACTUALLY... I'M SUPPOSED TO HOOK UP WITH HATTORI!
OH, THEN I'LL WAIT FOR HIM WITH YOU.
UH, THAT'S OKAY. ACUTALLY, IT'S NOT THAT IMPORTANT. I'LL JUST TALK TO HIM TOMORROW.
...?

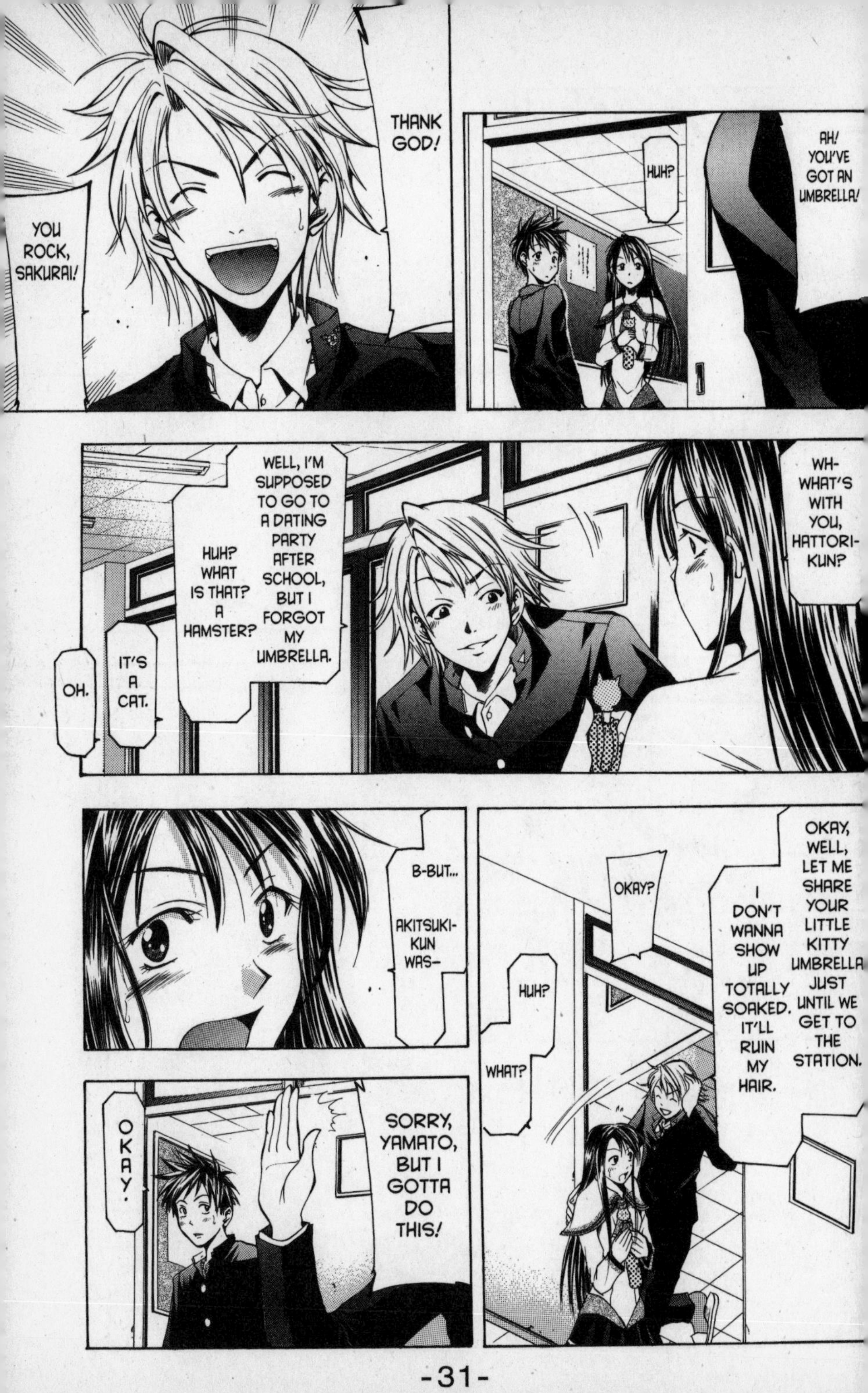
AH! YOU'VE GOT AN UMBRELLA!
HUH?
THANK GOD!
YOU ROCK, SAKURAI!
WH-WHAT'S WITH YOU, HATTORI-KUN?
WELL, I'M SUPPOSED TO GO TO A DATING PARTY AFTER SCHOOL, BUT I FORGOT MY UMBRELLA.
HUH? WHAT IS THAT? A HAMSTER?
IT'S A CAT.
OH.
OKAY, WELL, LET ME SHARE YOUR LITTLE KITTY UMBRELLA JUST UNTIL WE GET TO THE STATION.
I DON'T WANNA SHOW UP TOTALLY SOAKED. IT'LL RUIN MY HAIR.
OKAY?
HUH?
WHAT?
B-BUT...
AKITSUKI-KUN WAS—
SORRY, YAMATO, BUT I GOTTA DO THIS!
OKAY.

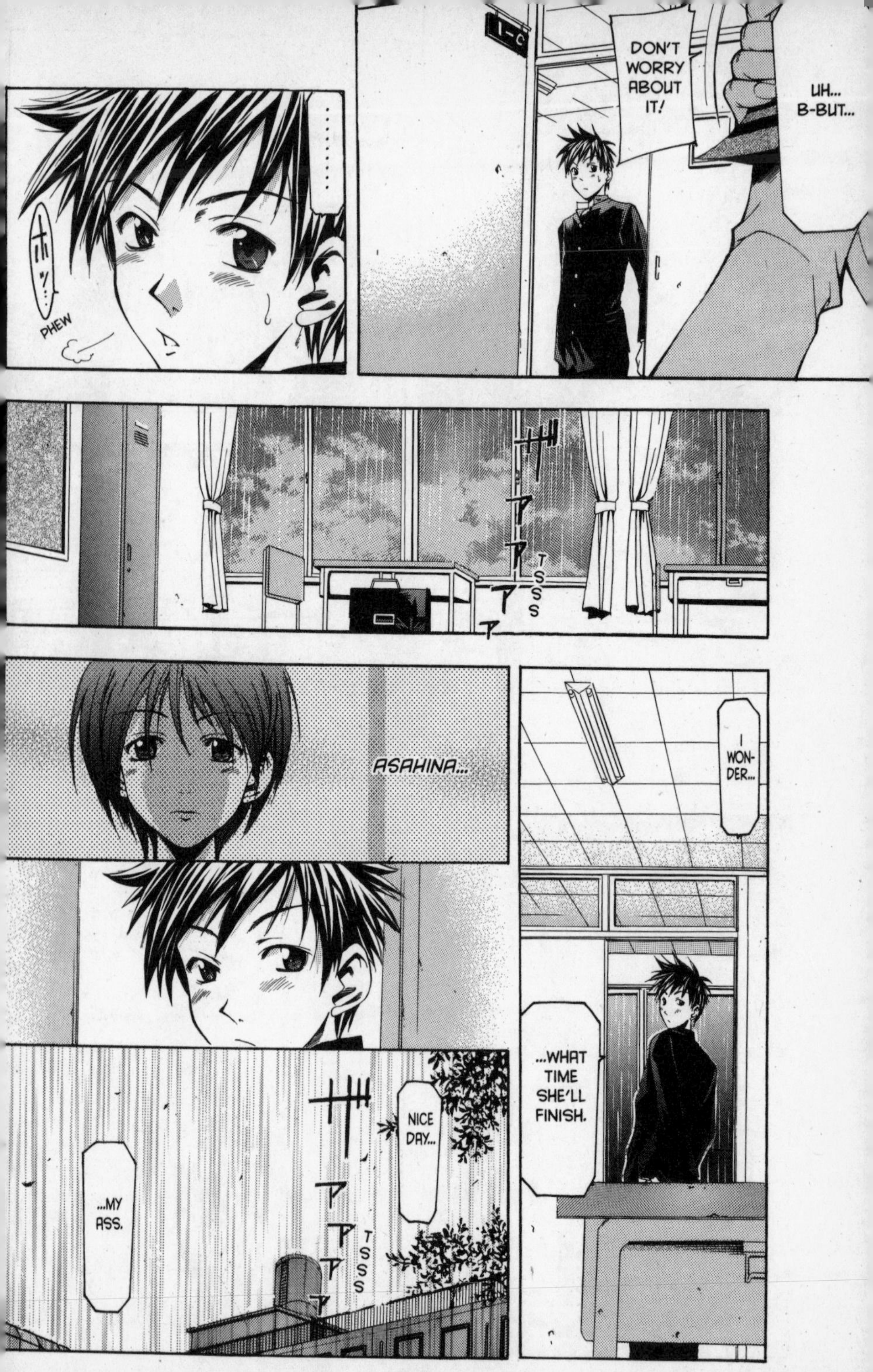
1-C
UH... B-BUT...
DON'T WORRY ABOUT IT!
......
ホッ...
PHEW
TSSS
I WONDER...
...WHAT TIME SHE'LL FINISH.
ASAHINA...
NICE DAY...
...MY ASS.
TSSS

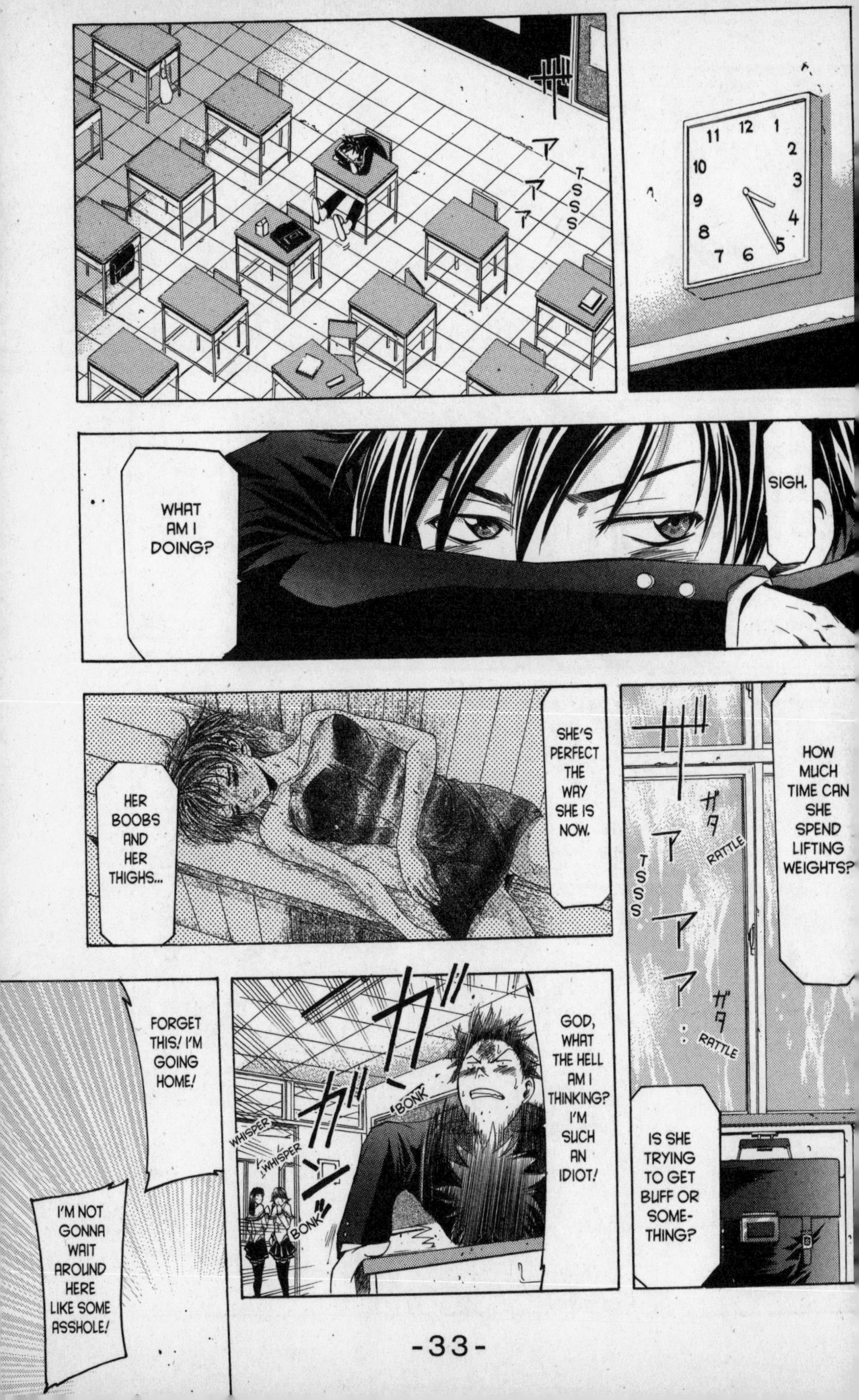
TSSS
SIGH.
WHAT AM I DOING?
HOW MUCH TIME CAN SHE SPEND LIFTING WEIGHTS?
TSSS
RATTLE
RATTLE
IS SHE TRYING TO GET BUFF OR SOME-THING?
SHE'S PERFECT THE WAY SHE IS NOW.
HER BOOBS AND HER THIGHS...
GOD, WHAT THE HELL AM I THINKING? I'M SUCH AN IDIOT!
BONK
WHISPER
WHISPER
BONK
FORGET THIS! I'M GOING HOME!
I'M NOT GONNA WAIT AROUND HERE LIKE SOME ASSHOLE!

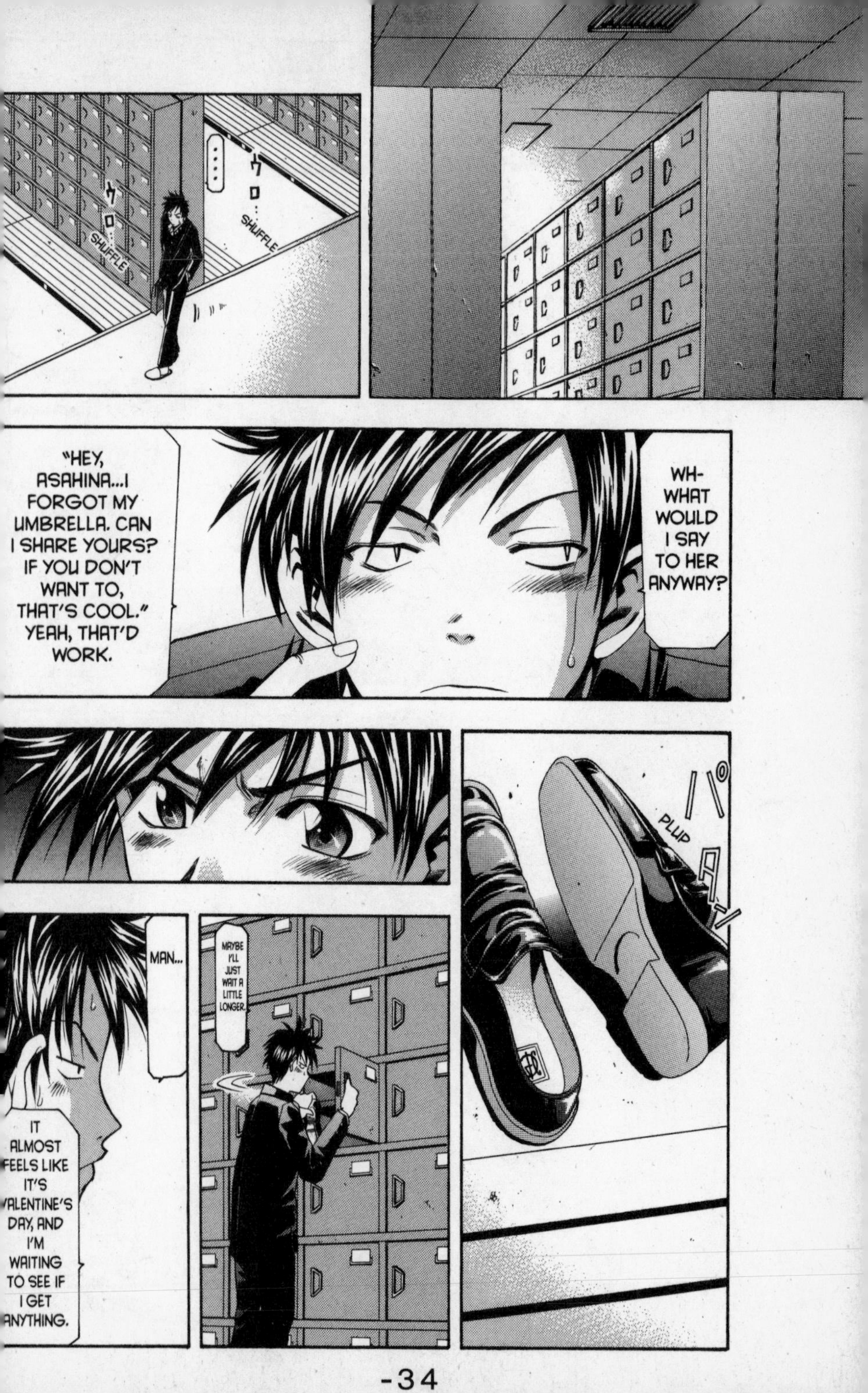
....
SHUFFLE
SHUFFLE
WH- WHAT WOULD I SAY TO HER ANYWAY?
"HEY, ASAHINA...I FORGOT MY UMBRELLA. CAN I SHARE YOURS? IF YOU DON'T WANT TO, THAT'S COOL." YEAH, THAT'D WORK.
PLUP
MAYBE I'LL JUST WAIT A LITTLE LONGER.
MAN...
IT ALMOST FEELS LIKE IT'S VALENTINE'S DAY, AND I'M WAITING TO SEE IF I GET ANYTHING.

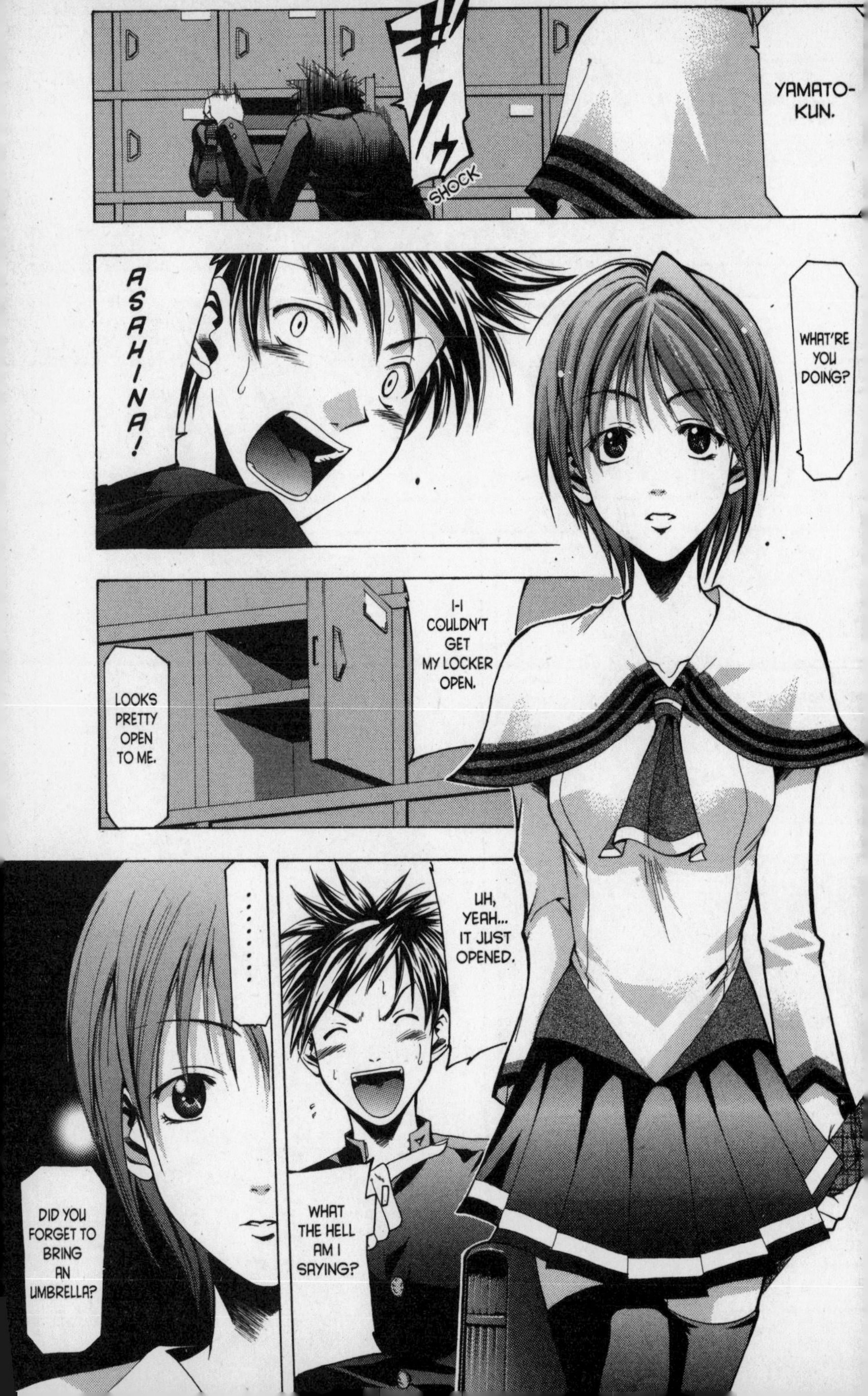
YAMATO-KUN.
SHOCK
WHAT'RE YOU DOING?
ASAHINA!
I-I COULDN'T GET MY LOCKER OPEN.
LOOKS PRETTY OPEN TO ME.
UH, YEAH... IT JUST OPENED.
WHAT THE HELL AM I SAYING?
......
DID YOU FORGET TO BRING AN UMBRELLA?

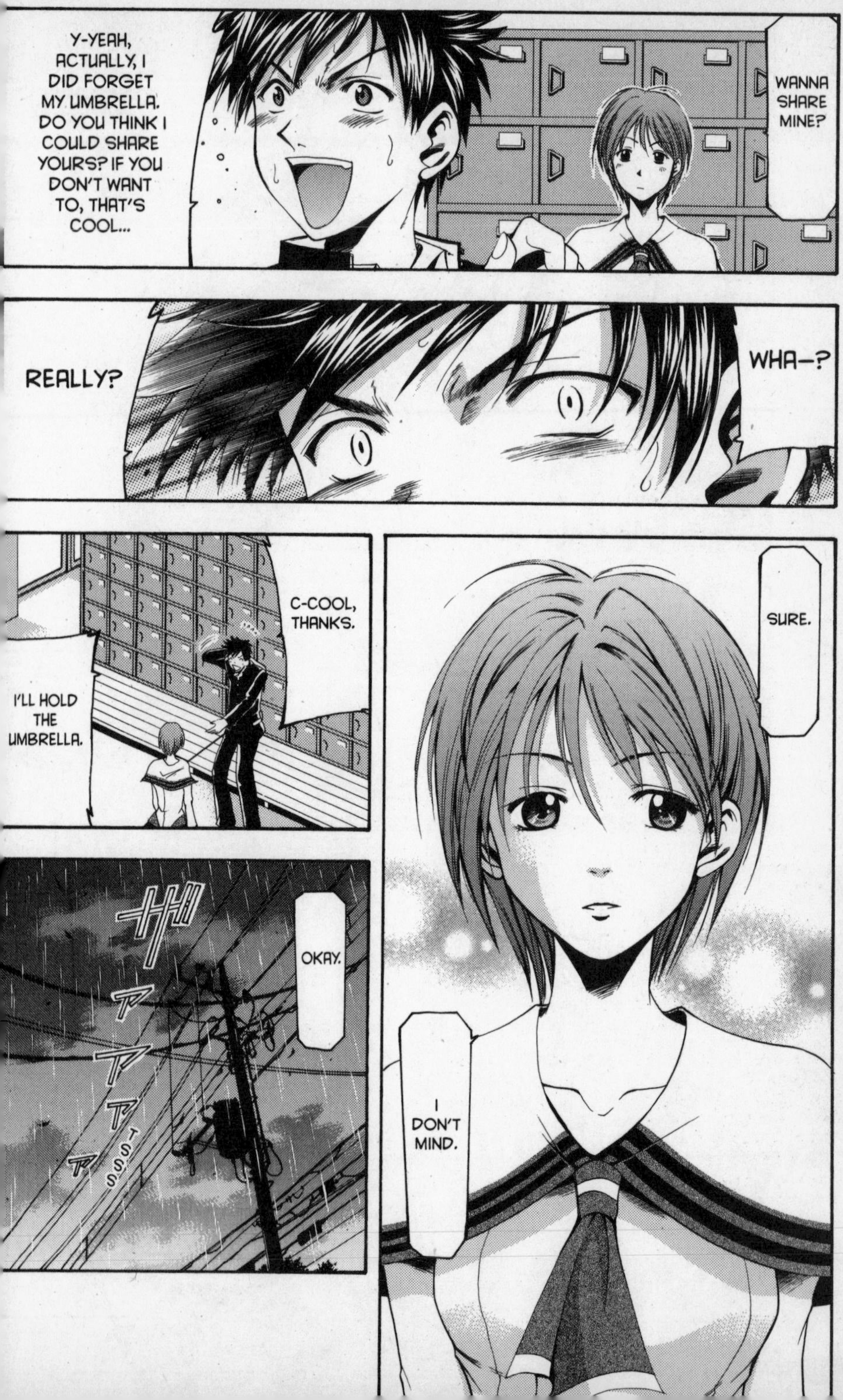
WANNA SHARE MINE?
Y-YEAH, ACTUALLY, I DID FORGET MY UMBRELLA. DO YOU THINK I COULD SHARE YOURS? IF YOU DON'T WANT TO, THAT'S COOL...
WHA-?
REALLY?
SURE.
I DON'T MIND.
C-COOL, THANKS.
I'LL HOLD THE UMBRELLA.
OKAY.
TSSS

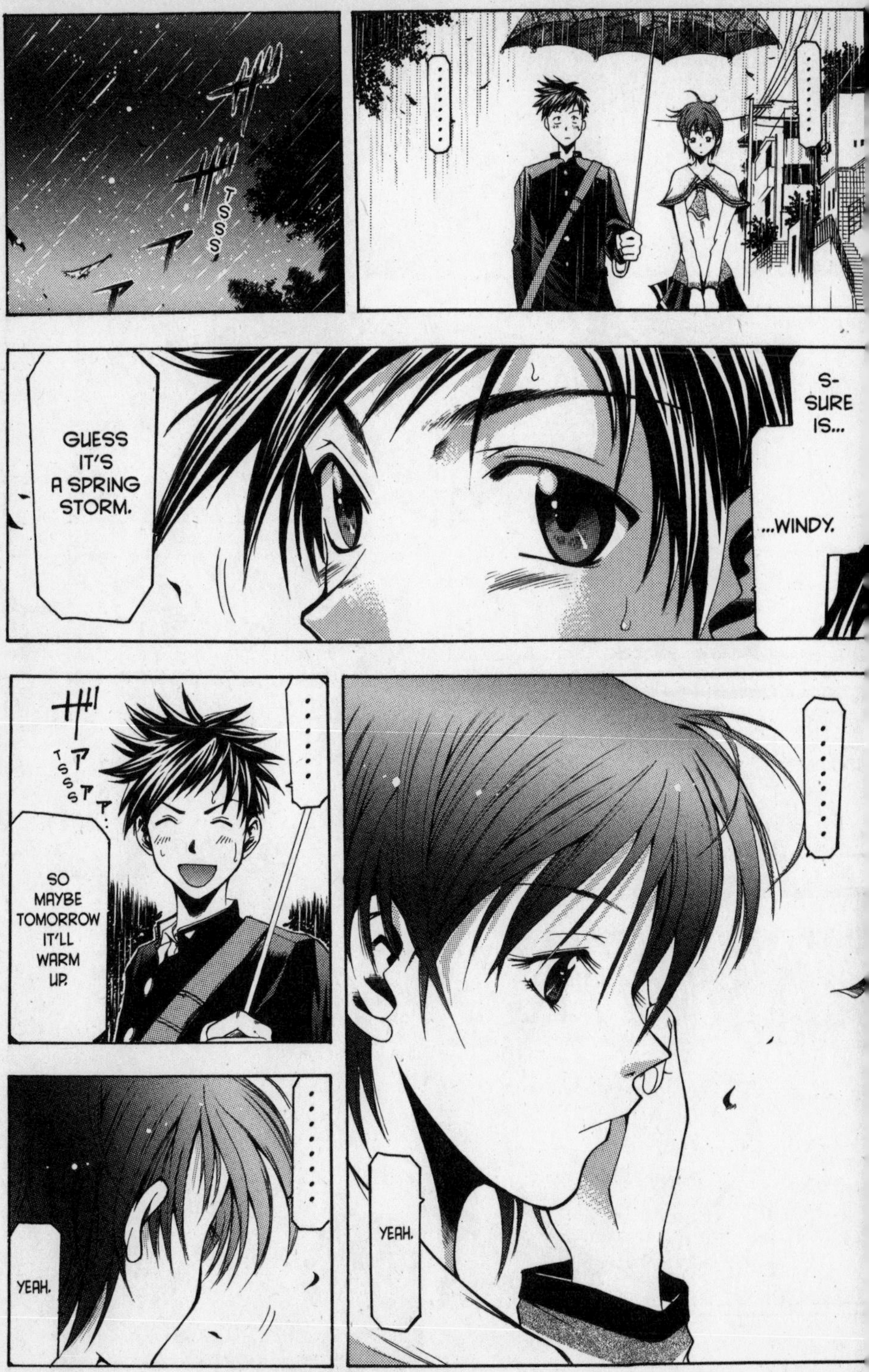
......
......
TSSS
S-SURE IS...
...WINDY.
GUESS IT'S A SPRING STORM.
......
YEAH.
......
TSSS
SO MAYBE TOMORROW IT'LL WARM UP.
......
YEAH.

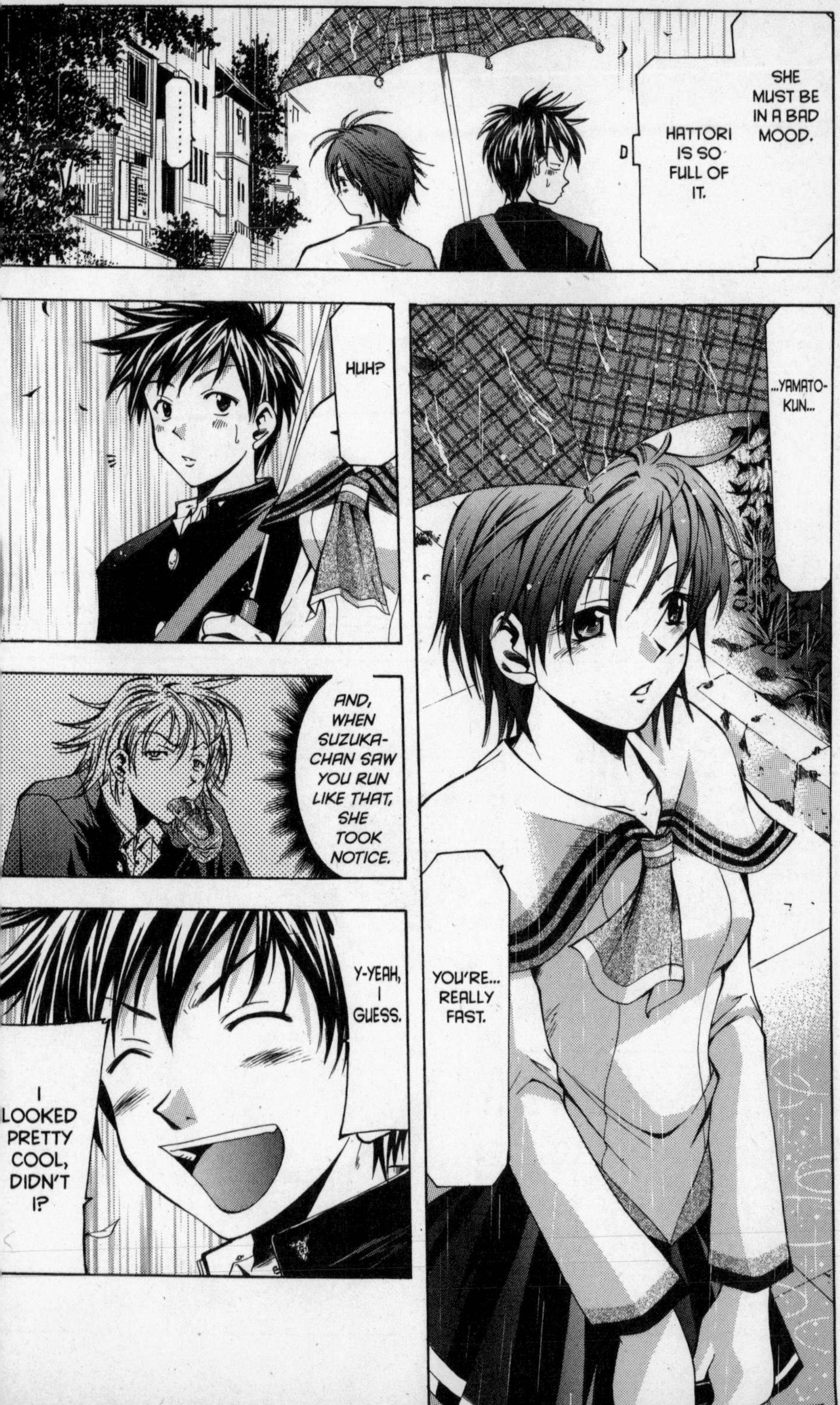
SHE MUST BE IN A BAD MOOD.
HATTORI IS SO FULL OF IT.
...YAMATO-KUN...
YOU'RE... REALLY FAST.
HUH?
AND, WHEN SUZUKA-CHAN SAW YOU RUN LIKE THAT, SHE TOOK NOTICE.
Y-YEAH, I GUESS.
I LOOKED PRETTY COOL, DIDN'T I?

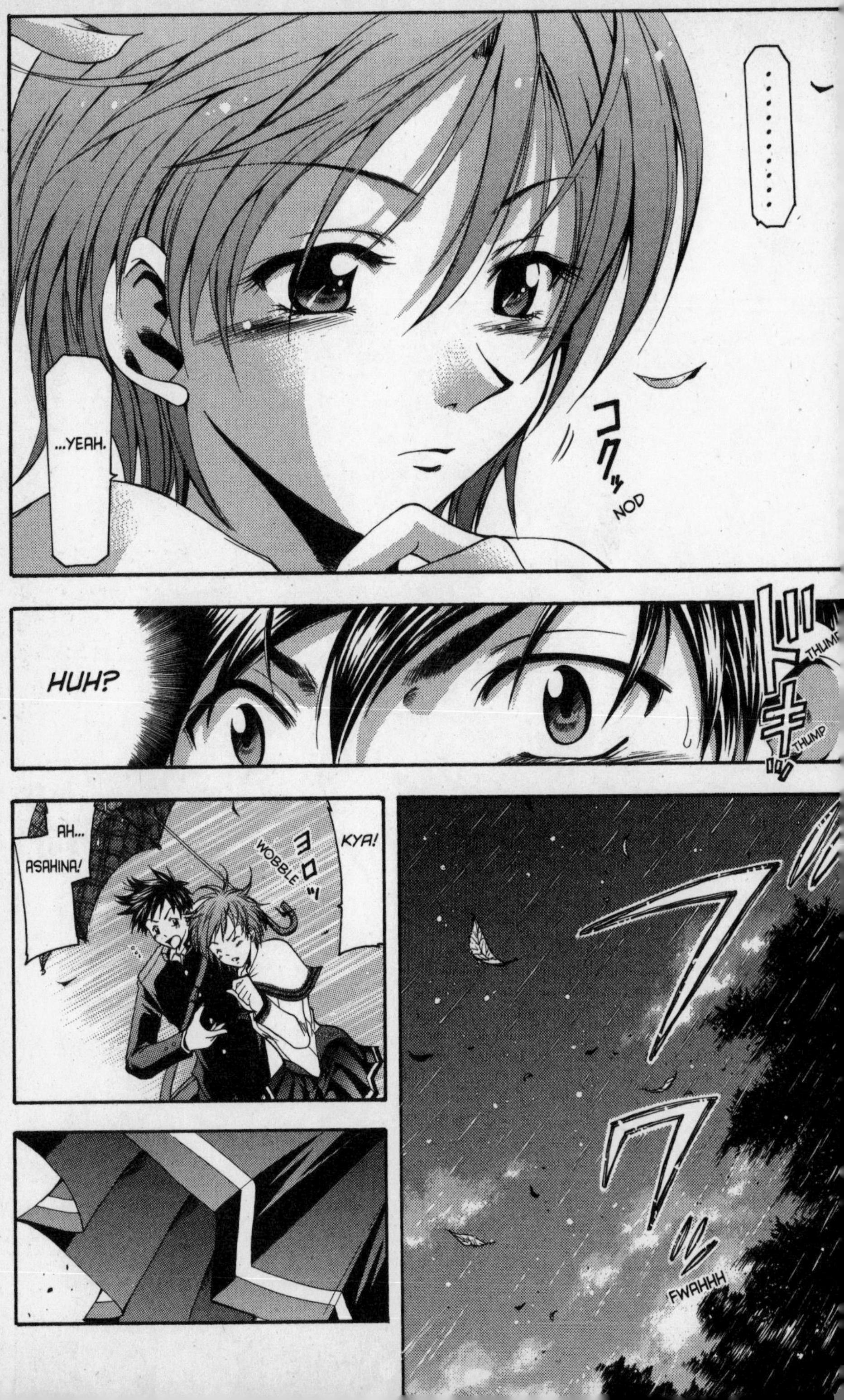
……
コクッ
NOD
...YEAH.
ドキッ
THUMP
THUMP
HUH?
ブワッ
FWAHHH
KYA!
ヨロッ
WOBBLE
AH... ASAHINA!
...

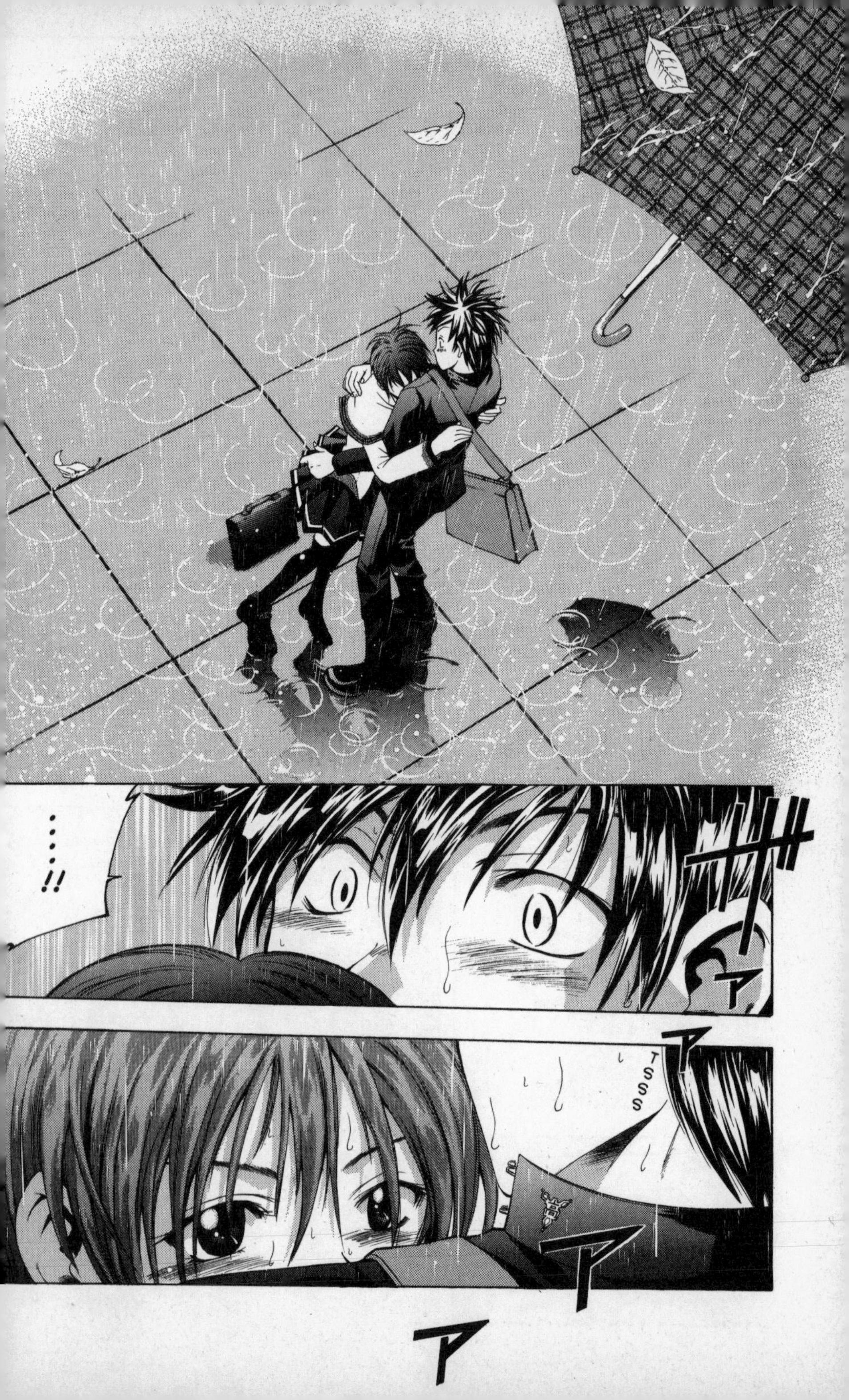
ザァアアア
....!!
TSSS

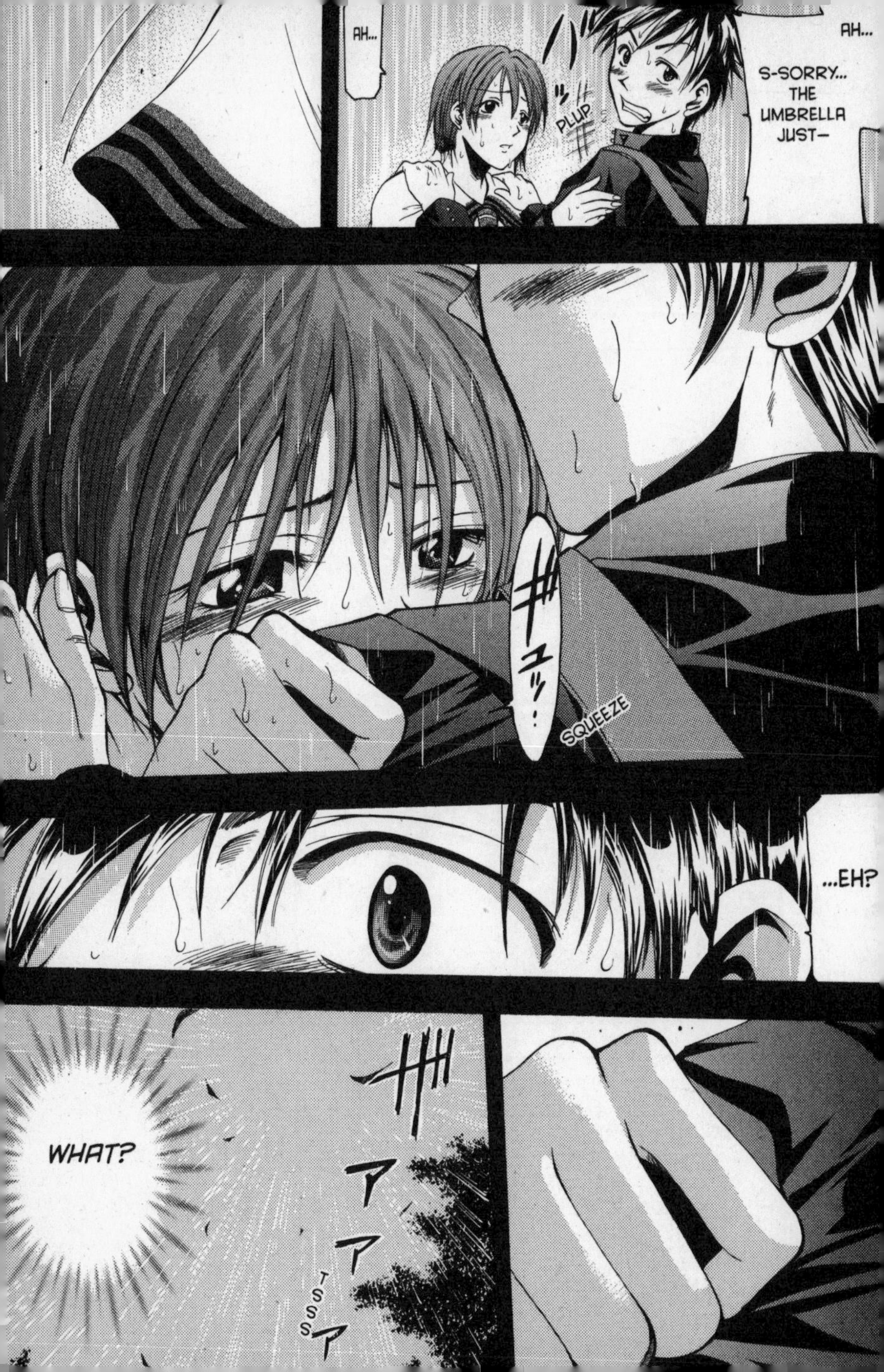
AH...
S-SORRY... THE UMBRELLA JUST—
PLUP
AH...
SQUEEZE
...EH?
WHAT?
TSSS

SUZUKA FOUR-PANEL THEATER NUMBER SIX

MR. FORGETFUL

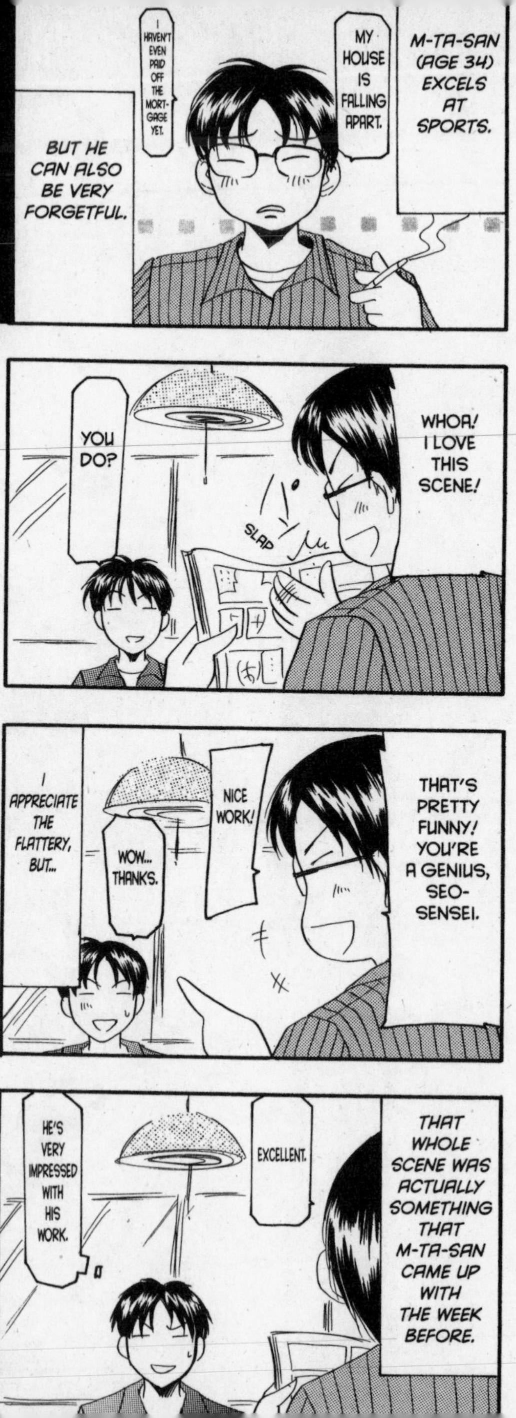
M-TA-SAN (AGE 34) EXCELS AT SPORTS.
MY HOUSE IS FALLING APART.
I HAVEN'T EVEN PAID OFF THE MORTGAGE YET.
BUT HE CAN ALSO BE VERY FORGETFUL.
WHOA! I LOVE THIS SCENE!
SLAP
YOU DO?
THAT'S PRETTY FUNNY! YOU'RE A GENIUS, SEO-SENSEI.
NICE WORK!
WOW... THANKS.
I APPRECIATE THE FLATTERY, BUT...
THAT WHOLE SCENE WAS ACTUALLY SOMETHING THAT M-TA-SAN CAME UP WITH THE WEEK BEFORE.
EXCELLENT.
HE'S VERY IMPRESSED WITH HIS WORK.

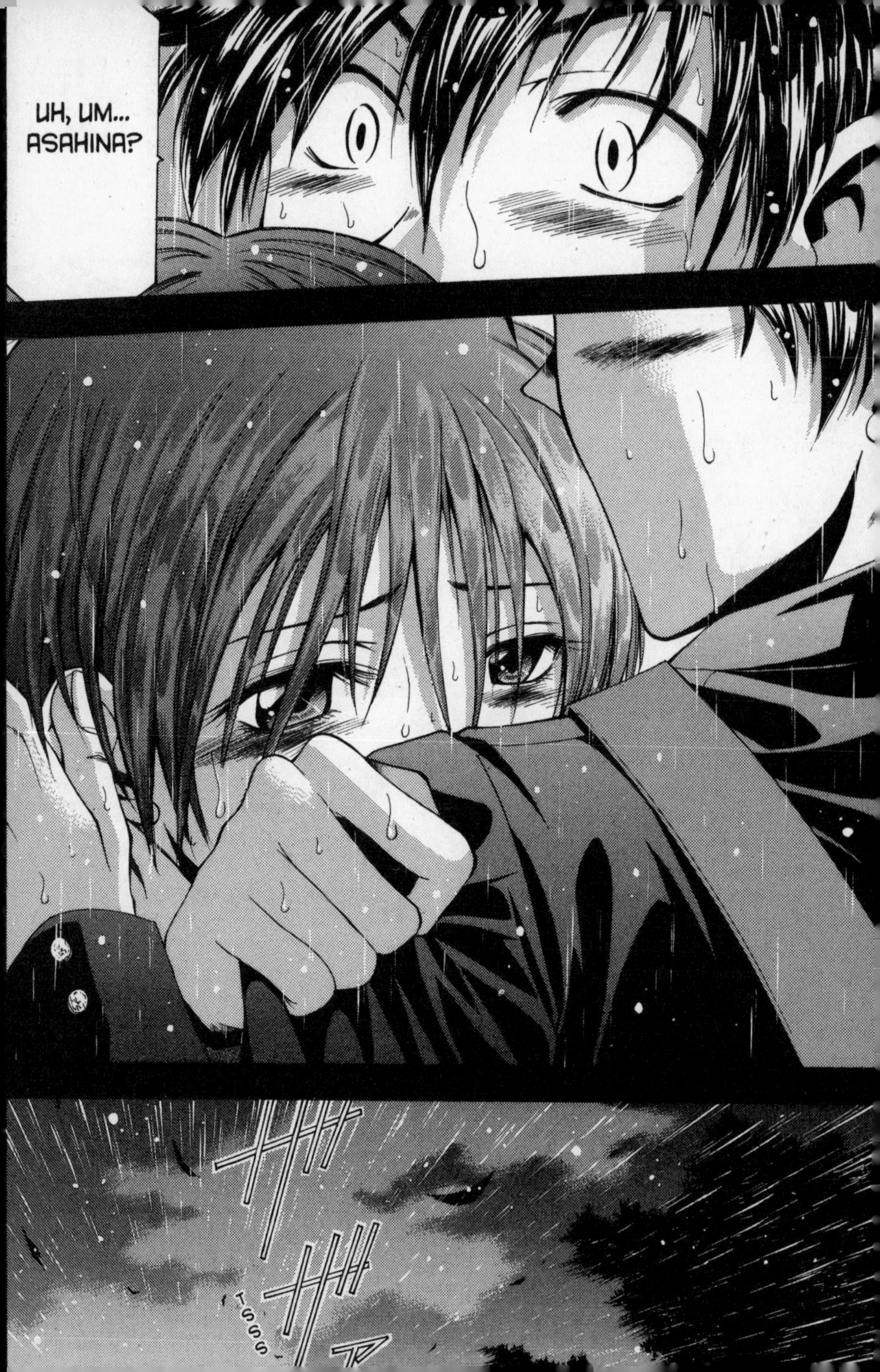
UH, UM... ASAHINA?
TSSS

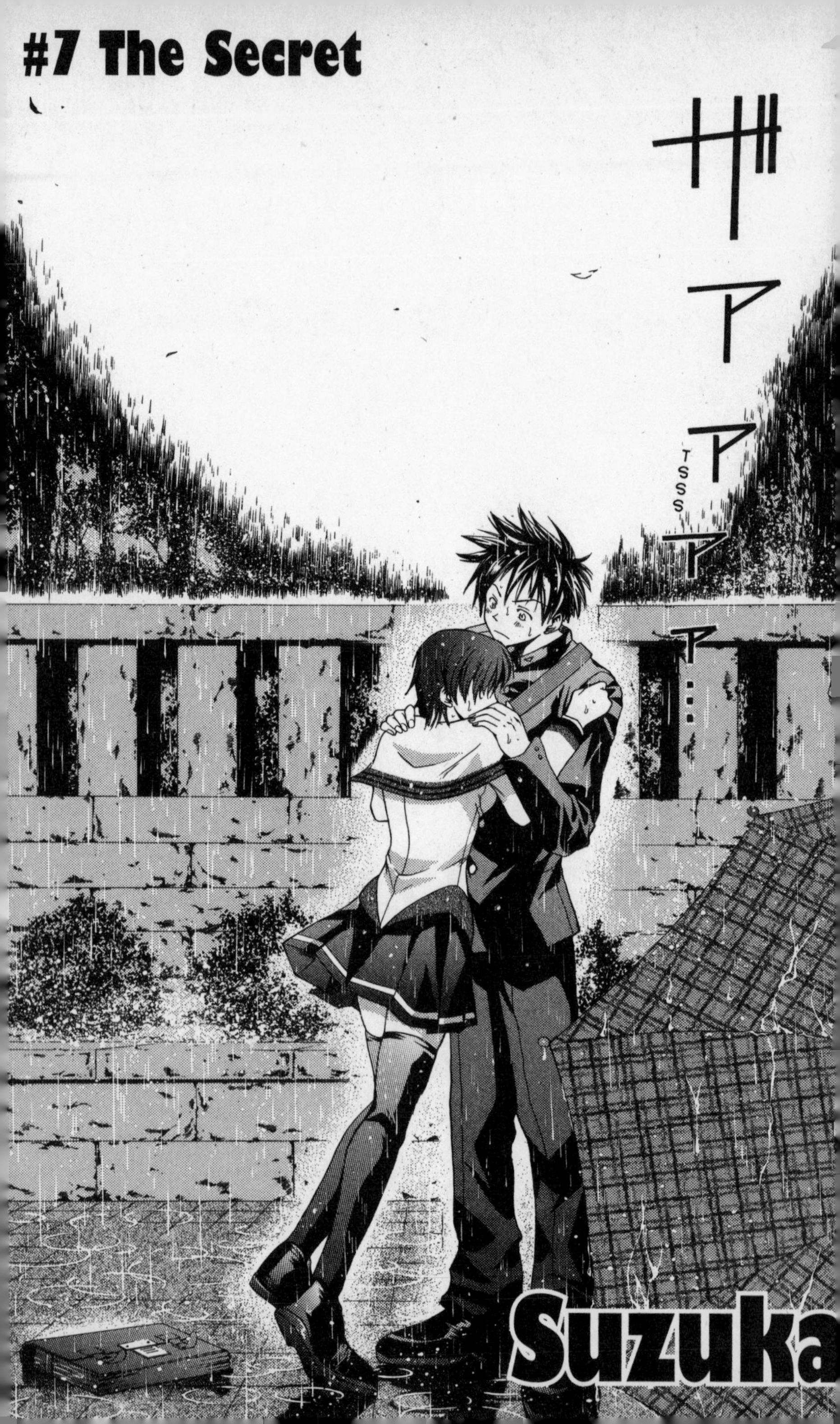
#7 The Secret
ザァァァァ…
TSSS
Suzuka

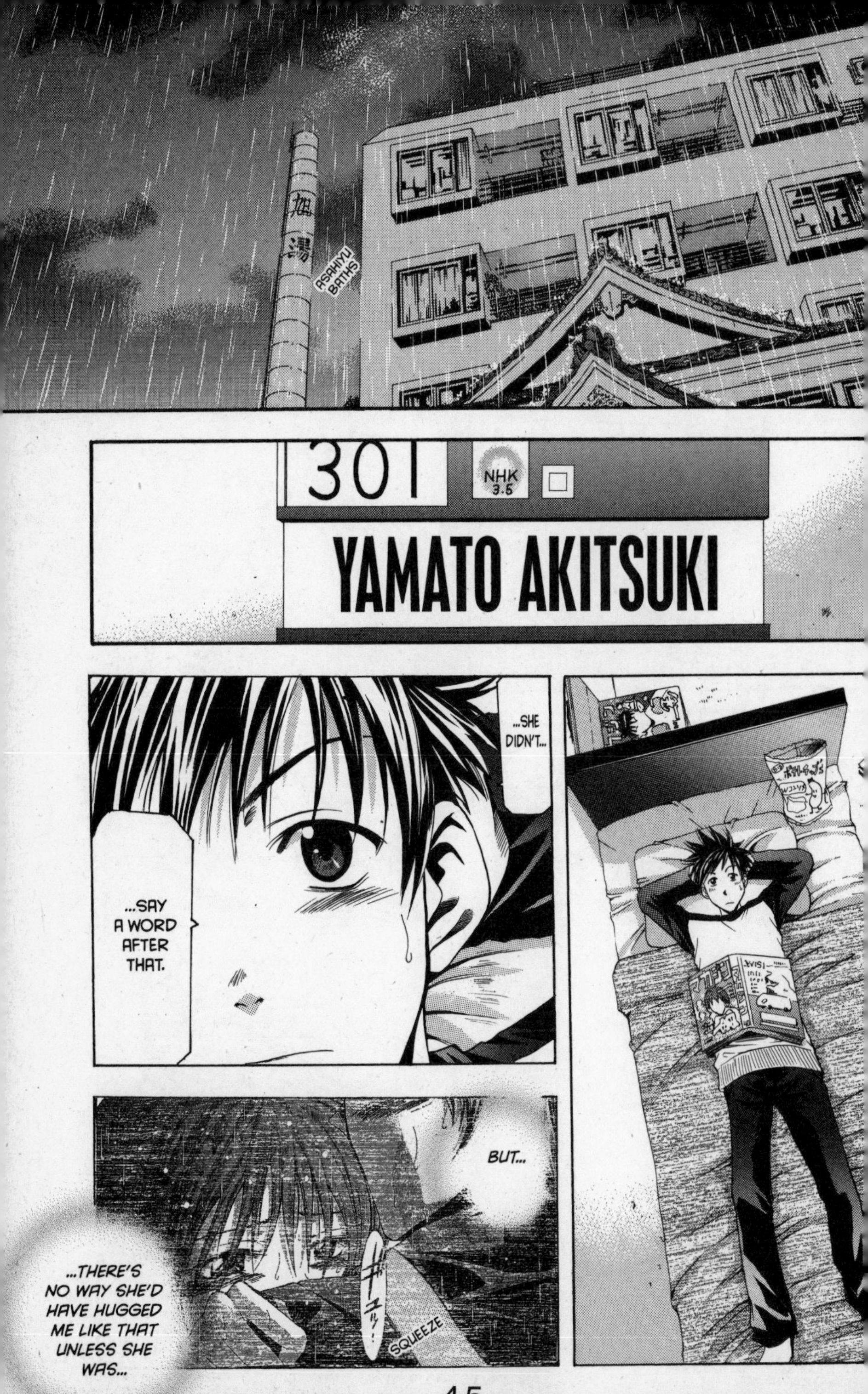
旭湯
ASAHIYU BATHS
301
NHK 3.5
YAMATO AKITSUKI
...SHE DIDN'T...
...SAY A WORD AFTER THAT.
BUT...
ギュッ
SQUEEZE
...THERE'S NO WAY SHE'D HAVE HUGGED ME LIKE THAT UNLESS SHE WAS...

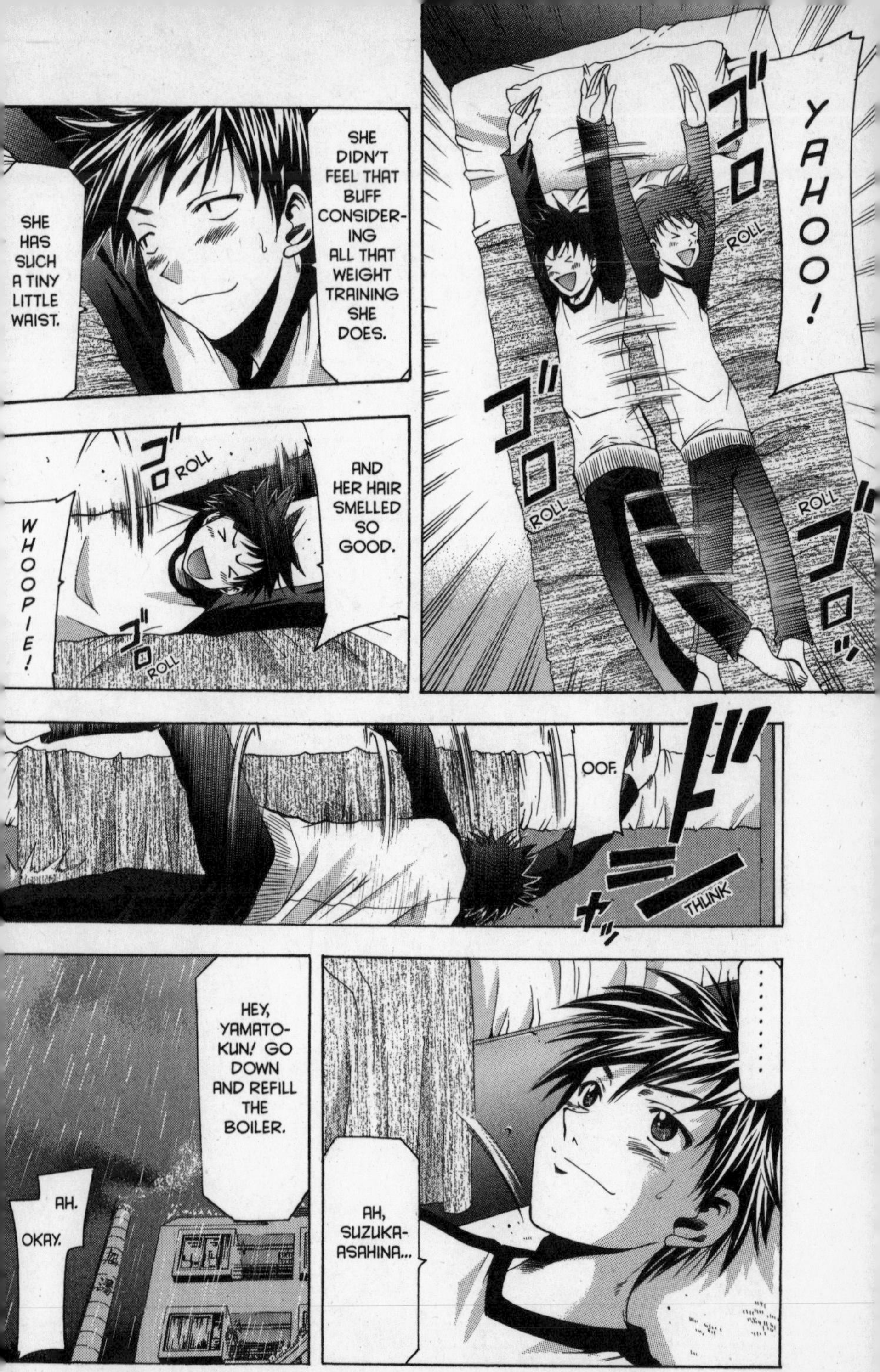
YAHOO!
ゴロ
ROLL
ROLL
ROLL
ゴロッ
SHE DIDN'T FEEL THAT BUFF CONSIDER-ING ALL THAT WEIGHT TRAINING SHE DOES.
SHE HAS SUCH A TINY LITTLE WAIST.
AND HER HAIR SMELLED SO GOOD.
ROLL
WHOOPIE!
ROLL
OOF.
THUNK
......
AH, SUZUKA-ASAHINA...
HEY, YAMATO-KUN! GO DOWN AND REFILL THE BOILER.
AH.
OKAY.

BATH

ASAHINA AND ME UNDER THE SAME UMBRELLA.

THAT'LL BE OUR LITTLE SECRET.

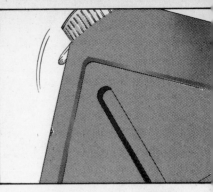

HEY, YAMATO-KUN.

WHAT'RE YOU SO HAPPY ABOUT?

MEOW.

BATH

SOMETHING GOOD HAPPEN AT SCHOOL?

WHA—

SHOCK

YUUKA-SAN.

LADIES BATH

HEY, WAIT!

WHAT'RE YOU BABBLING ABOUT?

NOTHING HAPPENED!

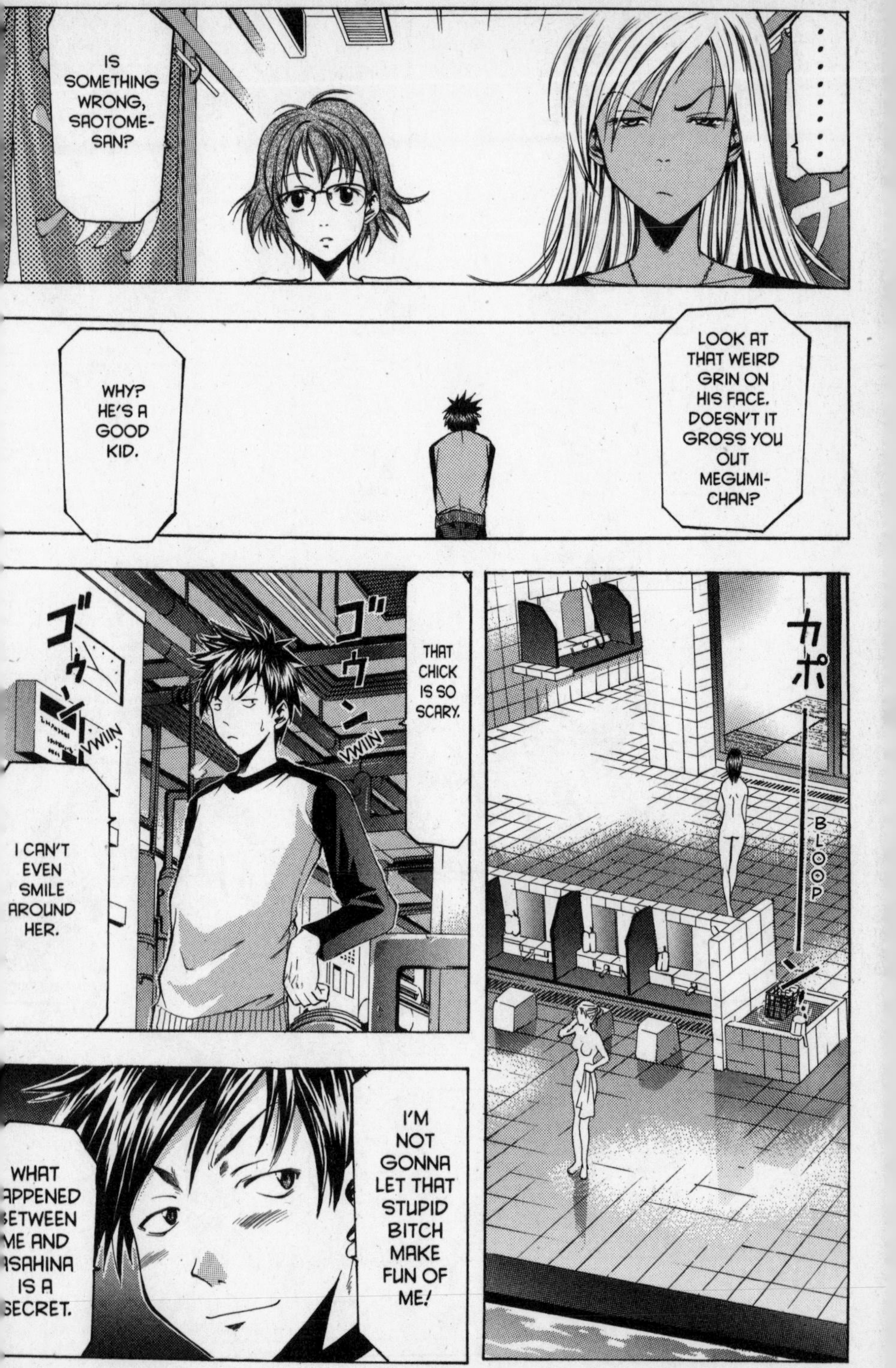
......
IS SOMETHING WRONG, SAOTOME-SAN?
LOOK AT THAT WEIRD GRIN ON HIS FACE. DOESN'T IT GROSS YOU OUT MEGUMI-CHAN?
WHY? HE'S A GOOD KID.
カポ
BLOOP
ゴウン
VWIIN
ゴウン
VWIIN
THAT CHICK IS SO SCARY.
I CAN'T EVEN SMILE AROUND HER.
I'M NOT GONNA LET THAT STUPID BITCH MAKE FUN OF ME!
WHAT APPENED ETWEEN ME AND SAHINA IS A ECRET.

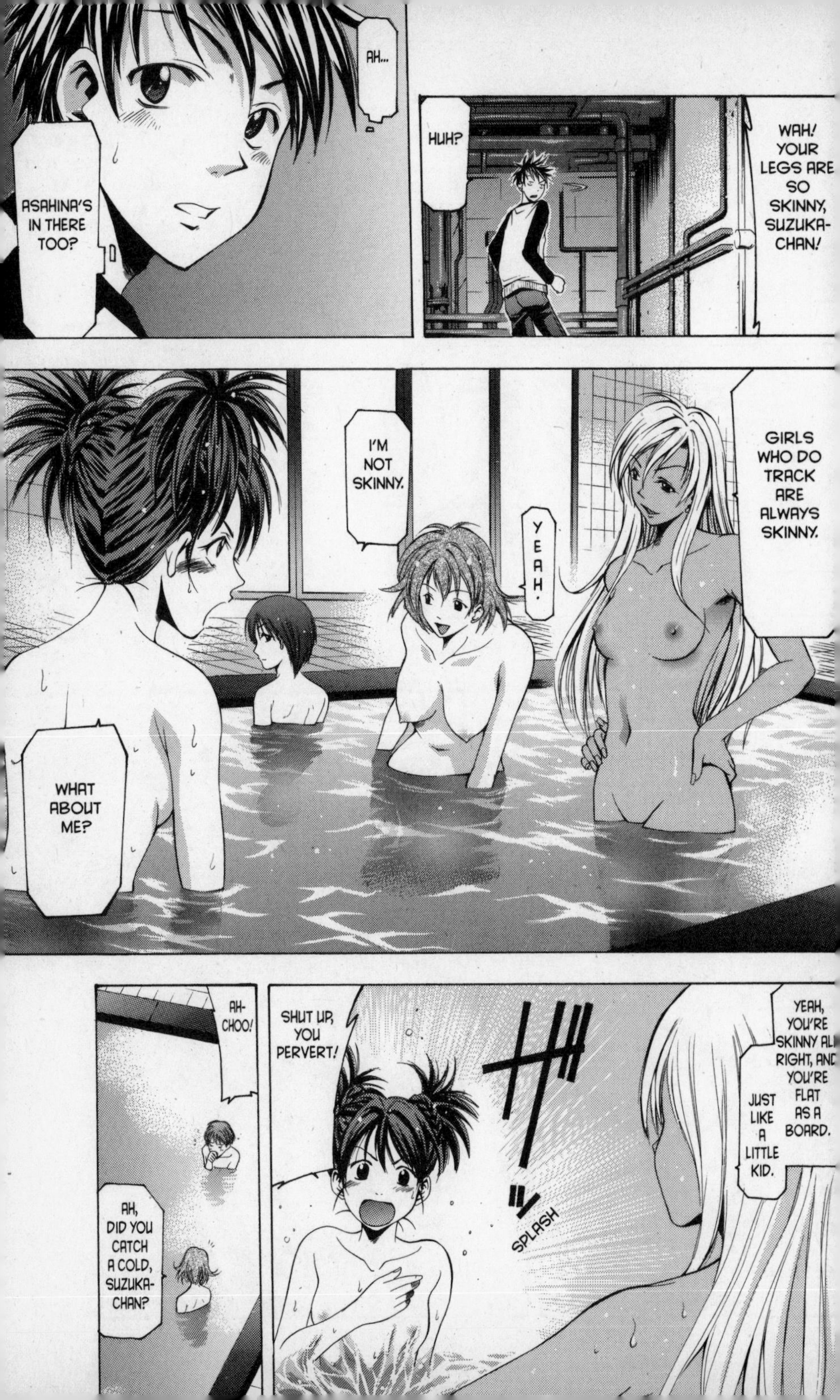
WAH! YOUR LEGS ARE SO SKINNY, SUZUKA-CHAN!
HUH?
AH...
ASAHINA'S IN THERE TOO?
GIRLS WHO DO TRACK ARE ALWAYS SKINNY.
YEAH.
I'M NOT SKINNY.
WHAT ABOUT ME?
YEAH, YOU'RE SKINNY AL RIGHT, AND YOU'RE FLAT AS A BOARD.
JUST LIKE A LITTLE KID.
SPLASH
SHUT UP, YOU PERVERT!
AH-CHOO!
AH, DID YOU CATCH A COLD, SUZUKA-CHAN?

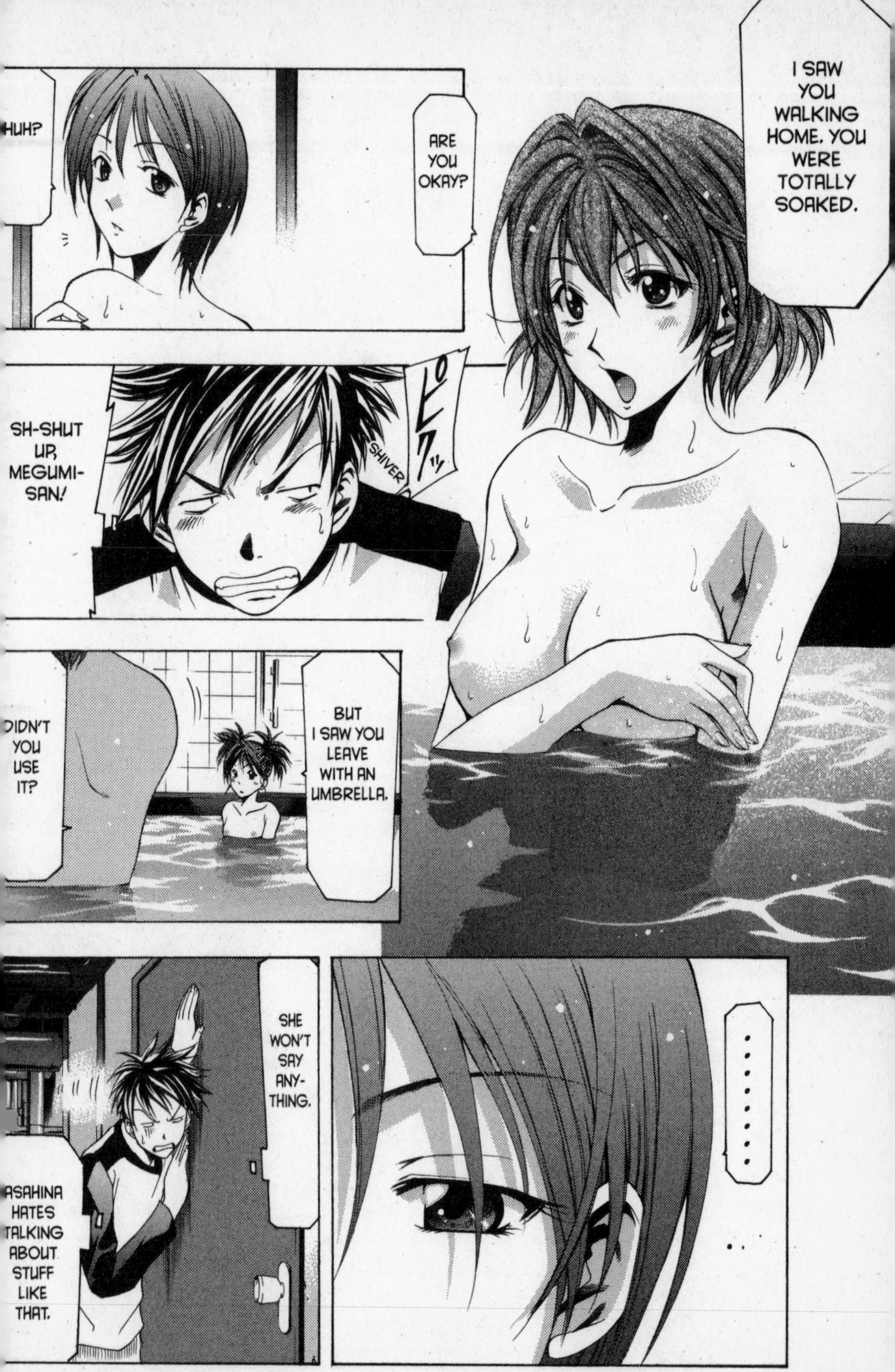
I SAW YOU WALKING HOME. YOU WERE TOTALLY SOAKED.
ARE YOU OKAY?
HUH?
SHIVER
SH-SHUT UP, MEGUMI-SAN!
BUT I SAW YOU LEAVE WITH AN UMBRELLA.
DIDN'T YOU USE IT?
....
..
SHE WON'T SAY ANY-THING.
ASAHINA HATES TALKING ABOUT STUFF LIKE THAT.

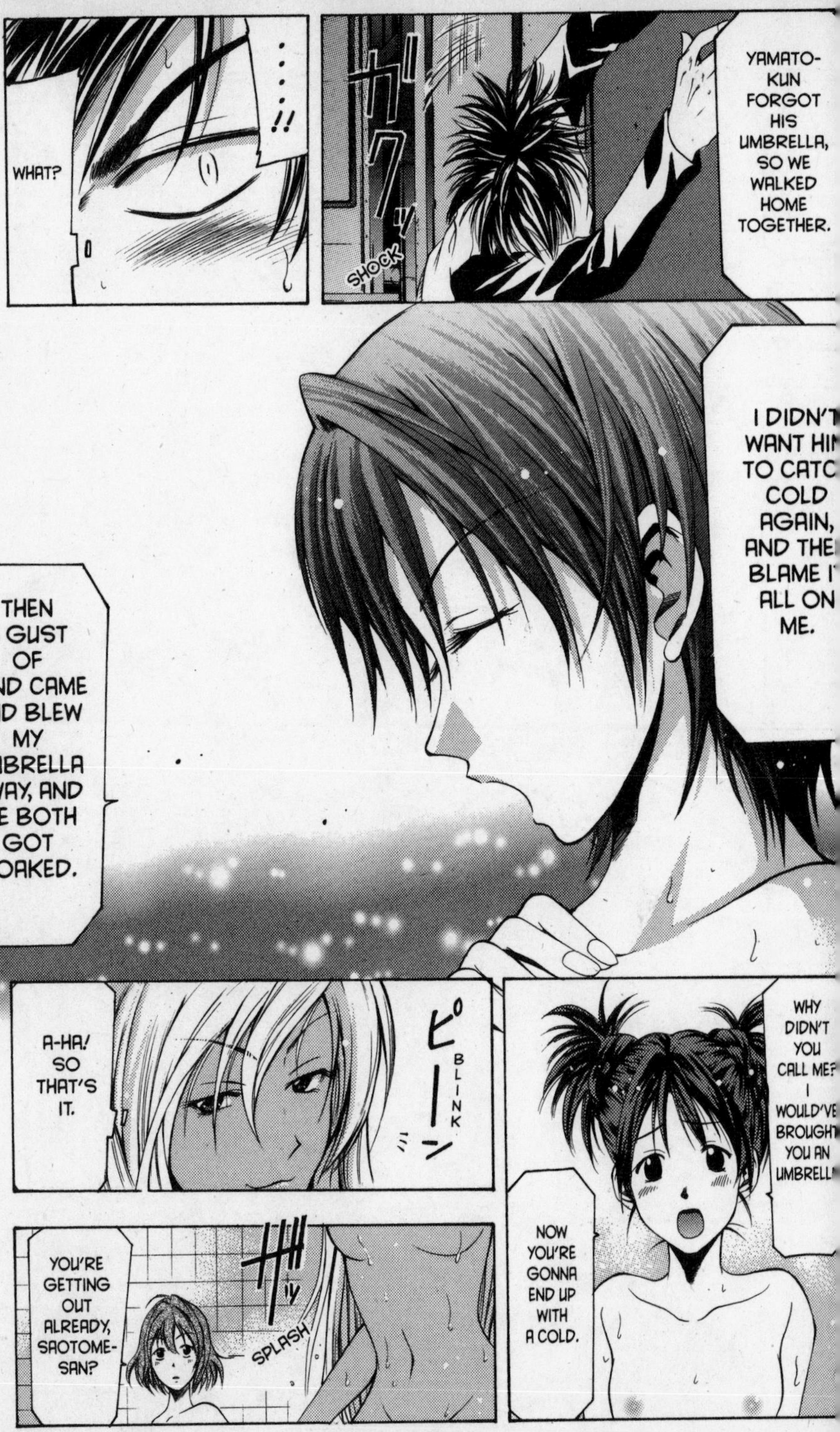
YAMATO-KUN FORGOT HIS UMBRELLA, SO WE WALKED HOME TOGETHER.
SHOCK
......!!
WHAT?
I DIDN'T WANT HI TO CATC COLD AGAIN, AND THE BLAME I ALL ON ME.
THEN A GUST OF WIND CAME AND BLEW MY UMBRELLA AWAY, AND WE BOTH GOT SOAKED.
WHY DIDN'T YOU CALL ME? I WOULD'VE BROUGHT YOU AN UMBRELL
NOW YOU'RE GONNA END UP WITH A COLD.
A-HA! SO THAT'S IT.
BLINK
YOU'RE GETTING OUT ALREADY, SAOTOME-SAN?
SPLASH

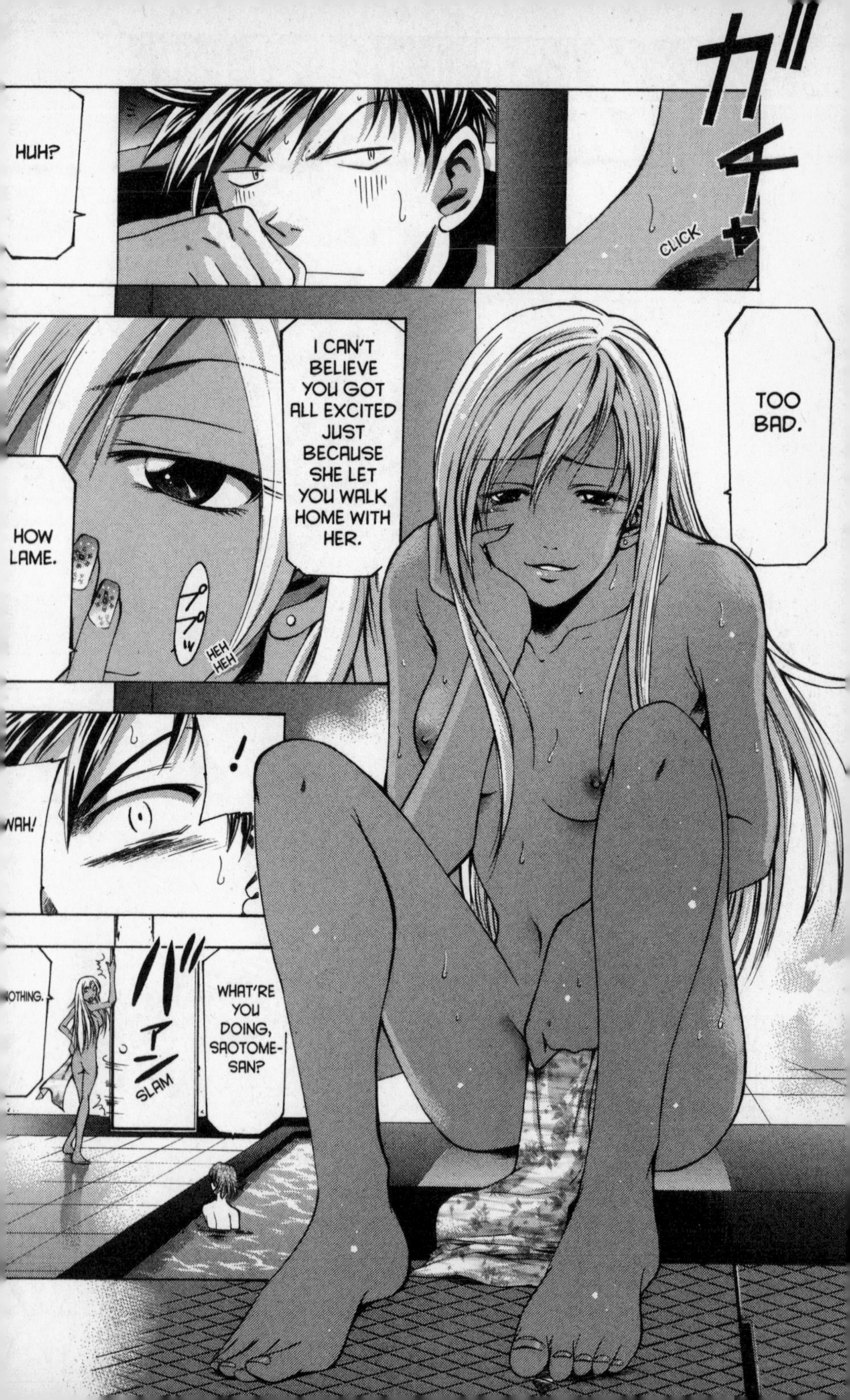
ガチャ
CLICK
HUH?
TOO BAD.
I CAN'T BELIEVE YOU GOT ALL EXCITED JUST BECAUSE SHE LET YOU WALK HOME WITH HER.
HOW LAME.
HEH HEH
!
WAH!
WHAT'RE YOU DOING, SAOTOME-SAN?
バァーン
SLAM
OTHING.

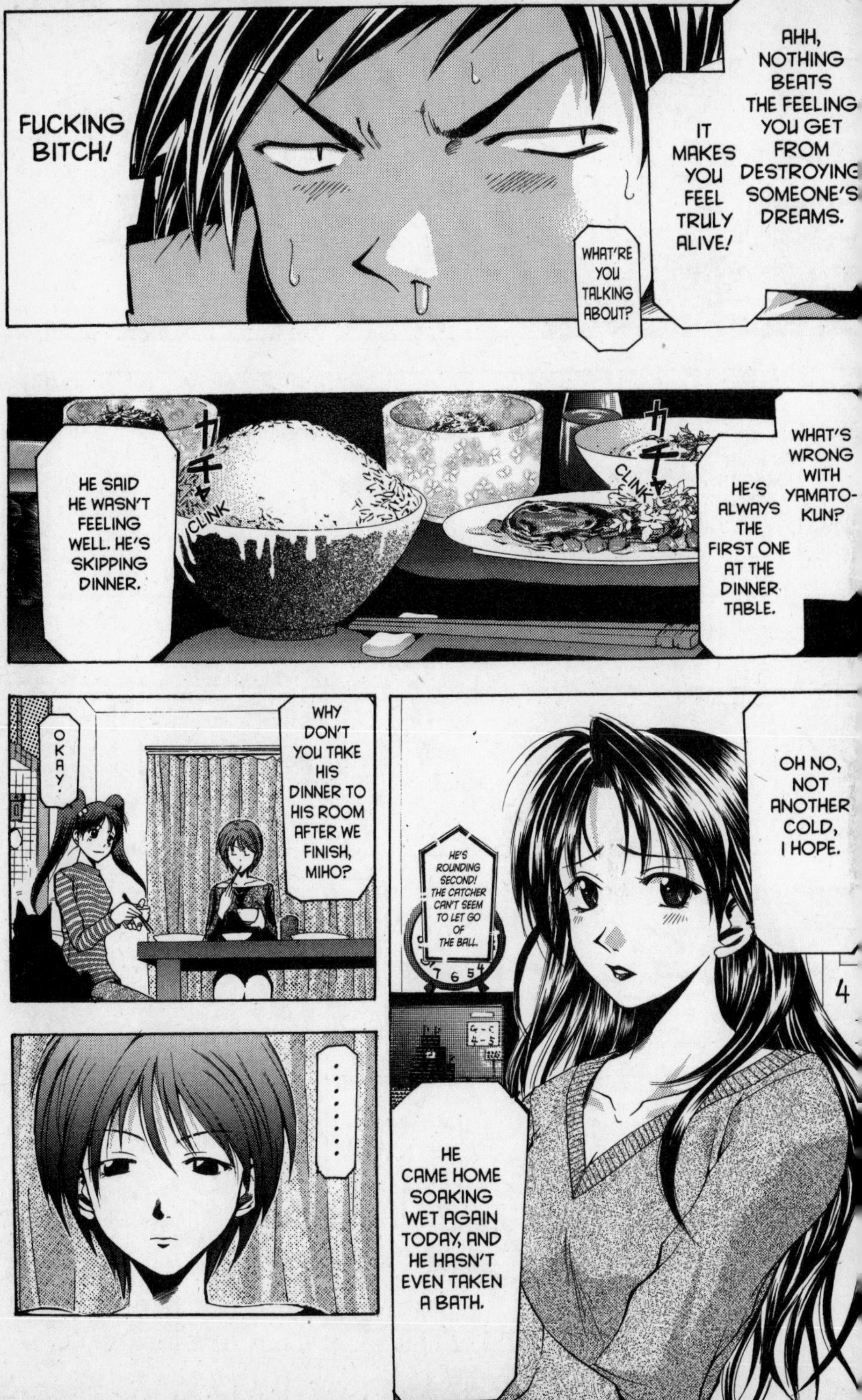
AHH, NOTHING BEATS THE FEELING YOU GET FROM DESTROYING SOMEONE'S DREAMS.
IT MAKES YOU FEEL TRULY ALIVE!
WHAT'RE YOU TALKING ABOUT?
FUCKING BITCH!
WHAT'S WRONG WITH YAMATO-KUN?
HE'S ALWAYS THE FIRST ONE AT THE DINNER TABLE.
カチャ
CLINK
カチャ
CLINK
HE SAID HE WASN'T FEELING WELL. HE'S SKIPPING DINNER.
OH NO, NOT ANOTHER COLD, I HOPE.
HE'S ROUNDING SECOND! THE CATCHER CAN'T SEEM TO LET GO OF THE BALL.
HE CAME HOME SOAKING WET AGAIN TODAY, AND HE HASN'T EVEN TAKEN A BATH.
WHY DON'T YOU TAKE HIS DINNER TO HIS ROOM AFTER WE FINISH, MIHO?
OKAY.
....

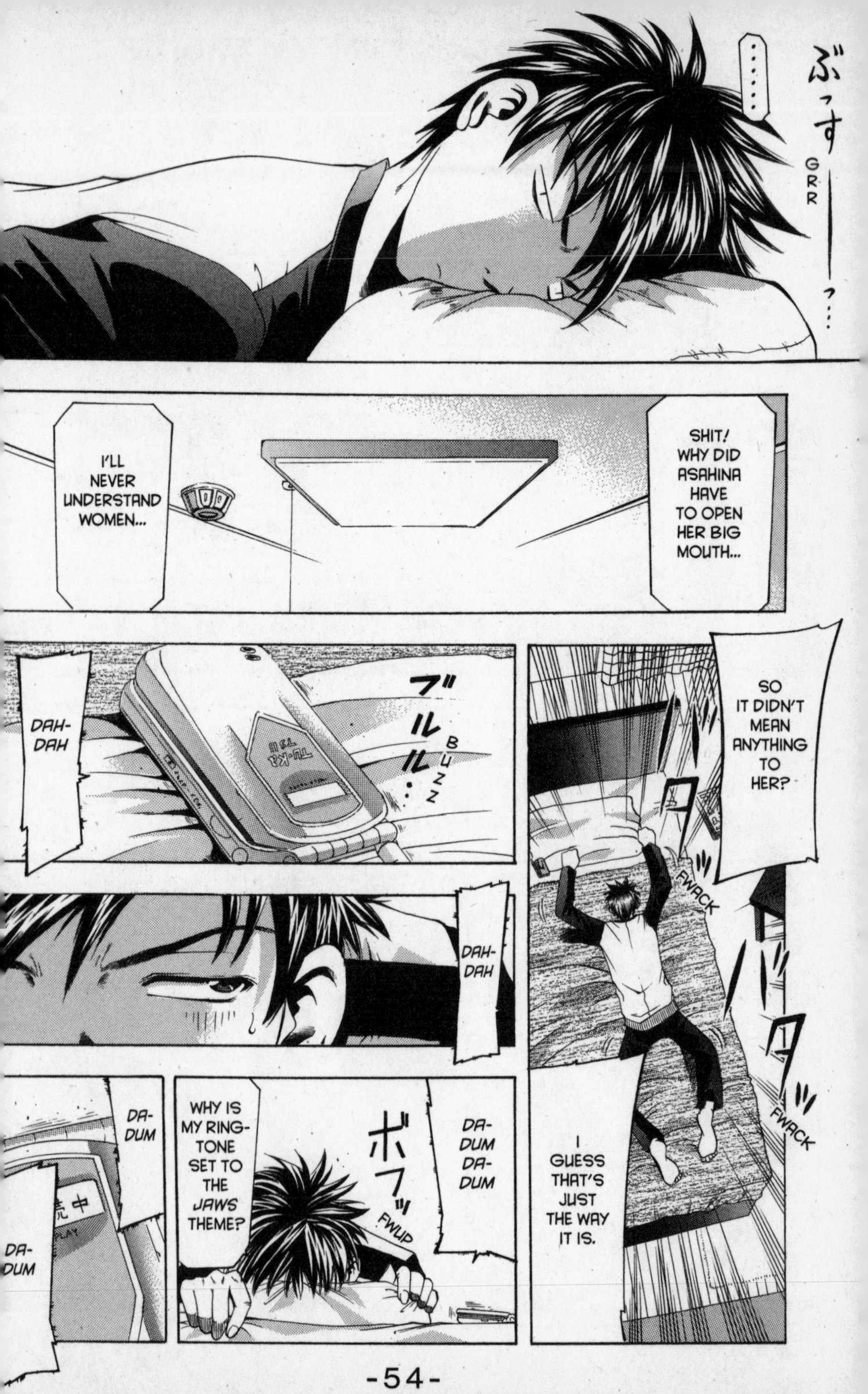

ぶっす
GRR
......
SHIT! WHY DID ASAHINA HAVE TO OPEN HER BIG MOUTH...
I'LL NEVER UNDERSTAND WOMEN...
SO IT DIDN'T MEAN ANYTHING TO HER?
FWACK
FWACK
I GUESS THAT'S JUST THE WAY IT IS.
ブルル...
BUZZ
DAH-DAH
DAH-DAH
DA-DUM DA-DUM
ボフッ
FWUP
WHY IS MY RING-TONE SET TO THE JAWS THEME?
DA-DUM
DA-DUM

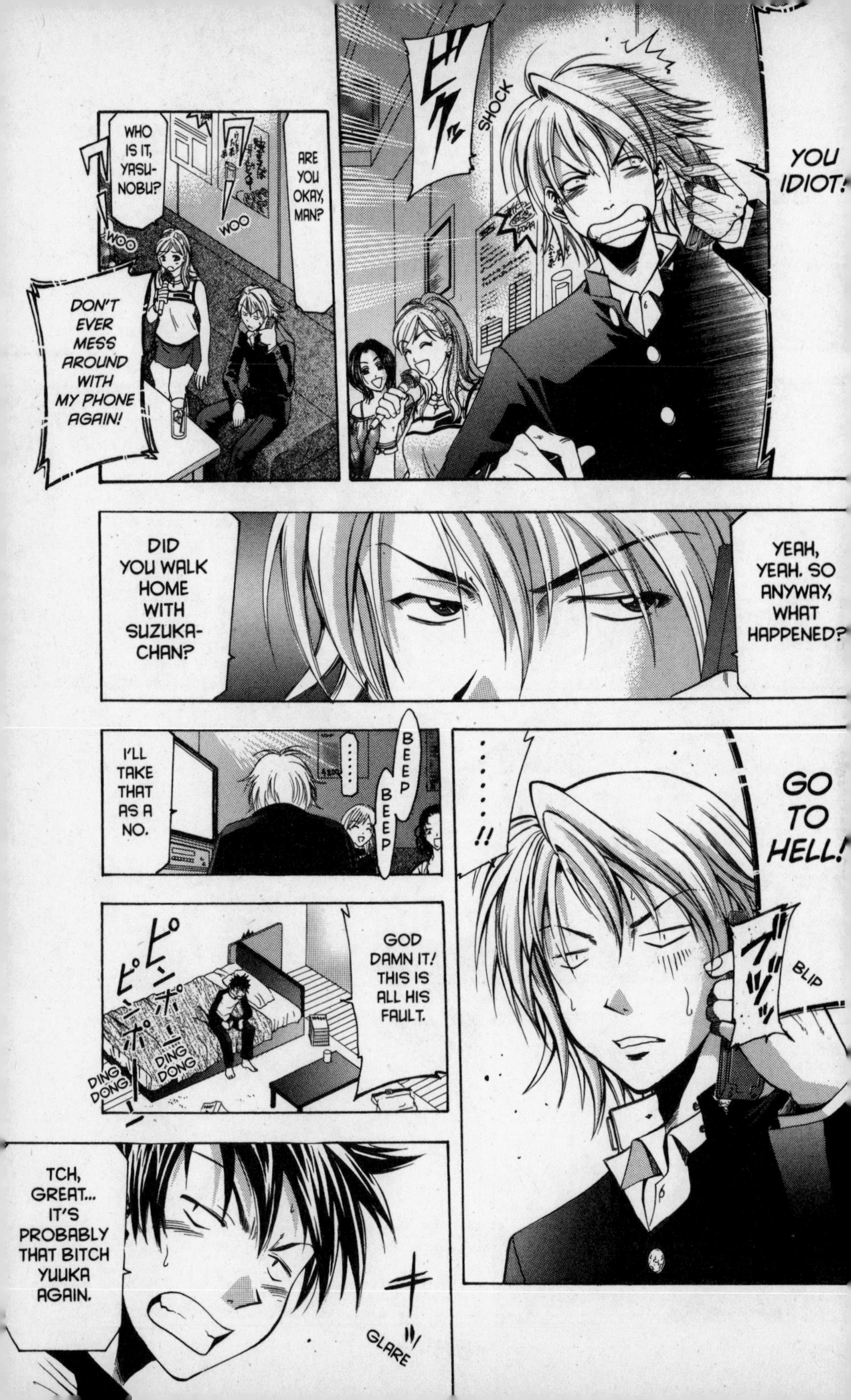
YOU IDIOT!
SHOCK
ARE YOU OKAY, MAN?
WHO IS IT, YASUNOBU?
WOO
WOO
DON'T EVER MESS AROUND WITH MY PHONE AGAIN!
YEAH, YEAH. SO ANYWAY, WHAT HAPPENED?
DID YOU WALK HOME WITH SUZUKA-CHAN?
GO TO HELL!
......!!
BLIP
BEEP BEEP
......
I'LL TAKE THAT AS A NO.
GOD DAMN IT! THIS IS ALL HIS FAULT.
DING DONG
DING DONG
TCH, GREAT... IT'S PROBABLY THAT BITCH YUUKA AGAIN.
GLARE

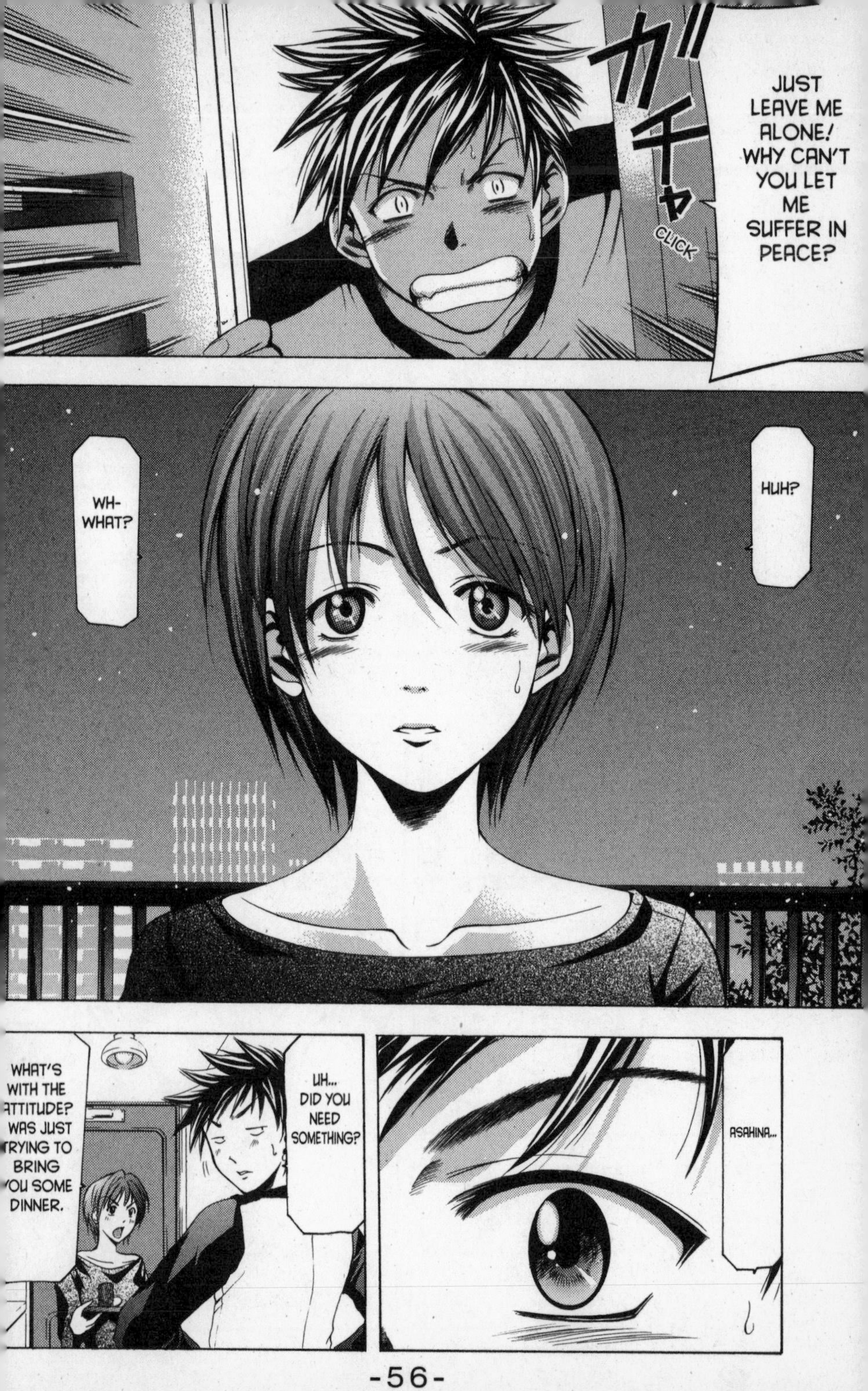
ガチャ
CLICK
JUST LEAVE ME ALONE! WHY CAN'T YOU LET ME SUFFER IN PEACE?
HUH?
WH- WHAT?
ASAHINA...
UH... DID YOU NEED SOMETHING?
WHAT'S WITH THE ATTITUDE? WAS JUST TRYING TO BRING YOU SOME DINNER.

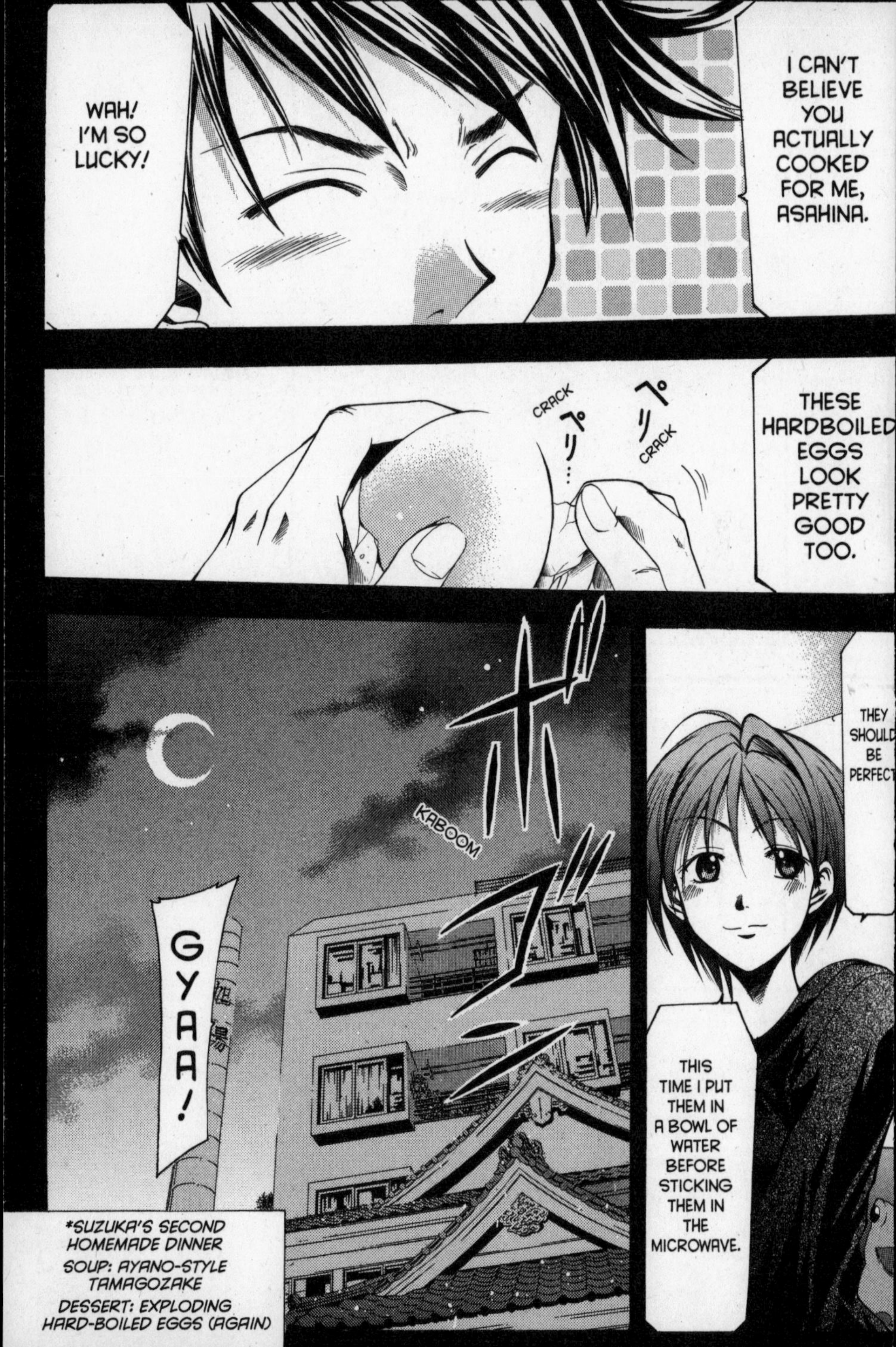
I CAN'T BELIEVE YOU ACTUALLY COOKED FOR ME, ASAHINA.
WAH! I'M SO LUCKY!
THESE HARDBOILED EGGS LOOK PRETTY GOOD TOO.
ペリ CRACK
ペリ… CRACK
THEY SHOULD BE PERFECT
THIS TIME I PUT THEM IN A BOWL OF WATER BEFORE STICKING THEM IN THE MICROWAVE.
KABOOM
GYAA!
*SUZUKA'S SECOND HOMEMADE DINNER
SOUP: AYANO-STYLE TAMAGOZAKE
DESSERT: EXPLODING HARD-BOILED EGGS (AGAIN)

SUZUKA FOUR-PANEL THEATER NUMBER SEVEN

TELLING IT LIKE IT IS

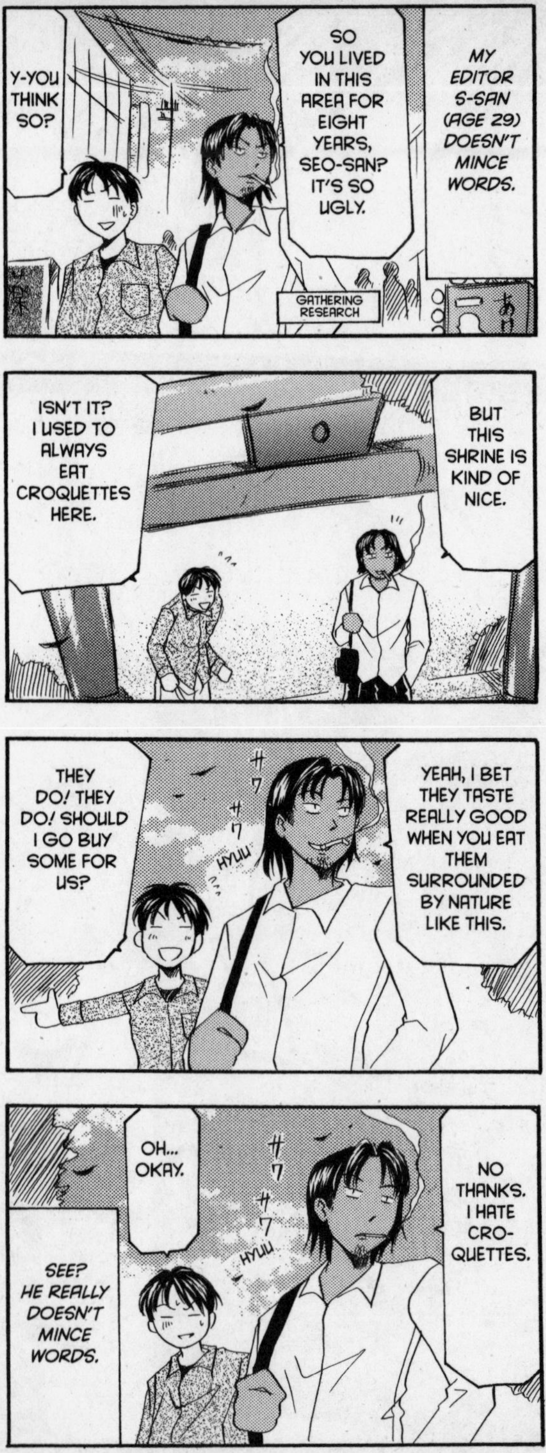
MY EDITOR S-SAN (AGE 29) DOESN'T MINCE WORDS.
SO YOU LIVED IN THIS AREA FOR EIGHT YEARS, SEO-SAN? IT'S SO UGLY.
GATHERING RESEARCH
Y-YOU THINK SO?
BUT THIS SHRINE IS KIND OF NICE.
ISN'T IT? I USED TO ALWAYS EAT CROQUETTES HERE.
YEAH, I BET THEY TASTE REALLY GOOD WHEN YOU EAT THEM SURROUNDED BY NATURE LIKE THIS.
サワ サワ
HYUU
THEY DO! THEY DO! SHOULD I GO BUY SOME FOR US?
NO THANKS. I HATE CRO-QUETTES.
サワ サワ
HYUU
OH... OKAY.
SEE? HE REALLY DOESN'T MINCE WORDS.

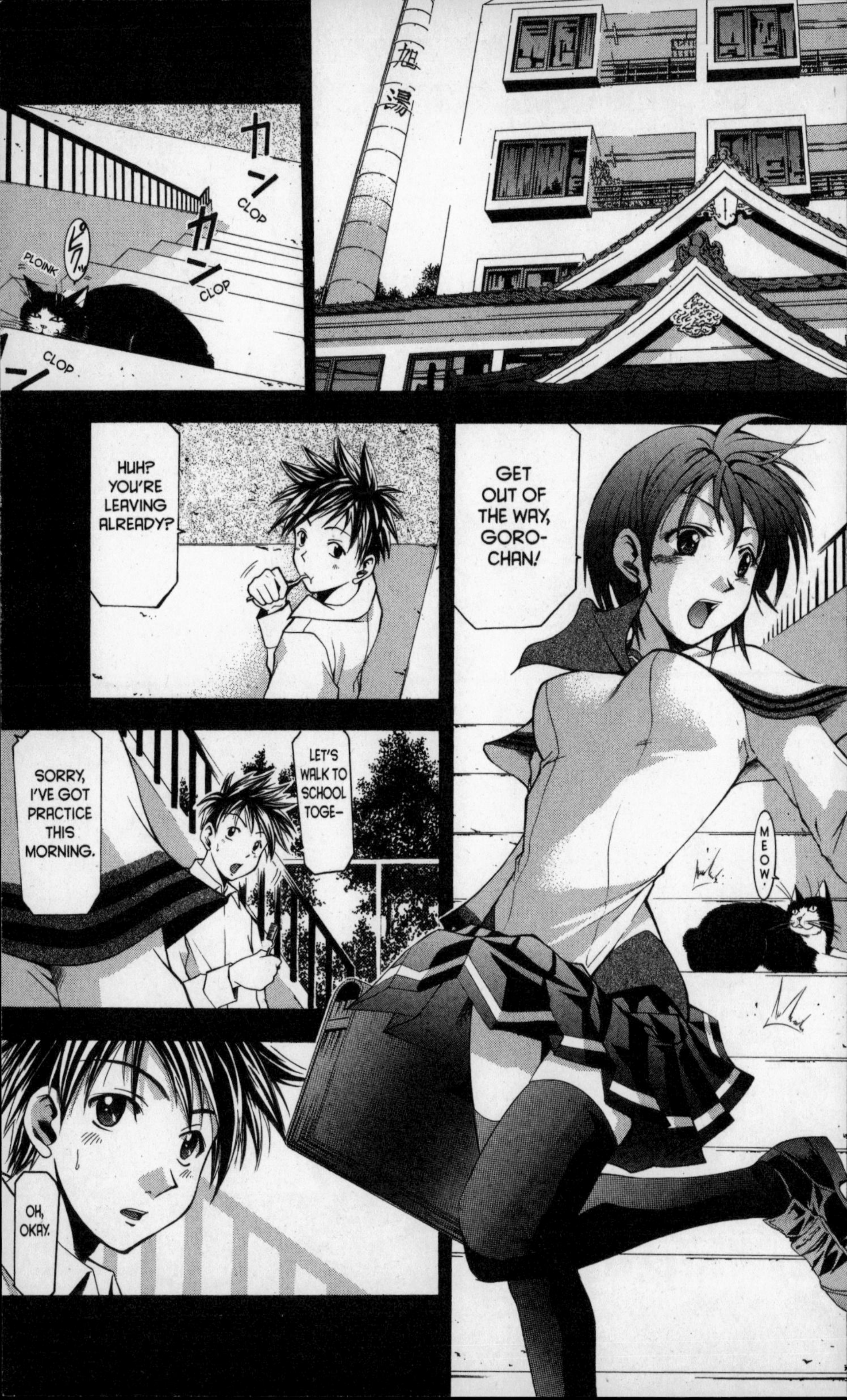
旭湯
カン
CLOP
カン
CLOP
ピク
PLOINK
CLOP
GET OUT OF THE WAY, GORO-CHAN!
MEOW!
HUH? YOU'RE LEAVING ALREADY?
LET'S WALK TO SCHOOL TOGE-
SORRY, I'VE GOT PRACTICE THIS MORNING.
OH, OKAY.

Suzuka

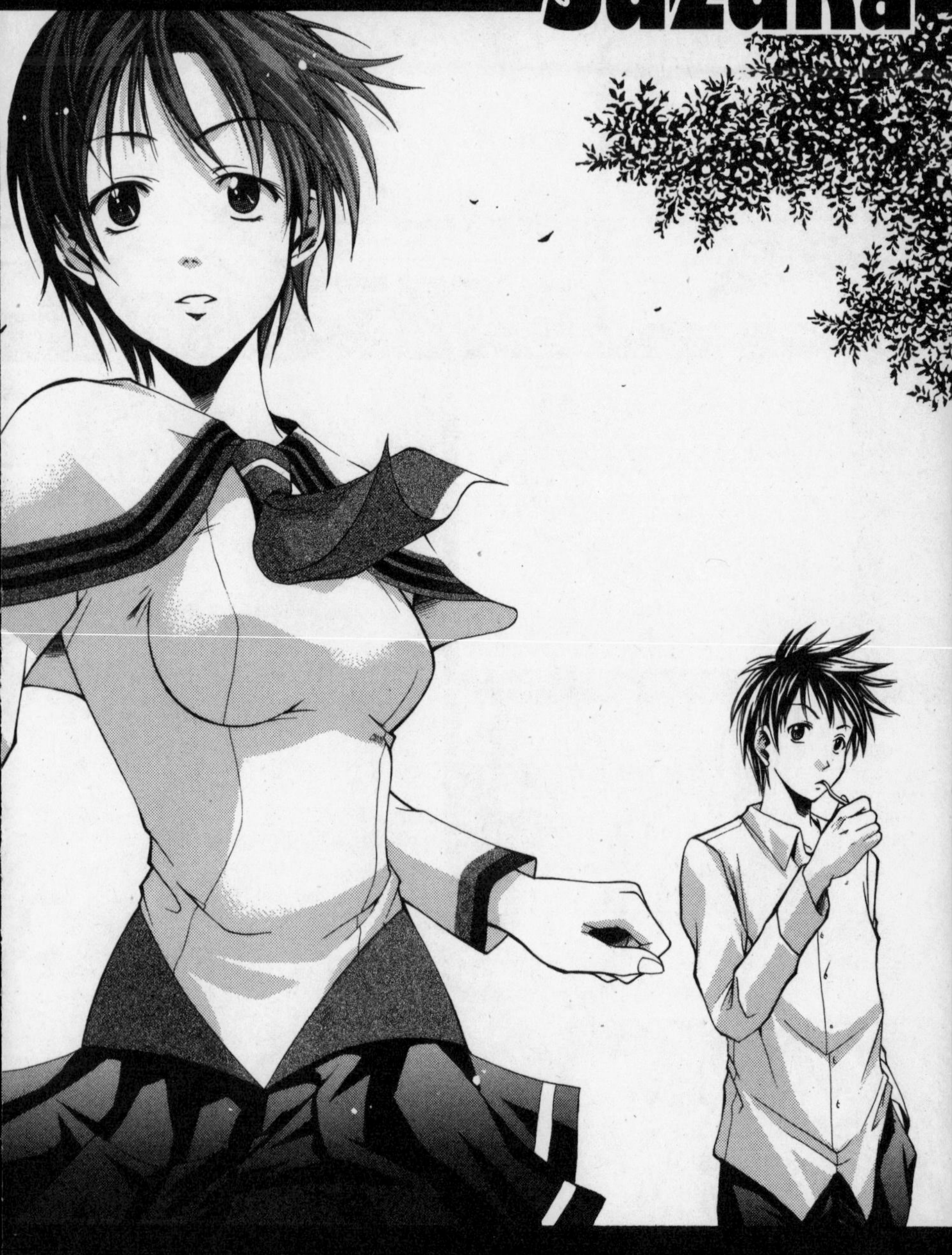

#8 Whirlwind

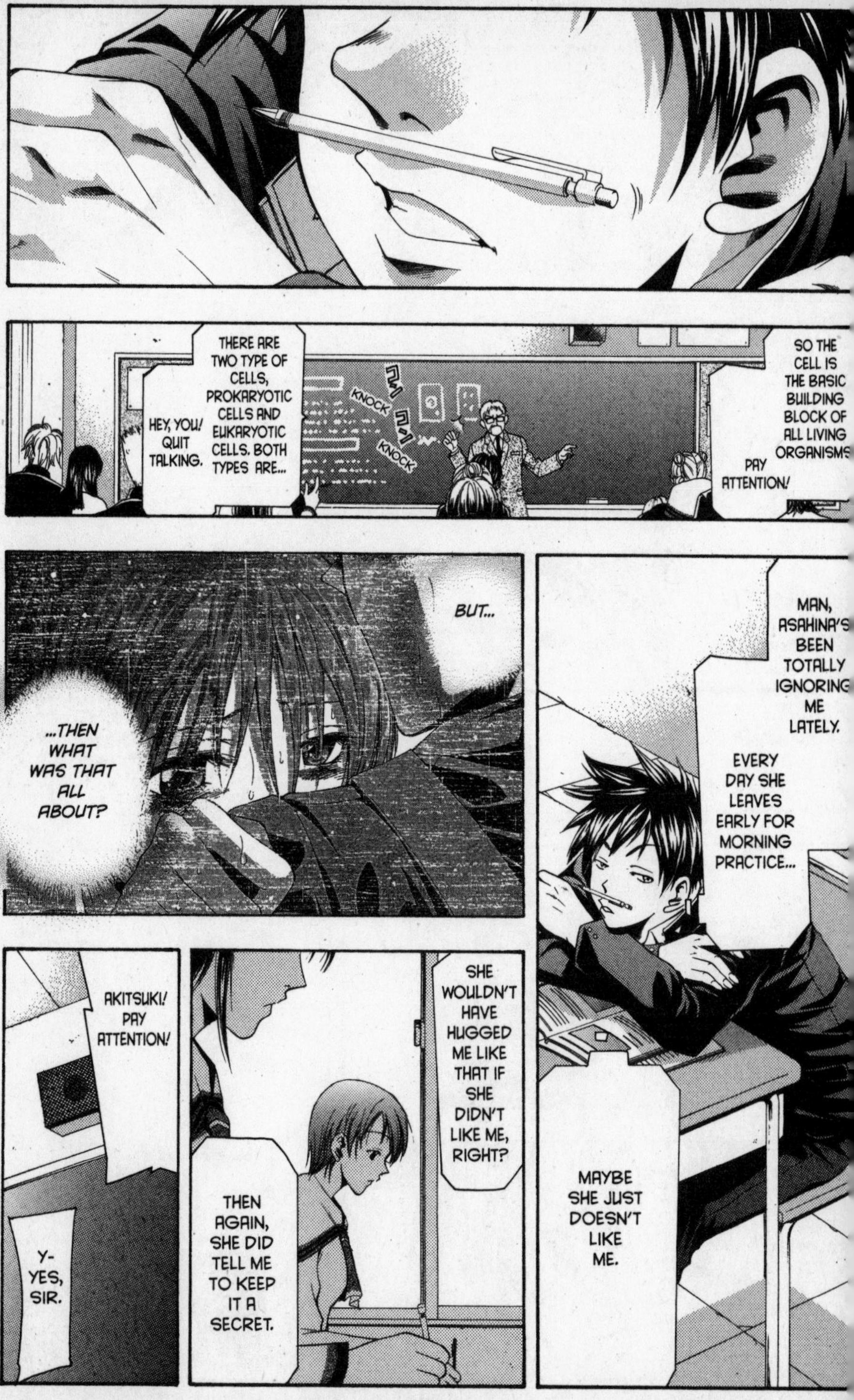
SO THE CELL IS THE BASIC BUILDING BLOCK OF ALL LIVING ORGANISMS
PAY ATTENTION!
KNOCK
KNOCK
THERE ARE TWO TYPE OF CELLS, PROKARYOTIC CELLS AND EUKARYOTIC CELLS. BOTH TYPES ARE...
HEY, YOU! QUIT TALKING.
MAN, ASAHINA'S BEEN TOTALLY IGNORING ME LATELY.
EVERY DAY SHE LEAVES EARLY FOR MORNING PRACTICE...
MAYBE SHE JUST DOESN'T LIKE ME.
BUT...
...THEN WHAT WAS THAT ALL ABOUT?
SHE WOULDN'T HAVE HUGGED ME LIKE THAT IF SHE DIDN'T LIKE ME, RIGHT?
THEN AGAIN, SHE DID TELL ME TO KEEP IT A SECRET.
AKITSUKI! PAY ATTENTION!
Y- YES, SIR.

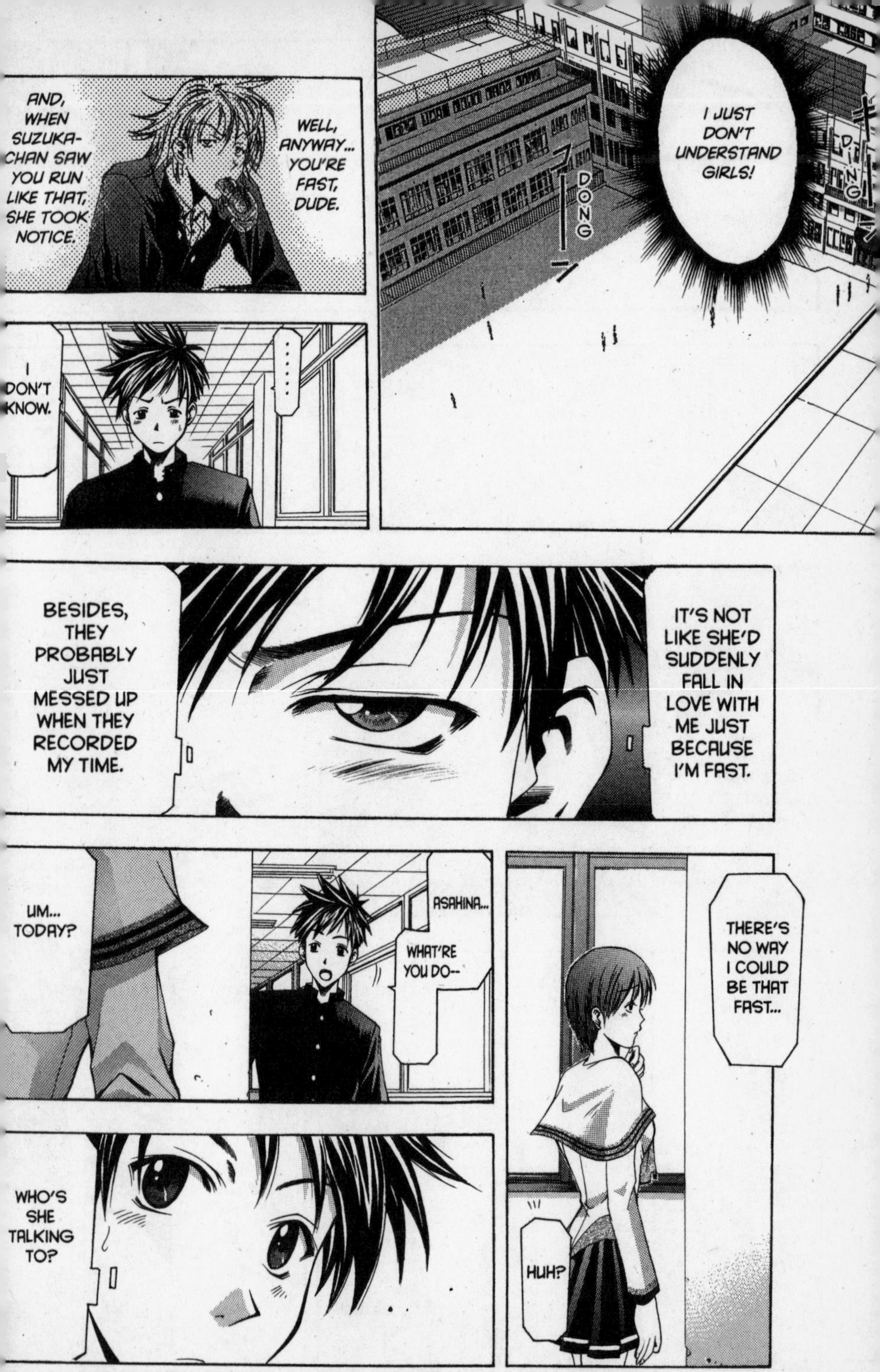
I JUST DON'T UNDERSTAND GIRLS!
DING
DONG
WELL, ANYWAY... YOU'RE FAST, DUDE.
AND, WHEN SUZUKA-CHAN SAW YOU RUN LIKE THAT, SHE TOOK NOTICE.
......
I DON'T KNOW.
IT'S NOT LIKE SHE'D SUDDENLY FALL IN LOVE WITH ME JUST BECAUSE I'M FAST.
BESIDES, THEY PROBABLY JUST MESSED UP WHEN THEY RECORDED MY TIME.
THERE'S NO WAY I COULD BE THAT FAST...
HUH?
ASAHINA...
WHAT'RE YOU DO--
UM... TODAY?
WHO'S SHE TALKING TO?

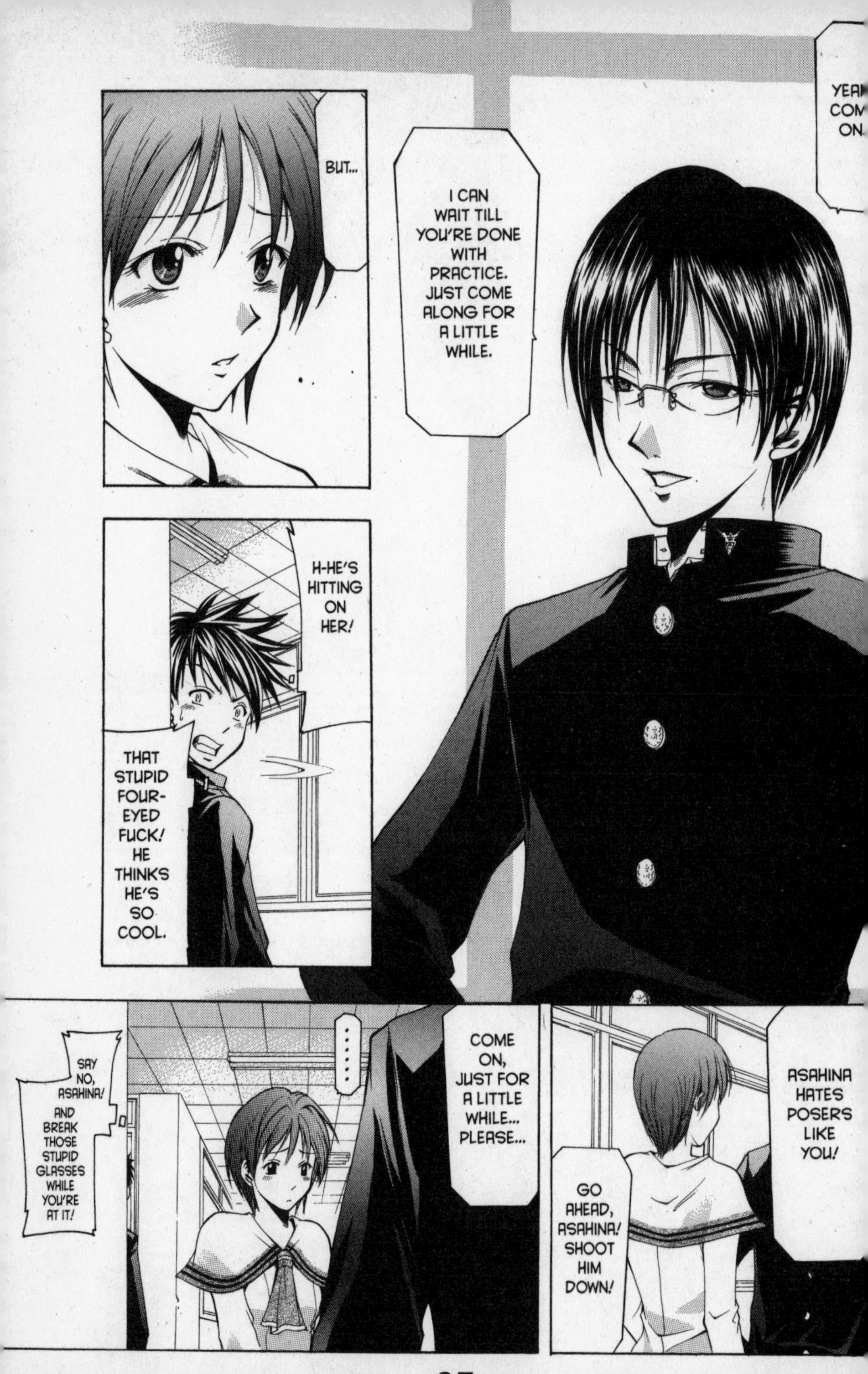

YEA COM ON.
I CAN WAIT TILL YOU'RE DONE WITH PRACTICE. JUST COME ALONG FOR A LITTLE WHILE.
BUT...
H-HE'S HITTING ON HER!
THAT STUPID FOUR-EYED FUCK! HE THINKS HE'S SO COOL.
ASAHINA HATES POSERS LIKE YOU!
GO AHEAD, ASAHINA! SHOOT HIM DOWN!
COME ON, JUST FOR A LITTLE WHILE... PLEASE...
......
SAY NO, ASAHINA!
AND BREAK THOSE STUPID GLASSES WHILE YOU'RE AT IT!

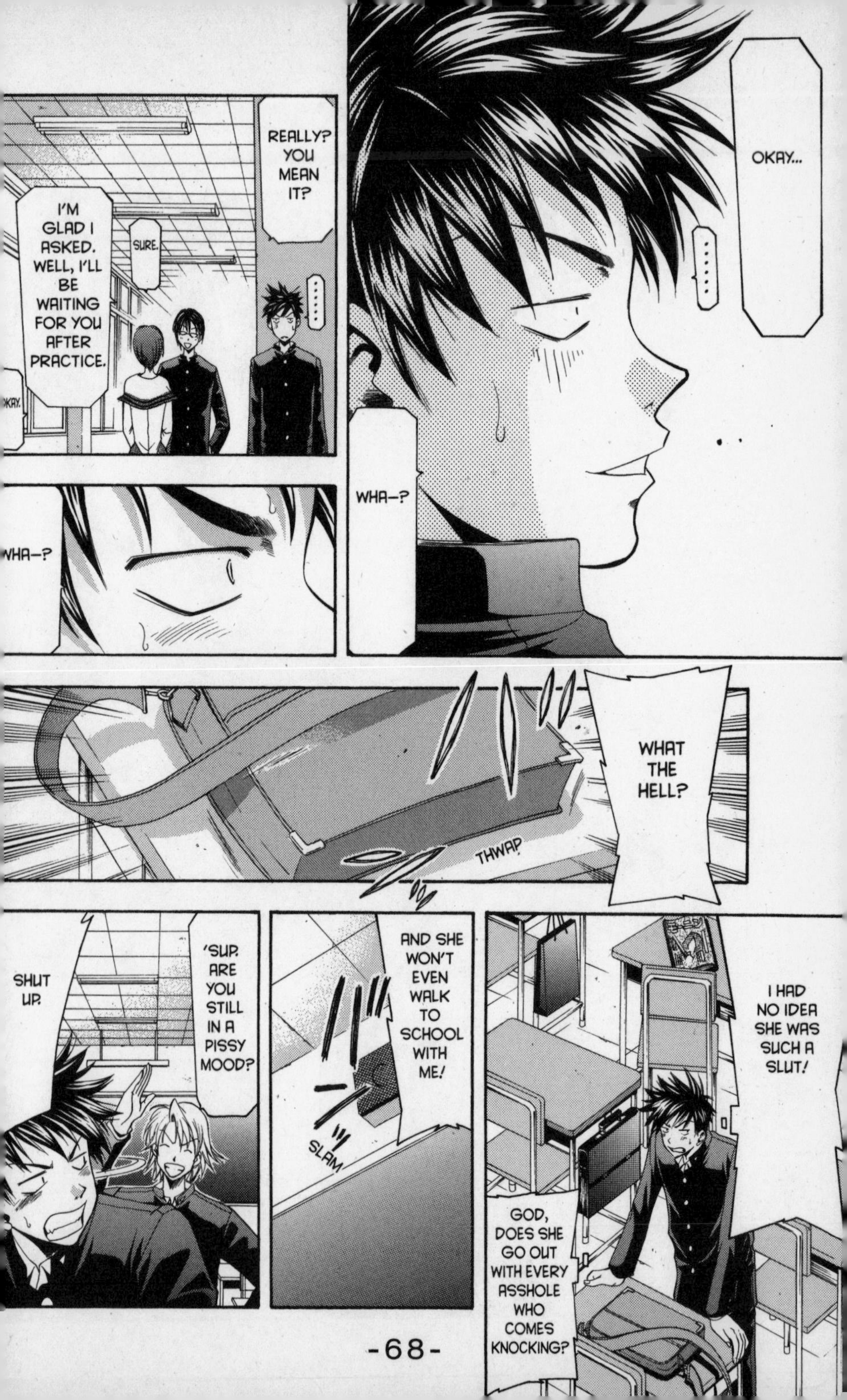
OKAY...
......
..
WHA-?
REALLY? YOU MEAN IT?
......
SURE.
I'M GLAD I ASKED. WELL, I'LL BE WAITING FOR YOU AFTER PRACTICE.
OKAY.
WHA-?
WHAT THE HELL?
THWAP
I HAD NO IDEA SHE WAS SUCH A SLUT!
GOD, DOES SHE GO OUT WITH EVERY ASSHOLE WHO COMES KNOCKING?
AND SHE WON'T EVEN WALK TO SCHOOL WITH ME!
SLAM
'SUP. ARE YOU STILL IN A PISSY MOOD?
SHUT UP.

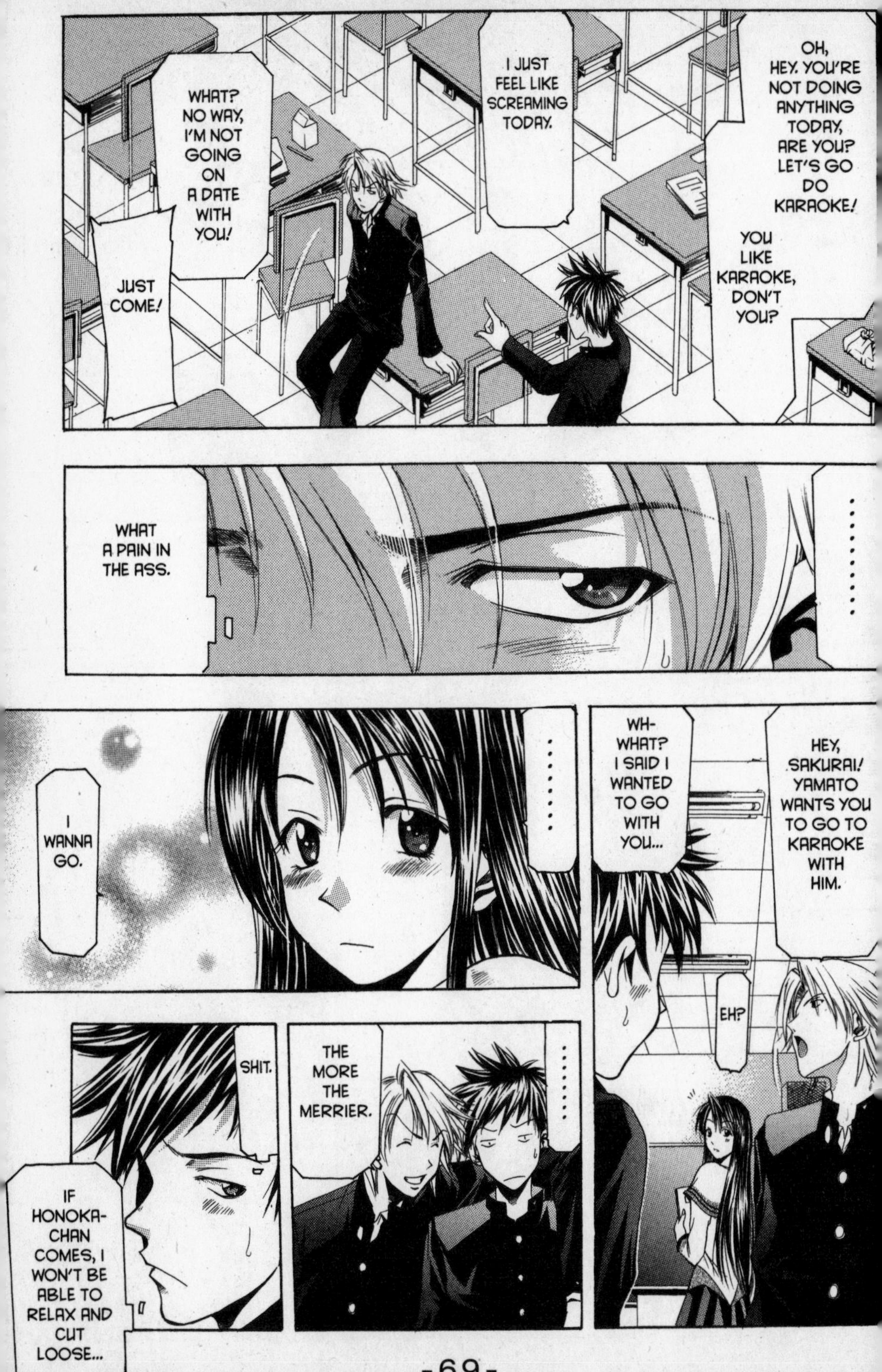
OH, HEY. YOU'RE NOT DOING ANYTHING TODAY, ARE YOU? LET'S GO DO KARAOKE!
YOU LIKE KARAOKE, DON'T YOU?
I JUST FEEL LIKE SCREAMING TODAY.
WHAT? NO WAY, I'M NOT GOING ON A DATE WITH YOU!
JUST COME!
......
WHAT A PAIN IN THE ASS.
HEY, SAKURAI! YAMATO WANTS YOU TO GO TO KARAOKE WITH HIM.
WH- WHAT? I SAID I WANTED TO GO WITH YOU...
EH?
......
I WANNA GO.
......
THE MORE THE MERRIER.
SHIT.
IF HONOKA-CHAN COMES, I WON'T BE ABLE TO RELAX AND CUT LOOSE...

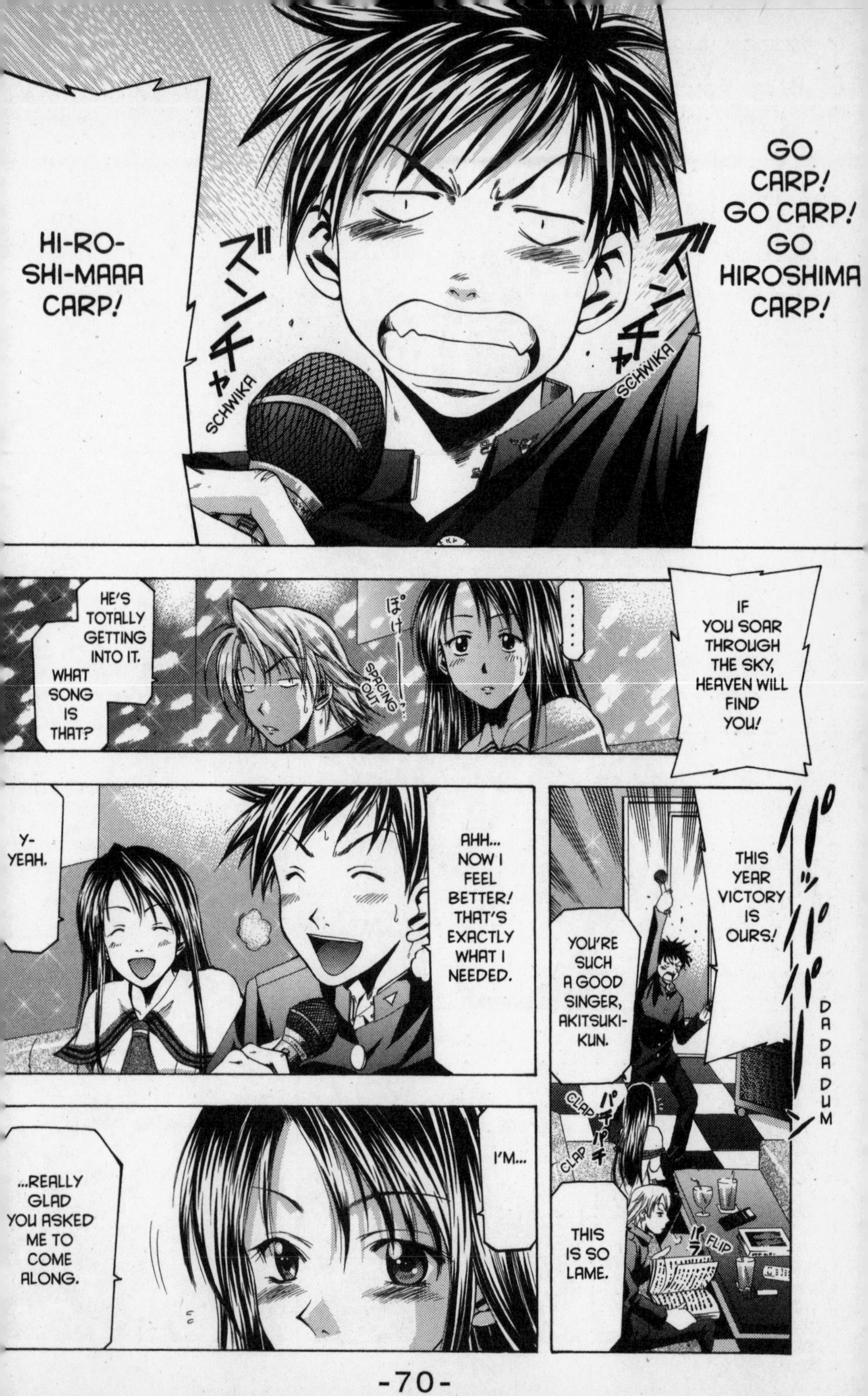
GO CARP! GO CARP! GO HIROSHIMA CARP!
ズンチャ
SCHWIKA
ズンチャ
SCHWIKA
HI-RO-SHI-MAAA CARP!
IF YOU SOAR THROUGH THE SKY, HEAVEN WILL FIND YOU!
......
ぽけー
SPACING OUT
HE'S TOTALLY GETTING INTO IT.
WHAT SONG IS THAT?
THIS YEAR VICTORY IS OURS!
パッパパパ
DA DA DA DUM
YOU'RE SUCH A GOOD SINGER, AKITSUKI-KUN.
パチパチ
CLAP CLAP
THIS IS SO LAME.
パラ
FLIP
AHH... NOW I FEEL BETTER! THAT'S EXACTLY WHAT I NEEDED.
Y-YEAH.
I'M...
...REALLY GLAD YOU ASKED ME TO COME ALONG.

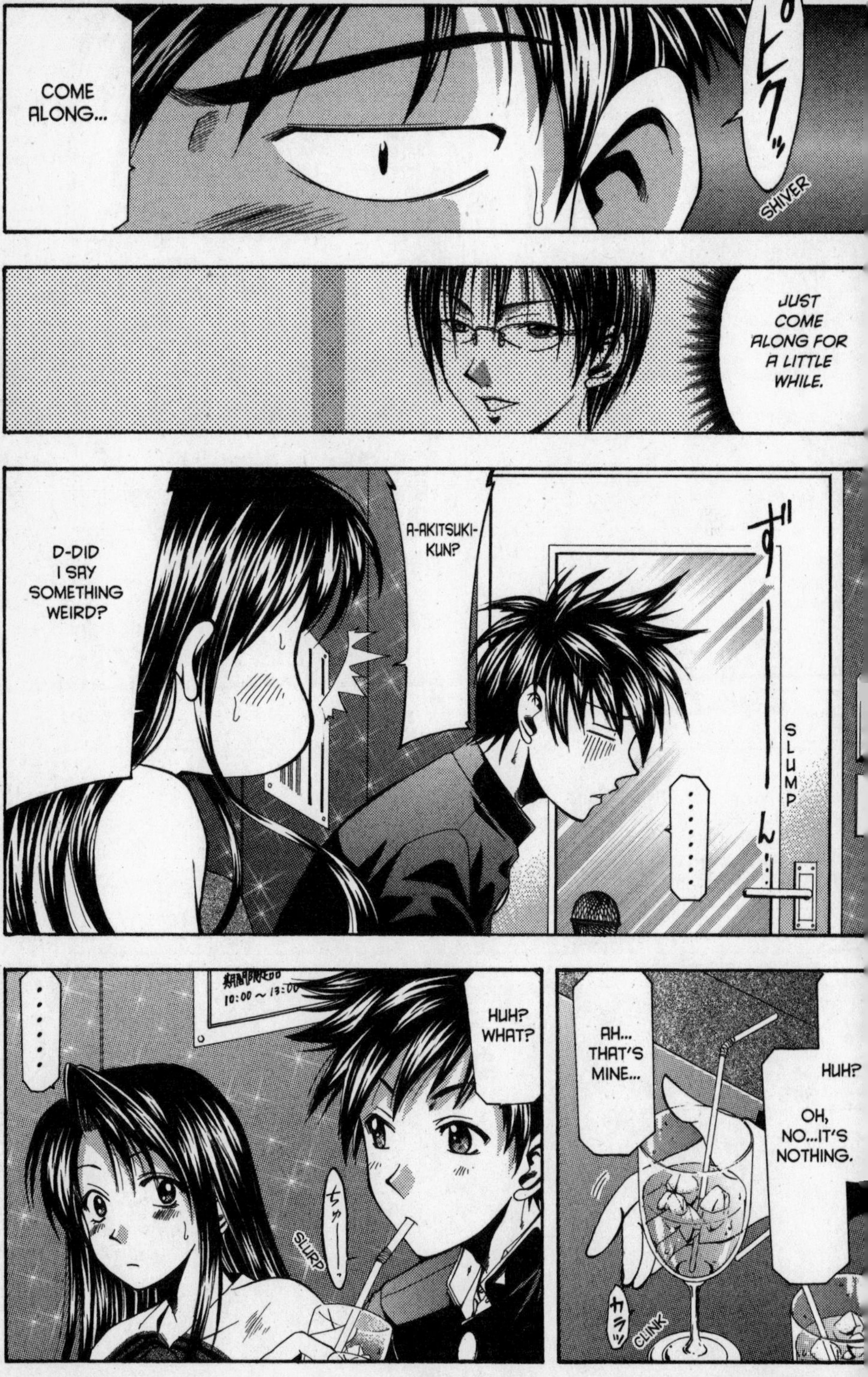
ピクッ
SHIVER
COME ALONG...
JUST COME ALONG FOR A LITTLE WHILE.
ずーん…
SLUMP
......
A-AKITSUKI-KUN?
D-DID I SAY SOMETHING WEIRD?
HUH?
OH, NO...IT'S NOTHING.
AH... THAT'S MINE...
カラッ
CLINK
HUH? WHAT?
ちゅー…
SLURP
......

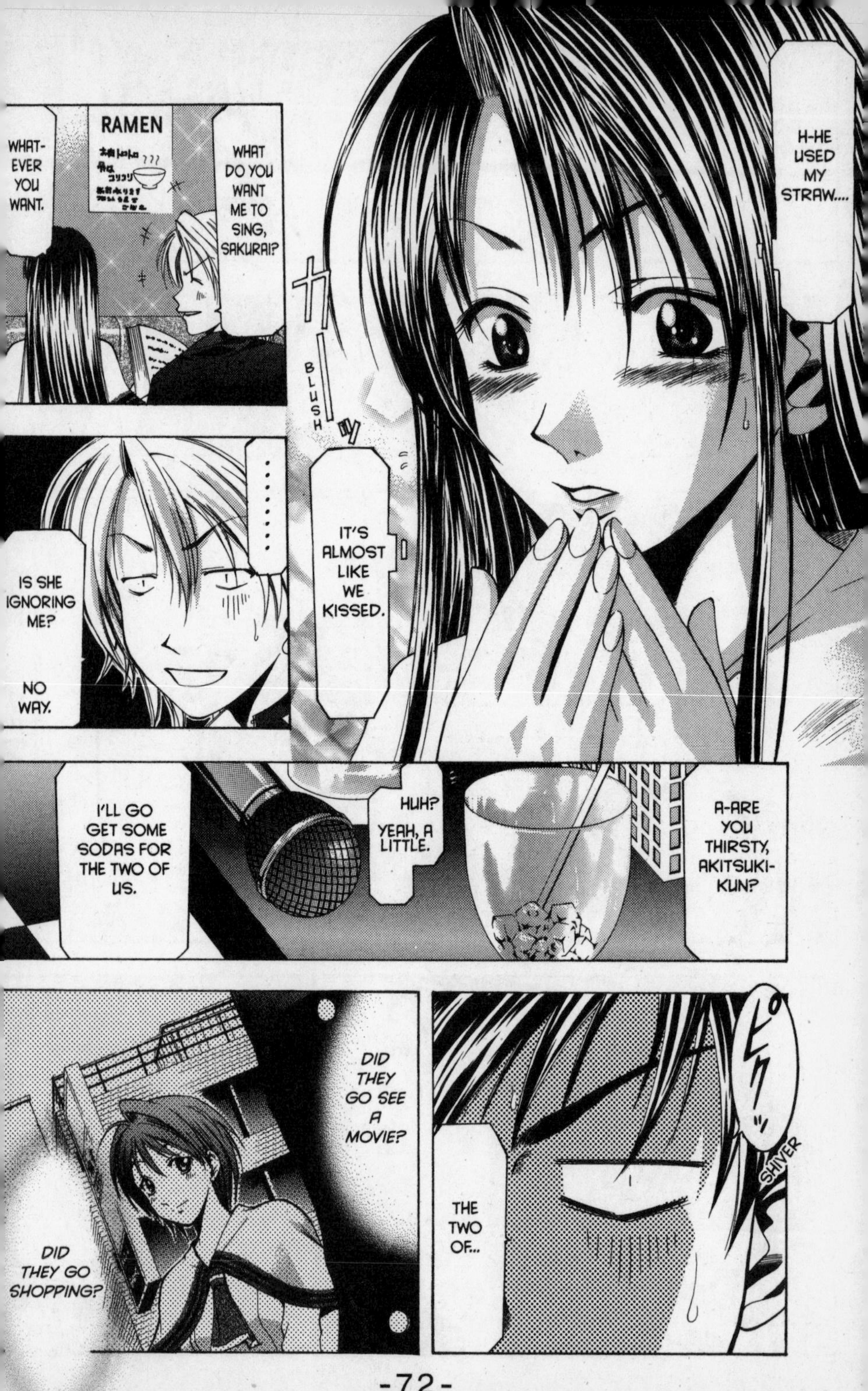
H-HE USED MY STRAW....
BLUSH
IT'S ALMOST LIKE WE KISSED.
RAMEN
WHAT DO YOU WANT ME TO SING, SAKURAI?
WHAT-EVER YOU WANT.
......
IS SHE IGNORING ME?
NO WAY.
A-ARE YOU THIRSTY, AKITSUKI-KUN?
HUH? YEAH, A LITTLE.
I'LL GO GET SOME SODAS FOR THE TWO OF US.
SHIVER
THE TWO OF...
DID THEY GO SEE A MOVIE?
DID THEY GO SHOPPING?

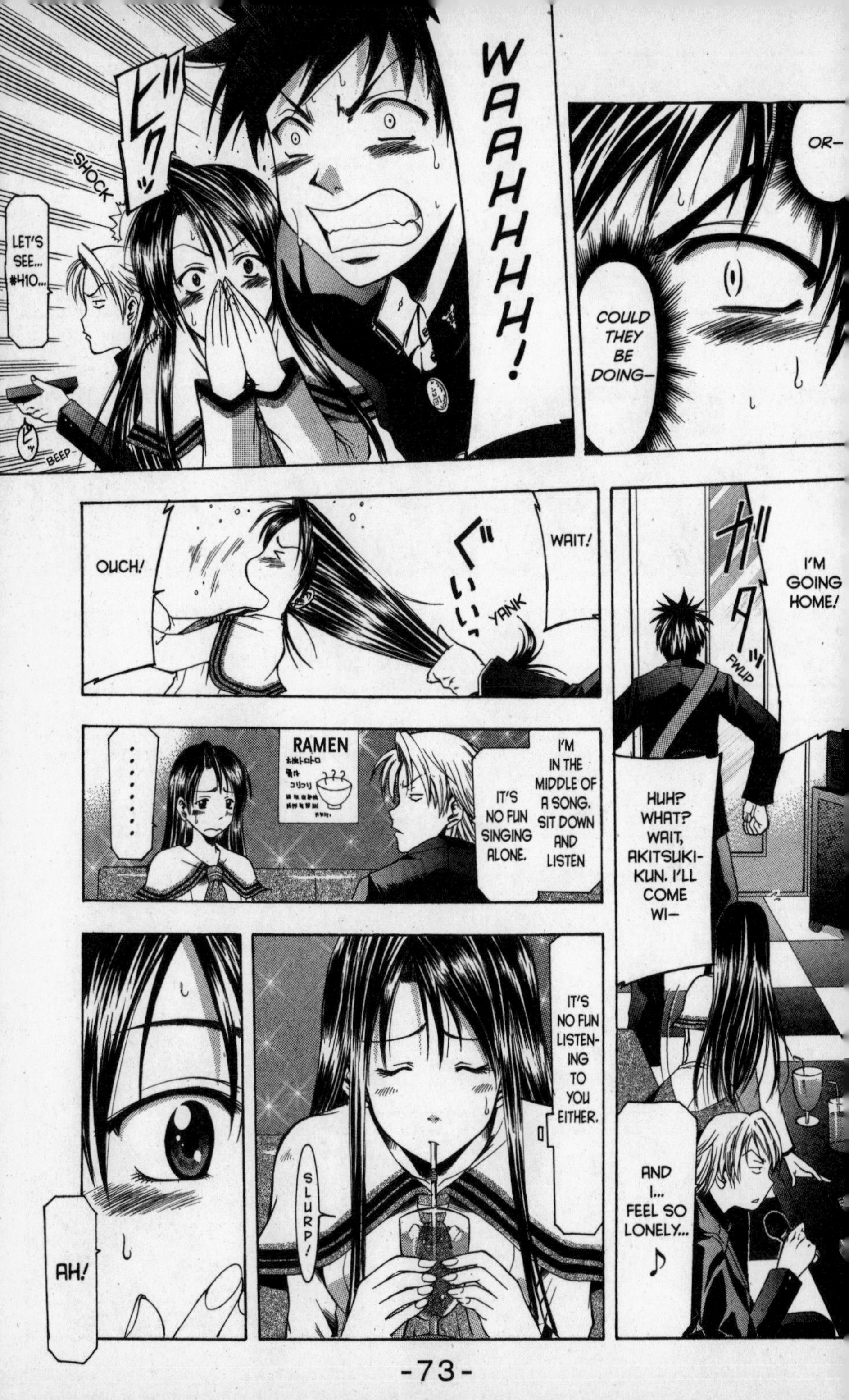
OR—
COULD THEY BE DOING—
WAAHHHHH!
SHOCK
LET'S SEE... #410...
BEEP
I'M GOING HOME!
FWUP
HUH? WHAT? WAIT, AKITSUKI-KUN. I'LL COME WI—
WAIT!
YANK
OUCH!
I'M IN THE MIDDLE OF A SONG. SIT DOWN AND LISTEN
IT'S NO FUN SINGING ALONE.
RAMEN
....
AND I... FEEL SO LONELY... ♪
IT'S NO FUN LISTENING TO YOU EITHER.
SLURP!
AH!

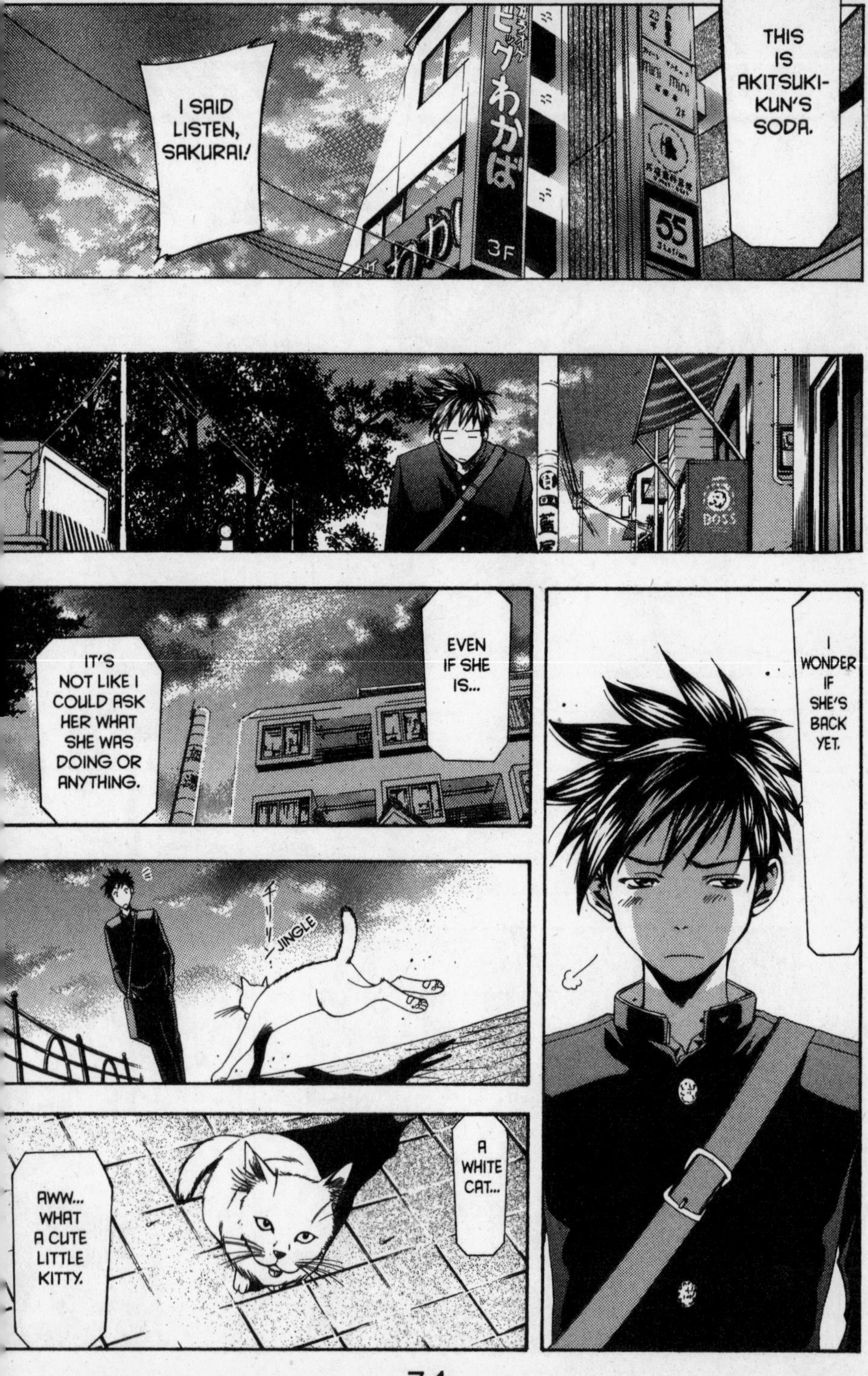
THIS IS AKITSUKI-KUN'S SODA.
I SAID LISTEN, SAKURAI!
I WONDER IF SHE'S BACK YET.
EVEN IF SHE IS...
IT'S NOT LIKE I COULD ASK HER WHAT SHE WAS DOING OR ANYTHING.
JINGLE
A WHITE CAT...
AWW... WHAT A CUTE LITTLE KITTY.

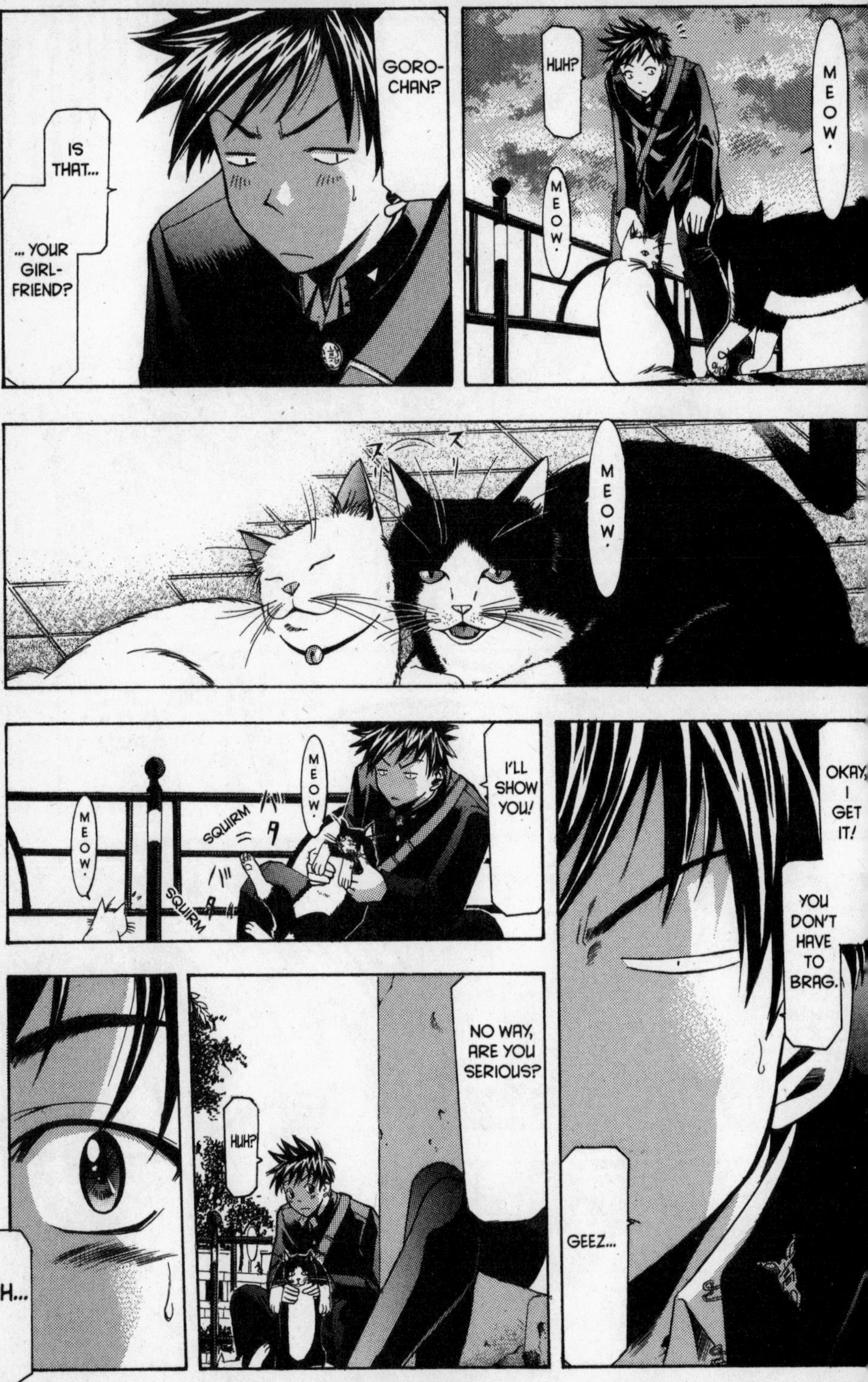
MEOW.
HUH?
MEOW.
GORO-CHAN?
IS THAT...
...YOUR GIRL-FRIEND?
MEOW.
OKAY, I GET IT!
YOU DON'T HAVE TO BRAG.
GEEZ...
I'LL SHOW YOU!
MEOW.
SQUIRM
MEOW.
SQUIRM
NO WAY, ARE YOU SERIOUS?
HUH?
AH...

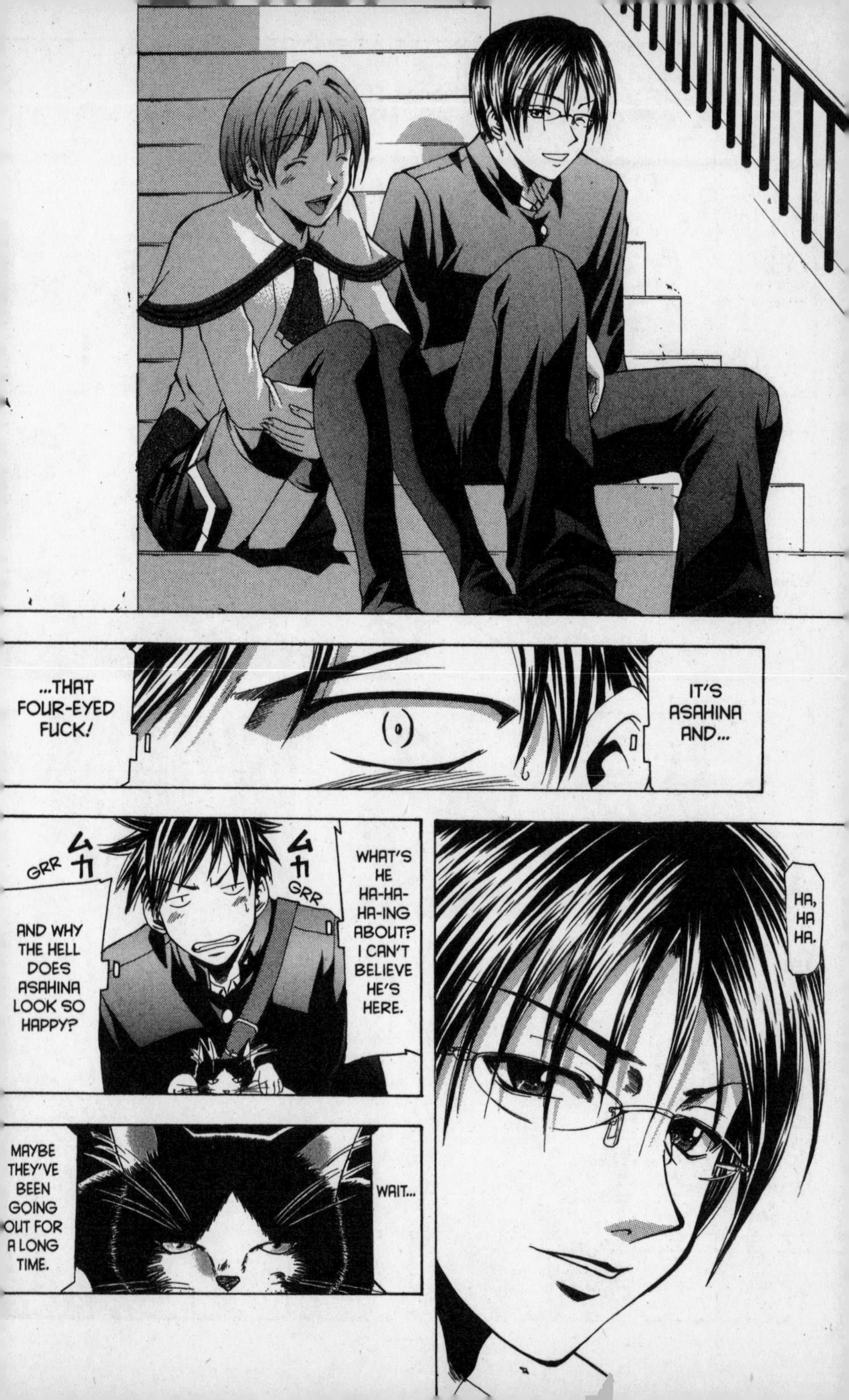
IT'S ASAHINA AND...
...THAT FOUR-EYED FUCK!
HA, HA HA.
WHAT'S HE HA-HA-HA-ING ABOUT? I CAN'T BELIEVE HE'S HERE.
ムカ GRR
ムカ GRR
AND WHY THE HELL DOES ASAHINA LOOK SO HAPPY?
WAIT...
MAYBE THEY'VE BEEN GOING OUT FOR A LONG TIME.

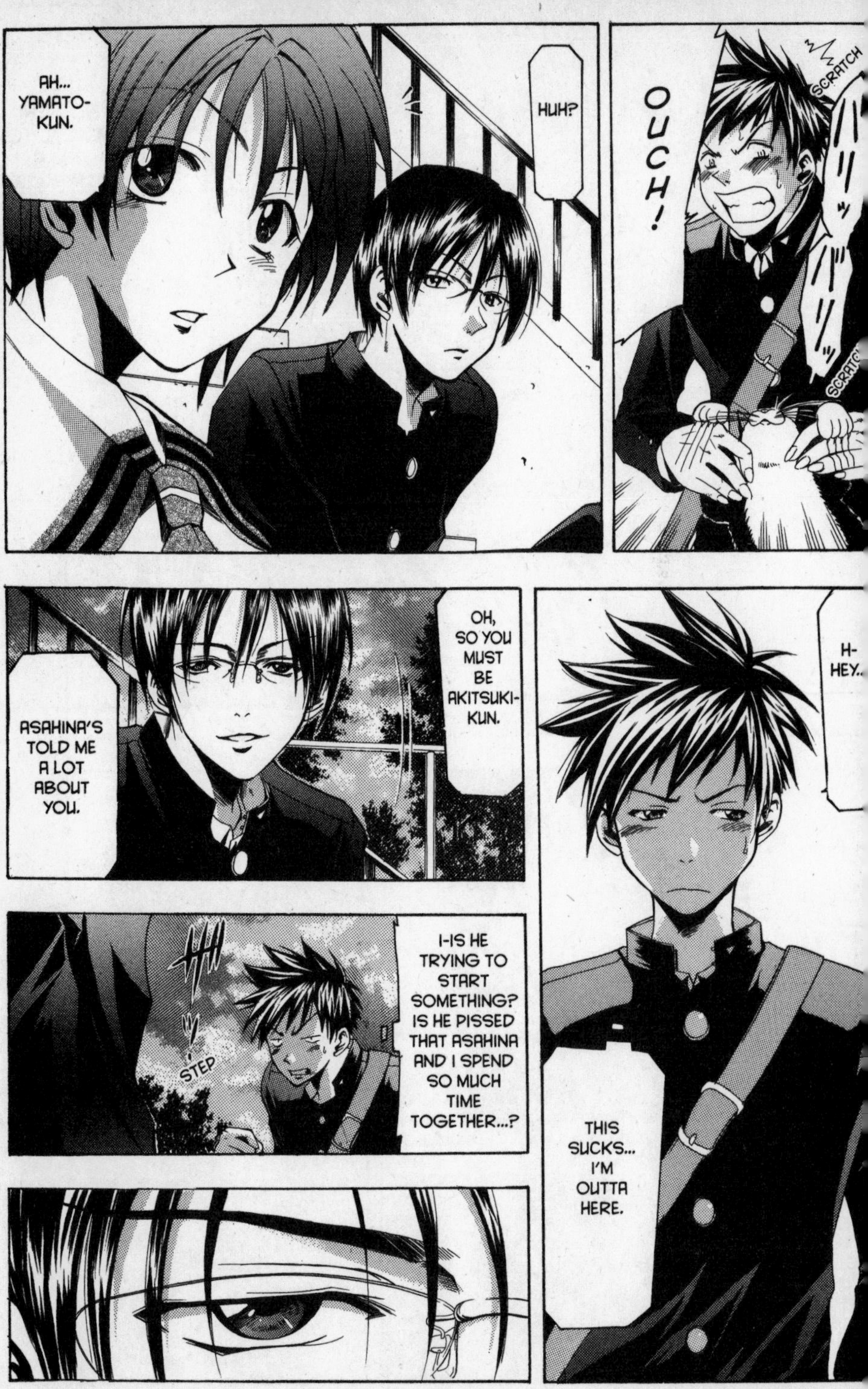
SCRATCH
OUCH!
SCRATCH
HUH?
AH... YAMATO-KUN.
H-HEY..
THIS SUCKS... I'M OUTTA HERE.
OH, SO YOU MUST BE AKITSUKI-KUN.
ASAHINA'S TOLD ME A LOT ABOUT YOU.
I-IS HE TRYING TO START SOMETHING? IS HE PISSED THAT ASAHINA AND I SPEND SO MUCH TIME TOGETHER...?
STEP

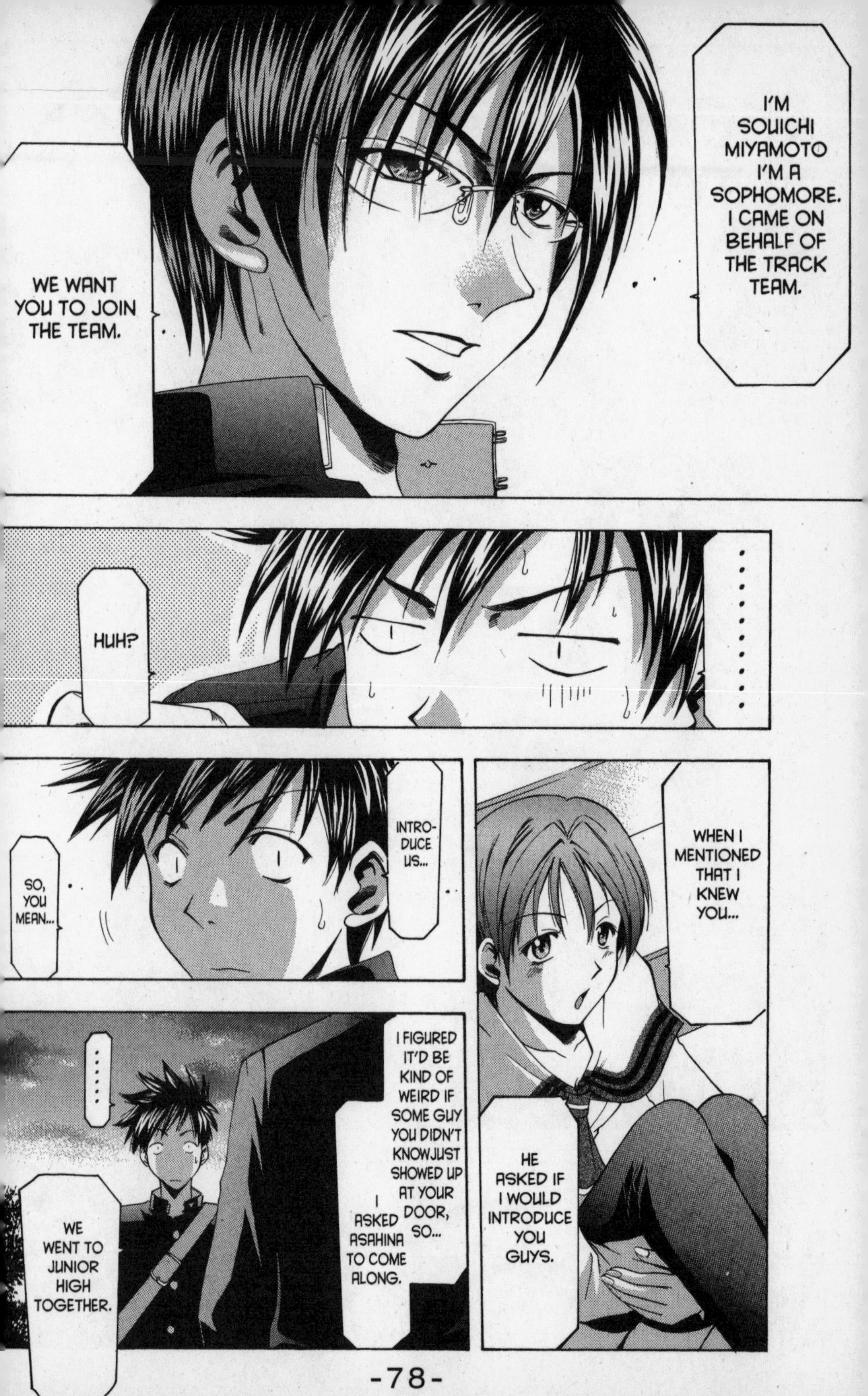
I'M SOUICHI MIYAMOTO I'M A SOPHOMORE. I CAME ON BEHALF OF THE TRACK TEAM.
WE WANT YOU TO JOIN THE TEAM.
......
HUH?
WHEN I MENTIONED THAT I KNEW YOU...
HE ASKED IF I WOULD INTRODUCE YOU GUYS.
INTRODUCE US...
SO, YOU MEAN...
I FIGURED IT'D BE KIND OF WEIRD IF SOME GUY YOU DIDN'T KNOWJUST SHOWED UP AT YOUR DOOR, SO...
I ASKED ASAHINA TO COME ALONG.
......
WE WENT TO JUNIOR HIGH TOGETHER.

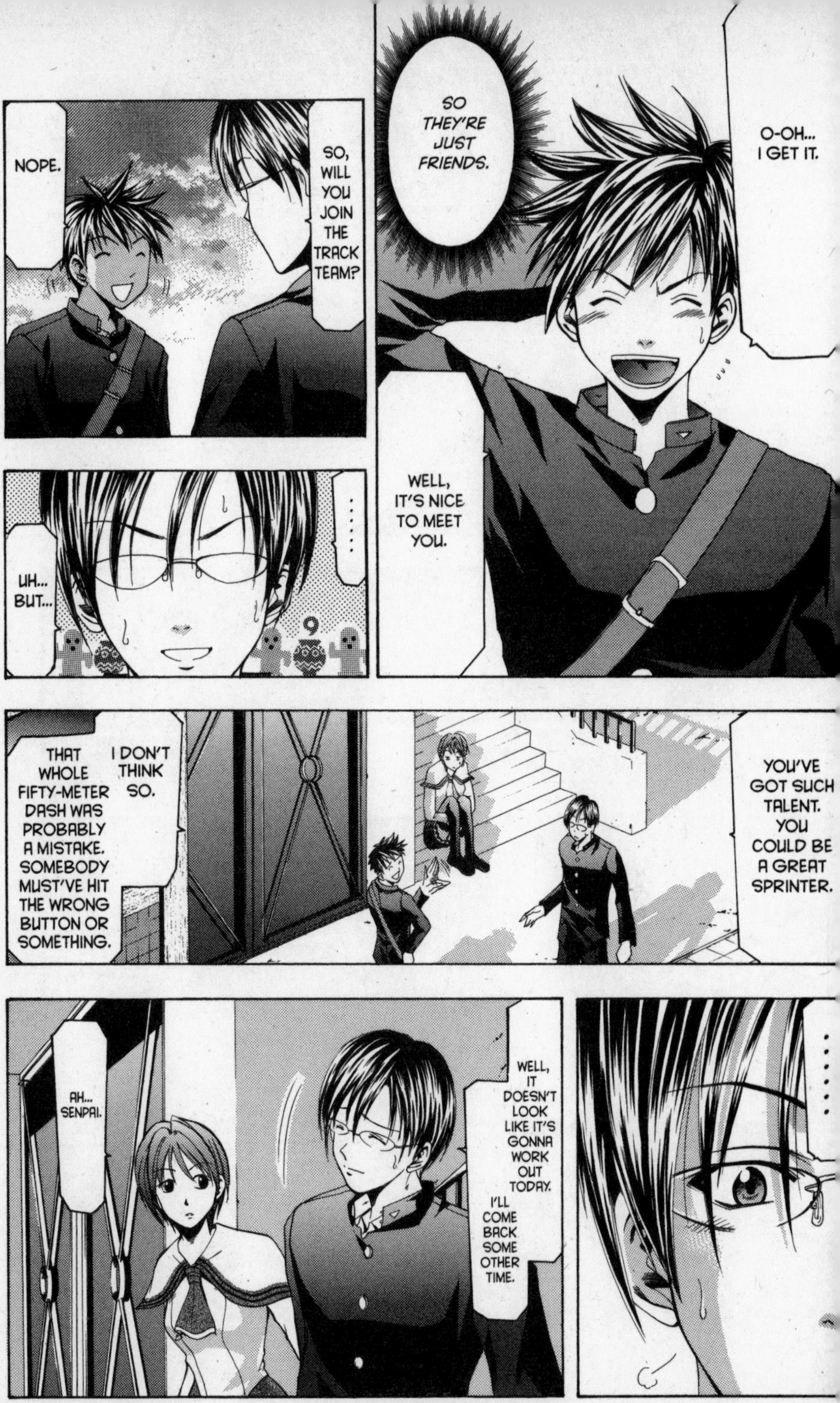
O-OH... I GET IT.
SO THEY'RE JUST FRIENDS.
WELL, IT'S NICE TO MEET YOU.
SO, WILL YOU JOIN THE TRACK TEAM?
NOPE.
......
UH... BUT...
YOU'VE GOT SUCH TALENT. YOU COULD BE A GREAT SPRINTER.
I DON'T THINK SO.
THAT WHOLE FIFTY-METER DASH WAS PROBABLY A MISTAKE. SOMEBODY MUST'VE HIT THE WRONG BUTTON OR SOMETHING.
......
WELL, IT DOESN'T LOOK LIKE IT'S GONNA WORK OUT TODAY. I'LL COME BACK SOME OTHER TIME.
AH... SENPAI.

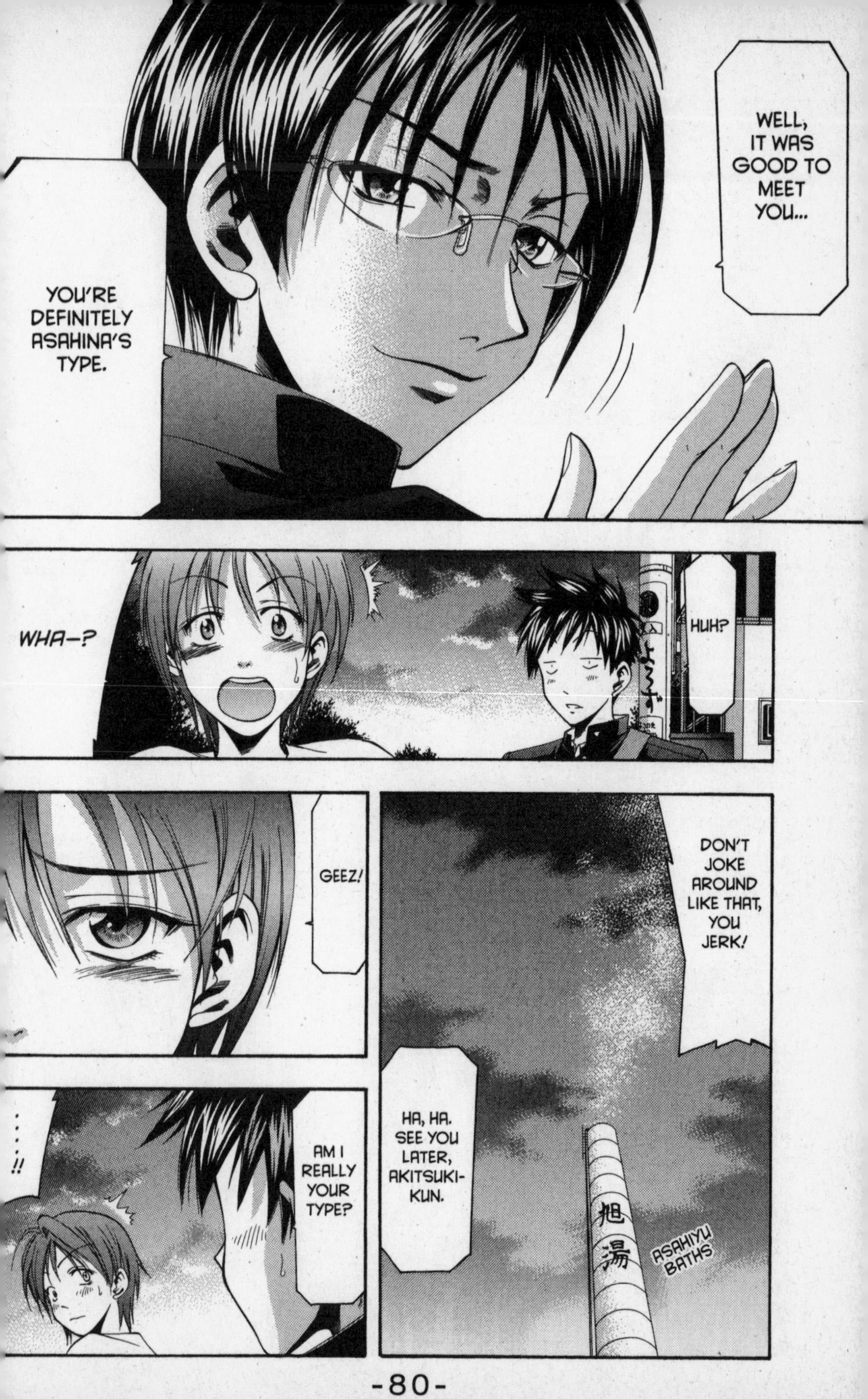
WELL, IT WAS GOOD TO MEET YOU...
YOU'RE DEFINITELY ASAHINA'S TYPE.
HUH?
WHA–?
DON'T JOKE AROUND LIKE THAT, YOU JERK!
HA, HA. SEE YOU LATER, AKITSUKI-KUN.
旭湯
ASAHIYU BATHS
GEEZ!
AM I REALLY YOUR TYPE?
......!!

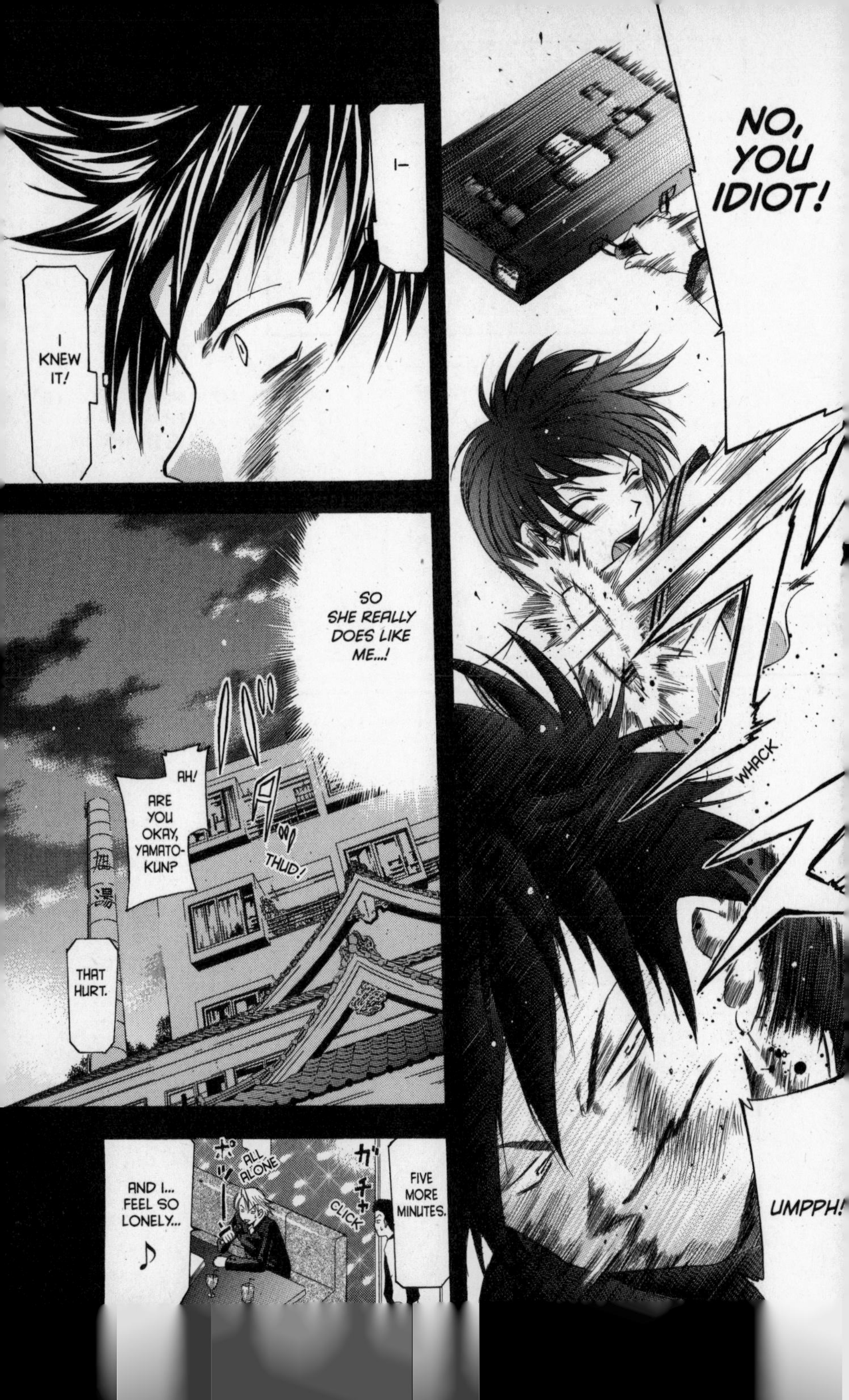
NO, YOU IDIOT!
WHACK
UMPPH!
I–
I KNEW IT!
SO SHE REALLY DOES LIKE ME...!
THUD!
AH! ARE YOU OKAY, YAMATO-KUN?
THAT HURT.
FIVE MORE MINUTES.
CLICK
ALL ALONE
AND I... FEEL SO LONELY... ♪

SUZUKA FOUR-PANEL THEATER NUMBER EIGHT

THE REASON

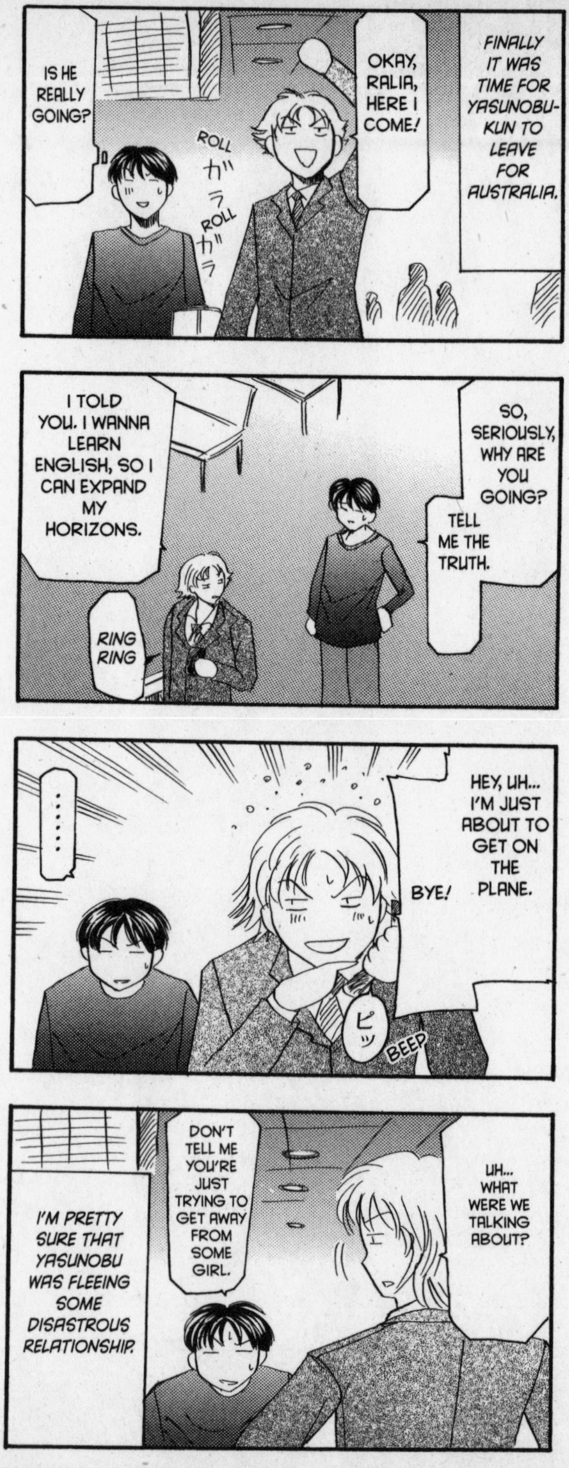
FINALLY IT WAS TIME FOR YASUNOBU-KUN TO LEAVE FOR AUSTRALIA.
OKAY, RALIA, HERE I COME!
ROLL ガラ
ROLL ガラ
IS HE REALLY GOING?
SO, SERIOUSLY, WHY ARE YOU GOING?
TELL ME THE TRUTH.
I TOLD YOU. I WANNA LEARN ENGLISH, SO I CAN EXPAND MY HORIZONS.
RING RING
HEY, UH... I'M JUST ABOUT TO GET ON THE PLANE.
BYE!
ピッ
BEEP
......
UH... WHAT WERE WE TALKING ABOUT?
DON'T TELL ME YOU'RE JUST TRYING TO GET AWAY FROM SOME GIRL.
I'M PRETTY SURE THAT YASUNOBU WAS FLEEING SOME DISASTROUS RELATIONSHIP.

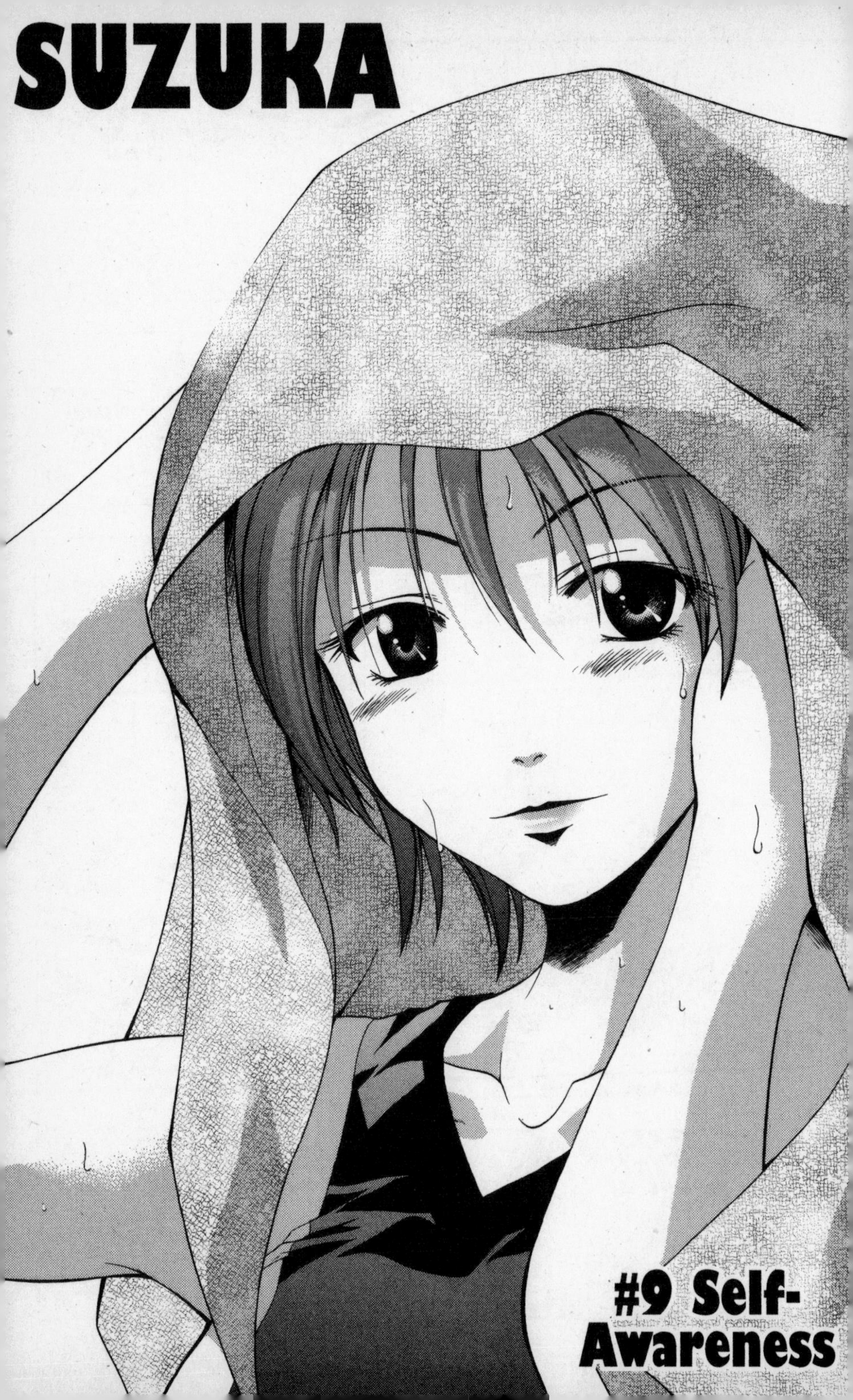
SUZUKA
#9 Self-Awareness

WHAT DOES IT MEAN WHEN A GIRL HUGS A GUY?

CHOMP CHOMP CHOMP

HUH?

I FIGURED YOU MIGHT KNOW. I MEAN, LIKE, PSYCHOLOGICALLY, WHAT'S GOING ON IN THEIR HEADS?

YEAH.

¥590
THE BAMBOO BURGER
SPRING SELECT MENU

PSYCHO-LOGICALLY, HUH?

WHY? DID SUZUKA-CHAN HUG YOU OR SOMETHING?

I GUESS IT MEANS SHE LIKES THE GUY.

N-NO, THIS IS JUST HYPOTHETICAL.

IT DIDN'T REALLY HAPPEN TO ME OR ANYTHING.

Y—

• • • • •

-84-

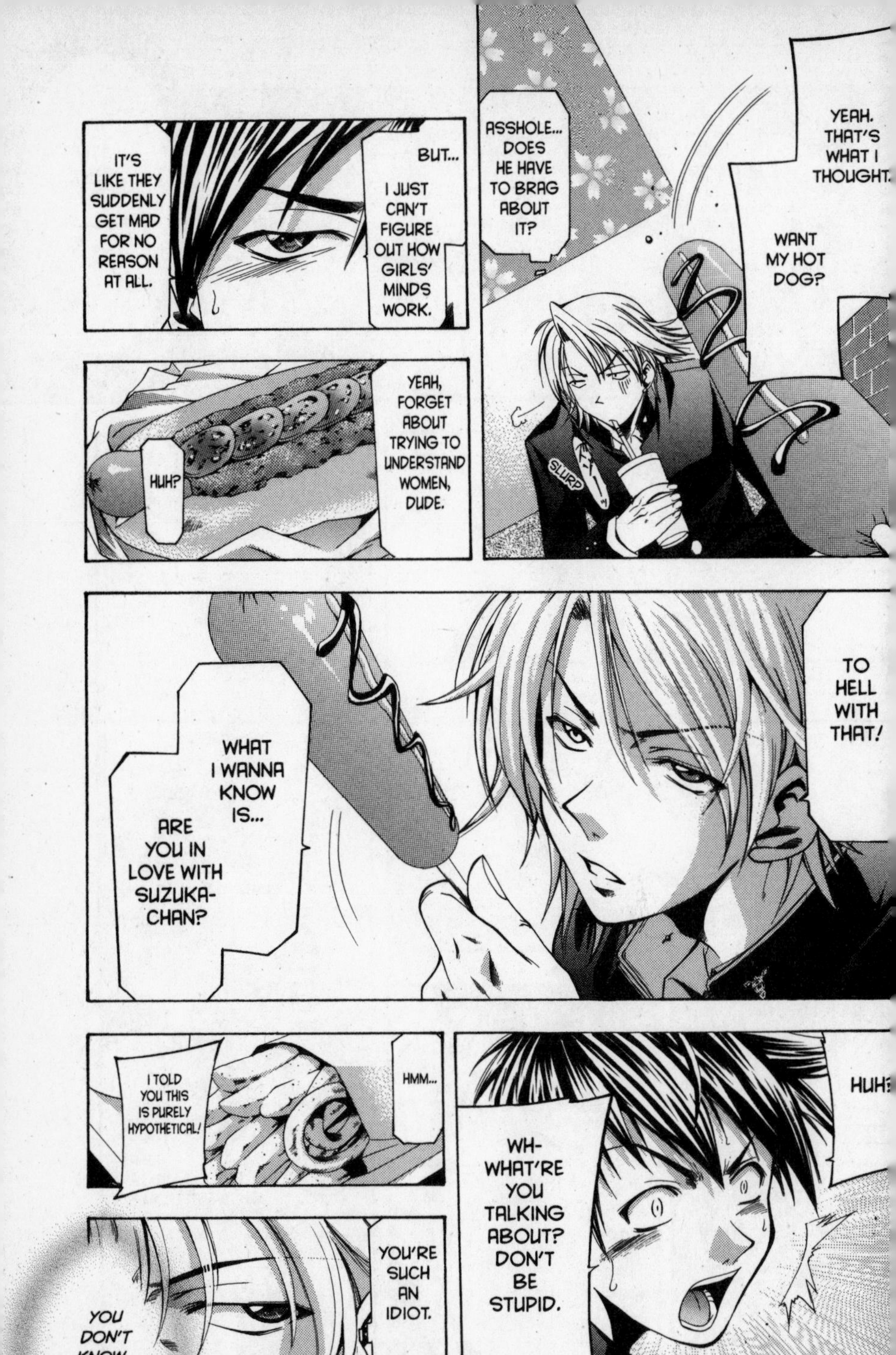
YEAH. THAT'S WHAT I THOUGHT.
WANT MY HOT DOG?
ASSHOLE... DOES HE HAVE TO BRAG ABOUT IT?
SLURP
BUT...
I JUST CAN'T FIGURE OUT HOW GIRLS' MINDS WORK.
IT'S LIKE THEY SUDDENLY GET MAD FOR NO REASON AT ALL.
YEAH, FORGET ABOUT TRYING TO UNDERSTAND WOMEN, DUDE.
HUH?
TO HELL WITH THAT!
WHAT I WANNA KNOW IS...
ARE YOU IN LOVE WITH SUZUKA-CHAN?
HUH?
WH-WHAT'RE YOU TALKING ABOUT? DON'T BE STUPID.
HMM...
I TOLD YOU THIS IS PURELY HYPOTHETICAL!
YOU'RE SUCH AN IDIOT.
YOU DON'T KNOW...

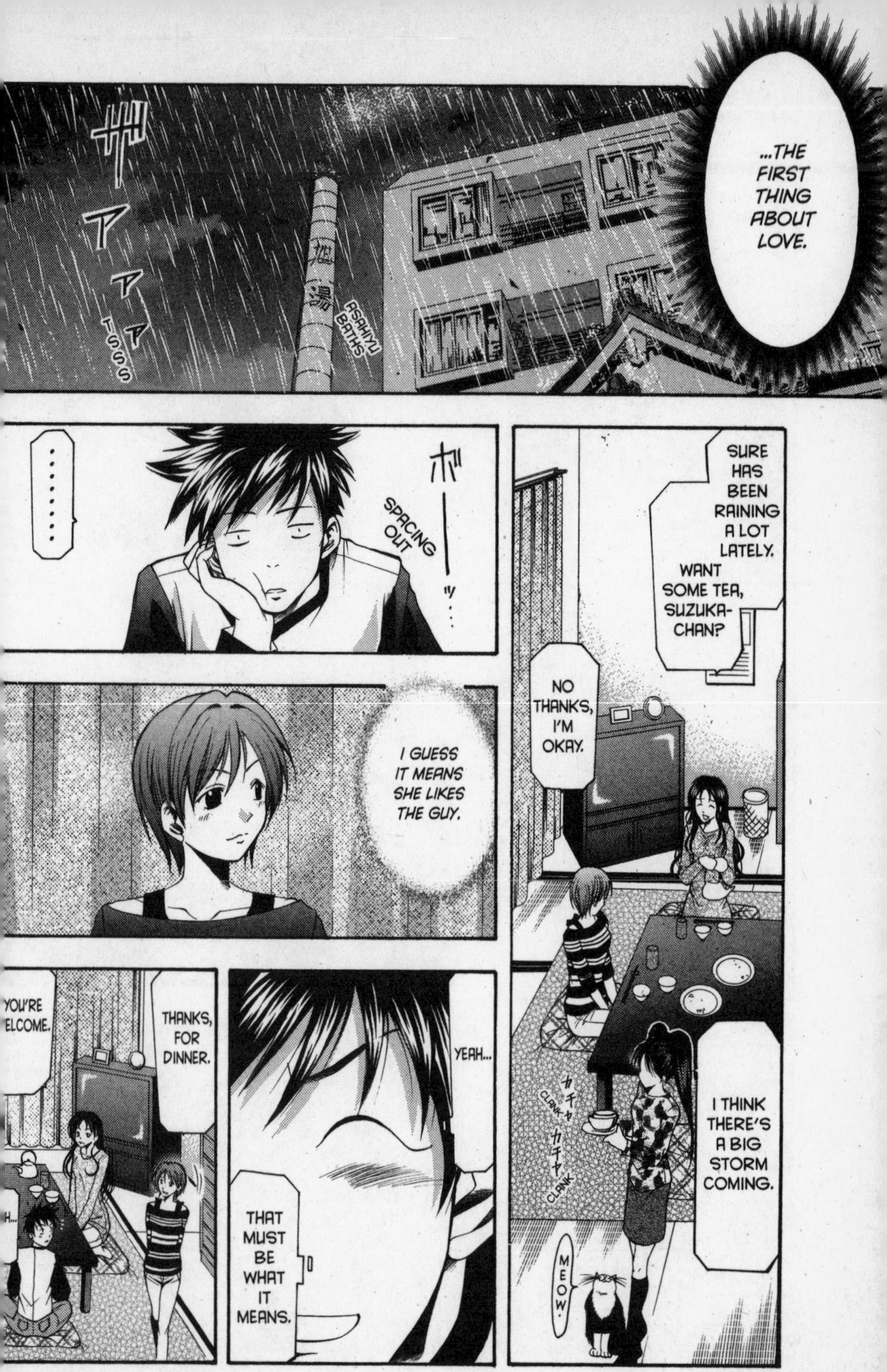
...THE FIRST THING ABOUT LOVE.
ASAHIYU BATHS
TSSS
SURE HAS BEEN RAINING A LOT LATELY.
WANT SOME TEA, SUZUKA-CHAN?
NO THANKS, I'M OKAY.
CLANK
CLANK
I THINK THERE'S A BIG STORM COMING.
MEOW.
SPACING OUT
....
I GUESS IT MEANS SHE LIKES THE GUY.
YEAH...
THAT MUST BE WHAT IT MEANS.
THANKS, FOR DINNER.
YOU'RE ELCOME.

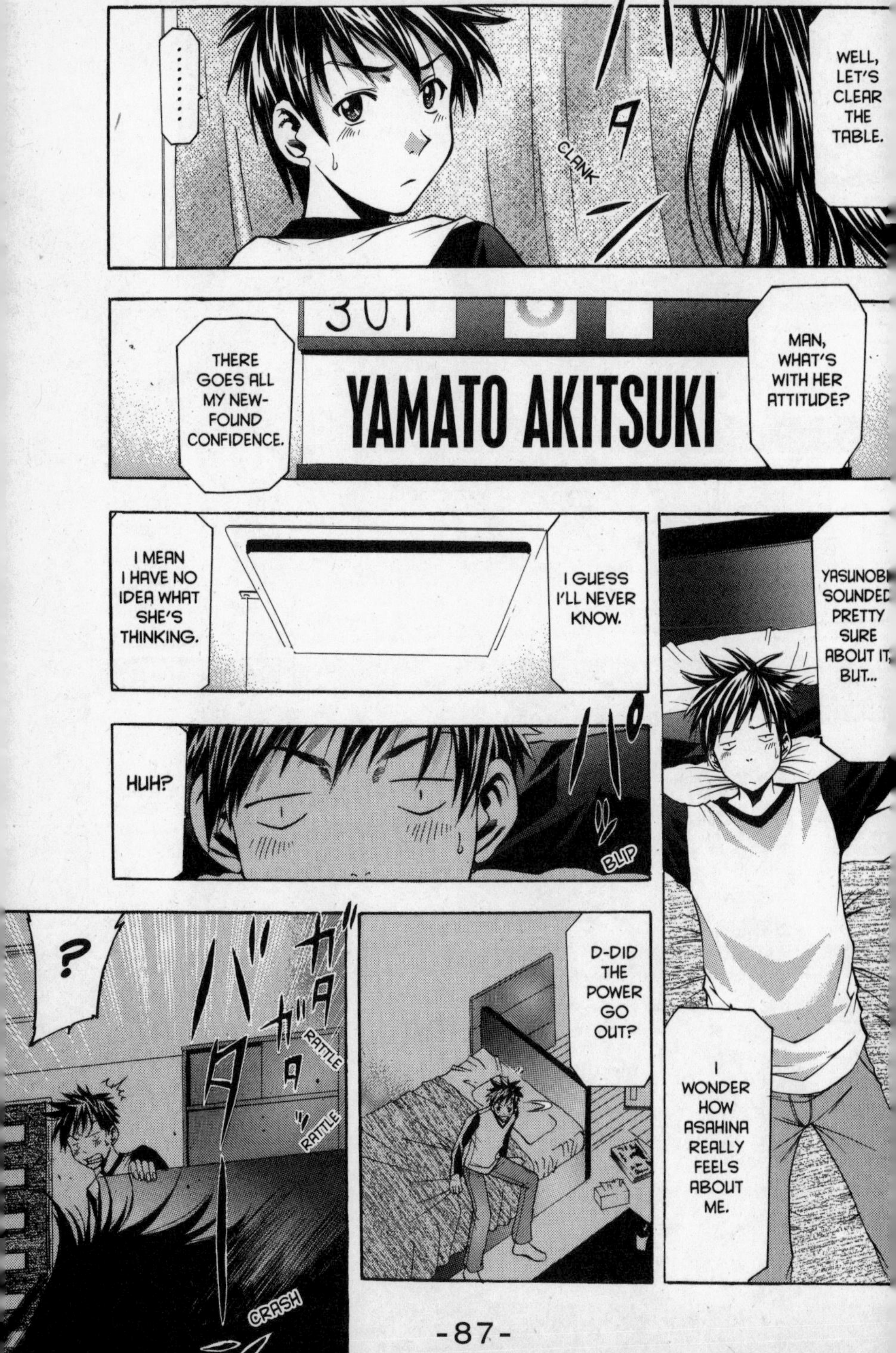
WELL, LET'S CLEAR THE TABLE.
CLANK
......
MAN, WHAT'S WITH HER ATTITUDE?
301
YAMATO AKITSUKI
THERE GOES ALL MY NEW-FOUND CONFIDENCE.
YASUNOBU SOUNDED PRETTY SURE ABOUT IT, BUT...
I WONDER HOW ASAHINA REALLY FEELS ABOUT ME.
I GUESS I'LL NEVER KNOW.
I MEAN I HAVE NO IDEA WHAT SHE'S THINKING.
BLIP
HUH?
D-DID THE POWER GO OUT?
RATTLE
RATTLE
?
CRASH

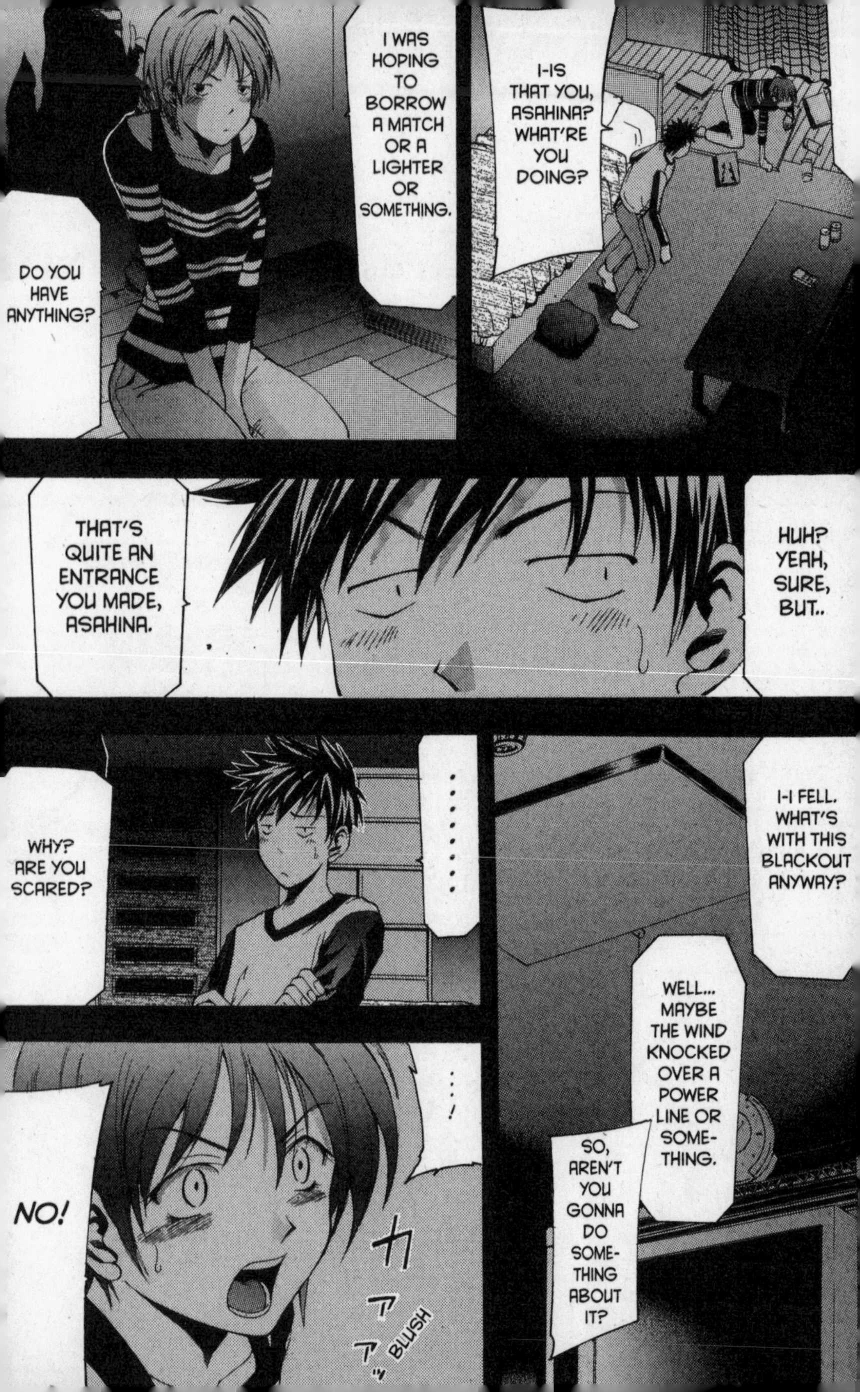
I-IS THAT YOU, ASAHINA? WHAT'RE YOU DOING?
I WAS HOPING TO BORROW A MATCH OR A LIGHTER OR SOMETHING.
DO YOU HAVE ANYTHING?
HUH? YEAH, SURE, BUT..
THAT'S QUITE AN ENTRANCE YOU MADE, ASAHINA.
I-I FELL. WHAT'S WITH THIS BLACKOUT ANYWAY?
WELL... MAYBE THE WIND KNOCKED OVER A POWER LINE OR SOME-THING.
SO, AREN'T YOU GONNA DO SOME-THING ABOUT IT?
....
WHY? ARE YOU SCARED?
...!
NO!
カァァッ
BLUSH

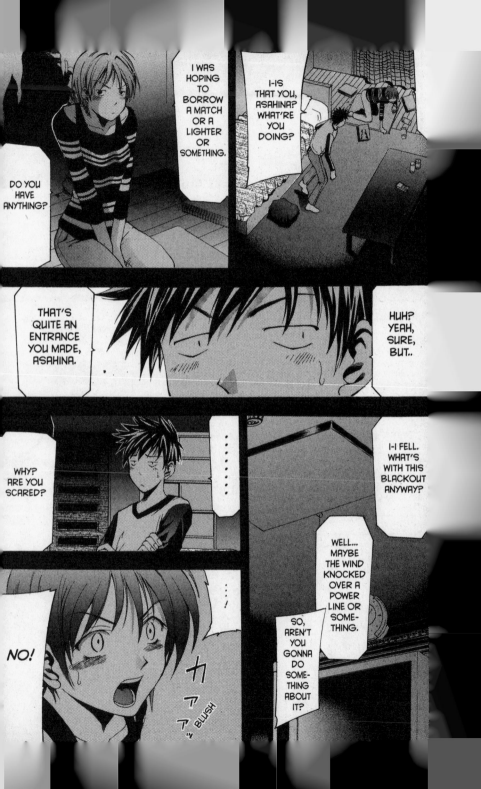

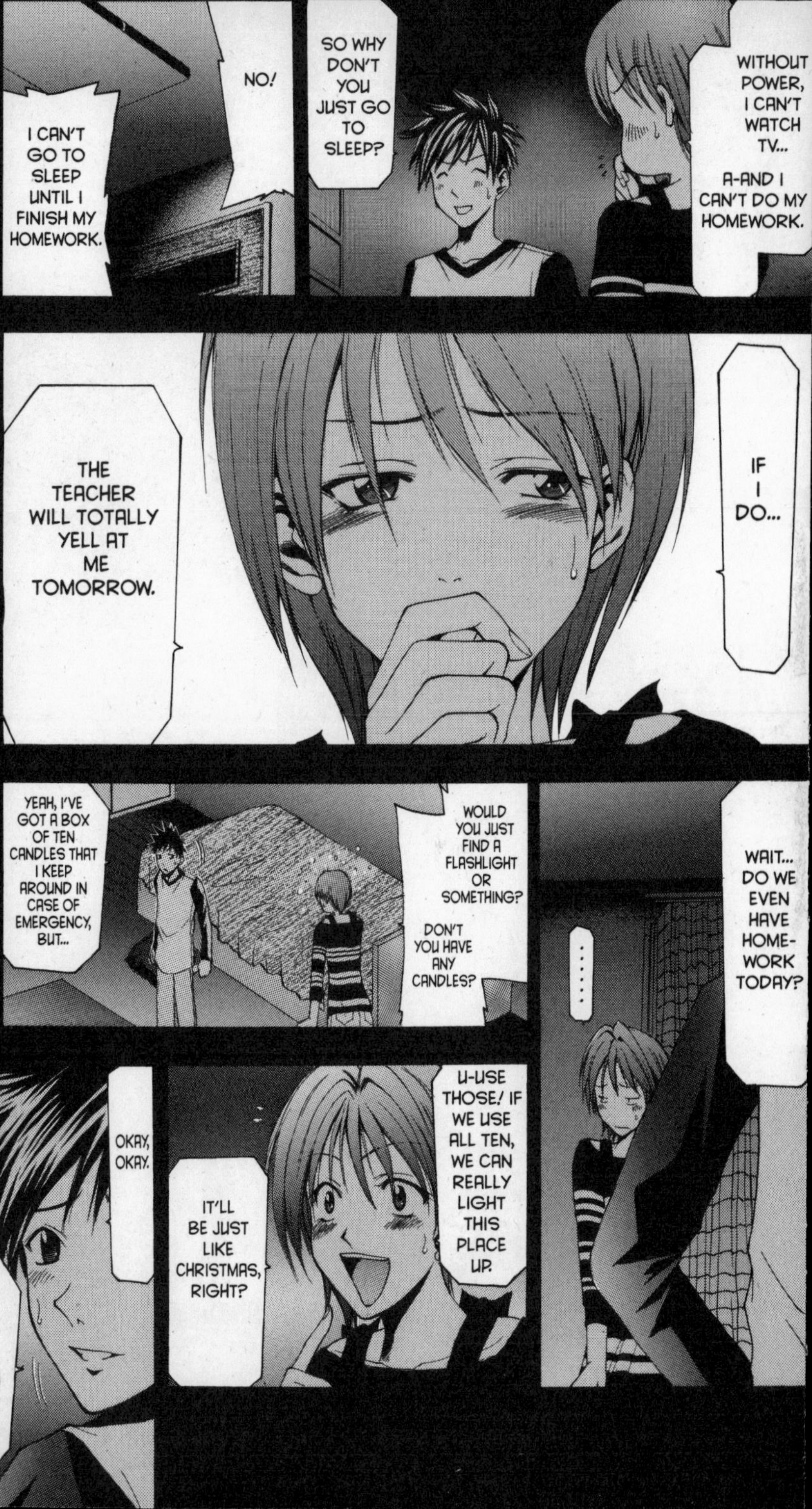

WITHOUT POWER, I CAN'T WATCH TV...
A-AND I CAN'T DO MY HOMEWORK.
SO WHY DON'T YOU JUST GO TO SLEEP?
NO!
I CAN'T GO TO SLEEP UNTIL I FINISH MY HOMEWORK.
IF I DO...
THE TEACHER WILL TOTALLY YELL AT ME TOMORROW.
WAIT... DO WE EVEN HAVE HOME-WORK TODAY?
......
WOULD YOU JUST FIND A FLASHLIGHT OR SOMETHING?
DON'T YOU HAVE ANY CANDLES?
YEAH, I'VE GOT A BOX OF TEN CANDLES THAT I KEEP AROUND IN CASE OF EMERGENCY, BUT...
U-USE THOSE! IF WE USE ALL TEN, WE CAN REALLY LIGHT THIS PLACE UP.
IT'LL BE JUST LIKE CHRISTMAS, RIGHT?
OKAY, OKAY.
I'LL LIGHT THEM UP! JUST HOLD ON A SEC.

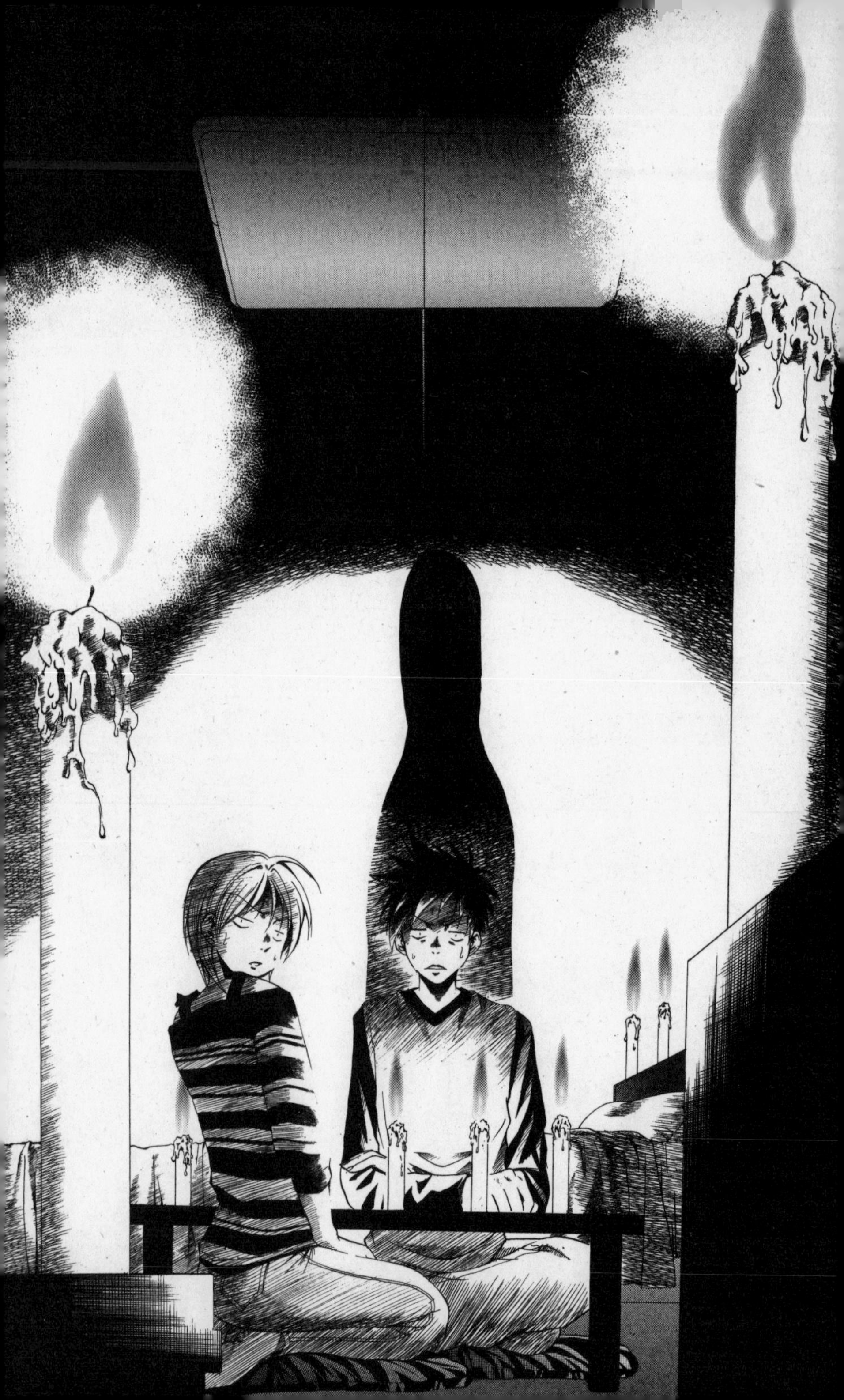

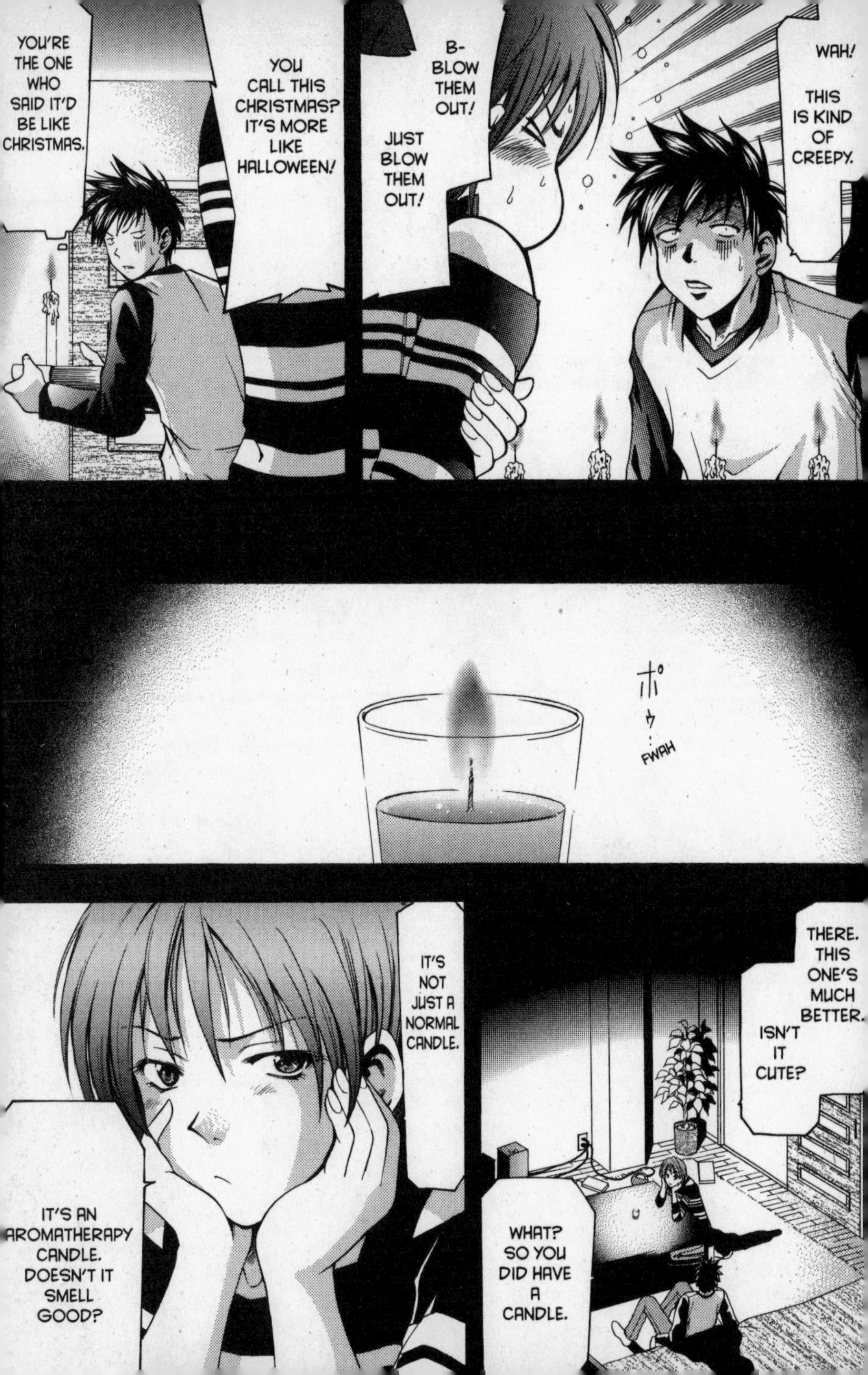
WAH!
THIS IS KIND OF CREEPY.
B-BLOW THEM OUT!
JUST BLOW THEM OUT!
YOU CALL THIS CHRISTMAS? IT'S MORE LIKE HALLOWEEN!
YOU'RE THE ONE WHO SAID IT'D BE LIKE CHRISTMAS.
ポゥ
FWAH
THERE. THIS ONE'S MUCH BETTER.
ISN'T IT CUTE?
WHAT? SO YOU DID HAVE A CANDLE.
IT'S NOT JUST A NORMAL CANDLE.
IT'S AN AROMATHERAPY CANDLE. DOESN'T IT SMELL GOOD?

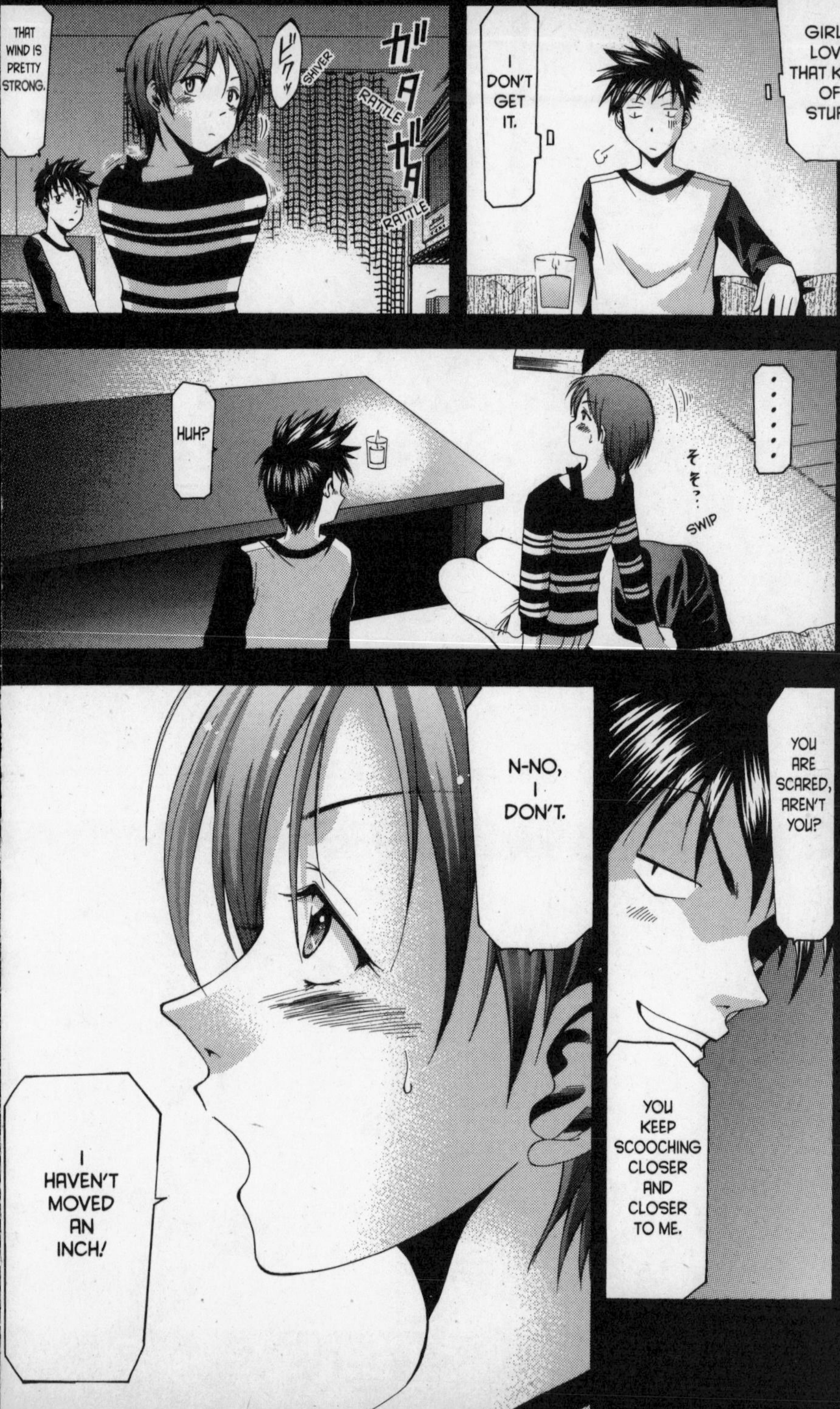
AROMATHERAPY.
GIRLS LOVE THAT KIND OF STUFF.
I DON'T GET IT.
ガタ RATTLE
ガタ RATTLE
ビクッ SHIVER
THAT WIND IS PRETTY STRONG.
......
そそっ... SWIP
HUH?
YOU ARE SCARED, AREN'T YOU?
YOU KEEP SCOOCHING CLOSER AND CLOSER TO ME.
N-NO, I DON'T.
I HAVEN'T MOVED AN INCH!

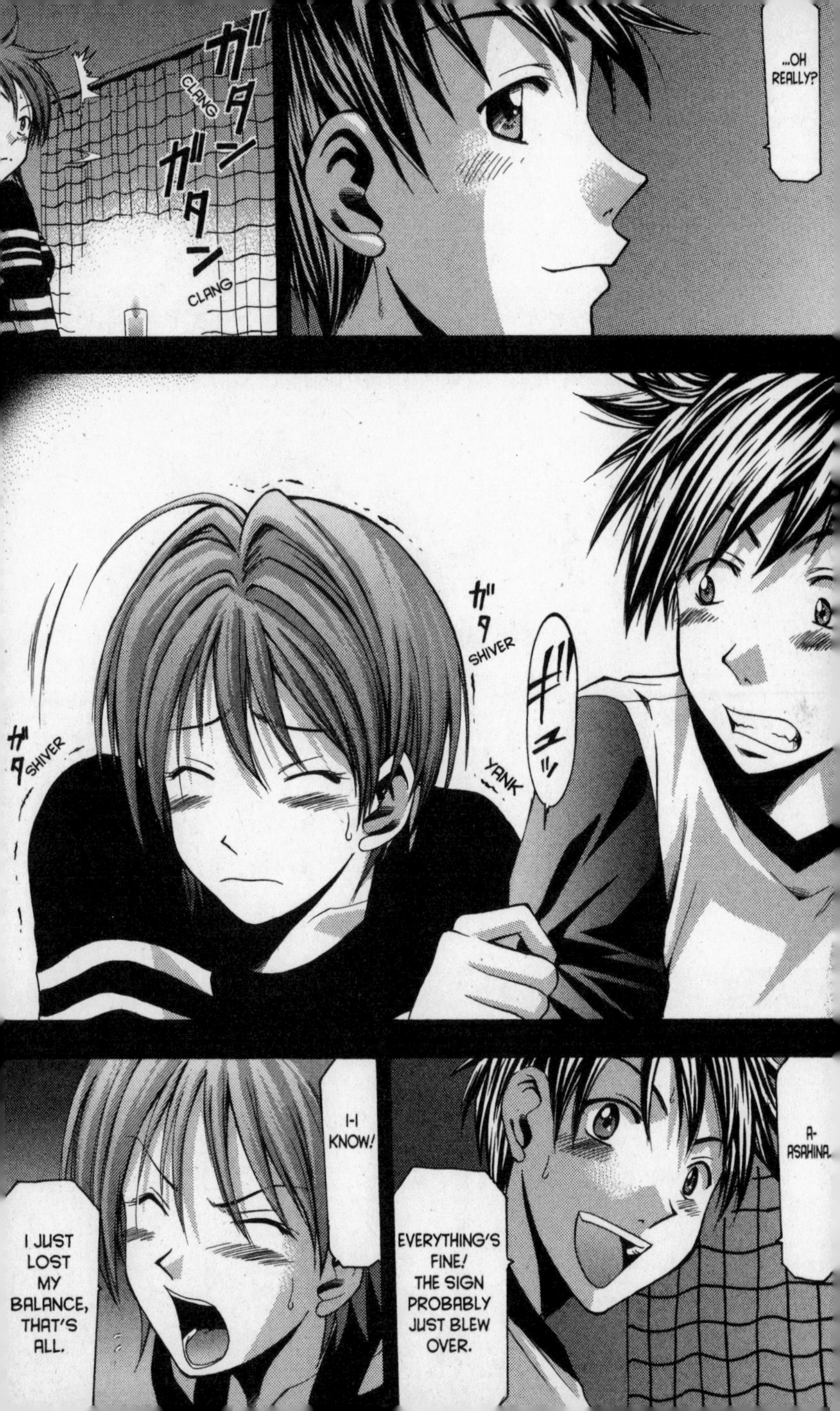
...OH REALLY?
ガタン
CLANG
ガタン
CLANG
ギュッ
YANK
ガタ
SHIVER
ガタ
SHIVER
A-ASAHINA.
EVERYTHING'S FINE! THE SIGN PROBABLY JUST BLEW OVER.
I-I KNOW!
I JUST LOST MY BALANCE, THAT'S ALL.

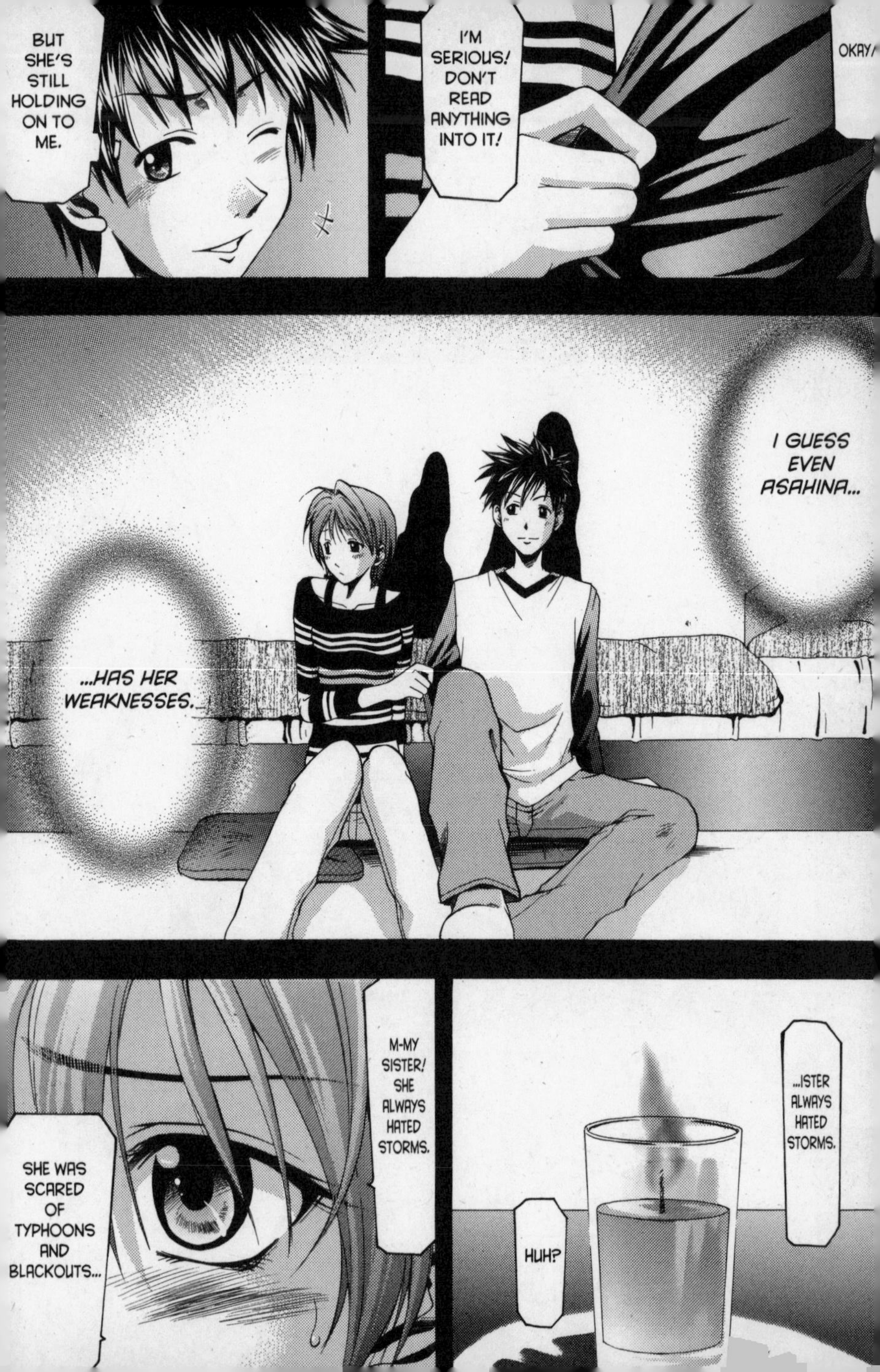
OKAY!
I'M SERIOUS! DON'T READ ANYTHING INTO IT!
BUT SHE'S STILL HOLDING ON TO ME.
I GUESS EVEN ASAHINA...
...HAS HER WEAKNESSES.
...ISTER ALWAYS HATED STORMS.
HUH?
M-MY SISTER! SHE ALWAYS HATED STORMS.
SHE WAS SCARED OF TYPHOONS AND BLACKOUTS...

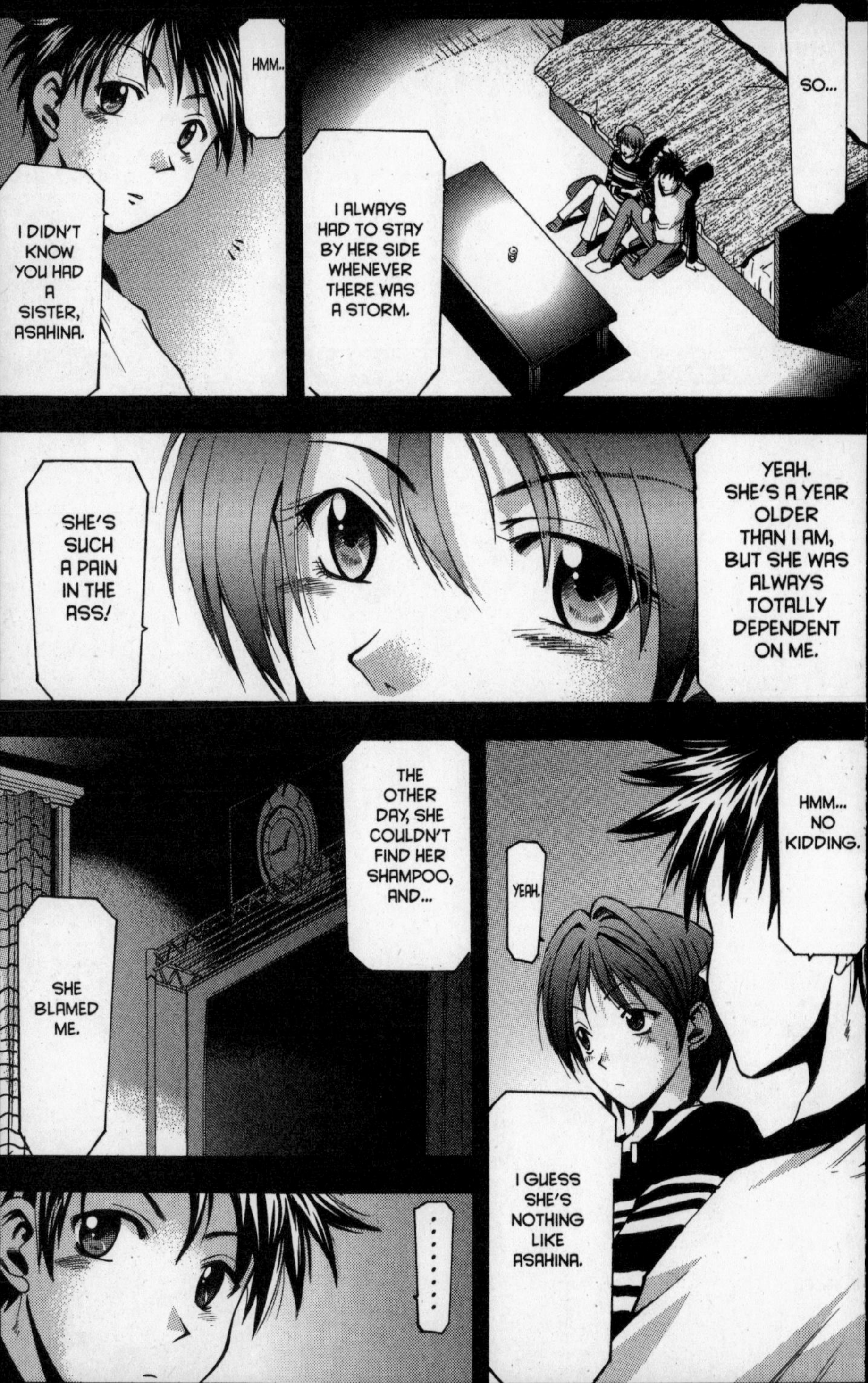
SO...
I ALWAYS HAD TO STAY BY HER SIDE WHENEVER THERE WAS A STORM.
HMM..
I DIDN'T KNOW YOU HAD A SISTER, ASAHINA.
YEAH. SHE'S A YEAR OLDER THAN I AM, BUT SHE WAS ALWAYS TOTALLY DEPENDENT ON ME.
SHE'S SUCH A PAIN IN THE ASS!
HMM... NO KIDDING.
YEAH.
I GUESS SHE'S NOTHING LIKE ASAHINA.
THE OTHER DAY, SHE COULDN'T FIND HER SHAMPOO, AND...
SHE BLAMED ME.
....

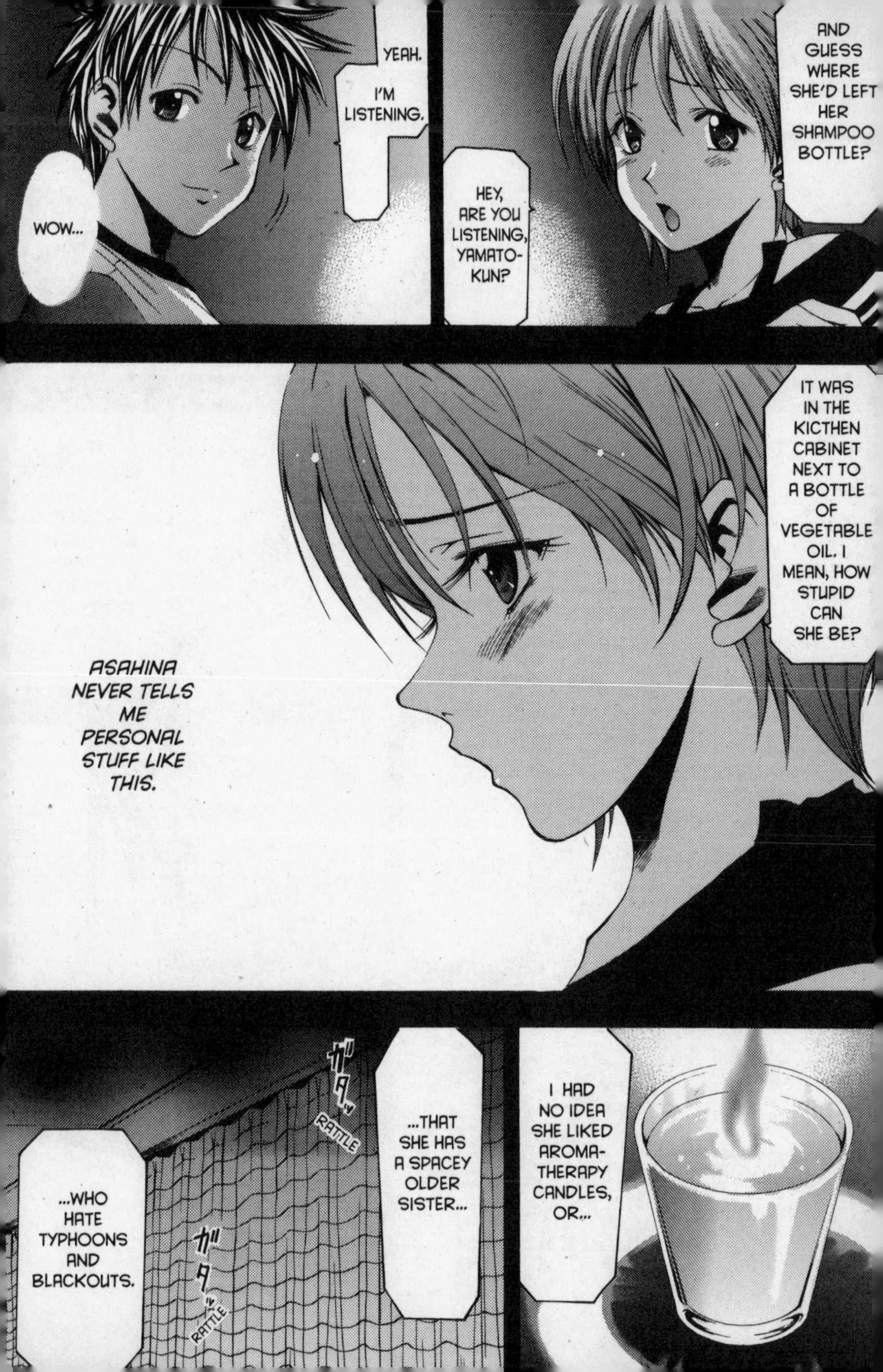
AND GUESS WHERE SHE'D LEFT HER SHAMPOO BOTTLE?
HEY, ARE YOU LISTENING, YAMATO-KUN?
YEAH.
I'M LISTENING.
WOW...
IT WAS IN THE KICTHEN CABINET NEXT TO A BOTTLE OF VEGETABLE OIL. I MEAN, HOW STUPID CAN SHE BE?
ASAHINA NEVER TELLS ME PERSONAL STUFF LIKE THIS.
I HAD NO IDEA SHE LIKED AROMA-THERAPY CANDLES, OR...
...THAT SHE HAS A SPACEY OLDER SISTER...
ガタッ
RATTLE
...WHO HATE TYPHOONS AND BLACKOUTS.
ガタッ
RATTLE

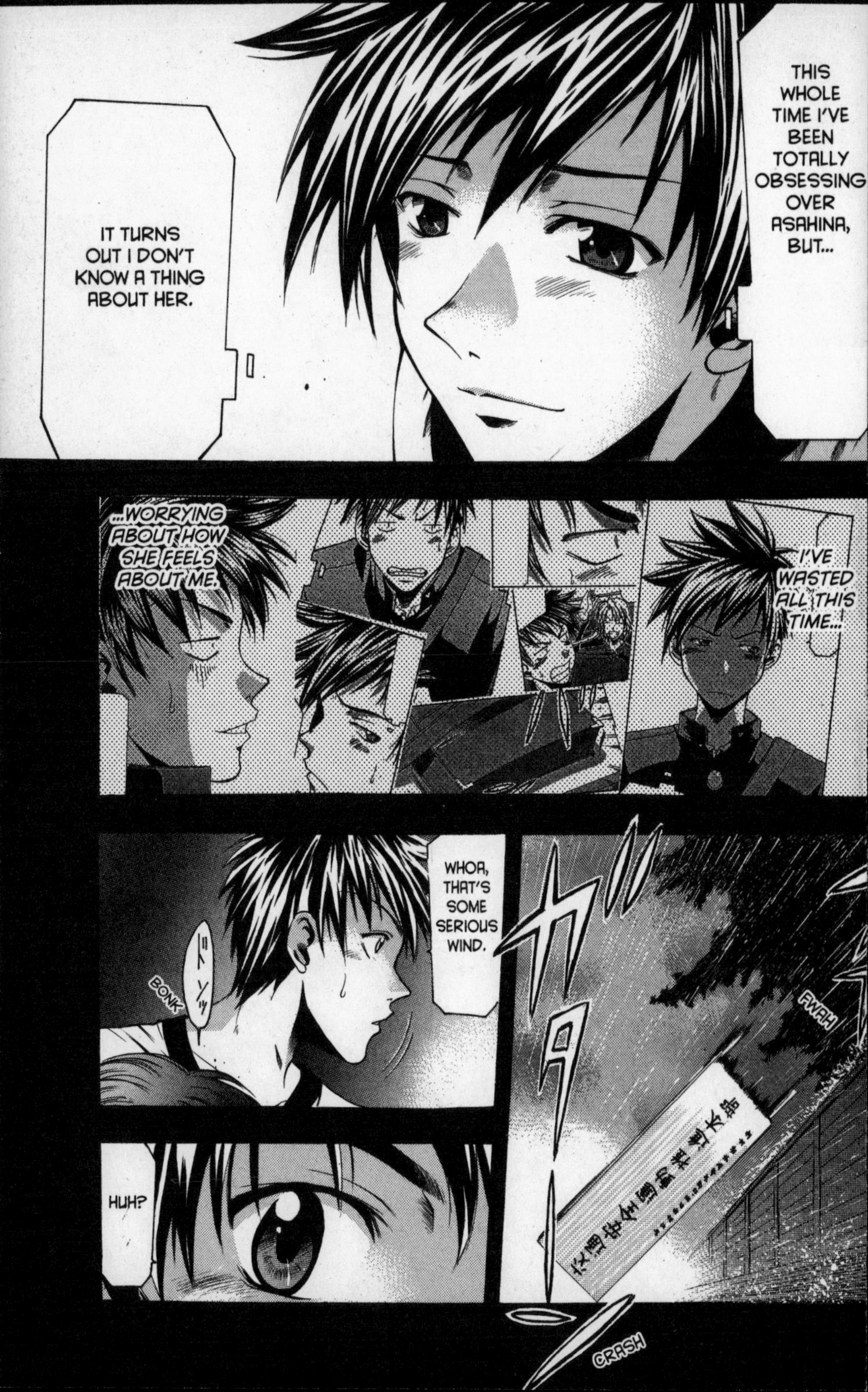
THIS WHOLE TIME I'VE BEEN TOTALLY OBSESSING OVER ASAHINA, BUT...
IT TURNS OUT I DON'T KNOW A THING ABOUT HER.
I'VE WASTED ALL THIS TIME...
...WORRYING ABOUT HOW SHE FEELS ABOUT ME.
ガタ
FWAH
CRASH
WHOA, THAT'S SOME SERIOUS WIND.
ドンッ
BONK
HUH?

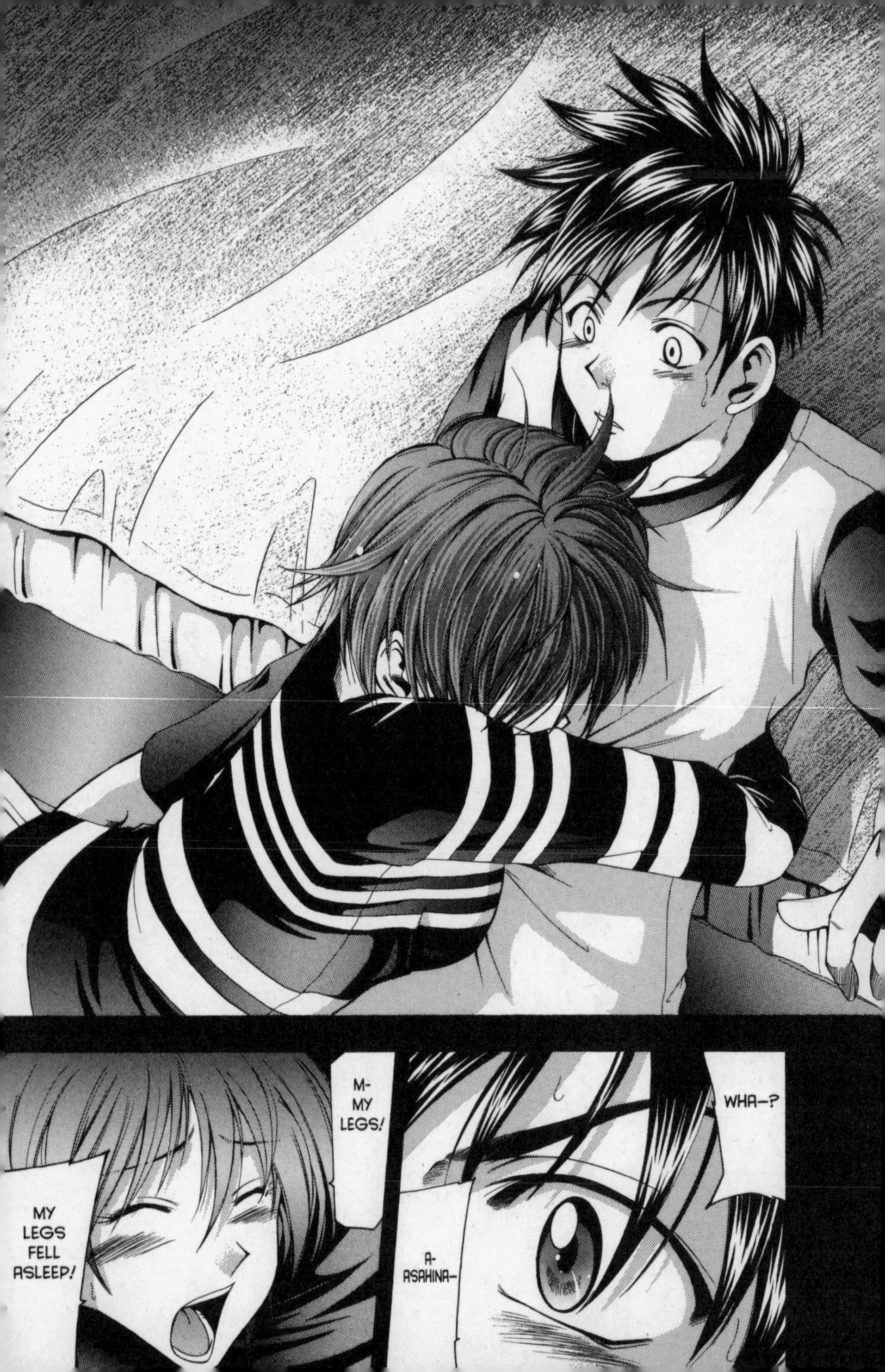
WHA-?
A-ASAHINA-
M-MY LEGS!
MY LEGS FELL ASLEEP!

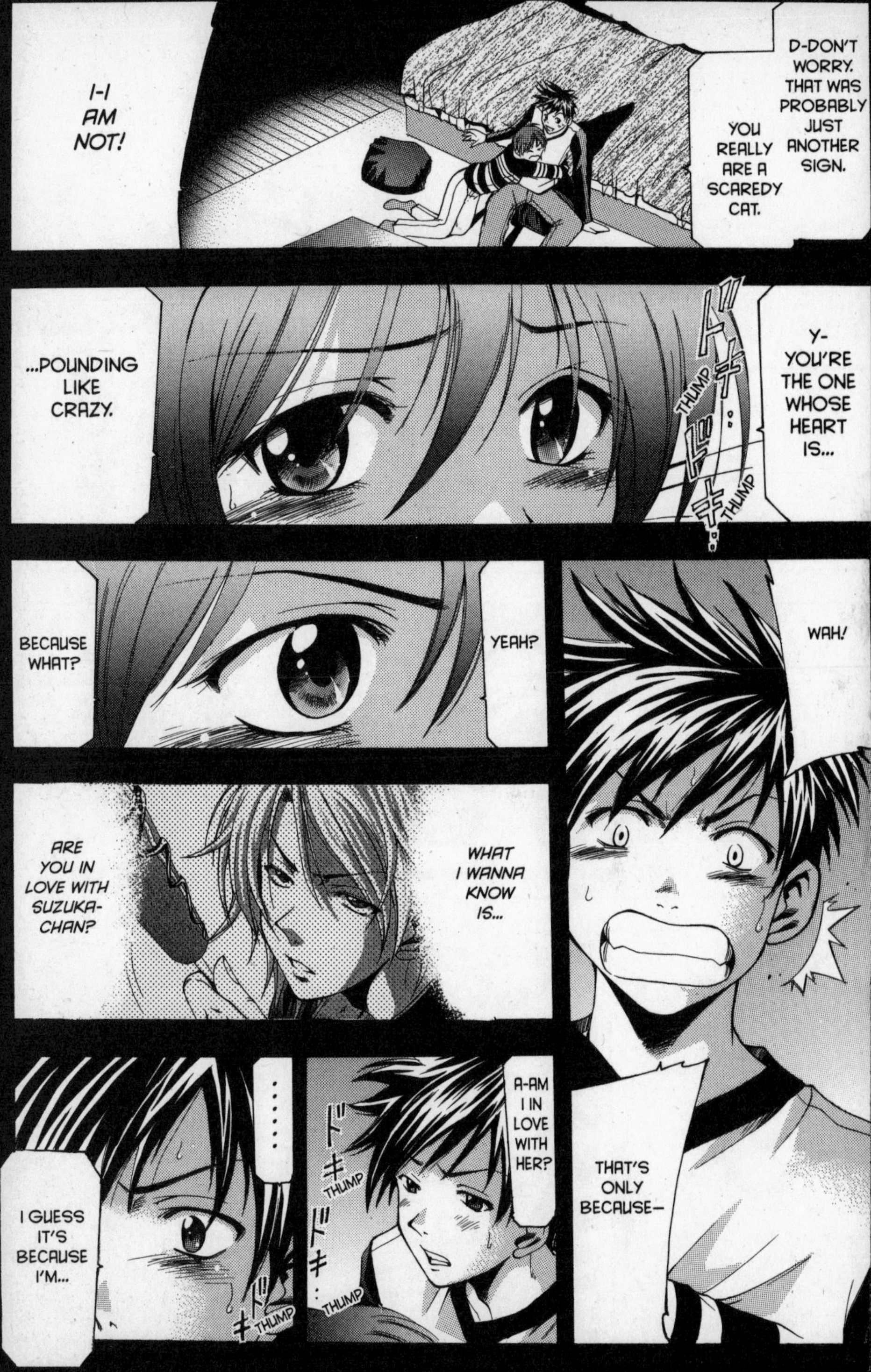
D-DON'T WORRY. THAT WAS PROBABLY JUST ANOTHER SIGN.
YOU REALLY ARE A SCAREDY CAT.
I-I AM NOT!
Y- YOU'RE THE ONE WHOSE HEART IS...
THUMP
THUMP
...POUNDING LIKE CRAZY.
WAH!
YEAH?
BECAUSE WHAT?
WHAT I WANNA KNOW IS...
ARE YOU IN LOVE WITH SUZUKA-CHAN?
THAT'S ONLY BECAUSE—
A-AM I IN LOVE WITH HER?
THUMP
THUMP
......
I GUESS IT'S BECAUSE I'M...
THUMP

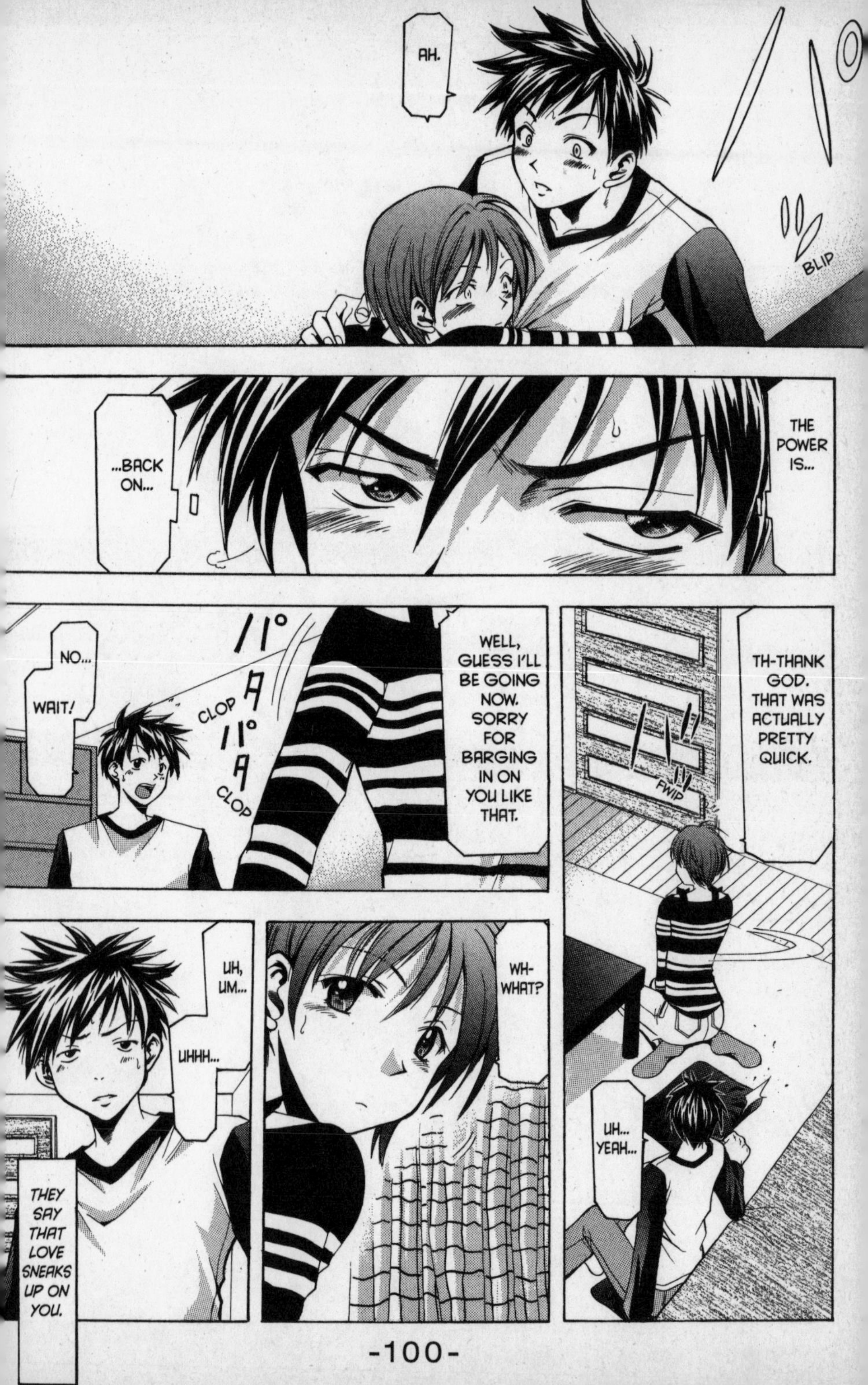
AH.
BLIP
THE POWER IS...
...BACK ON...
TH-THANK GOD. THAT WAS ACTUALLY PRETTY QUICK.
FWIP
UH... YEAH...
WELL, GUESS I'LL BE GOING NOW. SORRY FOR BARGING IN ON YOU LIKE THAT.
CLOP
CLOP
NO...
WAIT!
WH-WHAT?
UH, UM...
UHHH...
THEY SAY THAT LOVE SNEAKS UP ON YOU.

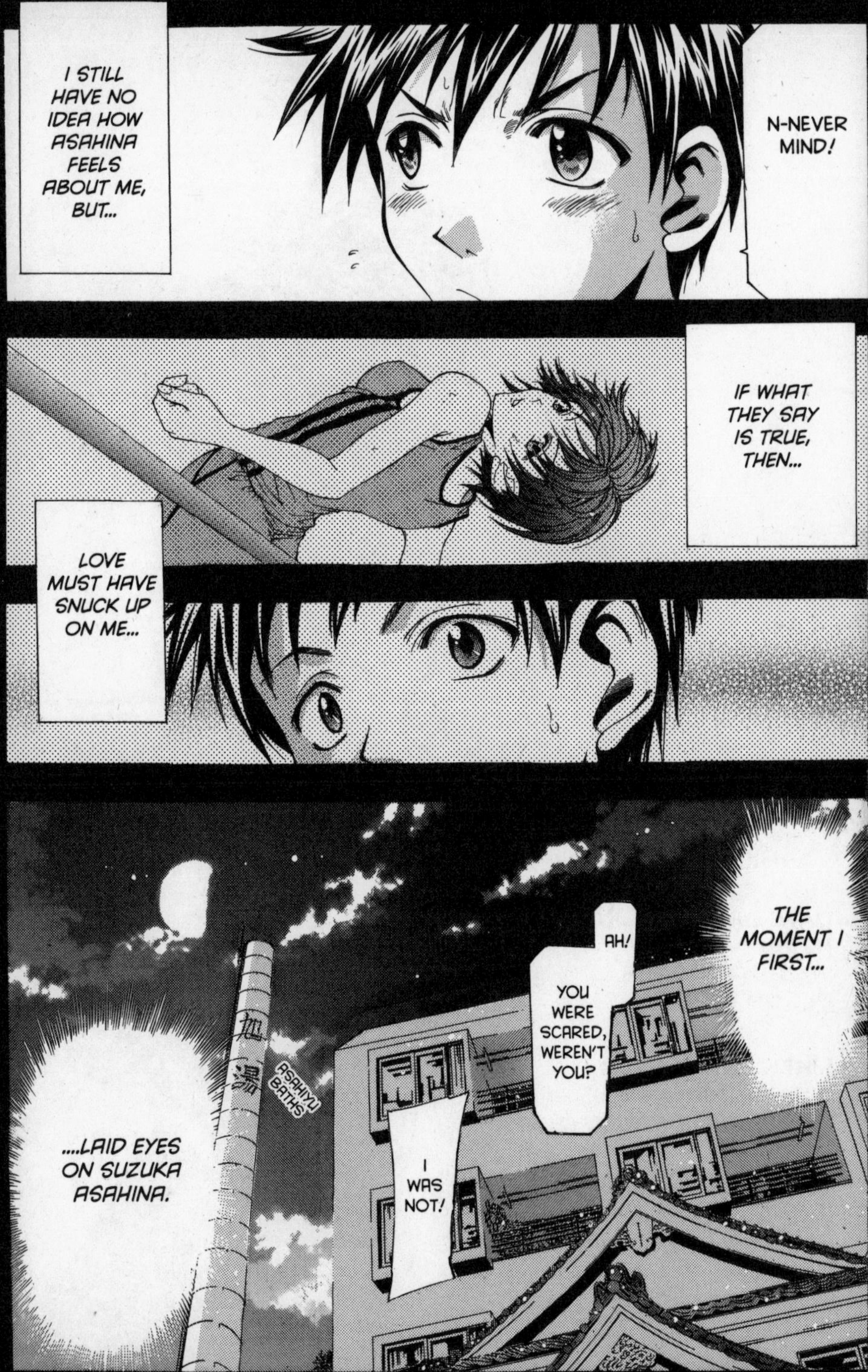
N-NEVER MIND!
I STILL HAVE NO IDEA HOW ASAHINA FEELS ABOUT ME, BUT...
IF WHAT THEY SAY IS TRUE, THEN...
LOVE MUST HAVE SNUCK UP ON ME...
THE MOMENT I FIRST...
AH!
YOU WERE SCARED, WEREN'T YOU?
I WAS NOT!
ASAHIYU BATHS
...LAID EYES ON SUZUKA ASAHINA.

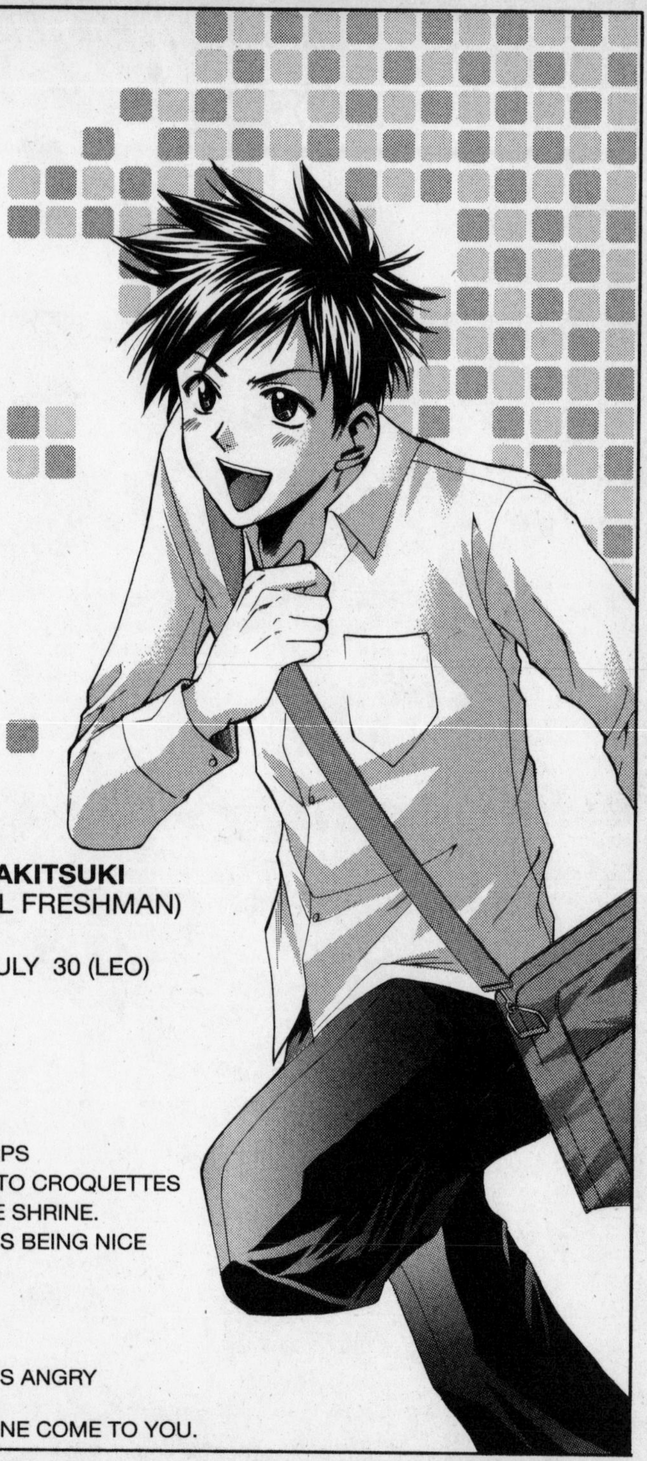

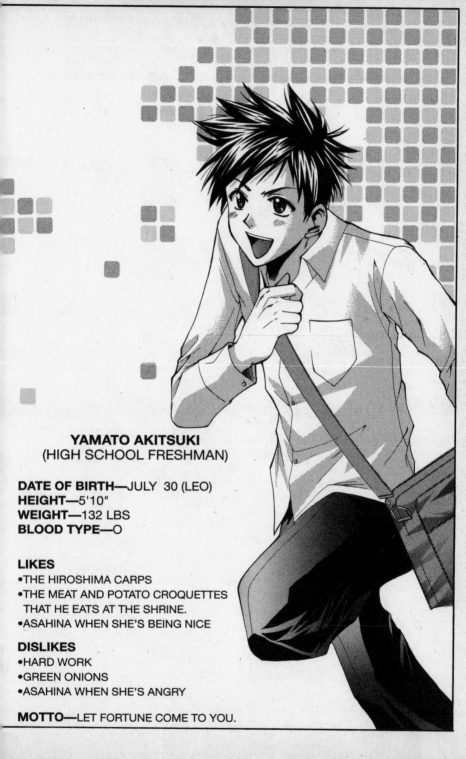

YAMATO AKITSUKI
(HIGH SCHOOL FRESHMAN)

DATE OF BIRTH—JULY 30 (LEO)
HEIGHT—5'10"
WEIGHT—132 LBS
BLOOD TYPE—O

LIKES
- THE HIROSHIMA CARPS
- THE MEAT AND POTATO CROQUETTES THAT HE EATS AT THE SHRINE.
- ASAHINA WHEN SHE'S BEING NICE

DISLIKES
- HARD WORK
- GREEN ONIONS
- ASAHINA WHEN SHE'S ANGRY

MOTTO—LET FORTUNE COME TO YOU.

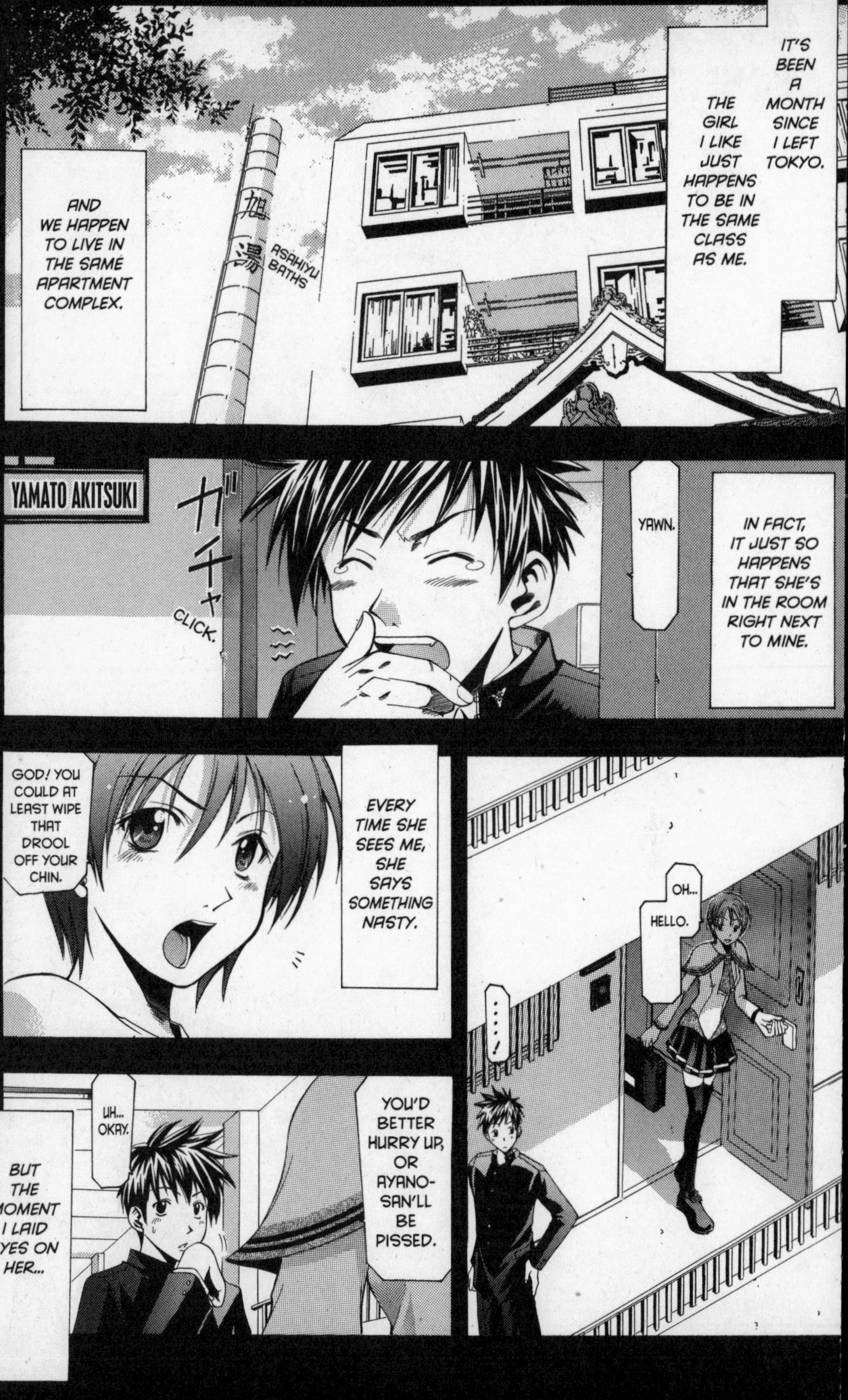
IT'S BEEN A MONTH SINCE I LEFT TOKYO.
THE GIRL I LIKE JUST HAPPENS TO BE IN THE SAME CLASS AS ME.
旭湯
ASAHIYU BATHS
AND WE HAPPEN TO LIVE IN THE SAME APARTMENT COMPLEX.
IN FACT, IT JUST SO HAPPENS THAT SHE'S IN THE ROOM RIGHT NEXT TO MINE.
YAWN.
ガチャ
CLICK.
YAMATO AKITSUKI
OH... HELLO.
......!
EVERY TIME SHE SEES ME, SHE SAYS SOMETHING NASTY.
GOD! YOU COULD AT LEAST WIPE THAT DROOL OFF YOUR CHIN.
YOU'D BETTER HURRY UP, OR AYANO-SAN'LL BE PISSED.
UH... OKAY.
BUT THE MOMENT I LAID EYES ON HER...

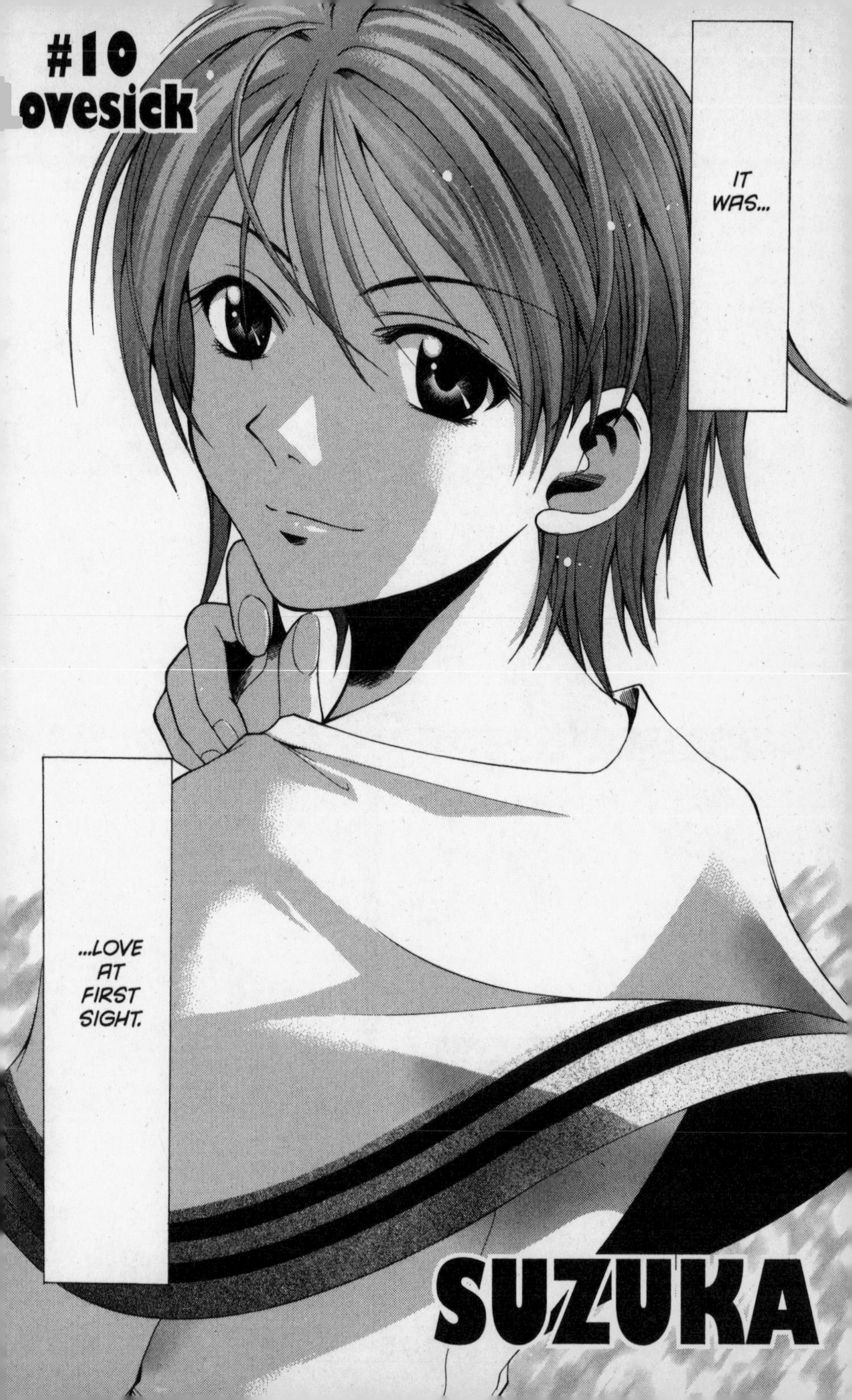
#10 Lovesick
IT WAS...
...LOVE AT FIRST SIGHT.
SUZUKA

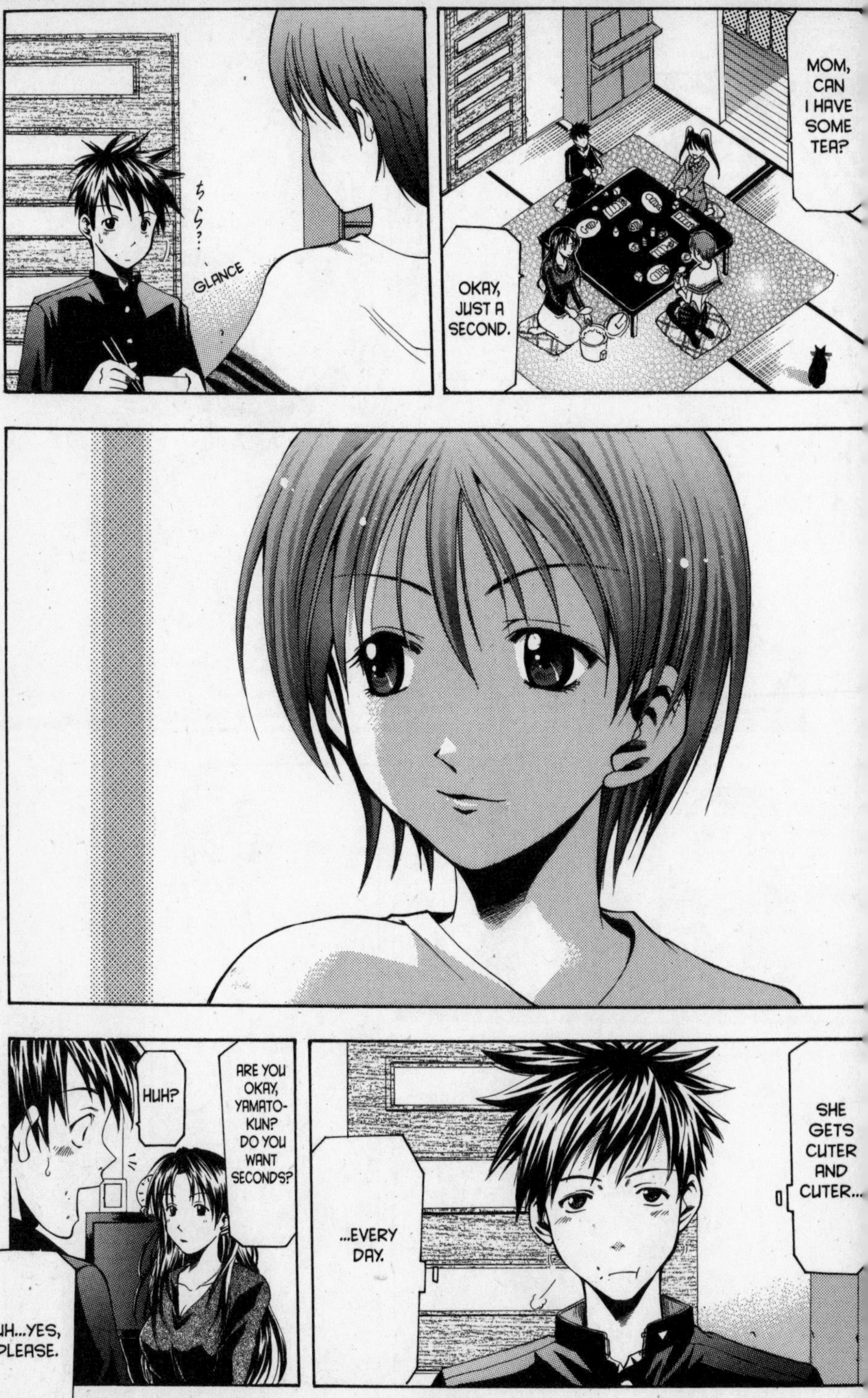
MOM, CAN I HAVE SOME TEA?
OKAY, JUST A SECOND.
ちら…
GLANCE
SHE GETS CUTER AND CUTER...
...EVERY DAY.
ARE YOU OKAY, YAMATO-KUN? DO YOU WANT SECONDS?
HUH?
UH...YES, PLEASE.

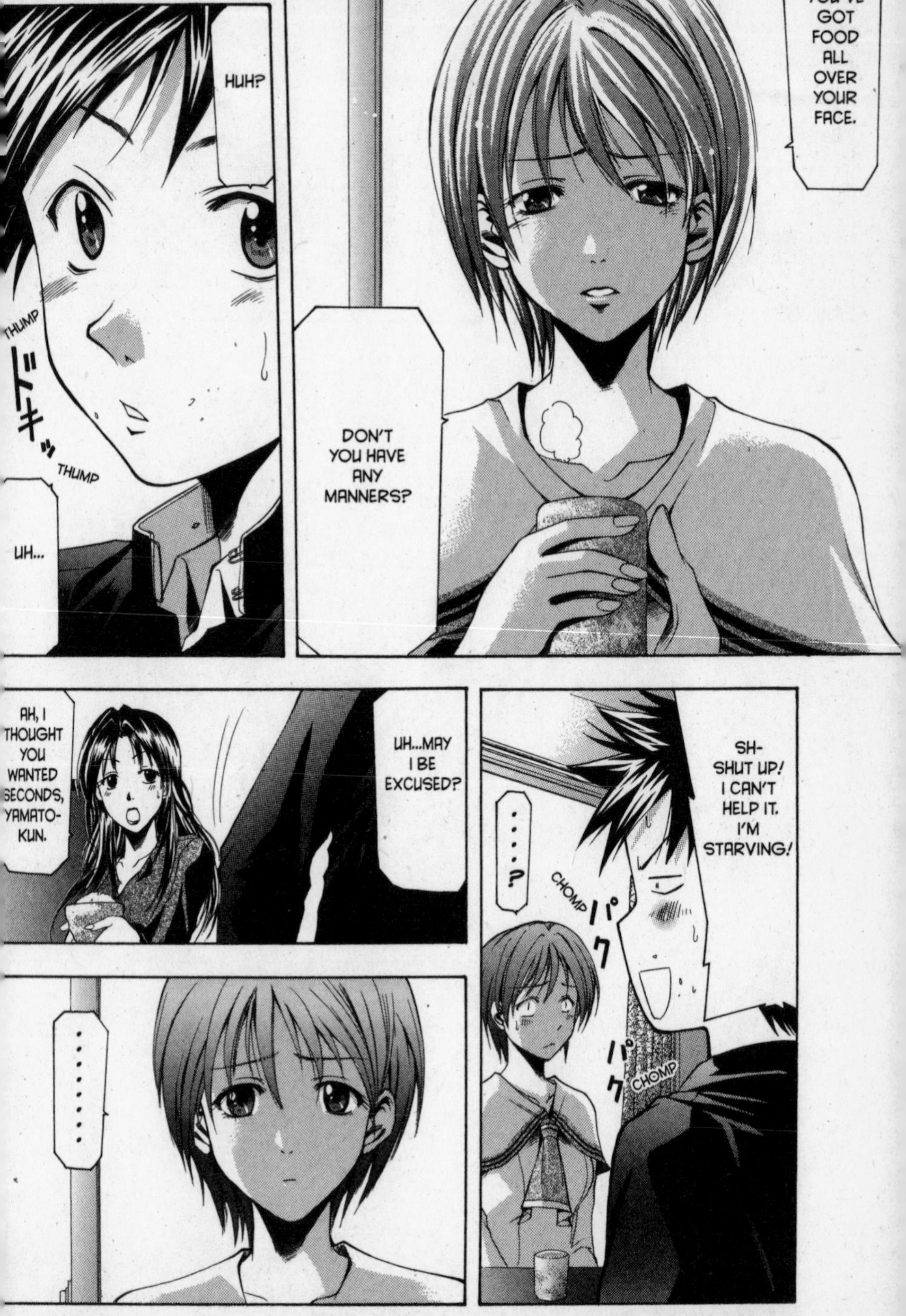
YOU'VE GOT FOOD ALL OVER YOUR FACE.
DON'T YOU HAVE ANY MANNERS?
HUH?
THUMP
ドキッ
THUMP
UH...
SH- SHUT UP! I CAN'T HELP IT. I'M STARVING!
....?
CHOMP
パク
パク
CHOMP
UH...MAY I BE EXCUSED?
AH, I THOUGHT YOU WANTED SECONDS, YAMATO-KUN.
......

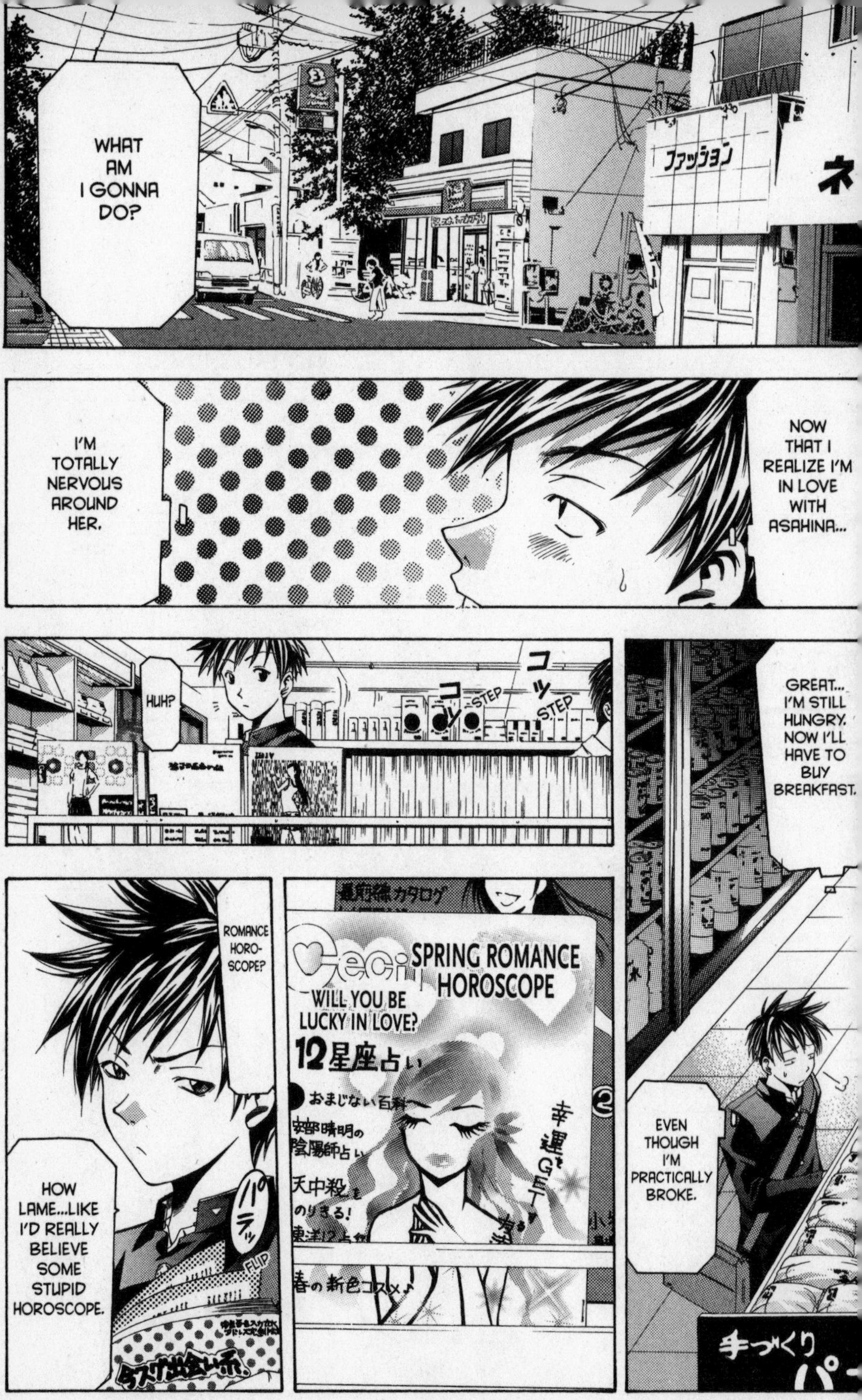
ファッション
WHAT AM I GONNA DO?
NOW THAT I REALIZE I'M IN LOVE WITH ASAHINA...
I'M TOTALLY NERVOUS AROUND HER.
GREAT... I'M STILL HUNGRY. NOW I'LL HAVE TO BUY BREAKFAST.
EVEN THOUGH I'M PRACTICALLY BROKE.
手づくり
コツ STEP
コツ STEP
HUH?
SPRING ROMANCE HOROSCOPE
WILL YOU BE LUCKY IN LOVE?
12星座占い
おまじない百科
安部晴明の陰陽師占い
天中殺をのりきる!
春の新色コスメ♪
幸運をGET
ROMANCE HORO-SCOPE?
パラッ FLIP
HOW LAME...LIKE I'D REALLY BELIEVE SOME STUPID HOROSCOPE.

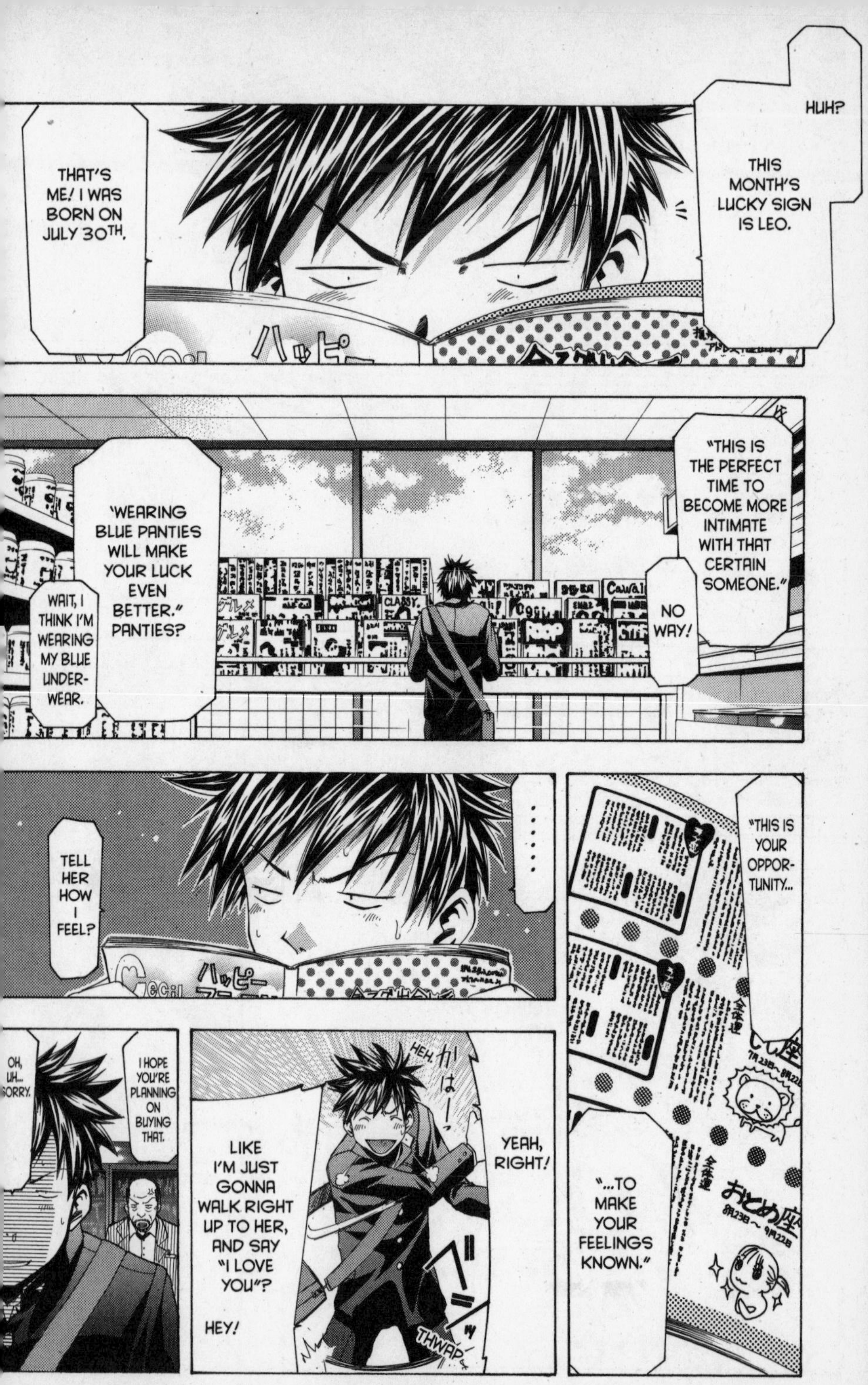
HUH?
THIS MONTH'S LUCKY SIGN IS LEO.
THAT'S ME! I WAS BORN ON JULY 30TH.
ハッピー
"THIS IS THE PERFECT TIME TO BECOME MORE INTIMATE WITH THAT CERTAIN SOMEONE."
NO WAY!
'WEARING BLUE PANTIES WILL MAKE YOUR LUCK EVEN BETTER." PANTIES?
WAIT, I THINK I'M WEARING MY BLUE UNDER-WEAR.
CLASSY
"THIS IS YOUR OPPOR-TUNITY...
しし座
"...TO MAKE YOUR FEELINGS KNOWN."
おとめ座
8月23日～9月22日
......
TELL HER HOW I FEEL?
ハッピー
YEAH, RIGHT!
HEH.
かはーっ
LIKE I'M JUST GONNA WALK RIGHT UP TO HER, AND SAY "I LOVE YOU"?
HEY!
THWAP
I HOPE YOU'RE PLANNING ON BUYING THAT.
OH, UH... SORRY.

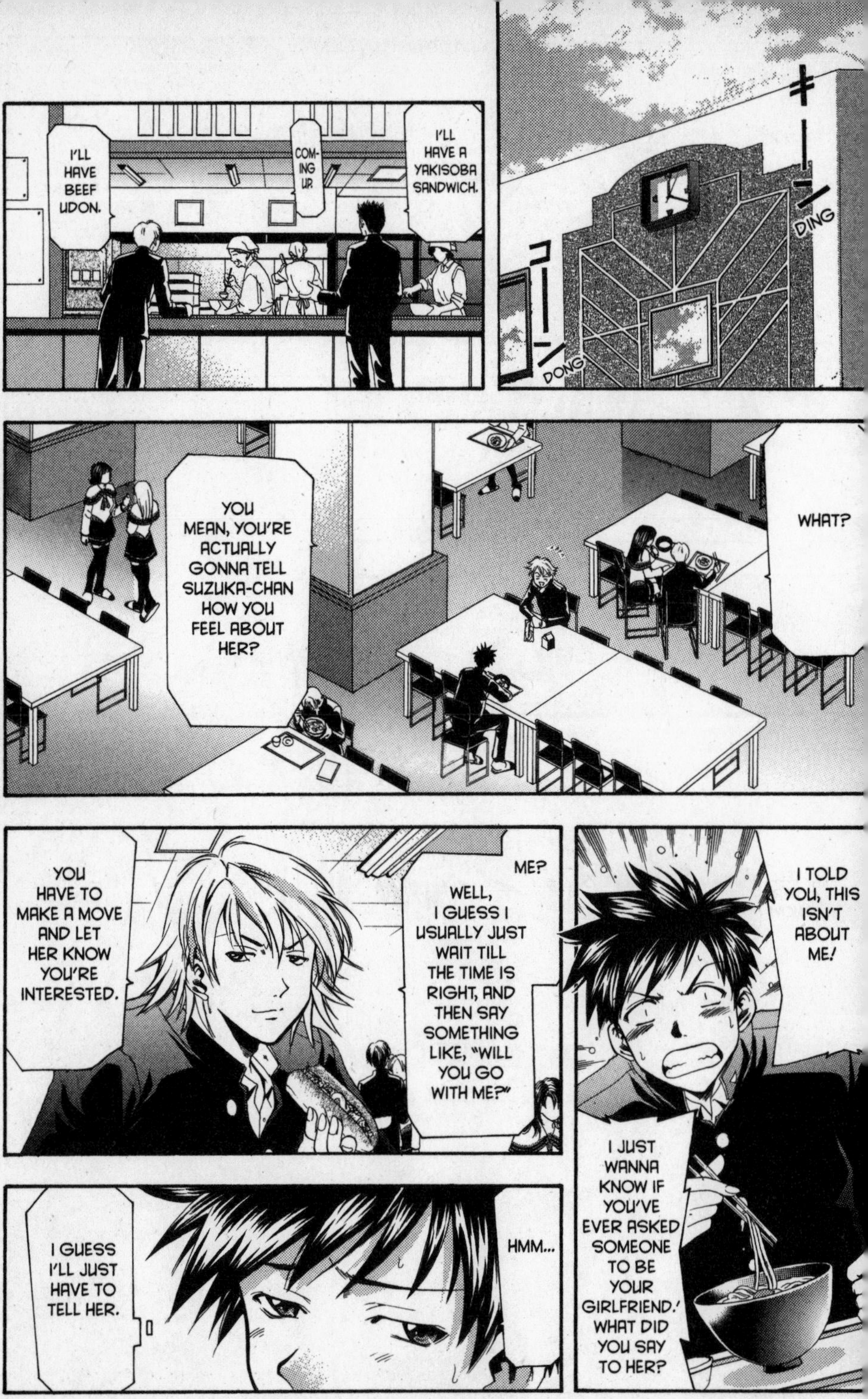
DING
DONG
I'LL HAVE A YAKISOBA SANDWICH.
COM-ING UP.
I'LL HAVE BEEF UDON.
WHAT?
YOU MEAN, YOU'RE ACTUALLY GONNA TELL SUZUKA-CHAN HOW YOU FEEL ABOUT HER?
I TOLD YOU, THIS ISN'T ABOUT ME!
I JUST WANNA KNOW IF YOU'VE EVER ASKED SOMEONE TO BE YOUR GIRLFRIEND.' WHAT DID YOU SAY TO HER?
ME?
WELL, I GUESS I USUALLY JUST WAIT TILL THE TIME IS RIGHT, AND THEN SAY SOMETHING LIKE, "WILL YOU GO WITH ME?"
YOU HAVE TO MAKE A MOVE AND LET HER KNOW YOU'RE INTERESTED.
HMM...
I GUESS I'LL JUST HAVE TO TELL HER.

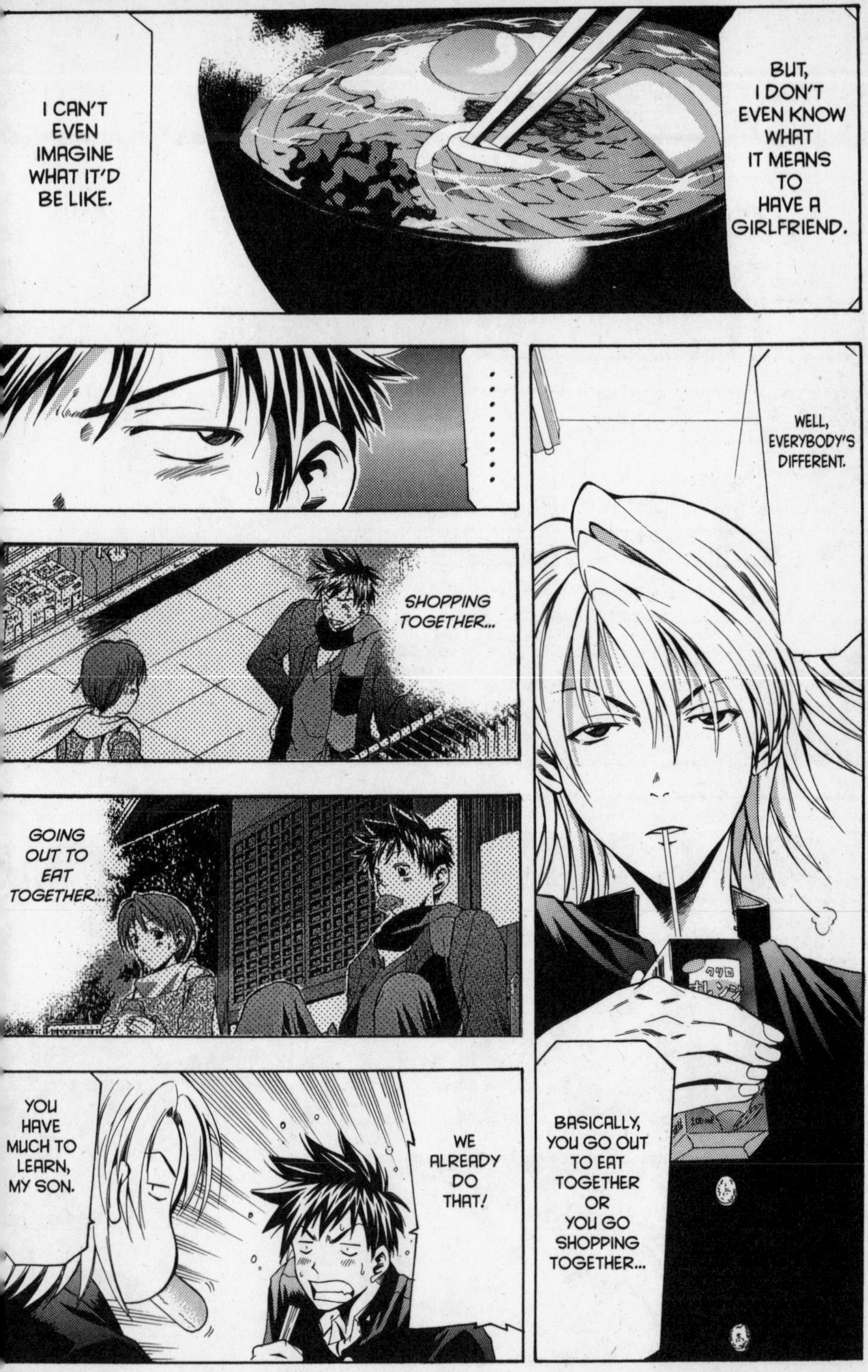
BUT, I DON'T EVEN KNOW WHAT IT MEANS TO HAVE A GIRLFRIEND.
I CAN'T EVEN IMAGINE WHAT IT'D BE LIKE.
WELL, EVERYBODY'S DIFFERENT.
BASICALLY, YOU GO OUT TO EAT TOGETHER OR YOU GO SHOPPING TOGETHER...
....
SHOPPING TOGETHER...
GOING OUT TO EAT TOGETHER...
WE ALREADY DO THAT!
YOU HAVE MUCH TO LEARN, MY SON.

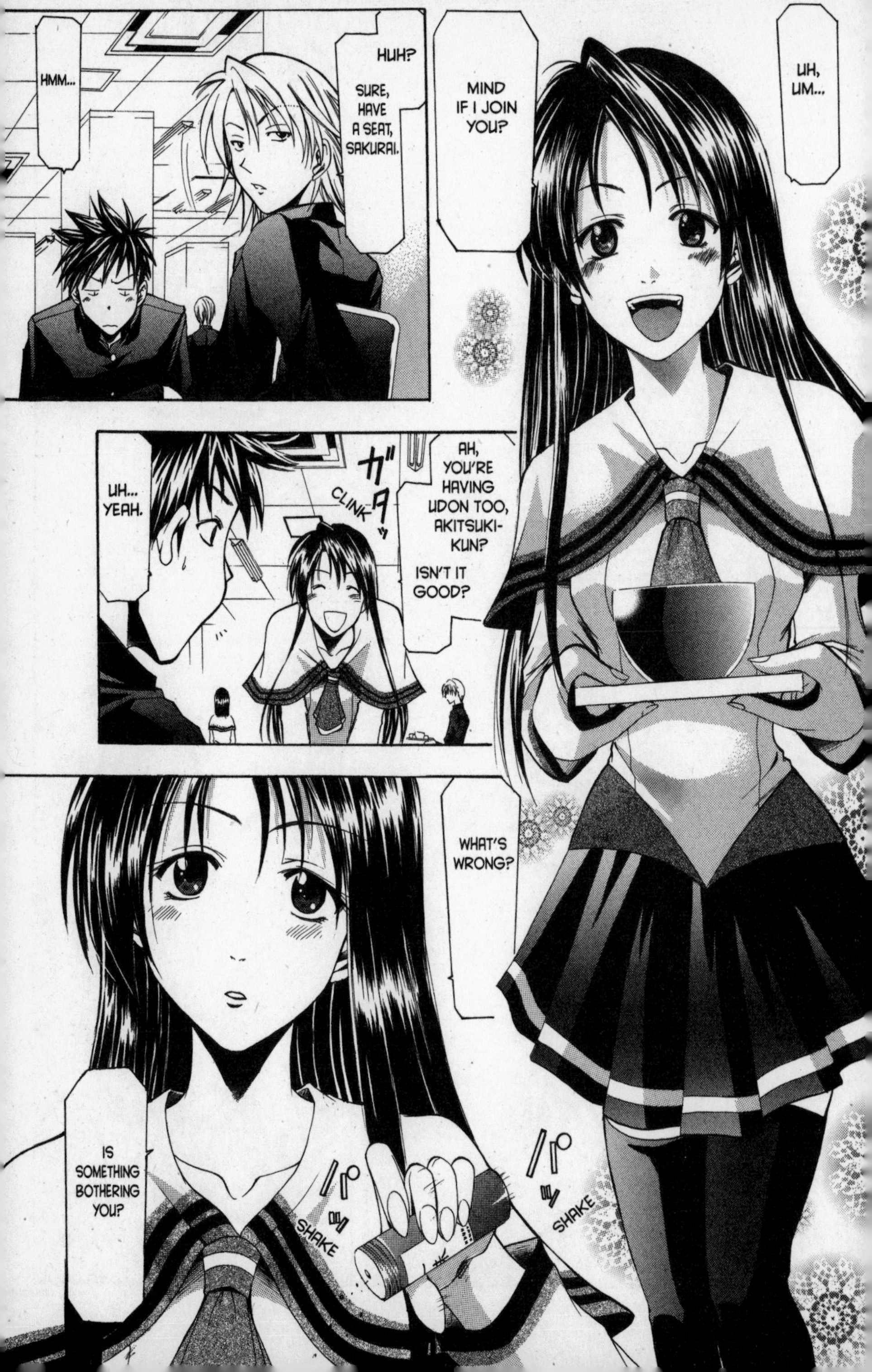
UH, UM...
MIND IF I JOIN YOU?
SHAKE
HUH?
SURE, HAVE A SEAT, SAKURAI.
HMM...
AH, YOU'RE HAVING UDON TOO, AKITSUKI-KUN?
ISN'T IT GOOD?
ガタッ
CLINK
UH... YEAH.
WHAT'S WRONG?
IS SOMETHING BOTHERING YOU?
SHAKE

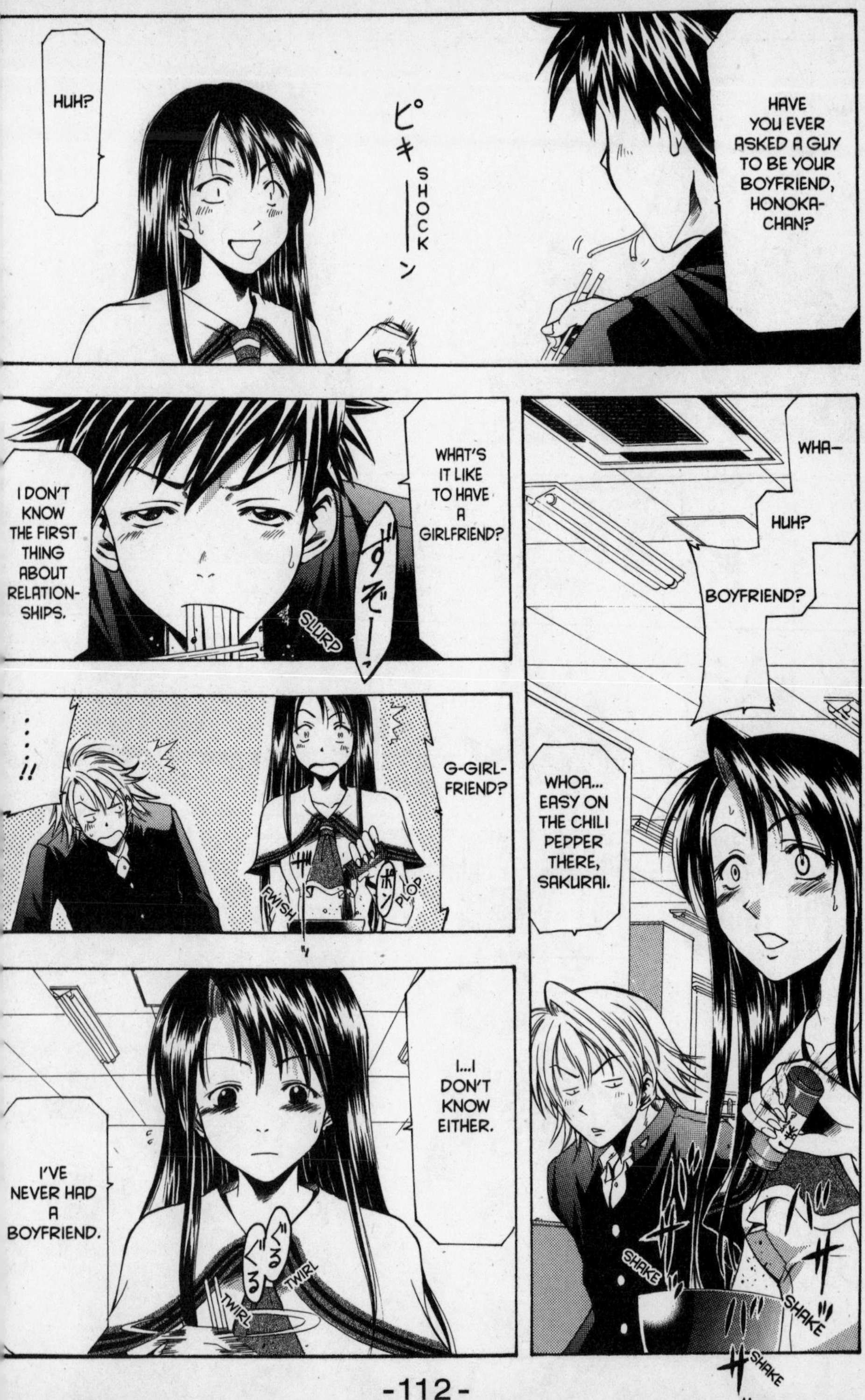
HAVE YOU EVER ASKED A GUY TO BE YOUR BOYFRIEND, HONOKA-CHAN?
ピキーン
SHOCK
HUH?
WHA-
HUH?
BOYFRIEND?
WHOA... EASY ON THE CHILI PEPPER THERE, SAKURAI.
SHAKE
SHAKE
SHAKE
WHAT'S IT LIKE TO HAVE A GIRLFRIEND?
ずぞーっ
SLURP
I DON'T KNOW THE FIRST THING ABOUT RELATIONSHIPS.
G-GIRLFRIEND?
ポン
PLOP
FWISH
...!!
I...I DON'T KNOW EITHER.
ぐるぐる
TWIRL
TWIRL
I'VE NEVER HAD A BOYFRIEND.

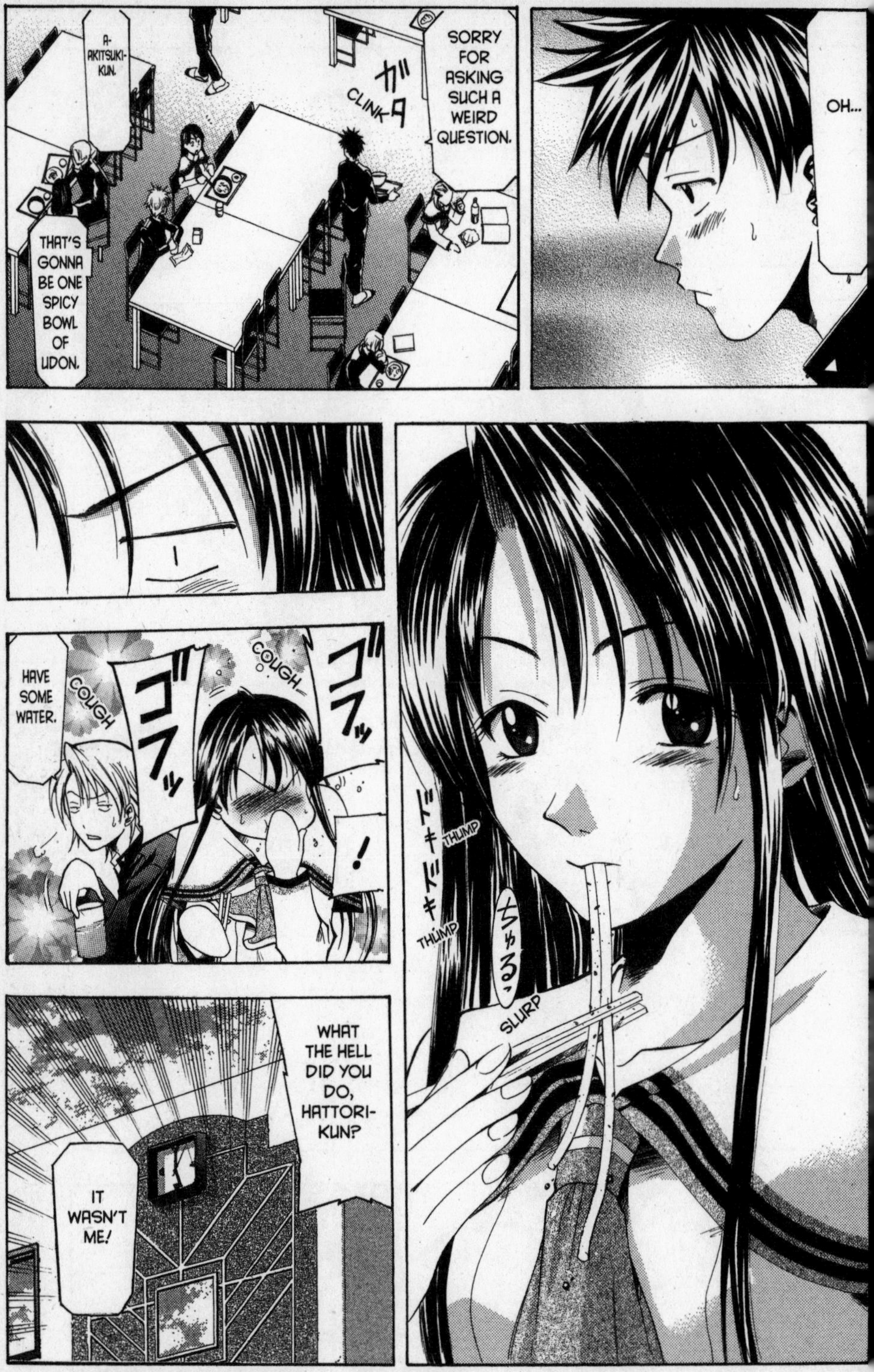
OH...
SORRY FOR ASKING SUCH A WEIRD QUESTION.
ガタ
CLINK
A-AKITSUKI-KUN.
THAT'S GONNA BE ONE SPICY BOWL OF UDON.
ドキドキ
THUMP
THUMP
ちゅるっ
SLURP
ゴフッ
COUGH
!
ゴフッ
COUGH
HAVE SOME WATER.
WHAT THE HELL DID YOU DO, HATTORI-KUN?
IT WASN'T ME!

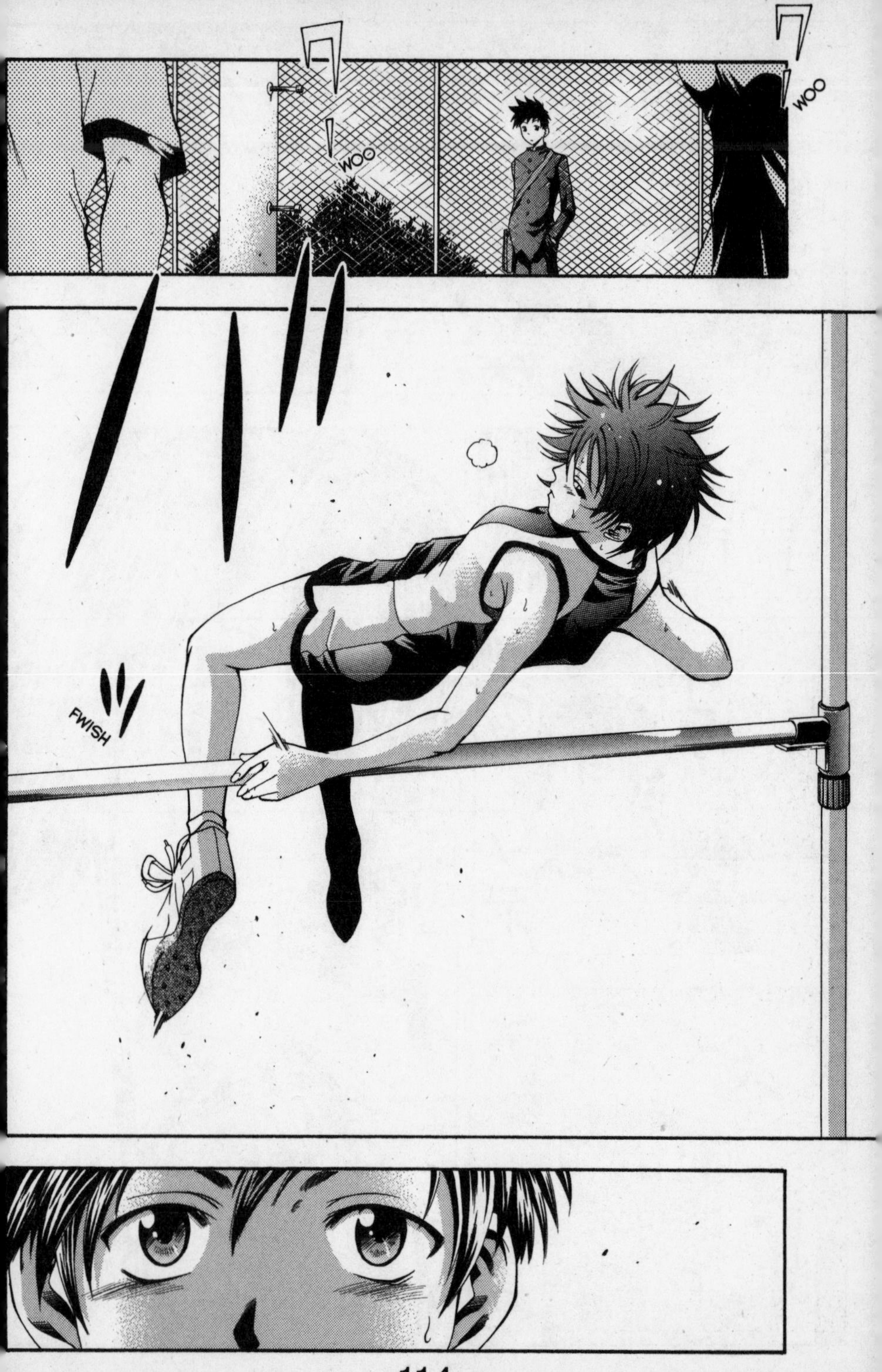
WOO
WOO
FWISH

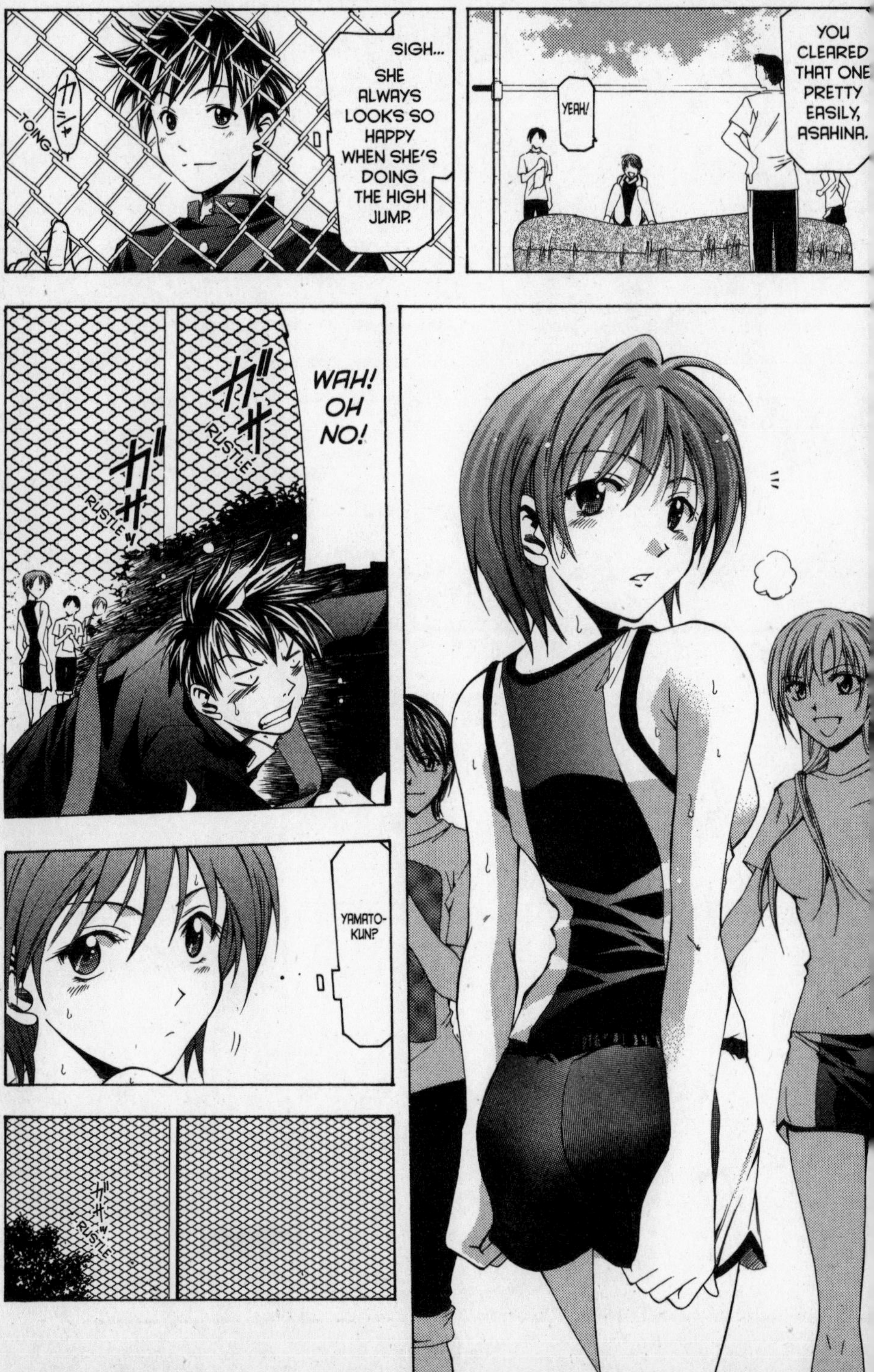
YOU CLEARED THAT ONE PRETTY EASILY, ASAHINA.
YEAH!
SIGH...
SHE ALWAYS LOOKS SO HAPPY WHEN SHE'S DOING THE HIGH JUMP.
TOING
WAH! OH NO!
ガサ
RUSTLE
ガサ
RUSTLE
YAMATO-KUN?
RUSTLE

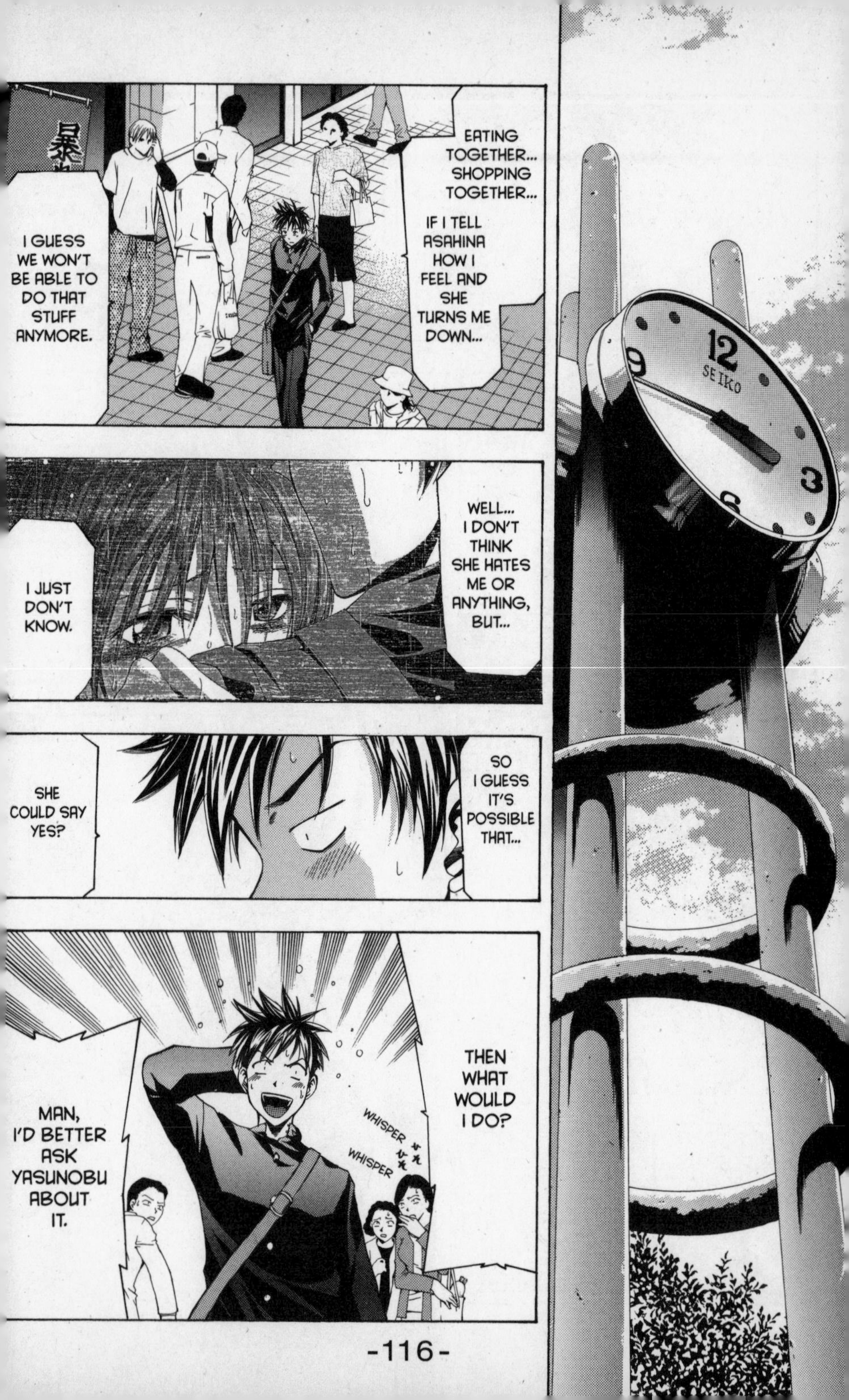
SEIKO
EATING TOGETHER... SHOPPING TOGETHER...
IF I TELL ASAHINA HOW I FEEL AND SHE TURNS ME DOWN...
I GUESS WE WON'T BE ABLE TO DO THAT STUFF ANYMORE.
WELL... I DON'T THINK SHE HATES ME OR ANYTHING, BUT...
I JUST DON'T KNOW.
SO I GUESS IT'S POSSIBLE THAT...
SHE COULD SAY YES?
THEN WHAT WOULD I DO?
WHISPER
WHISPER
MAN, I'D BETTER ASK YASUNOBU ABOUT IT.

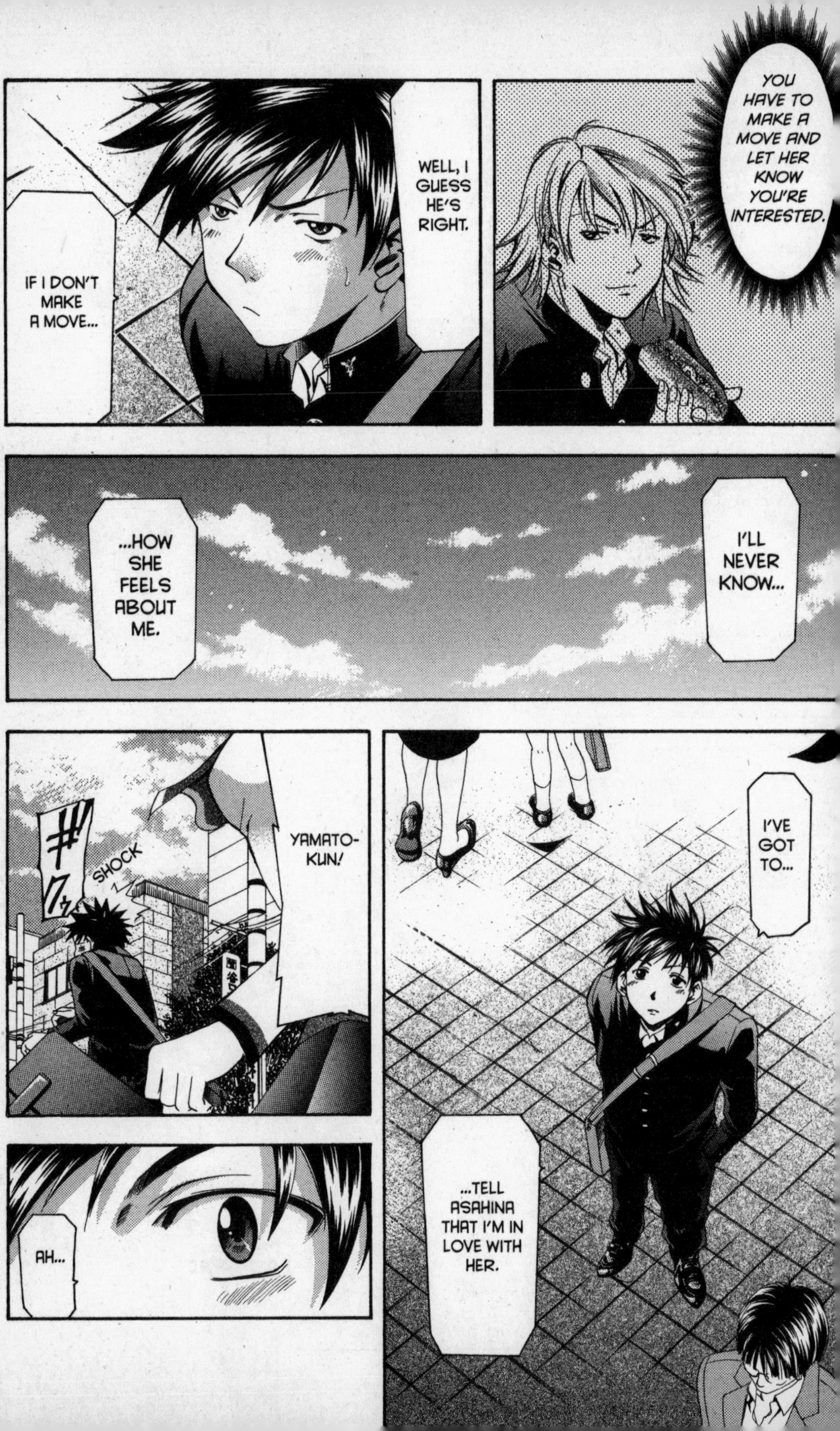
YOU HAVE TO MAKE A MOVE AND LET HER KNOW YOU'RE INTERESTED.
WELL, I GUESS HE'S RIGHT.
IF I DON'T MAKE A MOVE...
I'LL NEVER KNOW...
...HOW SHE FEELS ABOUT ME.
I'VE GOT TO...
...TELL ASAHINA THAT I'M IN LOVE WITH HER.
YAMATO-KUN!
SHOCK
AH...

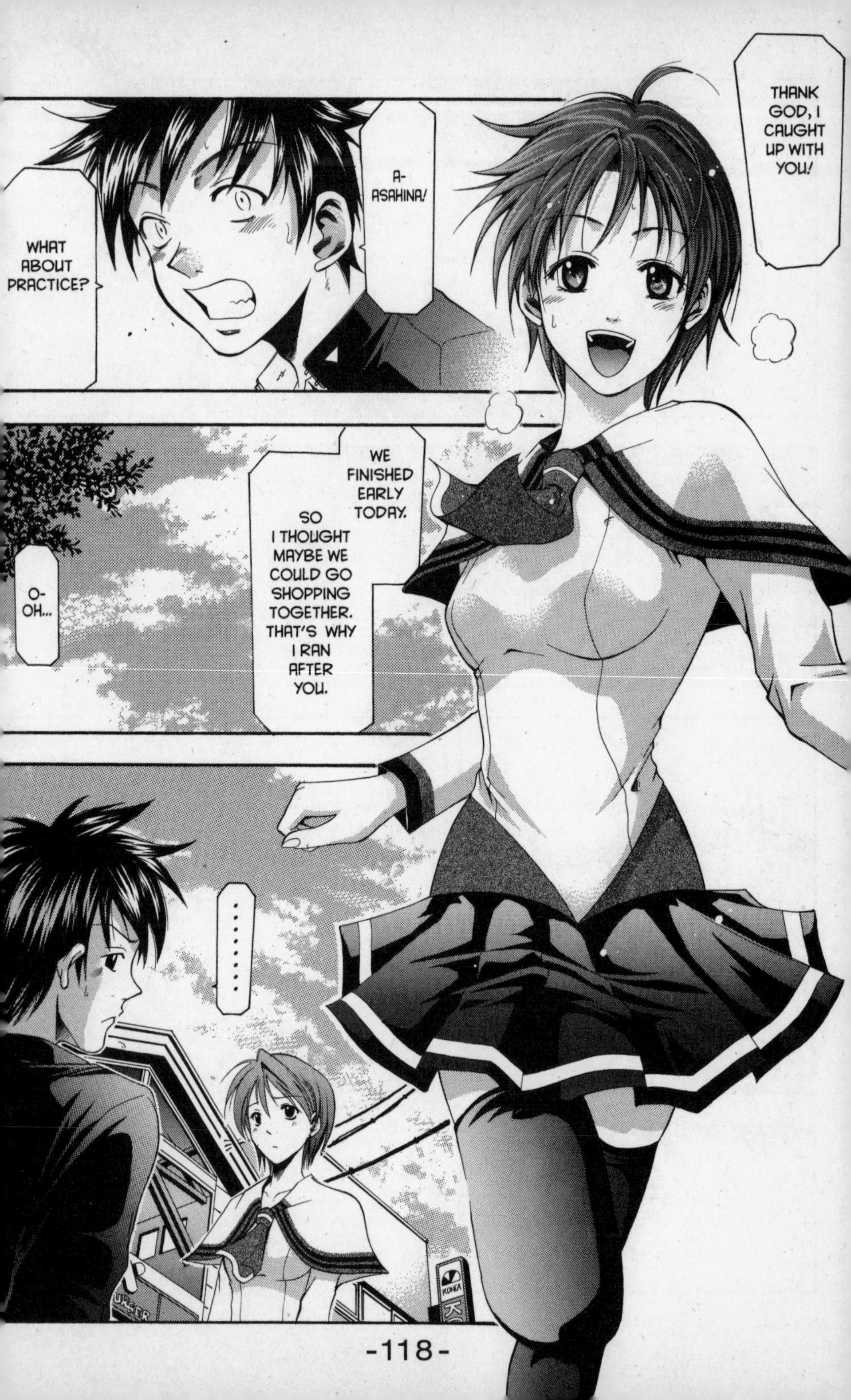
THANK GOD, I CAUGHT UP WITH YOU!
A- ASAHINA!
WHAT ABOUT PRACTICE?
WE FINISHED EARLY TODAY.
SO I THOUGHT MAYBE WE COULD GO SHOPPING TOGETHER. THAT'S WHY I RAN AFTER YOU.
O- OH...
....

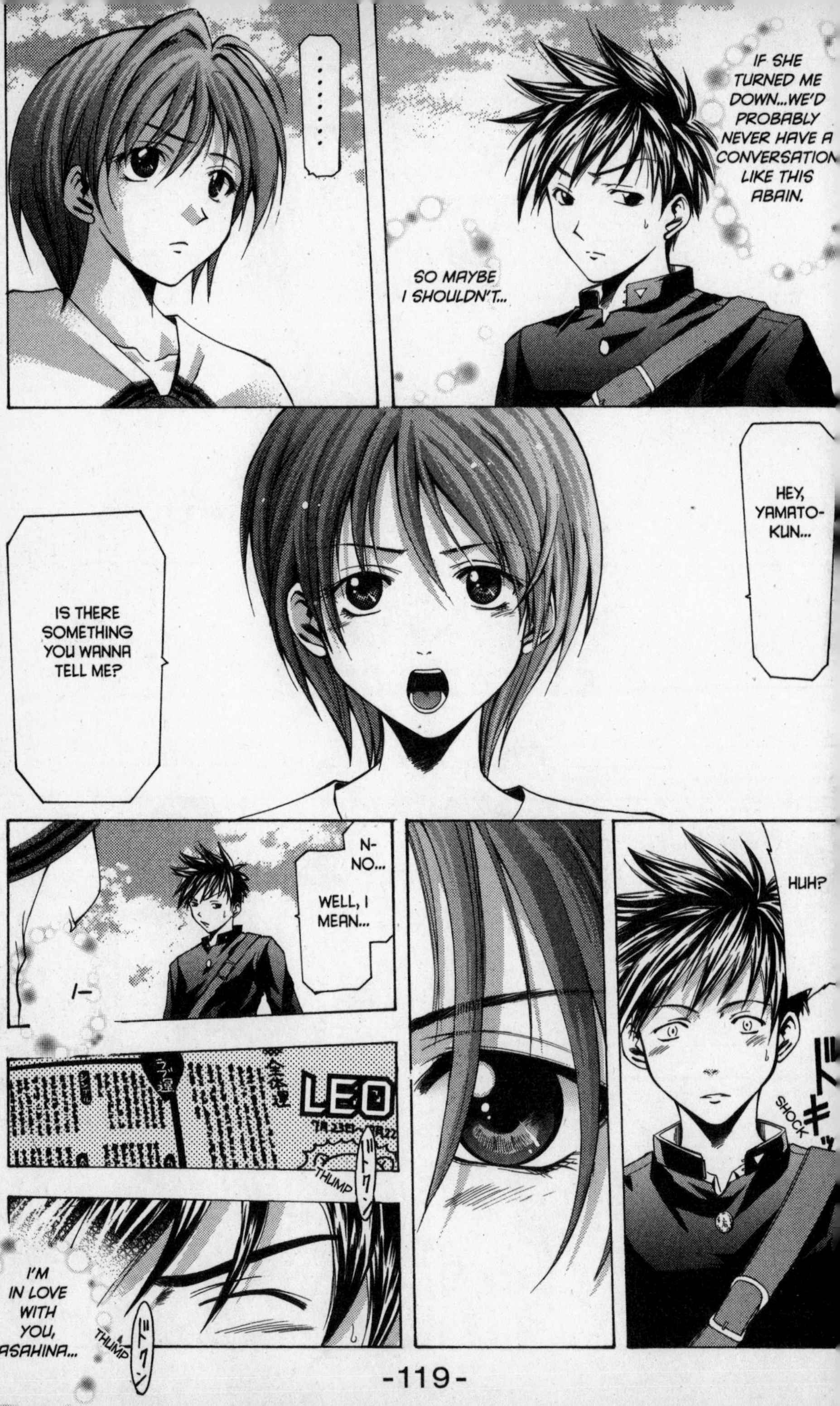
IF SHE TURNED ME DOWN...WE'D PROBABLY NEVER HAVE A CONVERSATION LIKE THIS AGAIN.
SO MAYBE I SHOULDN'T...
....
HEY, YAMATO-KUN...
IS THERE SOMETHING YOU WANNA TELL ME?
HUH?
ドキッ
SHOCK
N-NO...
WELL, I MEAN...
I—
LEO
ドクン
THUMP
I'M IN LOVE WITH YOU, ASAHINA...
ドクン
THUMP

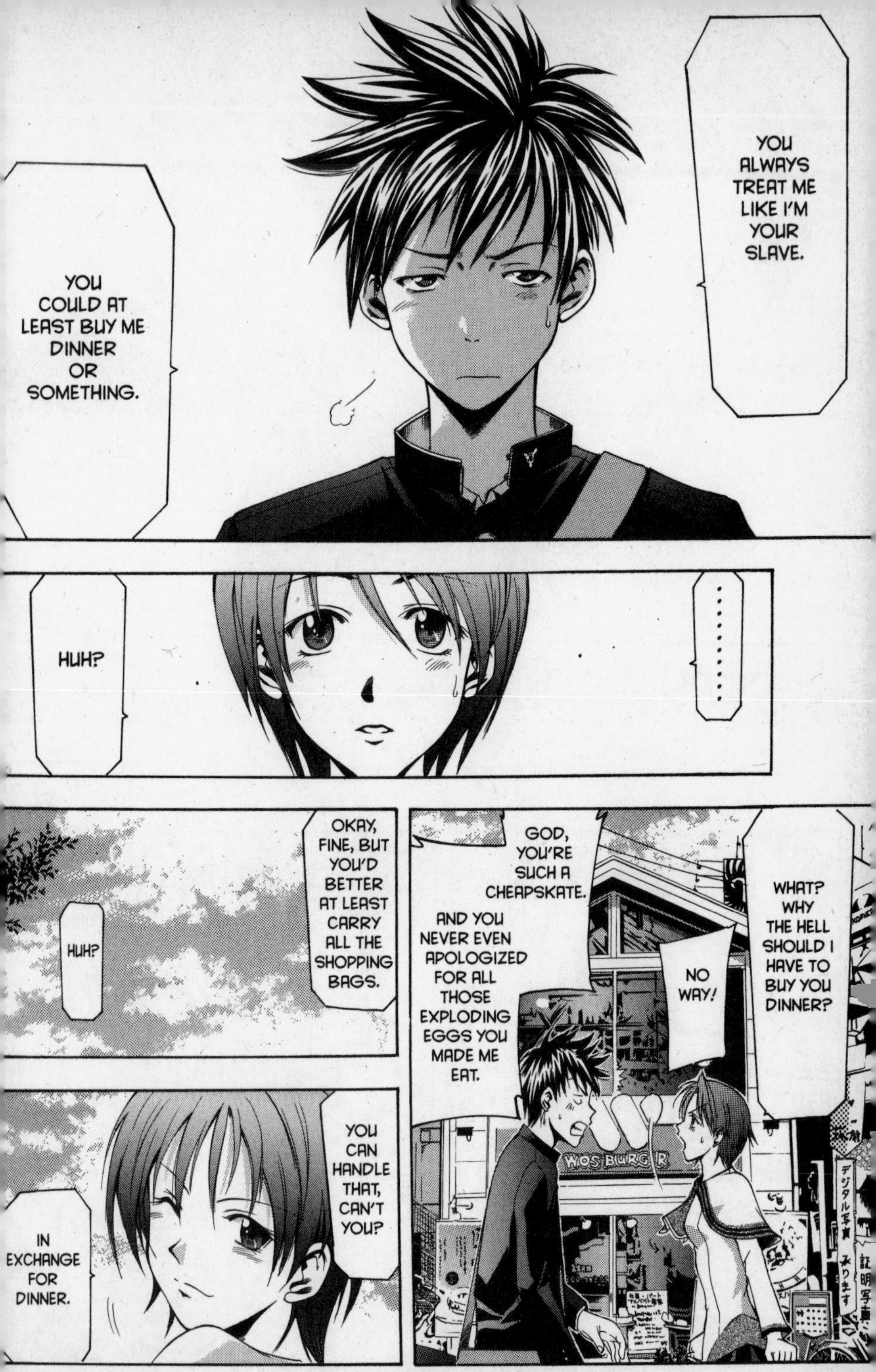
YOU ALWAYS TREAT ME LIKE I'M YOUR SLAVE.
YOU COULD AT LEAST BUY ME DINNER OR SOMETHING.
......
HUH?
WHAT? WHY THE HELL SHOULD I HAVE TO BUY YOU DINNER?
NO WAY!
GOD, YOU'RE SUCH A CHEAPSKATE.
AND YOU NEVER EVEN APOLOGIZED FOR ALL THOSE EXPLODING EGGS YOU MADE ME EAT.
WOS BURGER
OKAY, FINE, BUT YOU'D BETTER AT LEAST CARRY ALL THE SHOPPING BAGS.
HUH?
YOU CAN HANDLE THAT, CAN'T YOU?
IN EXCHANGE FOR DINNER.

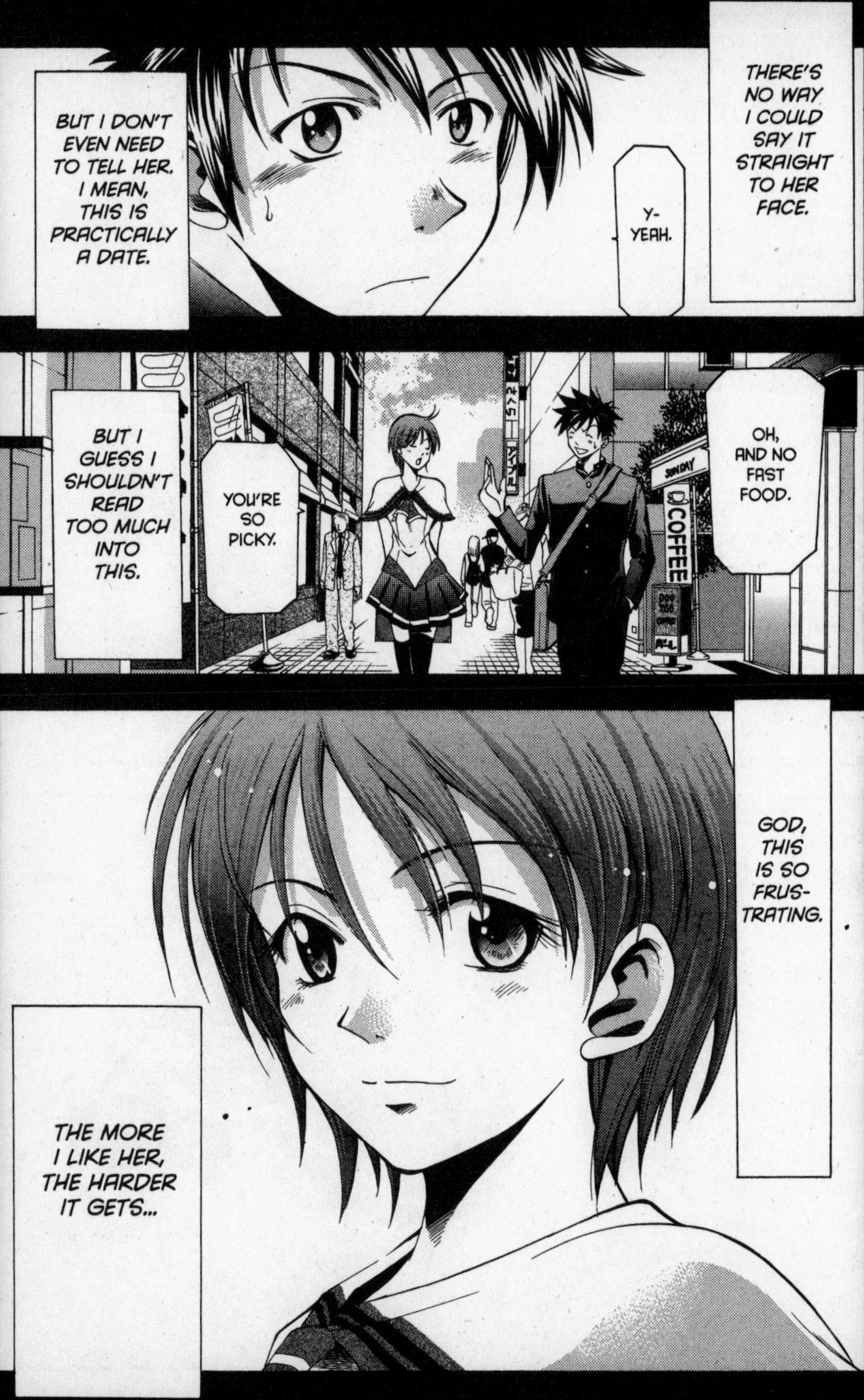
THERE'S NO WAY I COULD SAY IT STRAIGHT TO HER FACE.
Y-YEAH.
BUT I DON'T EVEN NEED TO TELL HER. I MEAN, THIS IS PRACTICALLY A DATE.
OH, AND NO FAST FOOD.
SUNDAY
COFFEE
YOU'RE SO PICKY.
BUT I GUESS I SHOULDN'T READ TOO MUCH INTO THIS.
GOD, THIS IS SO FRUS-TRATING.
THE MORE I LIKE HER, THE HARDER IT GETS...

CHARACTER PROFILE NO. 2

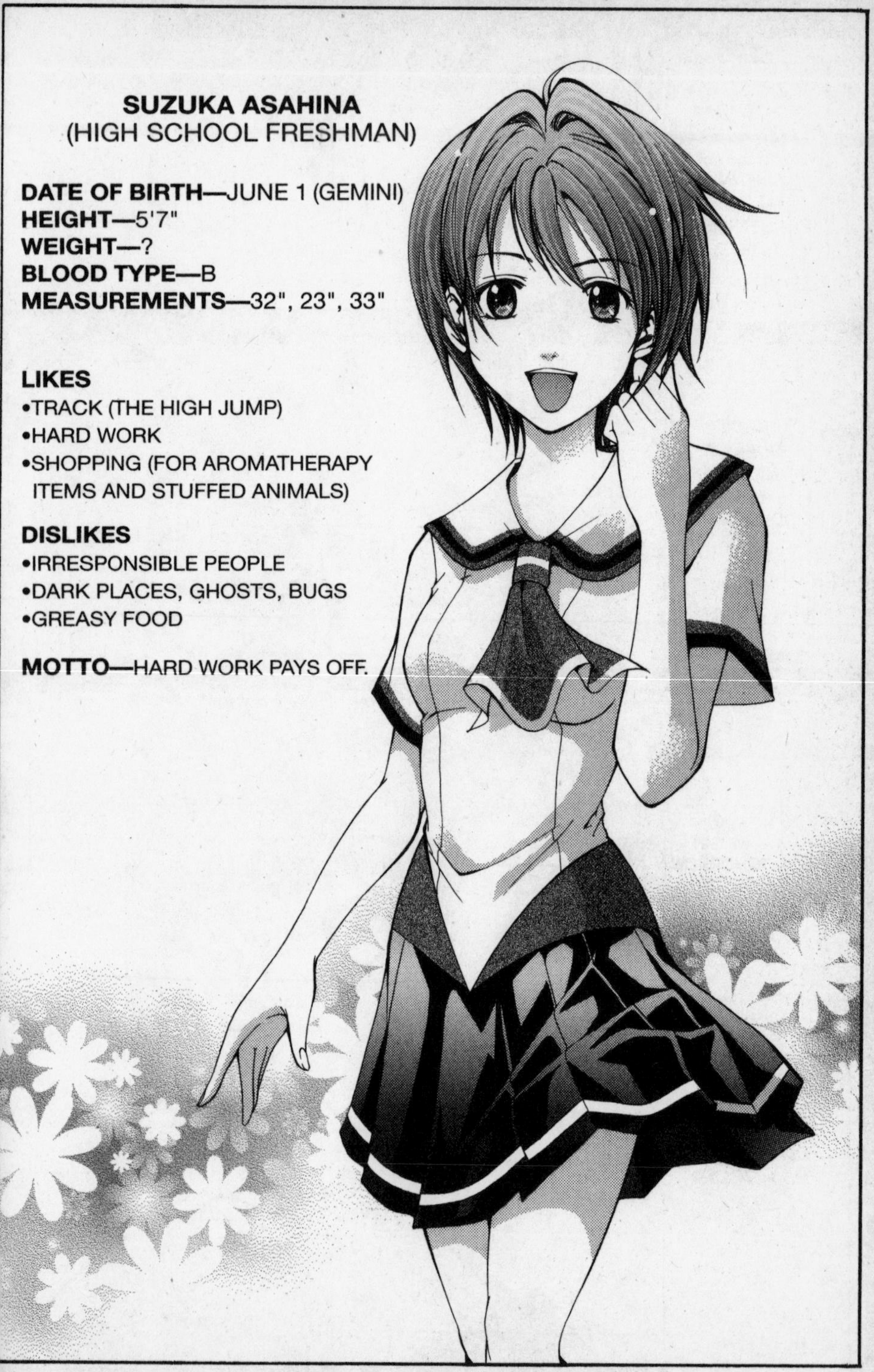

SUZUKA ASAHINA
(HIGH SCHOOL FRESHMAN)

DATE OF BIRTH—JUNE 1 (GEMINI)
HEIGHT—5'7"
WEIGHT—?
BLOOD TYPE—B
MEASUREMENTS—32", 23", 33"

LIKES
- TRACK (THE HIGH JUMP)
- HARD WORK
- SHOPPING (FOR AROMATHERAPY ITEMS AND STUFFED ANIMALS)

DISLIKES
- IRRESPONSIBLE PEOPLE
- DARK PLACES, GHOSTS, BUGS
- GREASY FOOD

MOTTO—HARD WORK PAYS OFF.

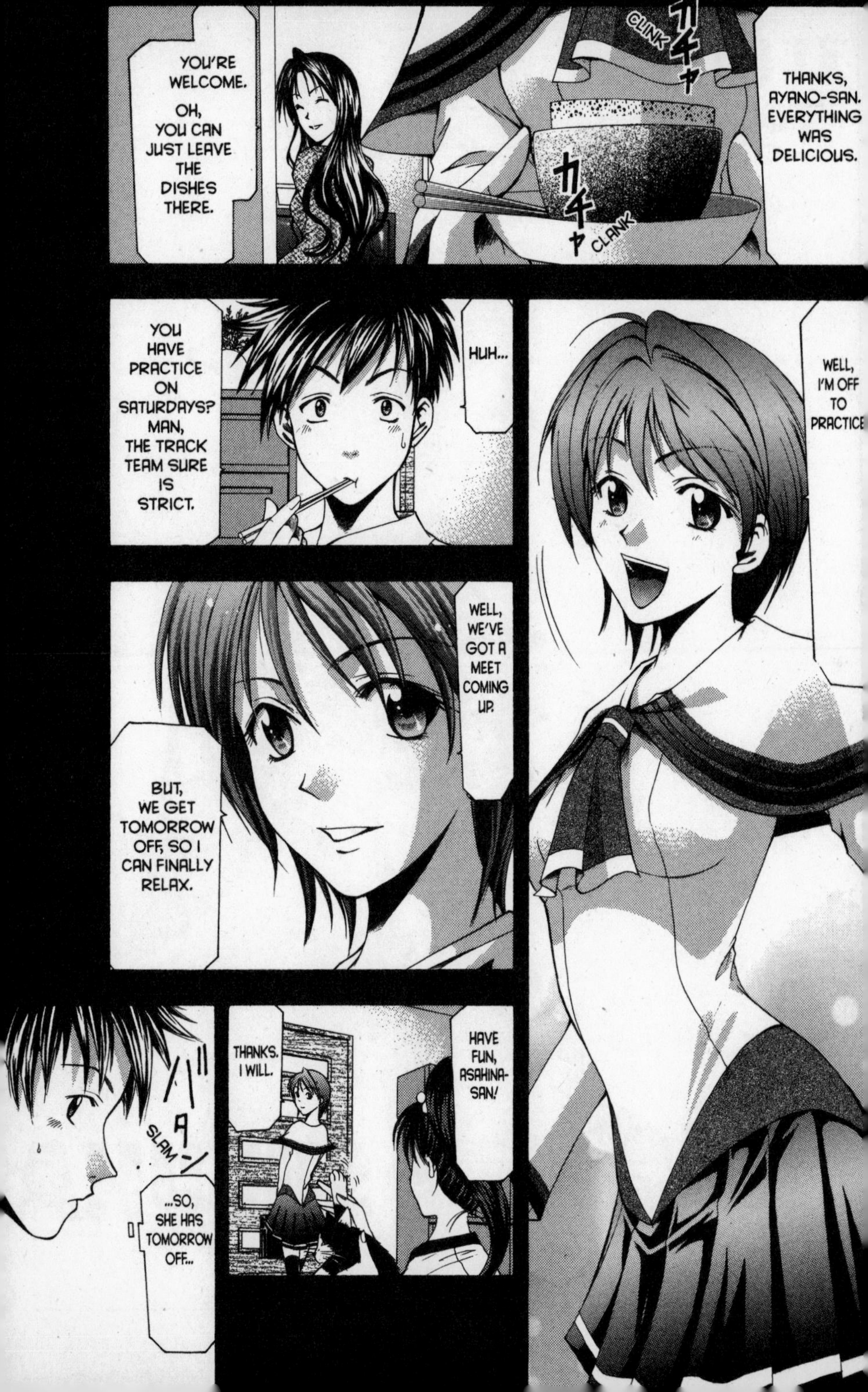
THANKS, AYANO-SAN. EVERYTHING WAS DELICIOUS.
CLINK
CLANK
YOU'RE WELCOME.
OH, YOU CAN JUST LEAVE THE DISHES THERE.
WELL, I'M OFF TO PRACTICE
HUH...
YOU HAVE PRACTICE ON SATURDAYS? MAN, THE TRACK TEAM SURE IS STRICT.
WELL, WE'VE GOT A MEET COMING UP.
BUT, WE GET TOMORROW OFF, SO I CAN FINALLY RELAX.
HAVE FUN, ASAHINA-SAN!
THANKS. I WILL.
SLAM
...SO, SHE HAS TOMORROW OFF...

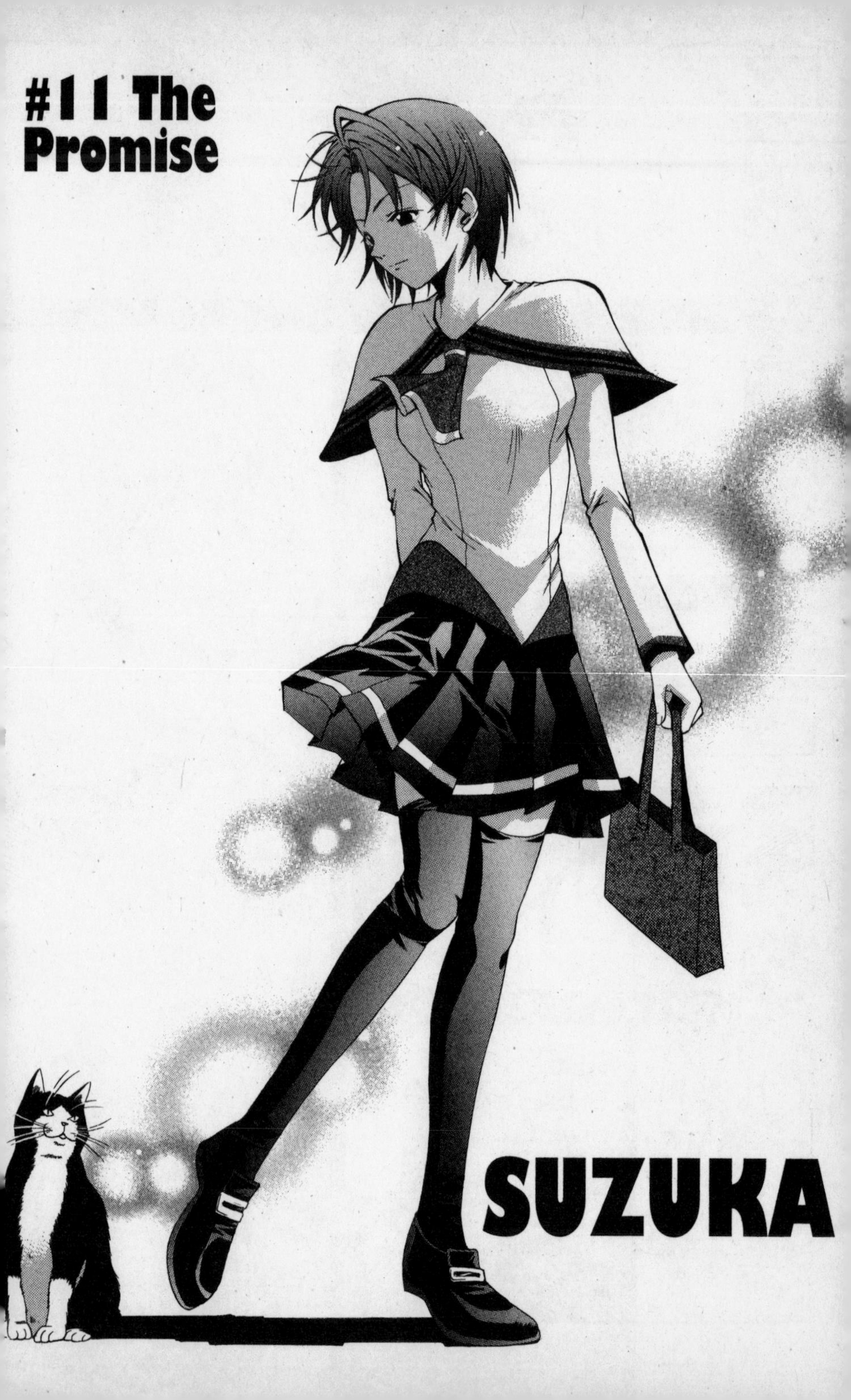
#11 The Promise
SUZUKA

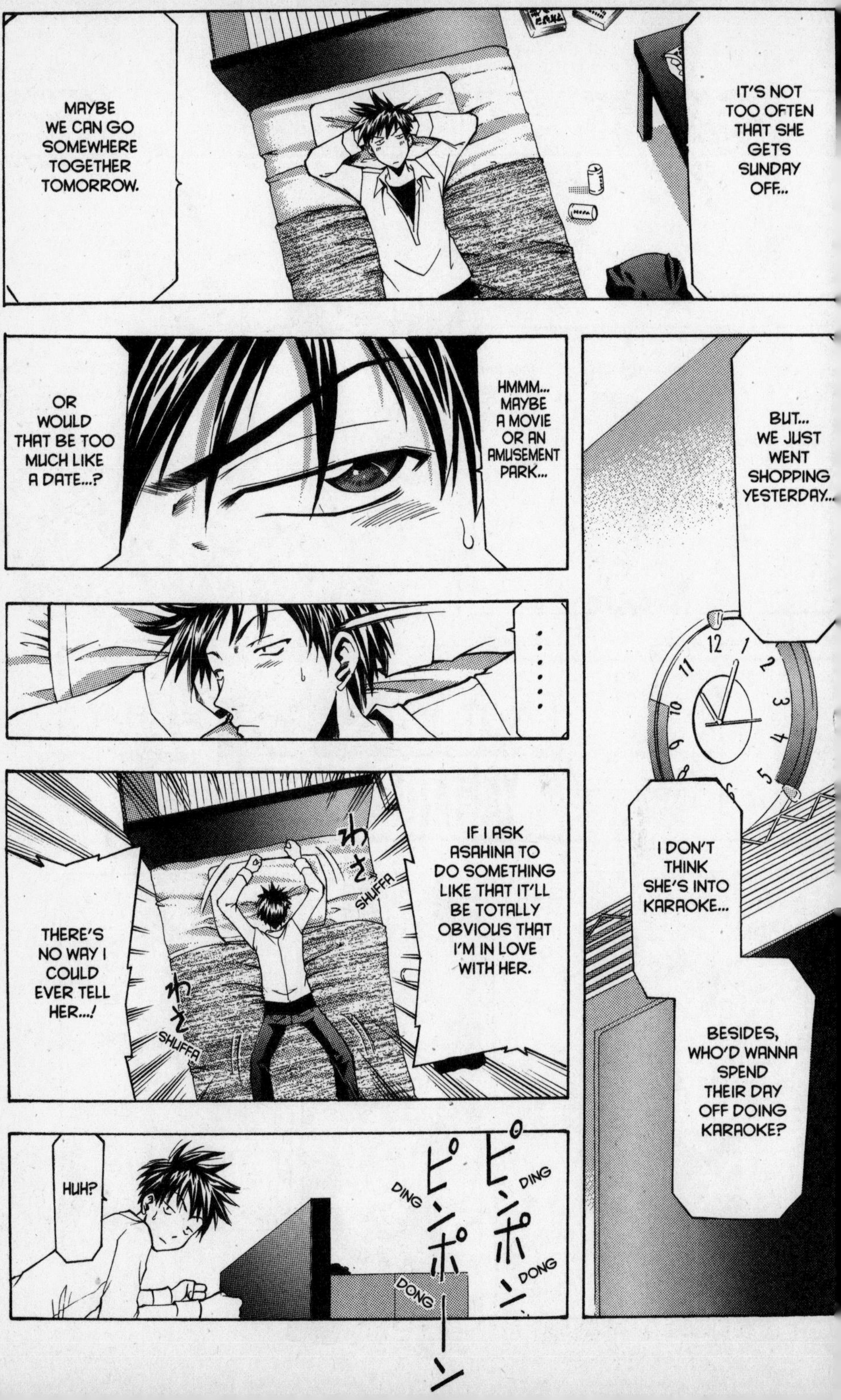
IT'S NOT TOO OFTEN THAT SHE GETS SUNDAY OFF...
MAYBE WE CAN GO SOMEWHERE TOGETHER TOMORROW.
BUT... WE JUST WENT SHOPPING YESTERDAY...
I DON'T THINK SHE'S INTO KARAOKE...
BESIDES, WHO'D WANNA SPEND THEIR DAY OFF DOING KARAOKE?
HMMM... MAYBE A MOVIE OR AN AMUSEMENT PARK...
OR WOULD THAT BE TOO MUCH LIKE A DATE...?
......
わさ SHUFFA
IF I ASK ASAHINA TO DO SOMETHING LIKE THAT IT'LL BE TOTALLY OBVIOUS THAT I'M IN LOVE WITH HER.
THERE'S NO WAY I COULD EVER TELL HER...!
わさ SHUFFA
ピンポン DING DONG
ピンポーン DING DONG
HUH?

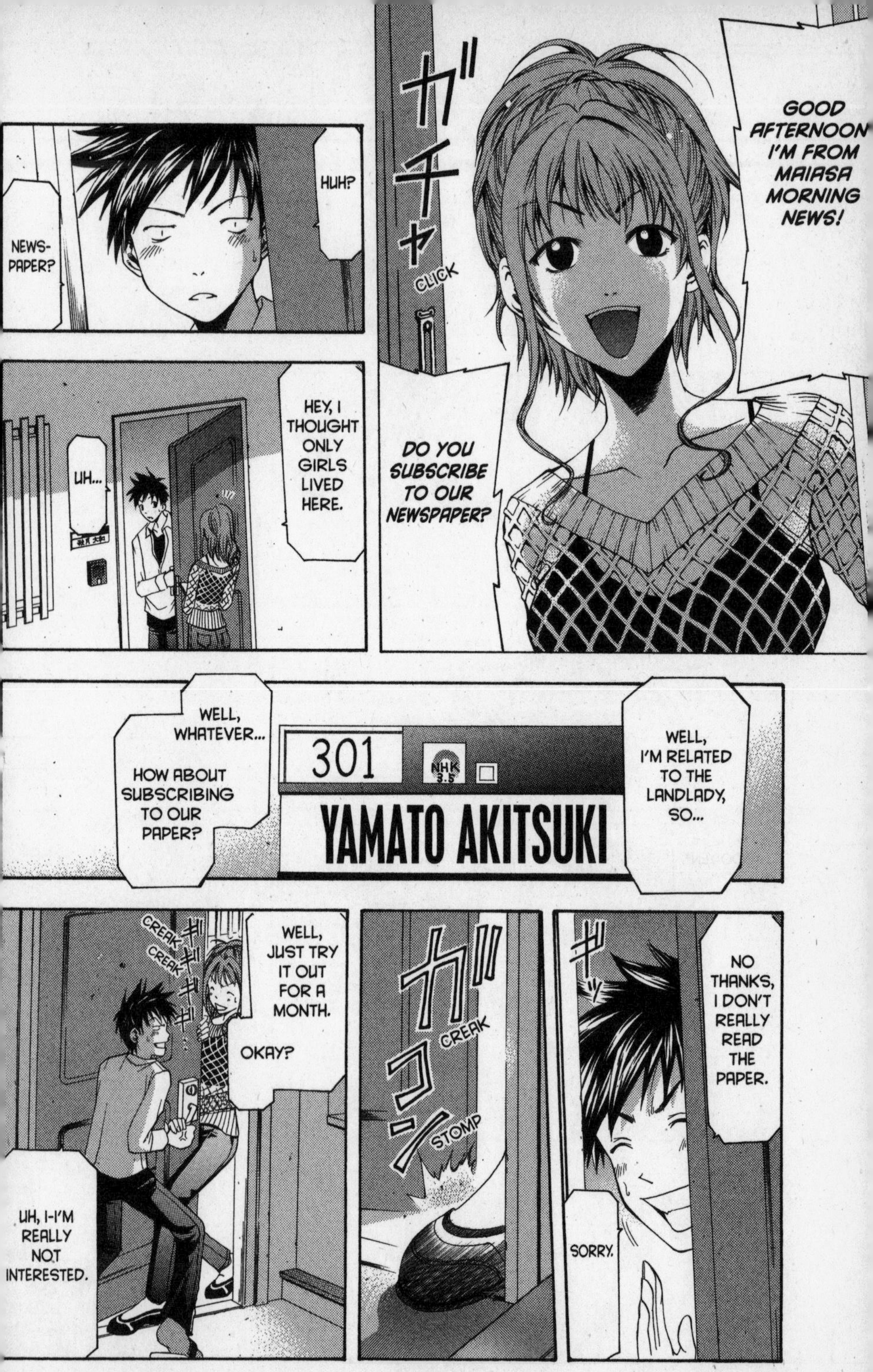
GOOD AFTERNOON I'M FROM MAIASA MORNING NEWS!
ガチャ
CLICK
DO YOU SUBSCRIBE TO OUR NEWSPAPER?
HUH?
NEWS-PAPER?
HEY, I THOUGHT ONLY GIRLS LIVED HERE.
UH...
WELL, I'M RELATED TO THE LANDLADY, SO...
301
NHK 3.5
YAMATO AKITSUKI
WELL, WHATEVER...
HOW ABOUT SUBSCRIBING TO OUR PAPER?
NO THANKS, I DON'T REALLY READ THE PAPER.
SORRY.
ガン
CREAK
STOMP
WELL, JUST TRY IT OUT FOR A MONTH.
OKAY?
CREAK CREAK
UH, I-I'M REALLY NOT INTERESTED.

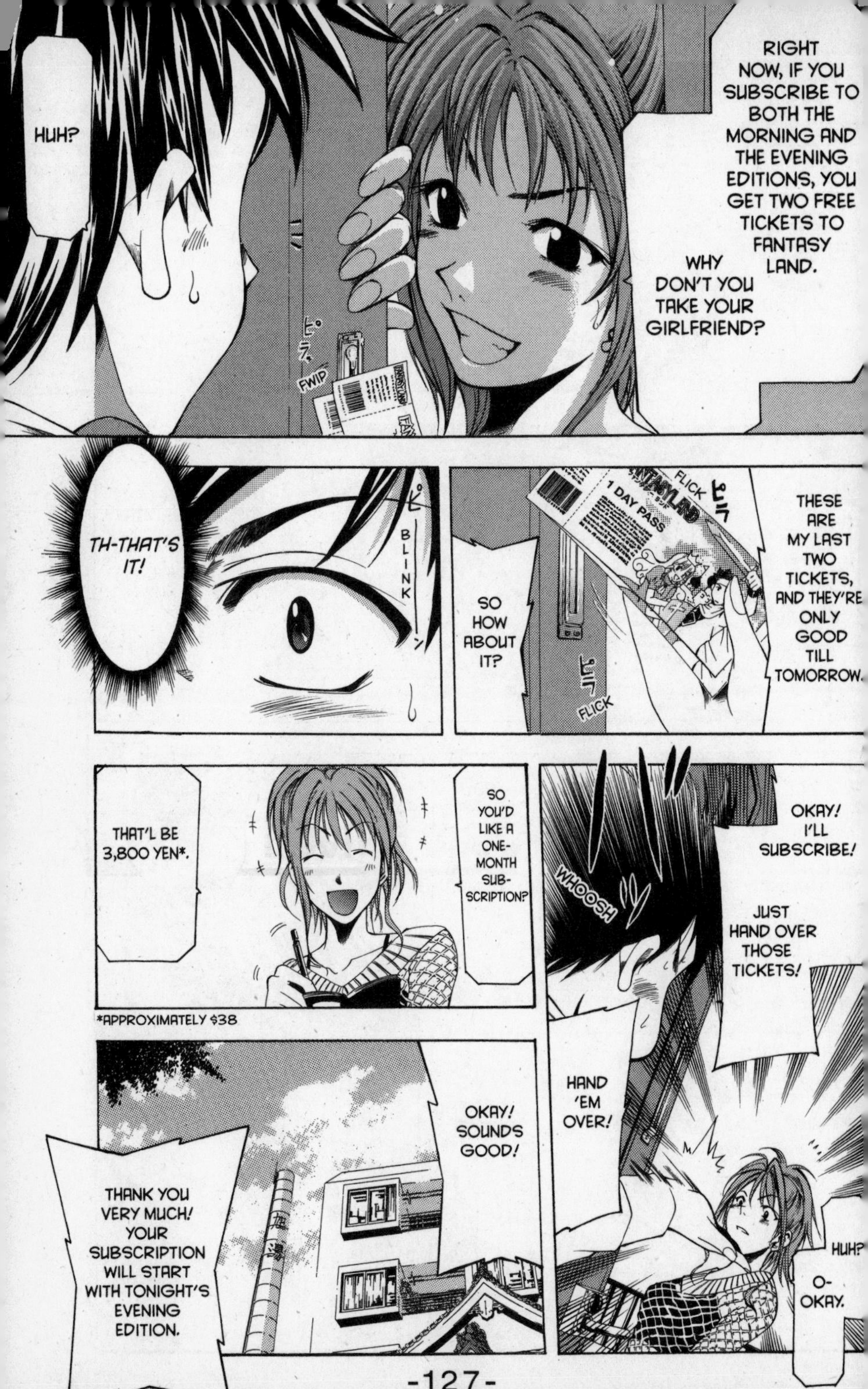
RIGHT NOW, IF YOU SUBSCRIBE TO BOTH THE MORNING AND THE EVENING EDITIONS, YOU GET TWO FREE TICKETS TO FANTASY LAND.
WHY DON'T YOU TAKE YOUR GIRLFRIEND?
FWIP
HUH?
THESE ARE MY LAST TWO TICKETS, AND THEY'RE ONLY GOOD TILL TOMORROW.
FANTASYLAND 1 DAY PASS
FLICK
FLICK
SO HOW ABOUT IT?
BLINK
TH-THAT'S IT!
OKAY! I'LL SUBSCRIBE!
JUST HAND OVER THOSE TICKETS!
WHOOSH
HAND 'EM OVER!
HUH?
O-OKAY.
SO YOU'D LIKE A ONE-MONTH SUBSCRIPTION?
THAT'L BE 3,800 YEN*.
*APPROXIMATELY $38
OKAY! SOUNDS GOOD!
THANK YOU VERY MUCH! YOUR SUBSCRIPTION WILL START WITH TONIGHT'S EVENING EDITION.

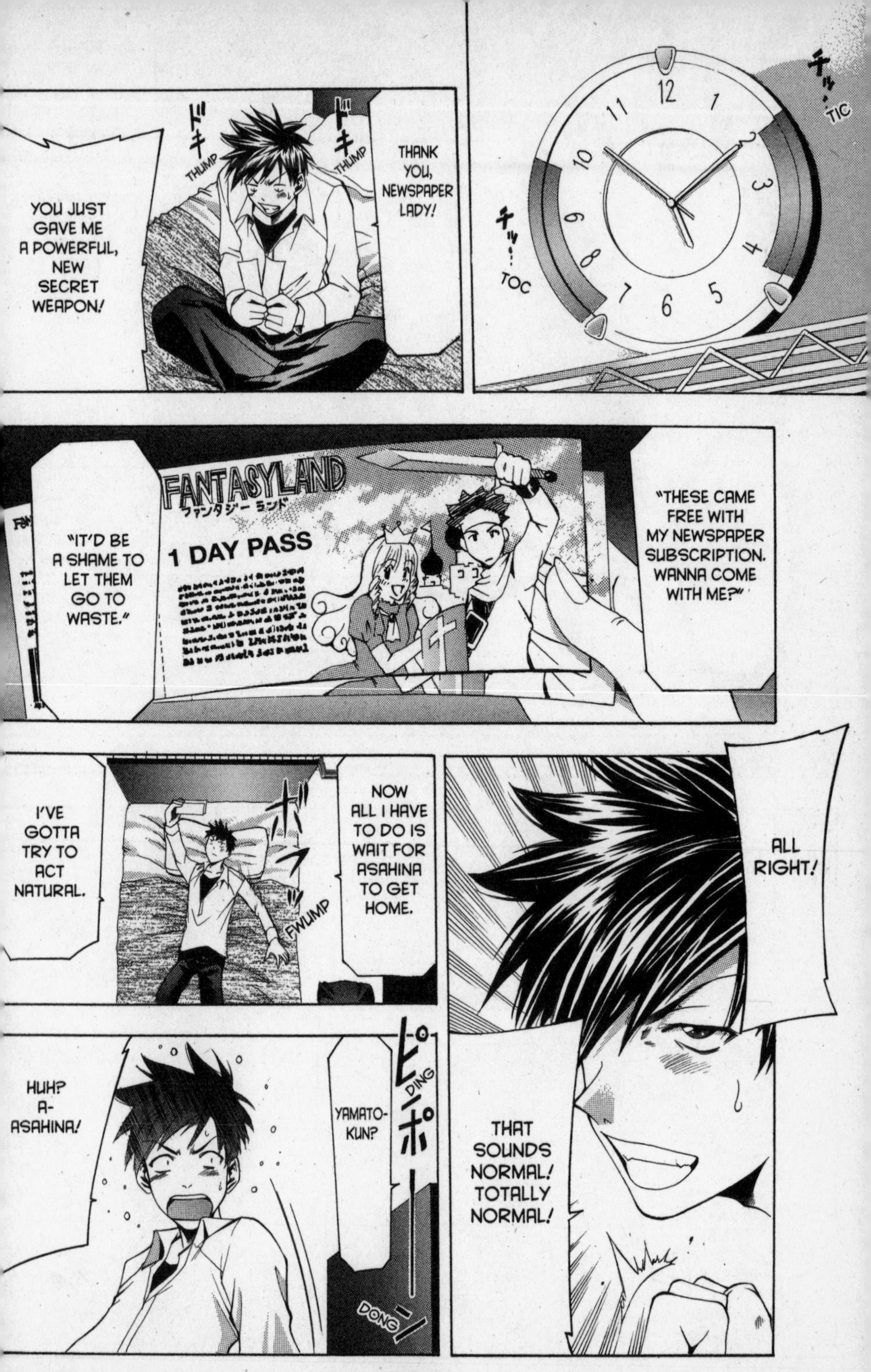
チッ
TIC
チッ
TOC
THANK YOU, NEWSPAPER LADY!
ドキ
THUMP
ドキ
THUMP
YOU JUST GAVE ME A POWERFUL, NEW SECRET WEAPON!
"THESE CAME FREE WITH MY NEWSPAPER SUBSCRIPTION. WANNA COME WITH ME?"
FANTASYLAND
ファンタジーランド
1 DAY PASS
"IT'D BE A SHAME TO LET THEM GO TO WASTE."
ALL RIGHT!
THAT SOUNDS NORMAL! TOTALLY NORMAL!
NOW ALL I HAVE TO DO IS WAIT FOR ASAHINA TO GET HOME.
FWUMP
I'VE GOTTA TRY TO ACT NATURAL.
ピ
DING
ポーン
DONG
YAMATO-KUN?
HUH? A-ASAHINA!

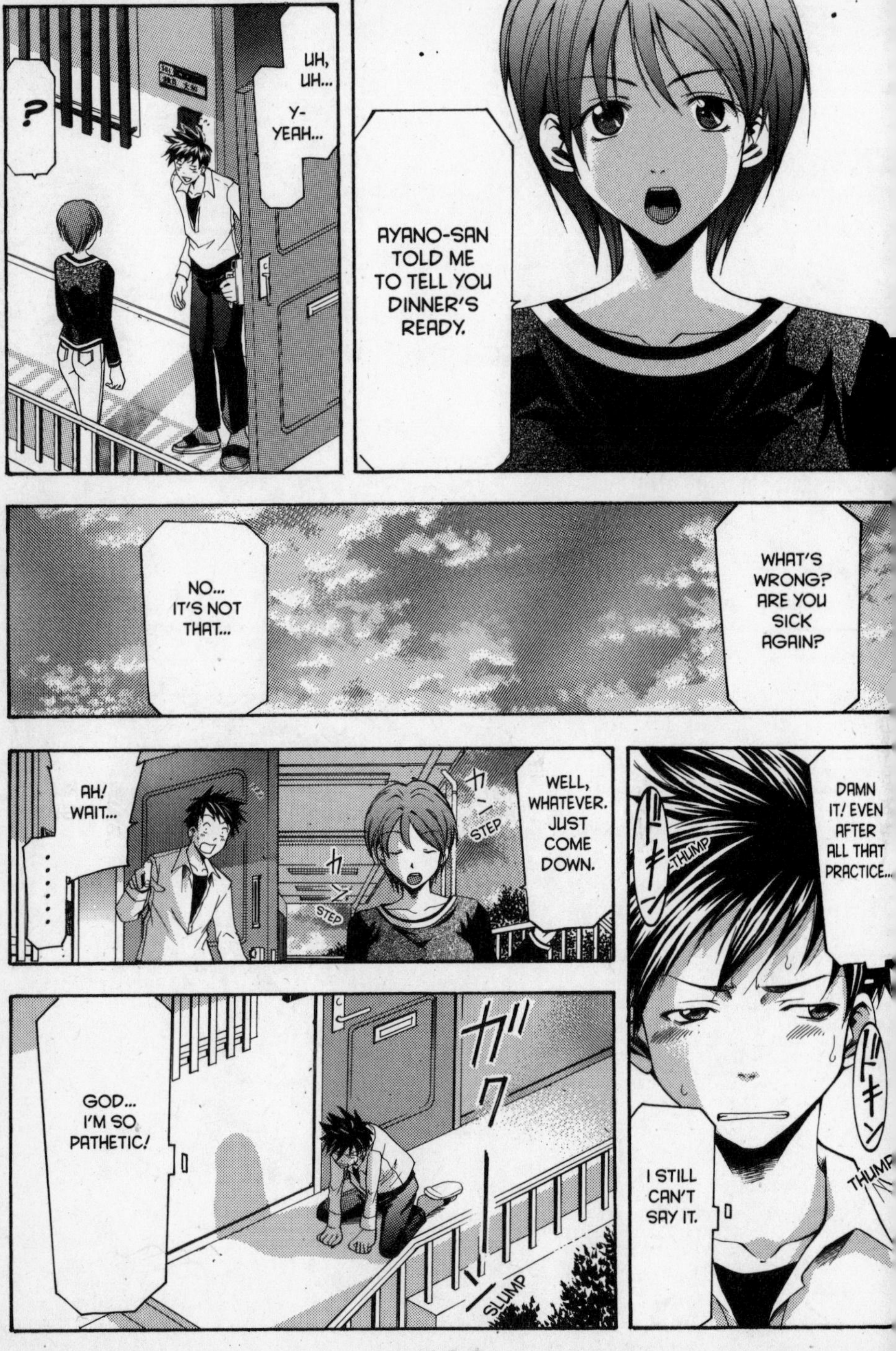
AYANO-SAN TOLD ME TO TELL YOU DINNER'S READY.
UH, UH...
Y- YEAH...
?
WHAT'S WRONG? ARE YOU SICK AGAIN?
NO... IT'S NOT THAT...
DAMN IT! EVEN AFTER ALL THAT PRACTICE...
THUMP
I STILL CAN'T SAY IT.
THUMP
WELL, WHATEVER. JUST COME DOWN.
STEP
STEP
AH! WAIT...
......
SLUMP
GOD... I'M SO PATHETIC!

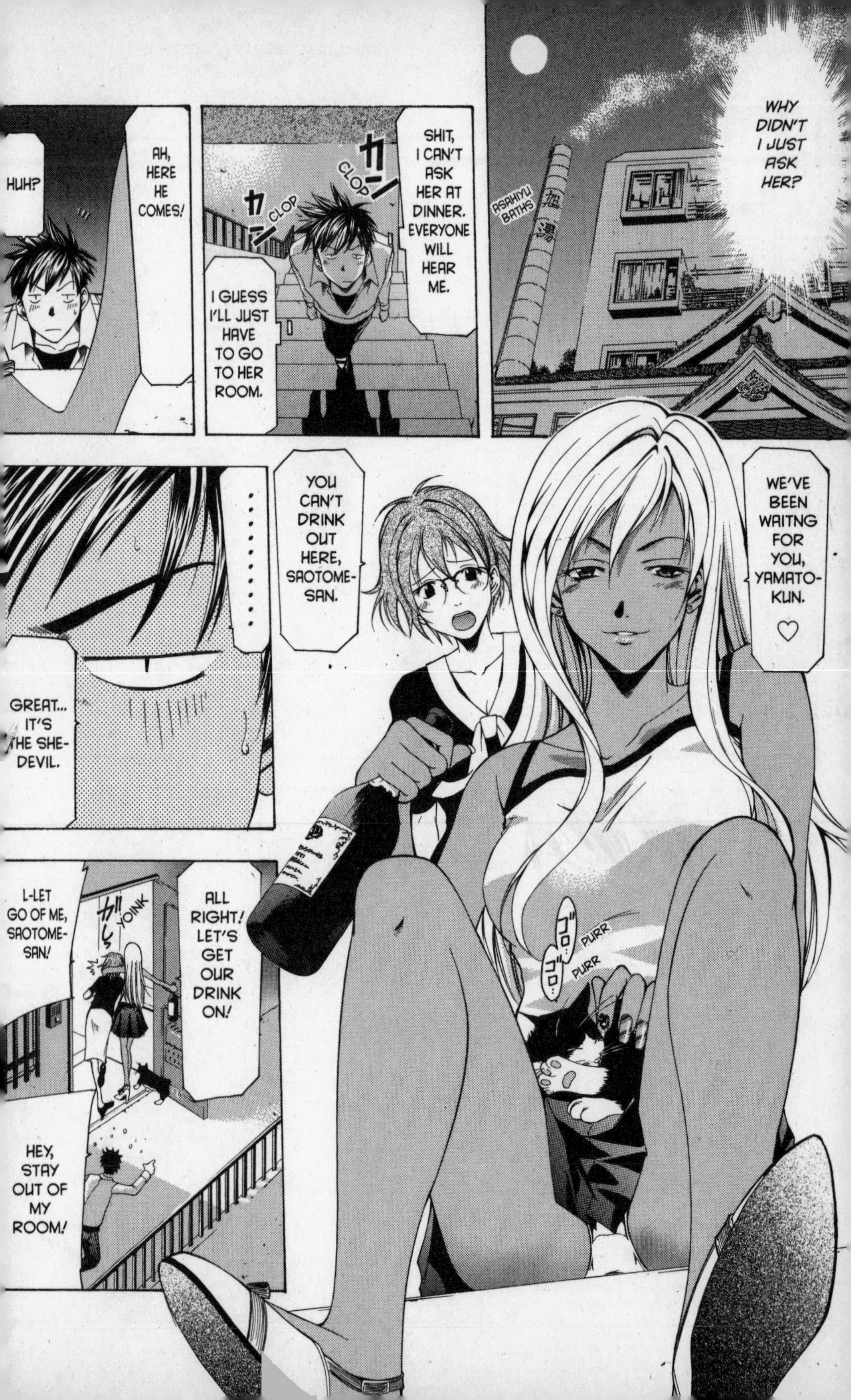
WHY DIDN'T I JUST ASK HER?
ASAHIYU BATHS
SHIT, I CAN'T ASK HER AT DINNER. EVERYONE WILL HEAR ME.
CLOP
CLOP
I GUESS I'LL JUST HAVE TO GO TO HER ROOM.
AH, HERE HE COMES!
HUH?
WE'VE BEEN WAITNG FOR YOU, YAMATO-KUN. ♡
YOU CAN'T DRINK OUT HERE, SAOTOME-SAN.
PURR
PURR
......
GREAT... IT'S THE SHE-DEVIL.
ALL RIGHT! LET'S GET OUR DRINK ON!
L-LET GO OF ME, SAOTOME-SAN!
YOINK
HEY, STAY OUT OF MY ROOM!

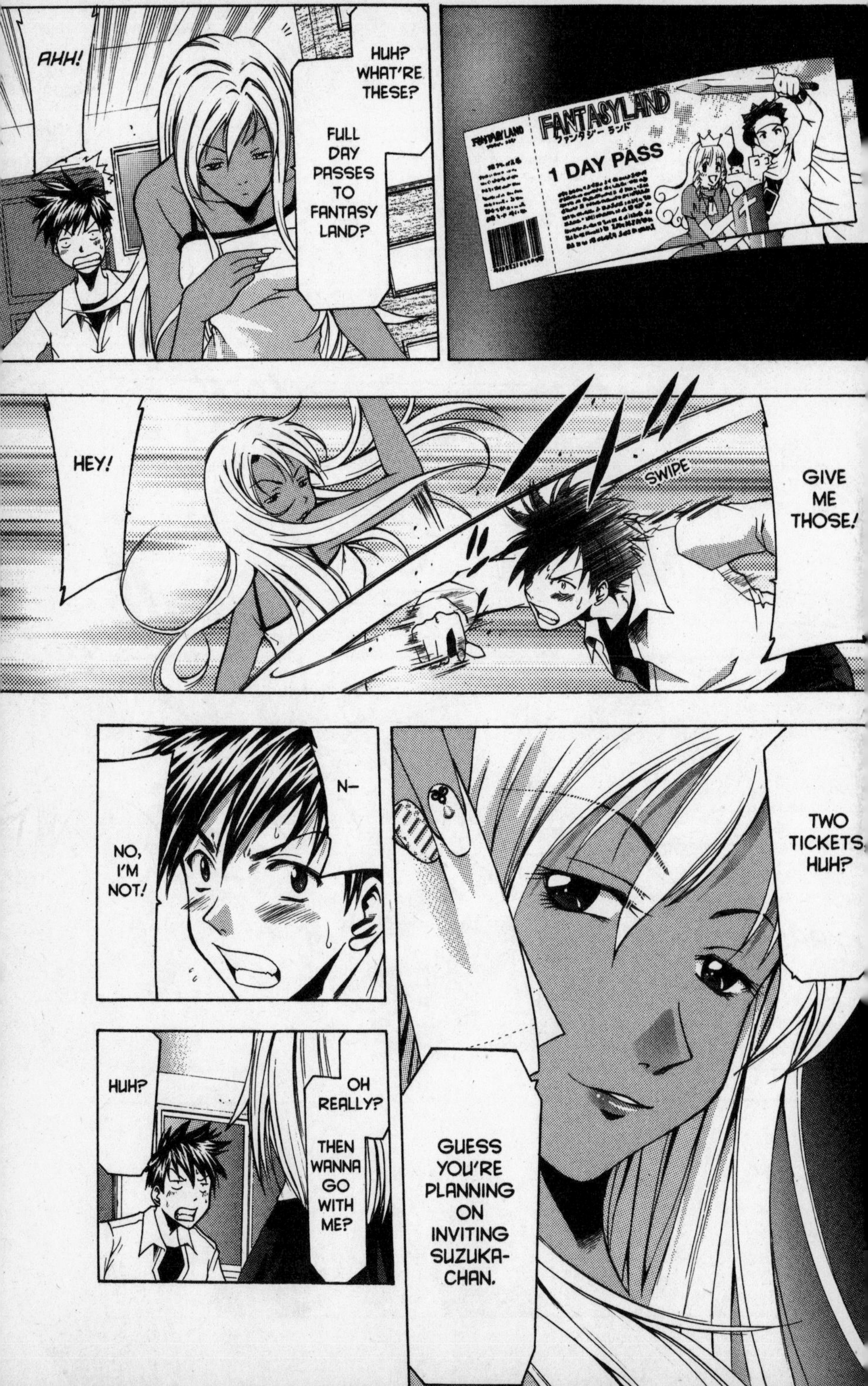
FANTASYLAND
ファンタジーランド
1 DAY PASS
HUH? WHAT'RE THESE?
FULL DAY PASSES TO FANTASY LAND?
AHH!
GIVE ME THOSE!
SWIPE
HEY!
TWO TICKETS, HUH?
GUESS YOU'RE PLANNING ON INVITING SUZUKA-CHAN.
N-
NO, I'M NOT!
OH REALLY?
THEN WANNA GO WITH ME?
HUH?

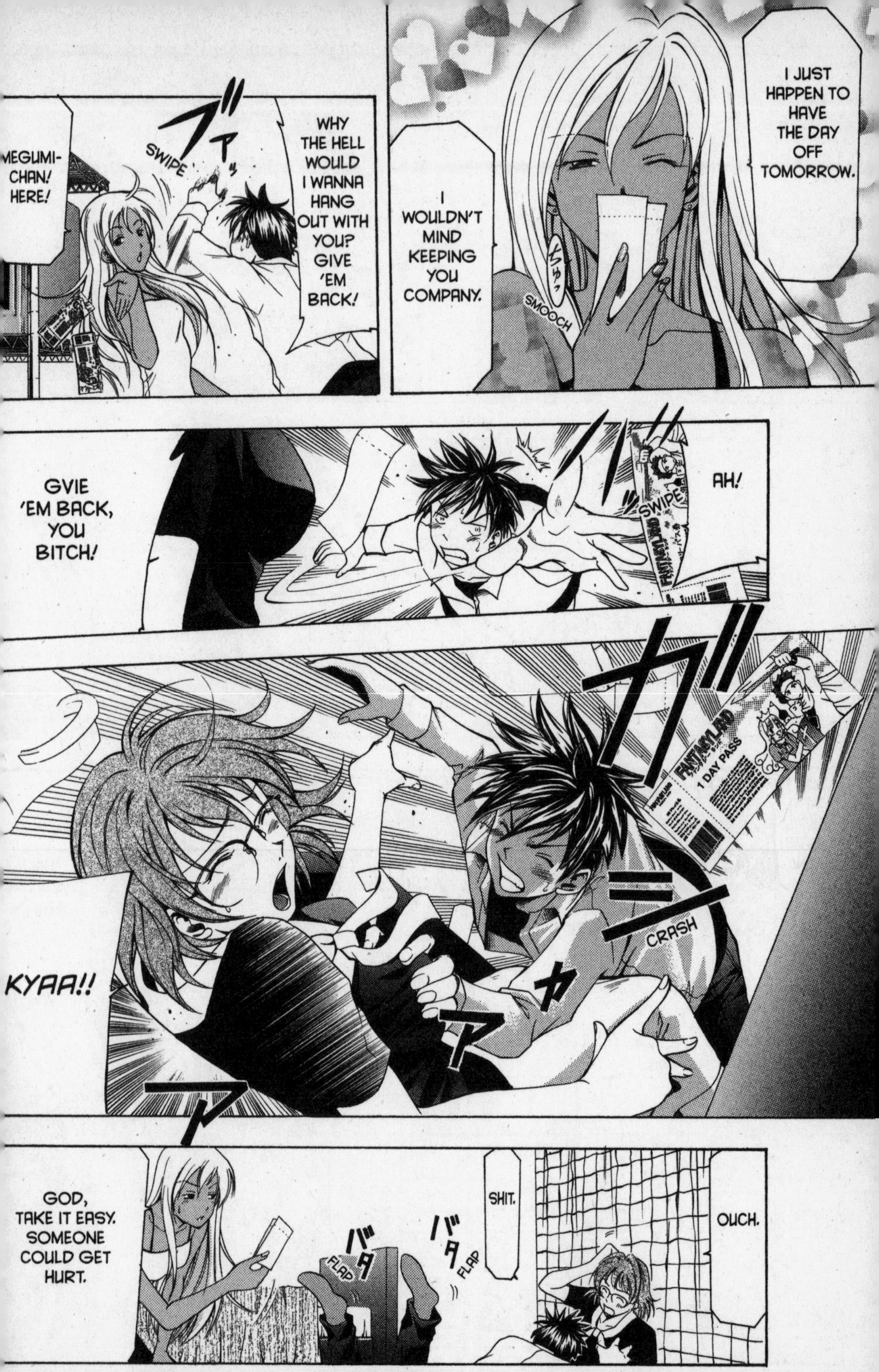
I JUST HAPPEN TO HAVE THE DAY OFF TOMORROW.
I WOULDN'T MIND KEEPING YOU COMPANY.
SMOOCH
WHY THE HELL WOULD I WANNA HANG OUT WITH YOU? GIVE 'EM BACK!
SWIPE
MEGUMI-CHAN! HERE!
AH!
SWIPE
GVIE 'EM BACK, YOU BITCH!
FANTASYLAND
1 DAY PASS
CRASH
KYAA!!
OUCH.
SHIT.
FLAP
FLAP
GOD, TAKE IT EASY. SOMEONE COULD GET HURT.

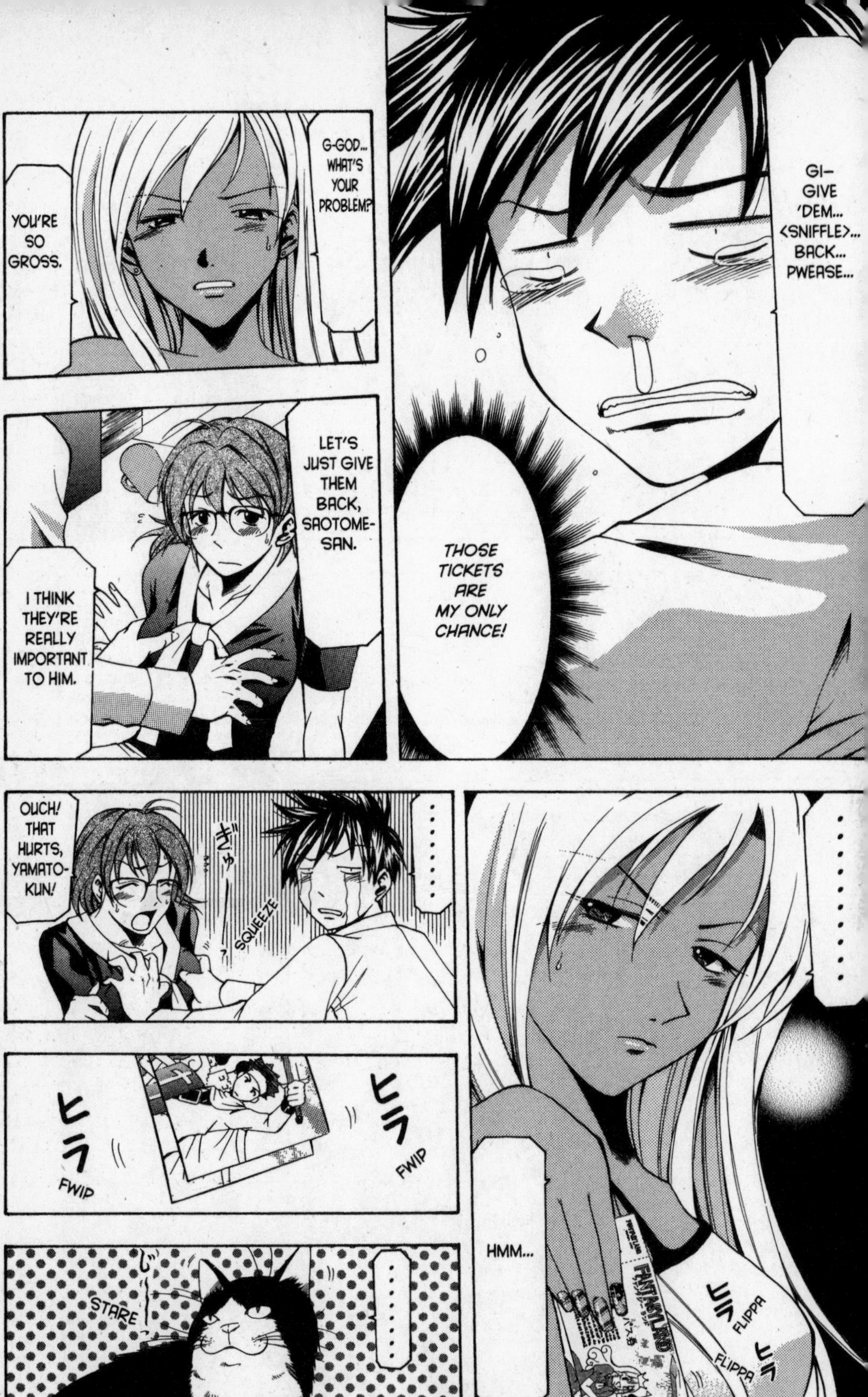
GI— GIVE 'DEM... <SNIFFLE>... BACK... PWEASE...
THOSE TICKETS ARE MY ONLY CHANCE!
G-GOD... WHAT'S YOUR PROBLEM?
YOU'RE SO GROSS.
LET'S JUST GIVE THEM BACK, SAOTOME-SAN.
I THINK THEY'RE REALLY IMPORTANT TO HIM.
......
HMM...
ヒラ FLIPPA
ヒラ FLIPPA
FANTASYLAND
......
OUCH! THAT HURTS, YAMATO-KUN!
ぎゅ SQUEEZE
ヒラ FWIP
ヒラ FWIP
......
じー STARE

WAH!

SLICE

BOING BOING

!

SWIPE

!

MEOW!

AWW... HE'S LIKE A NATURAL PAPER SHREDDER.

CRACK

THERE GOES MY ONLY CHANCE!

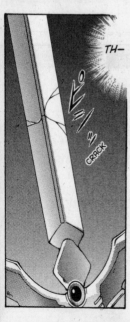

TH—

CRACK

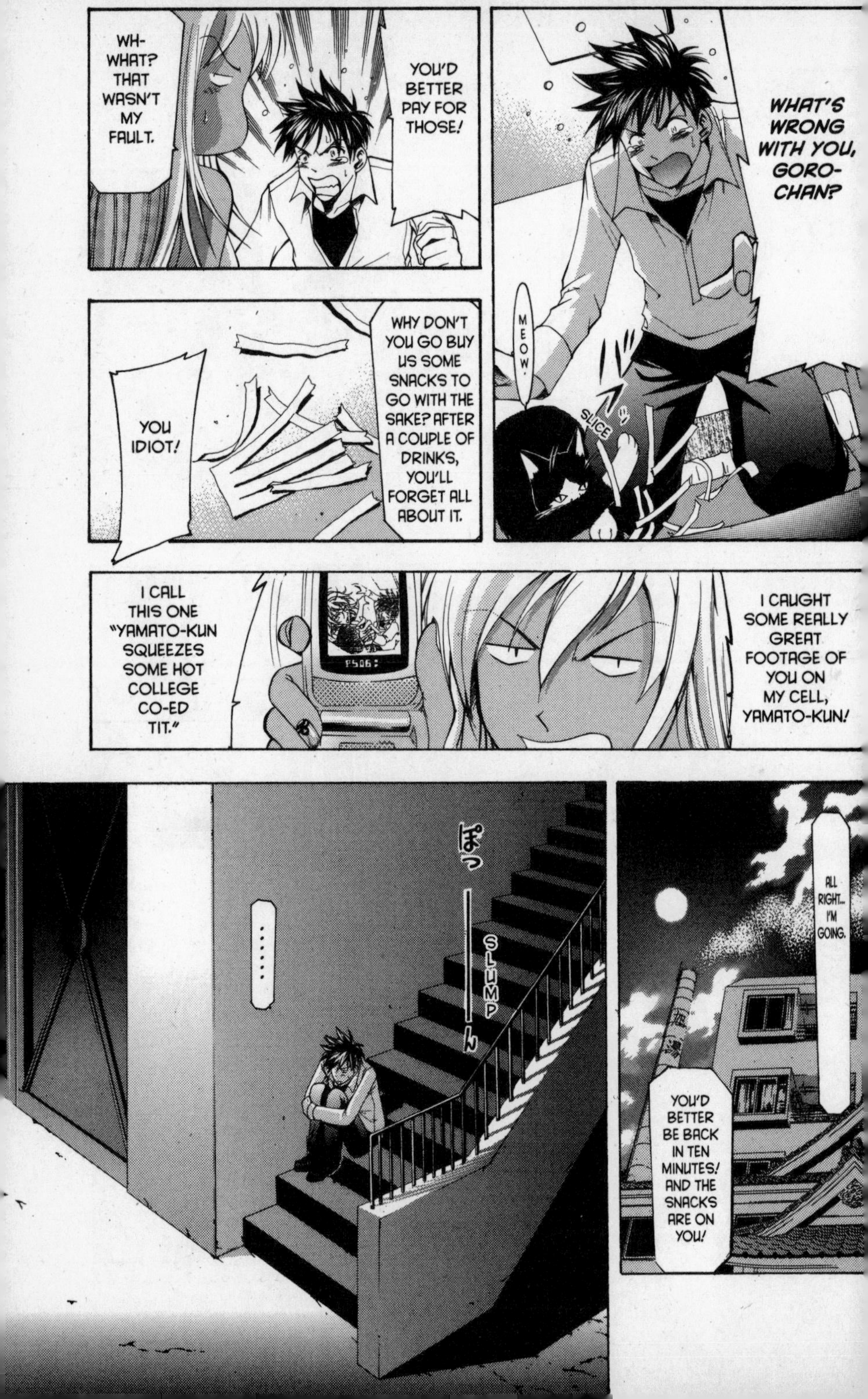

WHAT'S WRONG WITH YOU, GORO-CHAN?
MEOW.
SLICE
YOU'D BETTER PAY FOR THOSE!
WH-WHAT? THAT WASN'T MY FAULT.
WHY DON'T YOU GO BUY US SOME SNACKS TO GO WITH THE SAKE? AFTER A COUPLE OF DRINKS, YOU'LL FORGET ALL ABOUT IT.
YOU IDIOT!
I CAUGHT SOME REALLY GREAT FOOTAGE OF YOU ON MY CELL, YAMATO-KUN!
I CALL THIS ONE "YAMATO-KUN SQUEEZES SOME HOT COLLEGE CO-ED TIT."
ALL RIGHT... I'M GOING.
YOU'D BETTER BE BACK IN TEN MINUTES! AND THE SNACKS ARE ON YOU!
ぽっ———ん
SLUMP
......

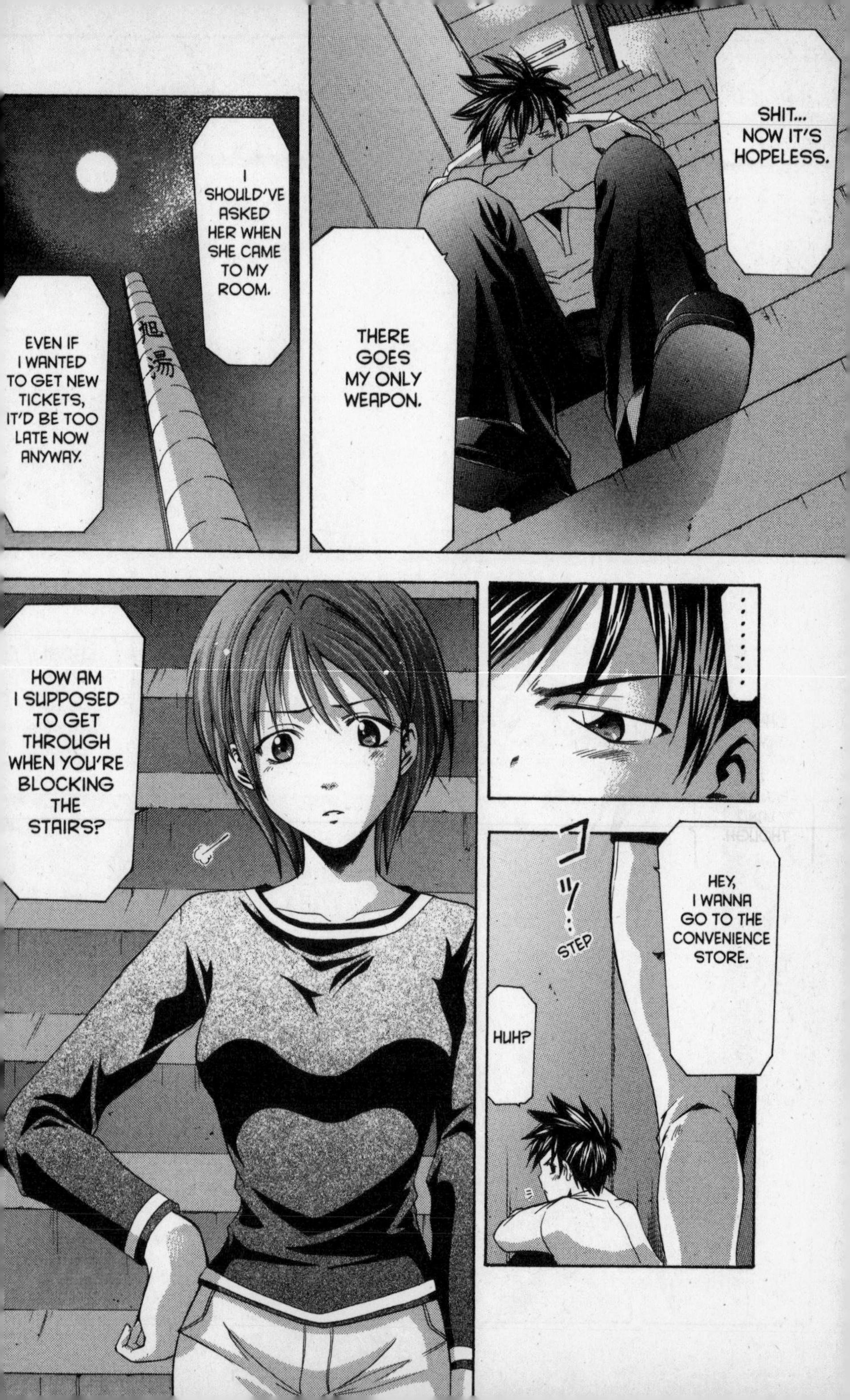
SHIT... NOW IT'S HOPELESS.
THERE GOES MY ONLY WEAPON.
I SHOULD'VE ASKED HER WHEN SHE CAME TO MY ROOM.
旭湯
EVEN IF I WANTED TO GET NEW TICKETS, IT'D BE TOO LATE NOW ANYWAY.
......
コッ
STEP
HEY, I WANNA GO TO THE CONVENIENCE STORE.
HUH?
HOW AM I SUPPOSED TO GET THROUGH WHEN YOU'RE BLOCKING THE STAIRS?

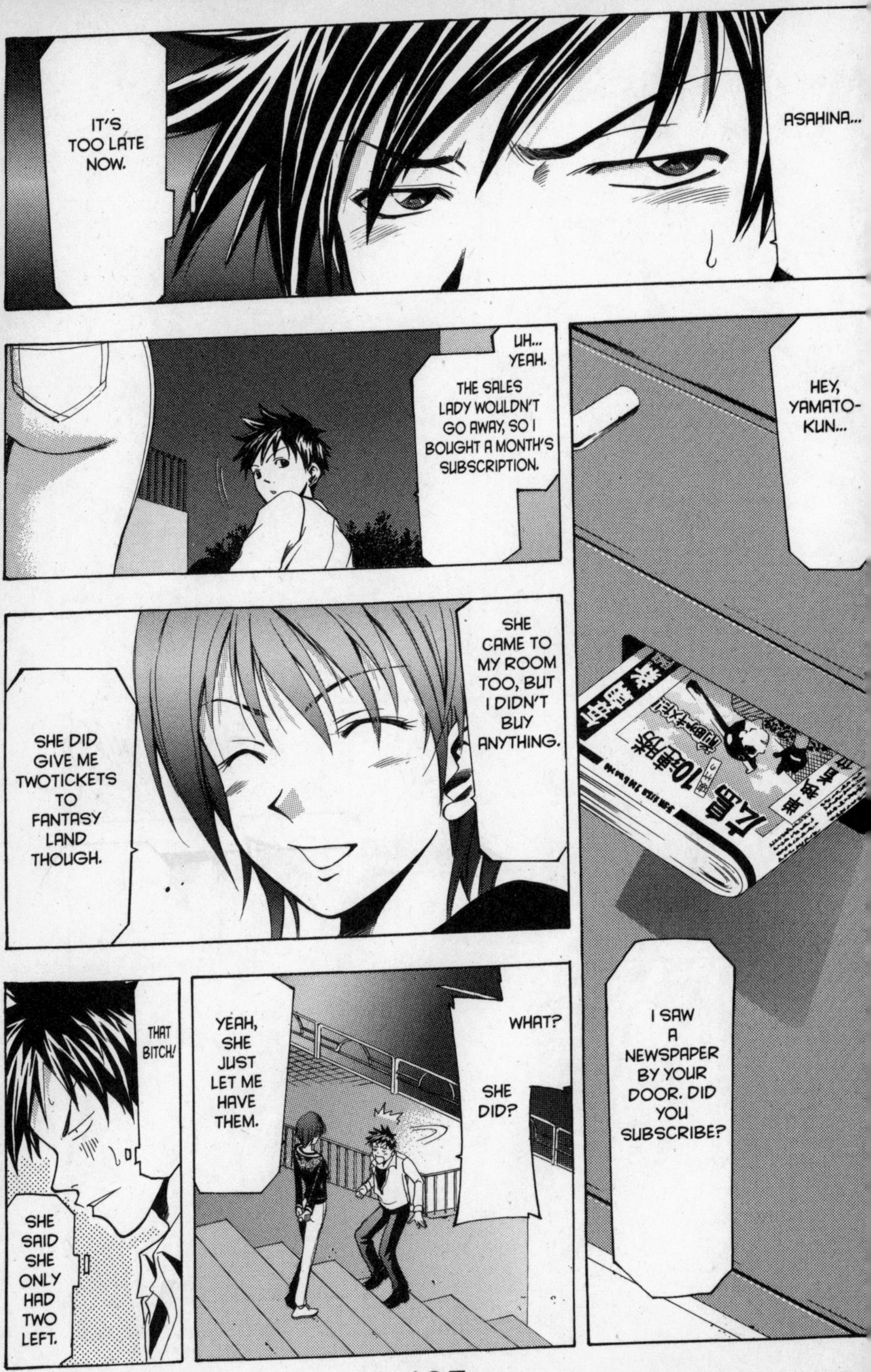
ASAHINA...
IT'S TOO LATE NOW.
HEY, YAMATO-KUN...
I SAW A NEWSPAPER BY YOUR DOOR. DID YOU SUBSCRIBE?
UH... YEAH.
THE SALES LADY WOULDN'T GO AWAY, SO I BOUGHT A MONTH'S SUBSCRIPTION.
SHE CAME TO MY ROOM TOO, BUT I DIDN'T BUY ANYTHING.
SHE DID GIVE ME TWOTICKETS TO FANTASY LAND THOUGH.
WHAT?
SHE DID?
YEAH, SHE JUST LET ME HAVE THEM.
THAT BITCH!
SHE SAID SHE ONLY HAD TWO LEFT.

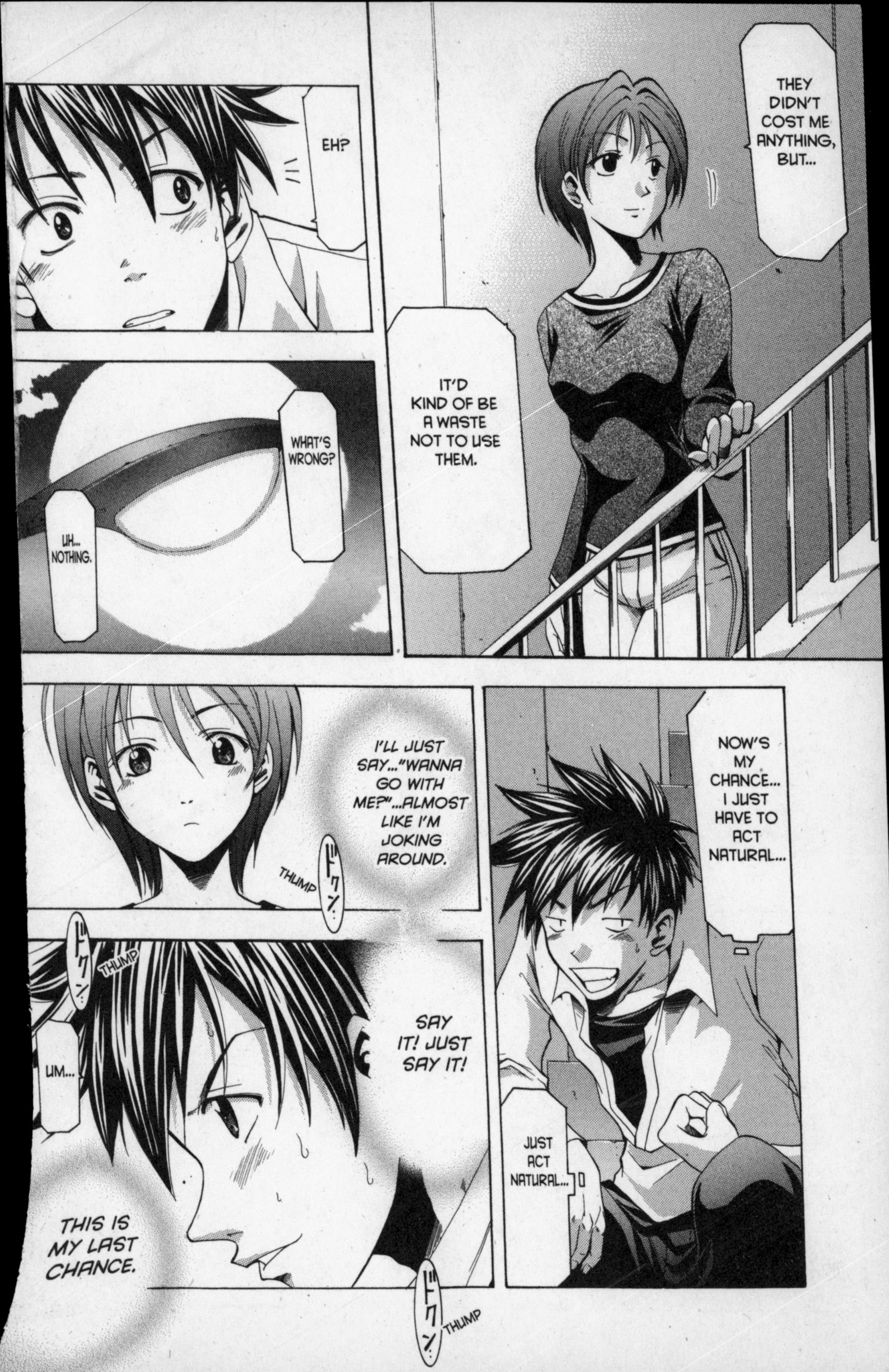
THEY DIDN'T COST ME ANYTHING, BUT...
IT'D KIND OF BE A WASTE NOT TO USE THEM.
EH?
WHAT'S WRONG?
UH... NOTHING.
NOW'S MY CHANCE... I JUST HAVE TO ACT NATURAL...
JUST ACT NATURAL...
I'LL JUST SAY..."WANNA GO WITH ME?"...ALMOST LIKE I'M JOKING AROUND.
ドクン
THUMP
ドクン
THUMP
UM...
SAY IT! JUST SAY IT!
THIS IS MY LAST CHANCE.
ドクン
THUMP

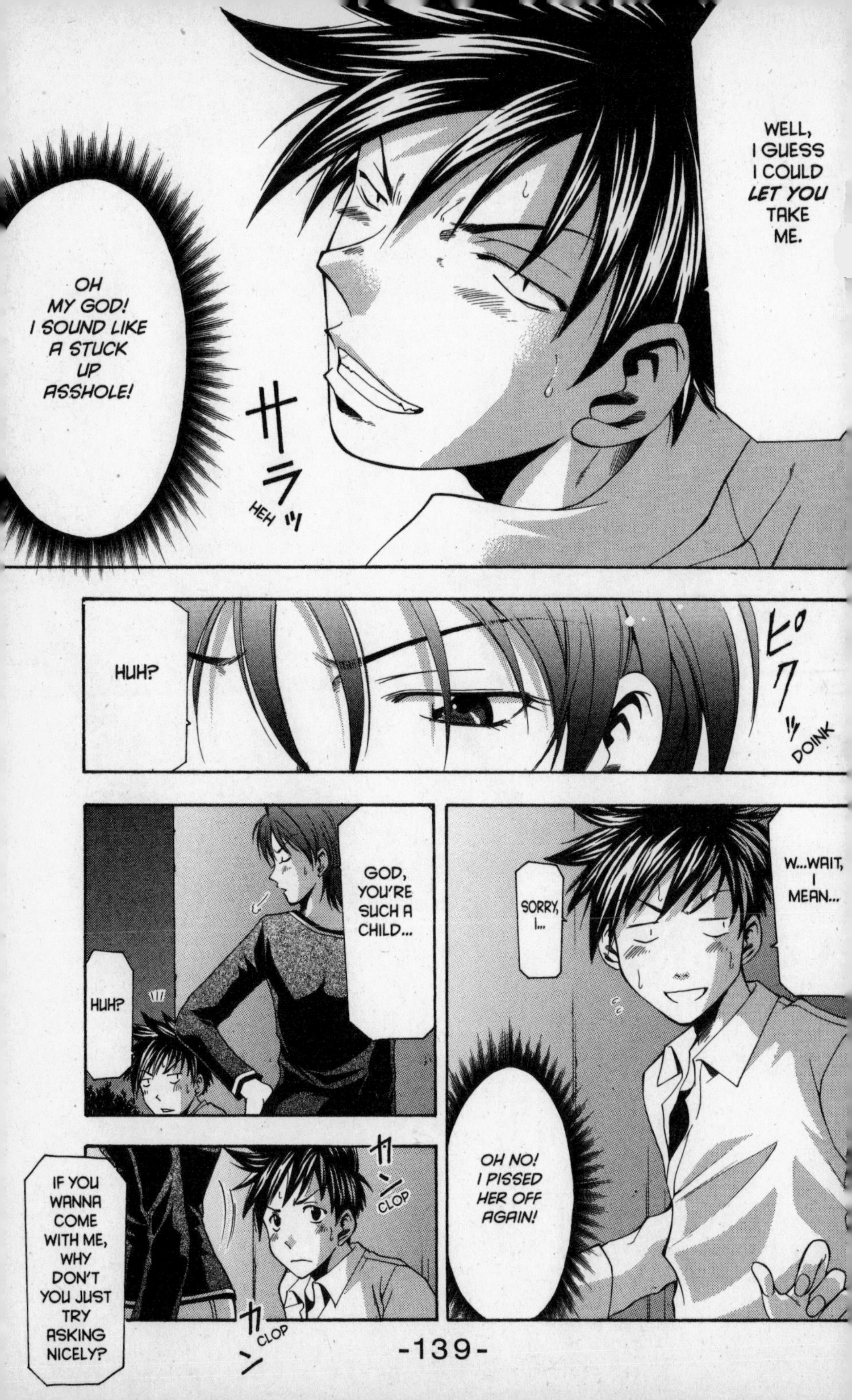
WELL, I GUESS I COULD *LET YOU* TAKE ME.
HEH
OH MY GOD! I SOUND LIKE A STUCK UP ASSHOLE!
DOINK
HUH?
W...WAIT, I MEAN...
SORRY, I...
OH NO! I PISSED HER OFF AGAIN!
GOD, YOU'RE SUCH A CHILD...
HUH?
CLOP
IF YOU WANNA COME WITH ME, WHY DON'T YOU JUST TRY ASKING NICELY?
CLOP

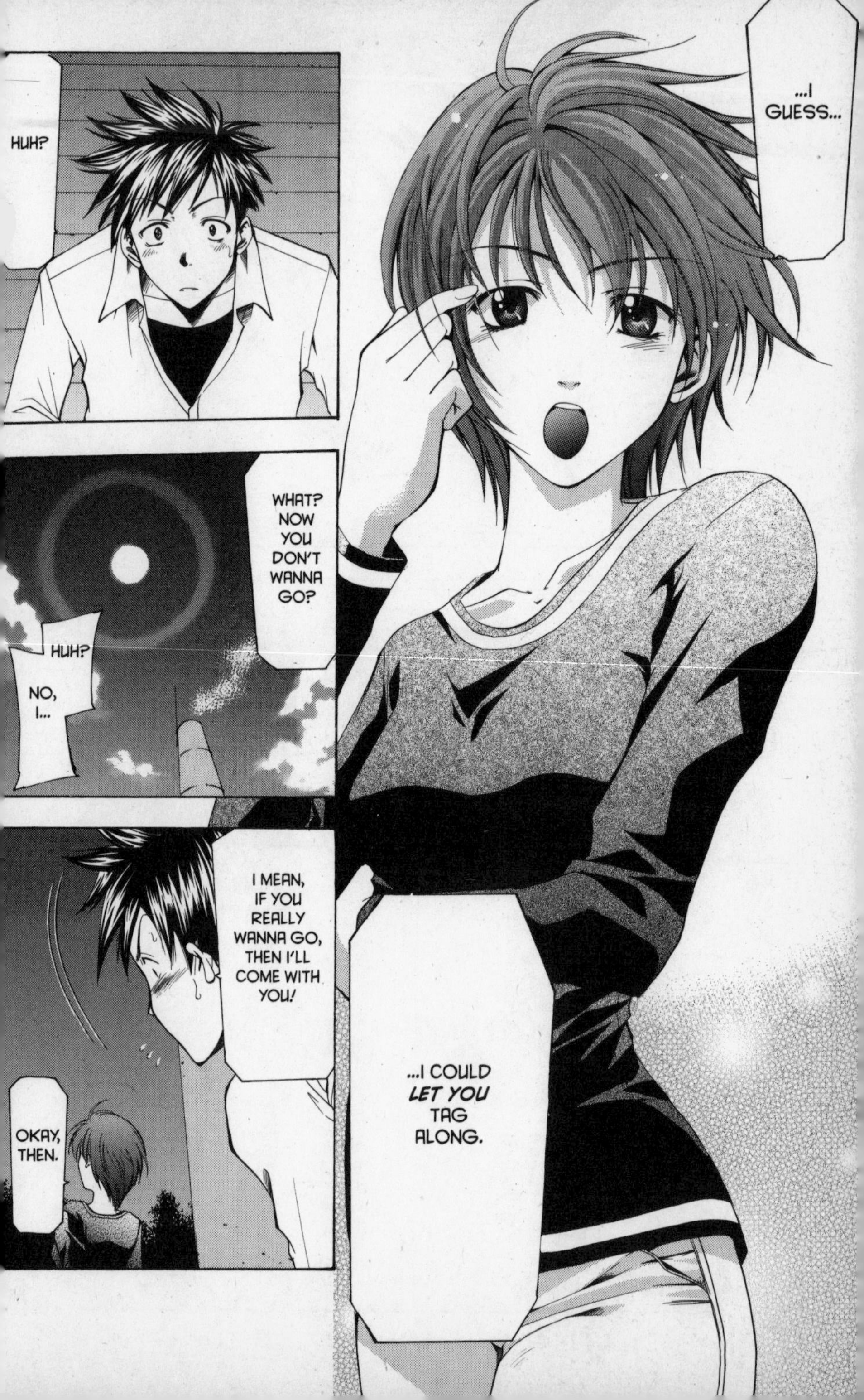
...I GUESS...
...I COULD *LET YOU* TAG ALONG.
HUH?
WHAT? NOW YOU DON'T WANNA GO?
HUH?
NO, I...
I MEAN, IF YOU REALLY WANNA GO, THEN I'LL COME WITH YOU!
OKAY, THEN.

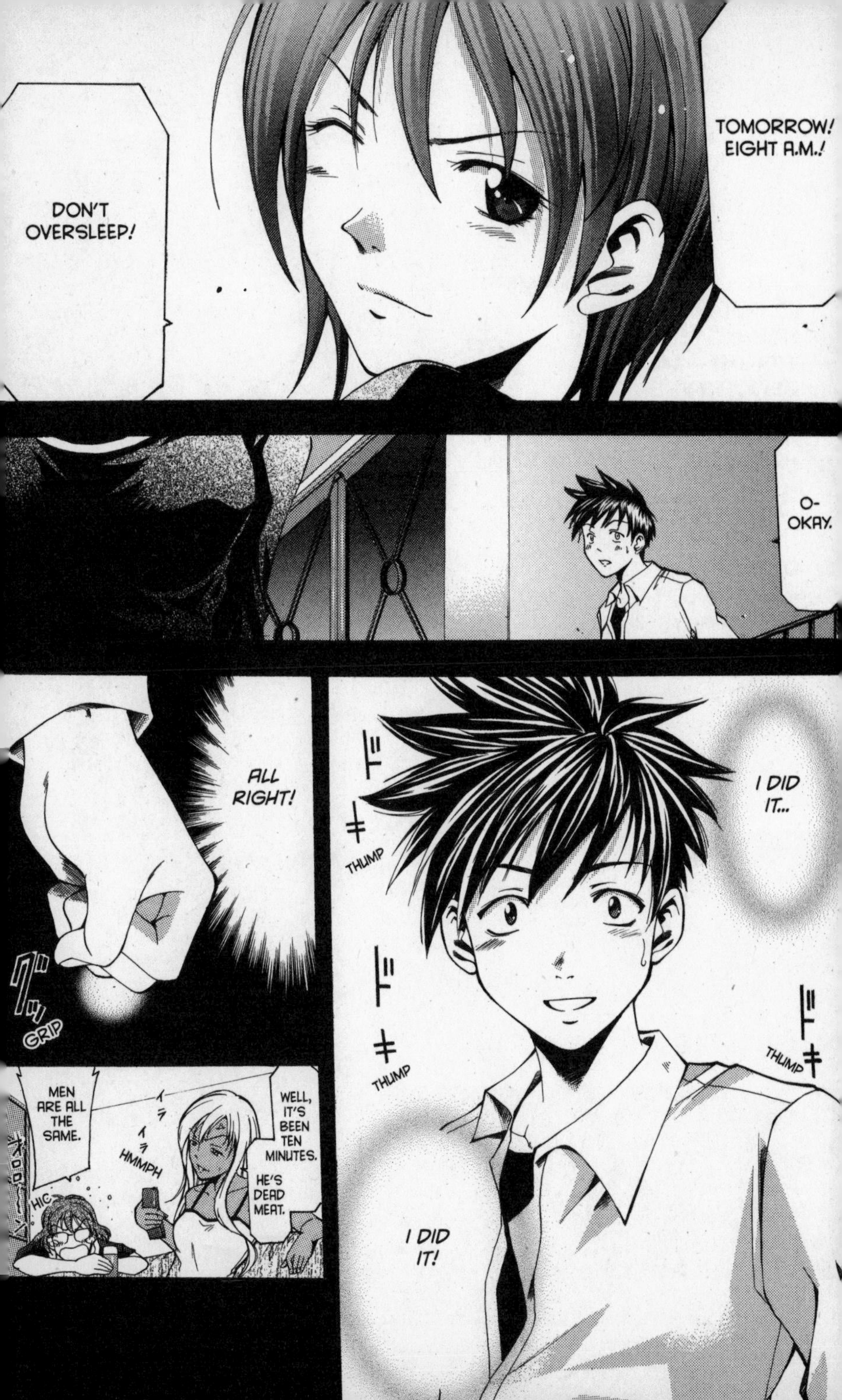
TOMORROW! EIGHT A.M.!
DON'T OVERSLEEP!
O- OKAY.
I DID IT...
ドキ
THUMP
ドキ
THUMP
ドキ
THUMP
I DID IT!
ALL RIGHT!
グッ
GRIP
WELL, IT'S BEEN TEN MINUTES.
HE'S DEAD MEAT.
イラ
イラ
HMMPH
MEN ARE ALL THE SAME.
HIC

YASUNOBU HATTORI
(HIGH SCHOOL FRESHMAN)

DATE OF BIRTH—DECEMBER 16
(SAGITTARIUS)
HEIGHT—5'10"
WEIGHT—140 LBS
BLOOD TYPE—O

LIKES
•GIRLS (ESPECIALLY OLDER ONES)
•DATING
•KARAOKE

DISLIKES
•GETTING UP EARLY
•OTHER GUYS
•NEEDY CHICKS

MOTTO—BIGAMY IS BEAUTIFUL.

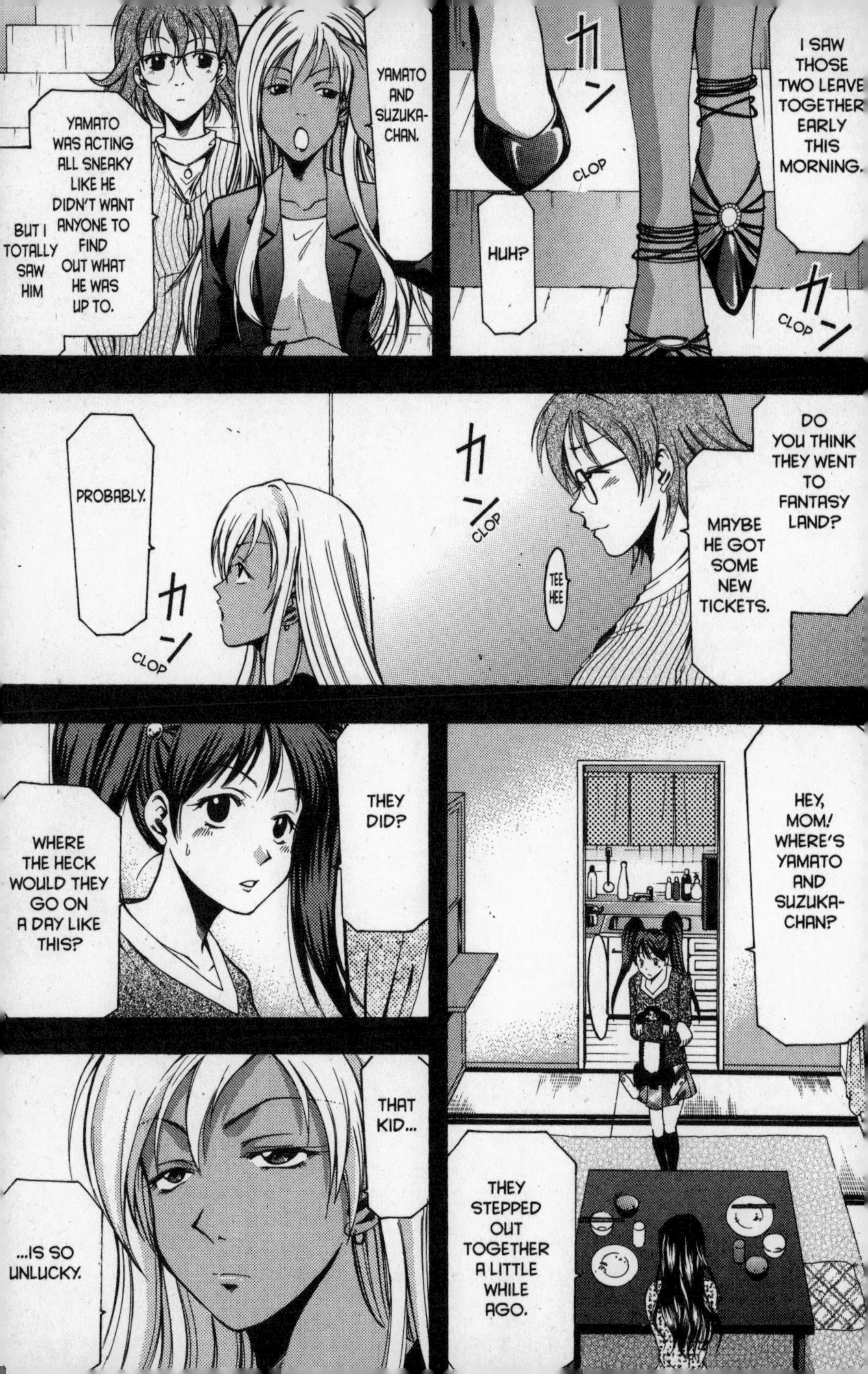
I SAW THOSE TWO LEAVE TOGETHER EARLY THIS MORNING.
CLOP
HUH?
CLOP
YAMATO AND SUZUKA-CHAN.
YAMATO WAS ACTING ALL SNEAKY LIKE HE DIDN'T WANT ANYONE TO FIND OUT WHAT HE WAS UP TO.
BUT I TOTALLY SAW HIM
DO YOU THINK THEY WENT TO FANTASY LAND?
MAYBE HE GOT SOME NEW TICKETS.
TEE HEE
CLOP
PROBABLY.
CLOP
HEY, MOM! WHERE'S YAMATO AND SUZUKA-CHAN?
THEY STEPPED OUT TOGETHER A LITTLE WHILE AGO.
THEY DID?
WHERE THE HECK WOULD THEY GO ON A DAY LIKE THIS?
THAT KID...
...IS SO UNLUCKY.

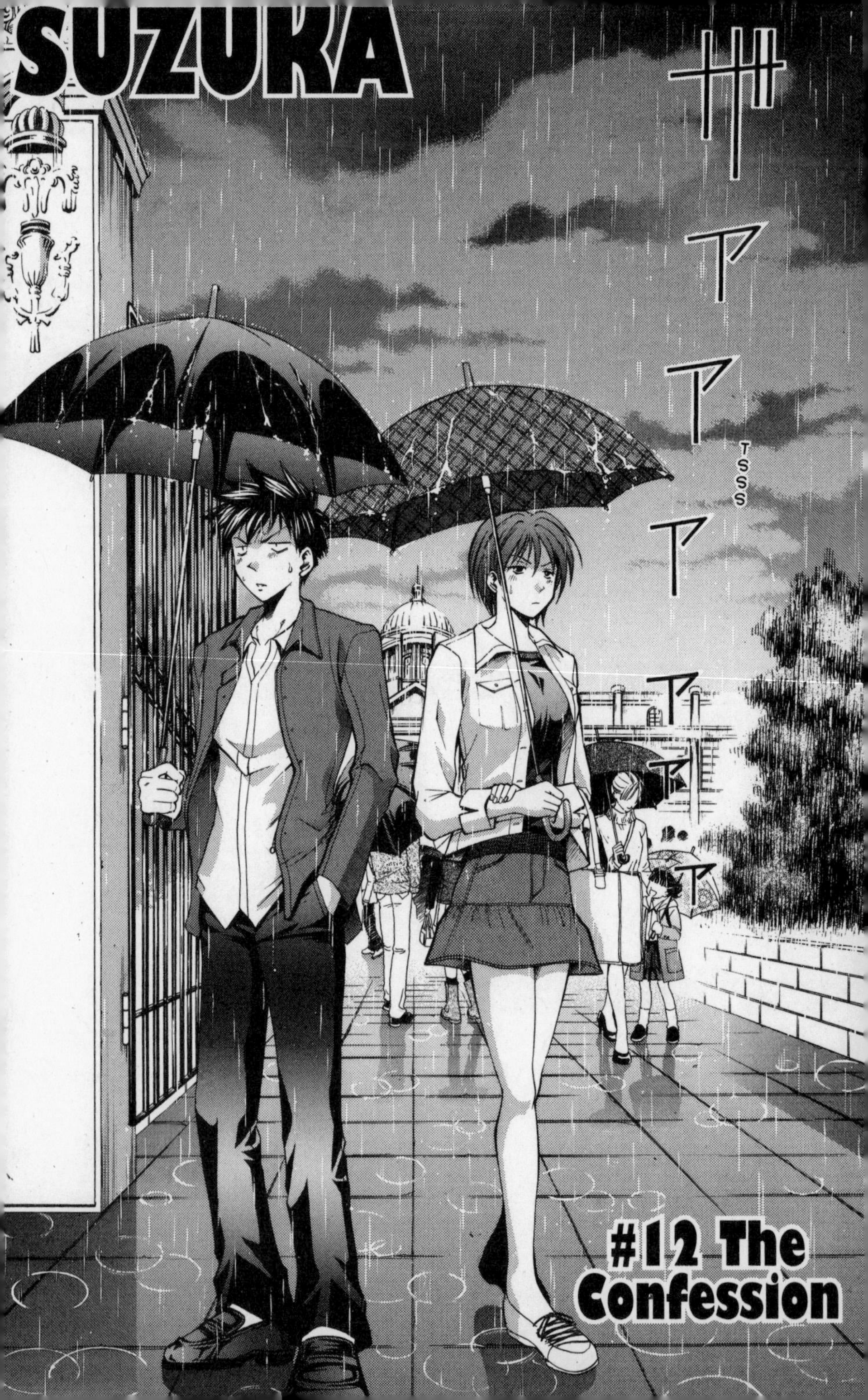
SUZUKA
ザアアアアアア
TSSS
#12 The Confession

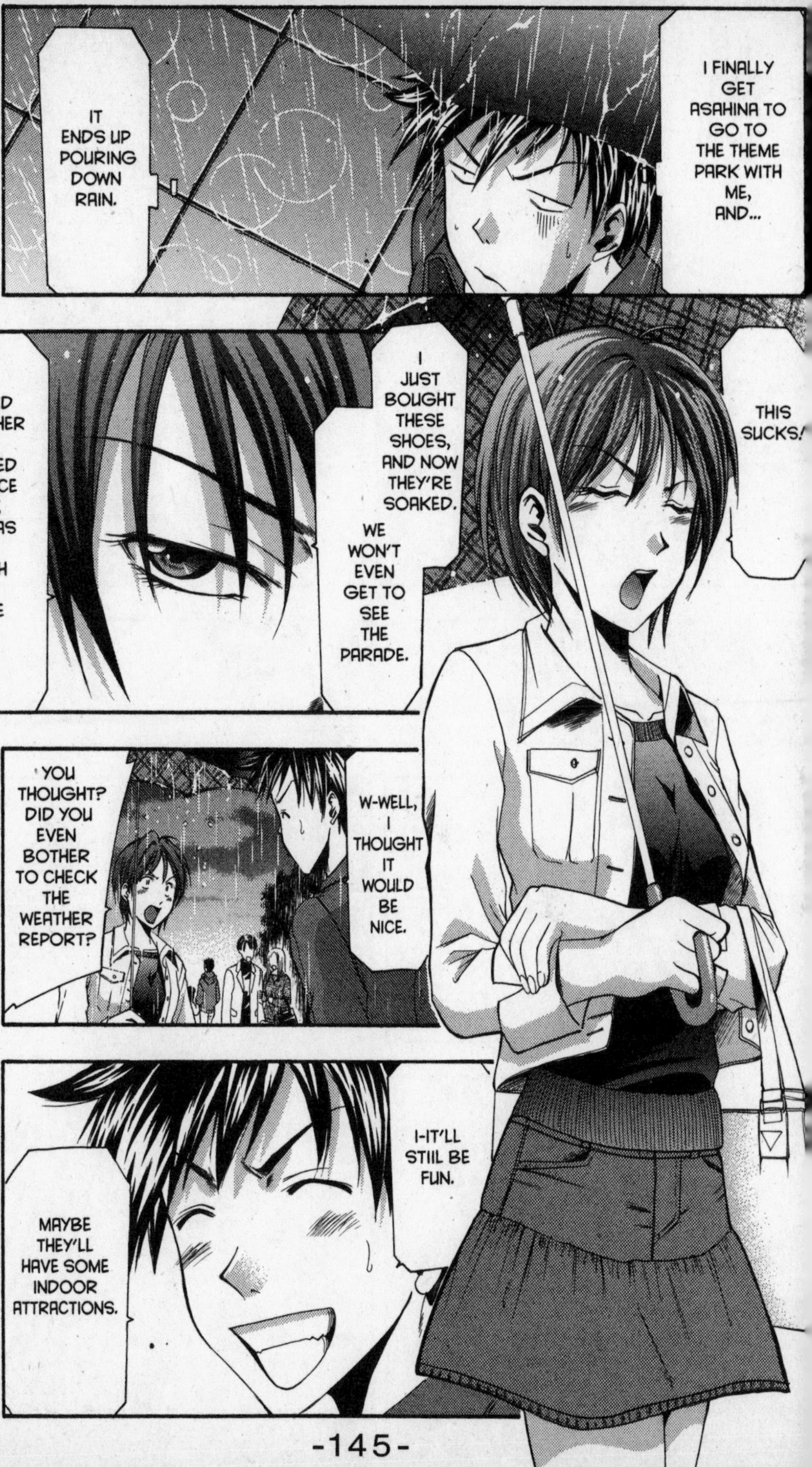
I FINALLY GET ASAHINA TO GO TO THE THEME PARK WITH ME, AND...
IT ENDS UP POURING DOWN RAIN.
THIS SUCKS!
I JUST BOUGHT THESE SHOES, AND NOW THEY'RE SOAKED.
WE WON'T EVEN GET TO SEE THE PARADE.
YOU SAID THE WEATHER WAS SUPPOSED TO BE NICE TODAY, AND I WAS DUMB ENOUGH TO BELIEVE YOU.
W-WELL, I THOUGHT IT WOULD BE NICE.
YOU THOUGHT? DID YOU EVEN BOTHER TO CHECK THE WEATHER REPORT?
I-IT'LL STIIL BE FUN.
MAYBE THEY'LL HAVE SOME INDOOR ATTRACTIONS.

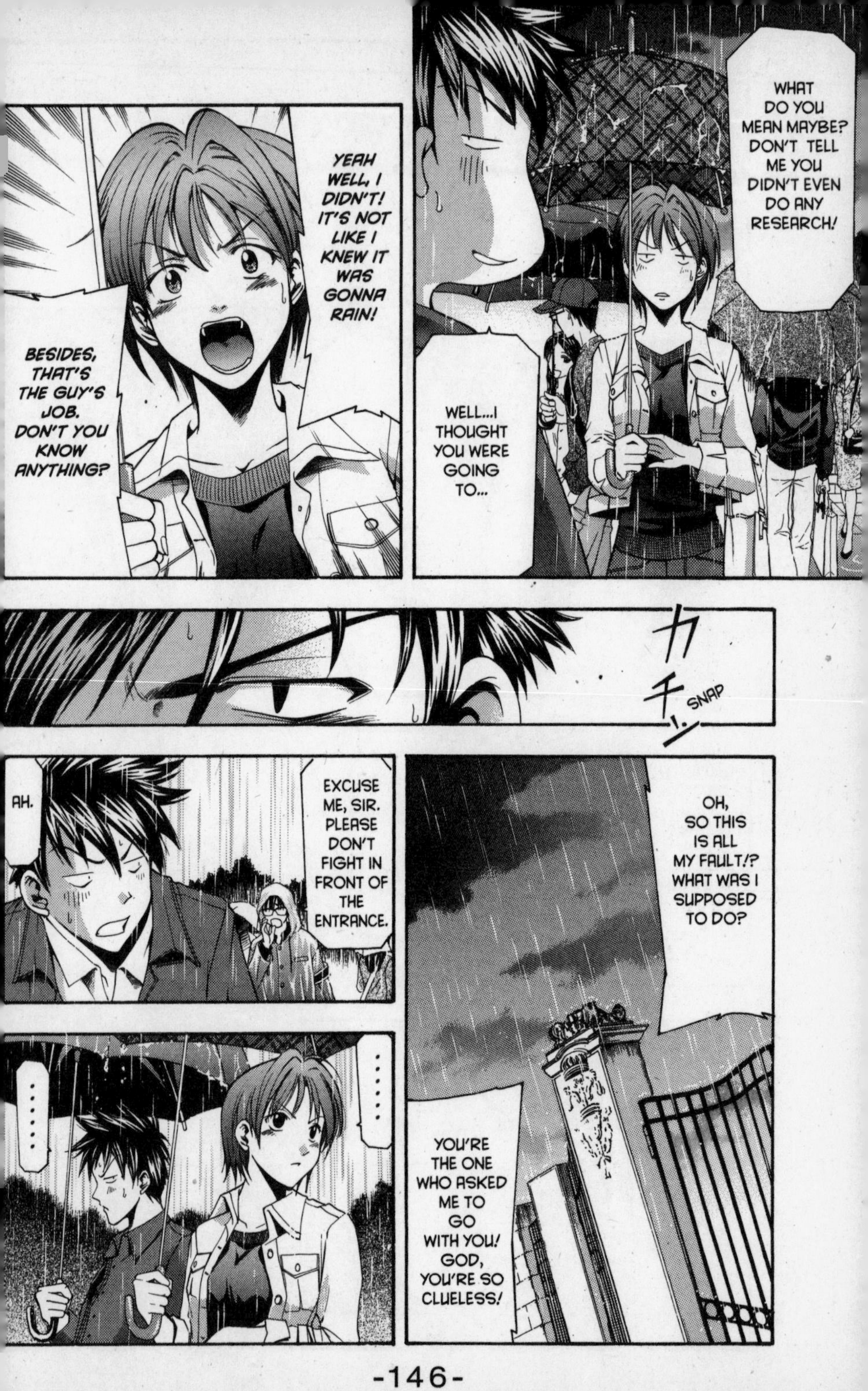
WHAT DO YOU MEAN MAYBE? DON'T TELL ME YOU DIDN'T EVEN DO ANY RESEARCH!
WELL...I THOUGHT YOU WERE GOING TO...
YEAH WELL, I DIDN'T! IT'S NOT LIKE I KNEW IT WAS GONNA RAIN!
BESIDES, THAT'S THE GUY'S JOB. DON'T YOU KNOW ANYTHING?
カチ！
SNAP
OH, SO THIS IS ALL MY FAULT!? WHAT WAS I SUPPOSED TO DO?
YOU'RE THE ONE WHO ASKED ME TO GO WITH YOU! GOD, YOU'RE SO CLUELESS!
EXCUSE ME, SIR. PLEASE DON'T FIGHT IN FRONT OF THE ENTRANCE.
AH.
......
......

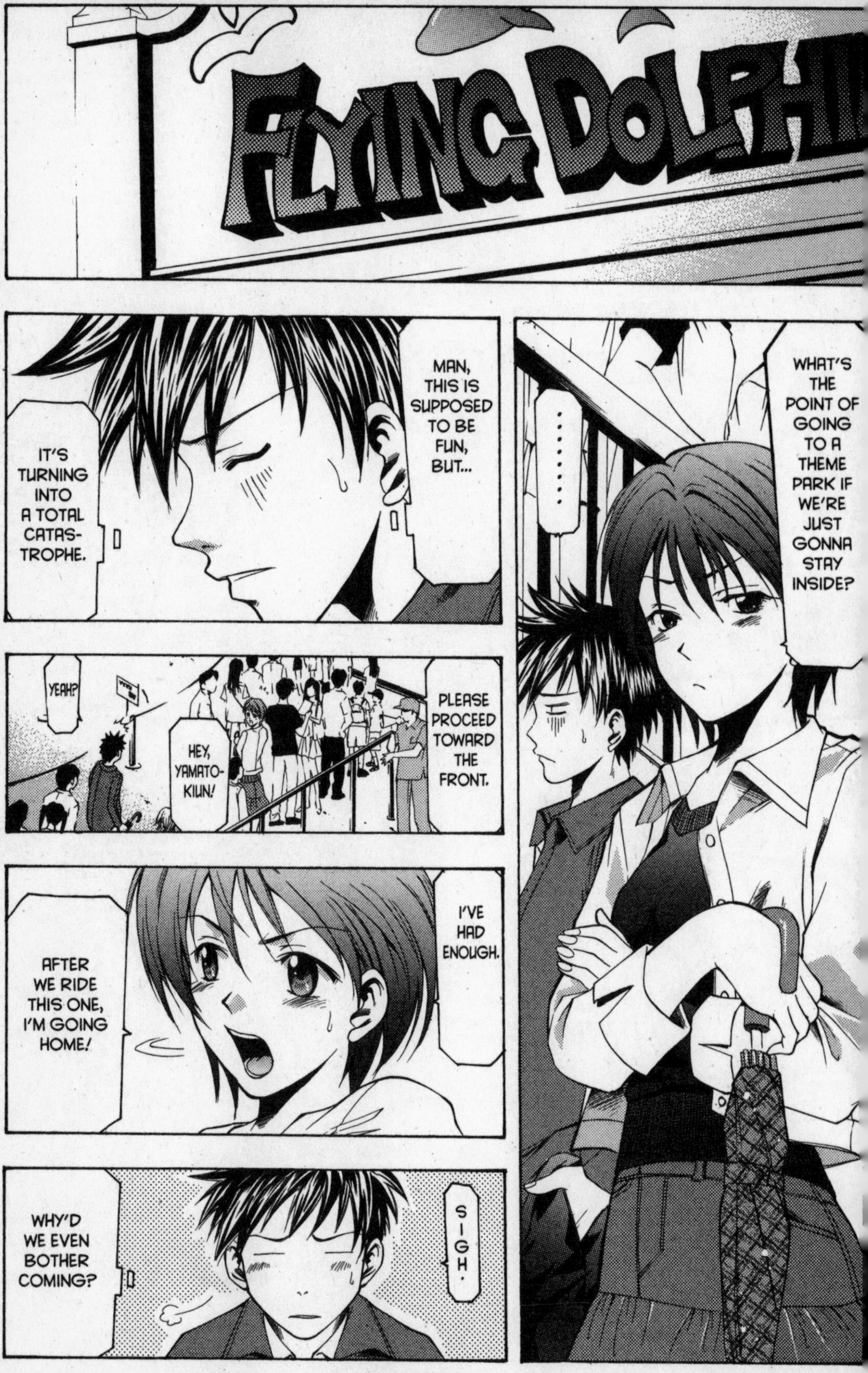
FLYING DOLPHI
WHAT'S THE POINT OF GOING TO A THEME PARK IF WE'RE JUST GONNA STAY INSIDE?
....
MAN, THIS IS SUPPOSED TO BE FUN, BUT...
IT'S TURNING INTO A TOTAL CATAS-TROPHE.
PLEASE PROCEED TOWARD THE FRONT.
HEY, YAMATO-KUN!
YEAH?
I'VE HAD ENOUGH.
AFTER WE RIDE THIS ONE, I'M GOING HOME!
SIGH
WHY'D WE EVEN BOTHER COMING?

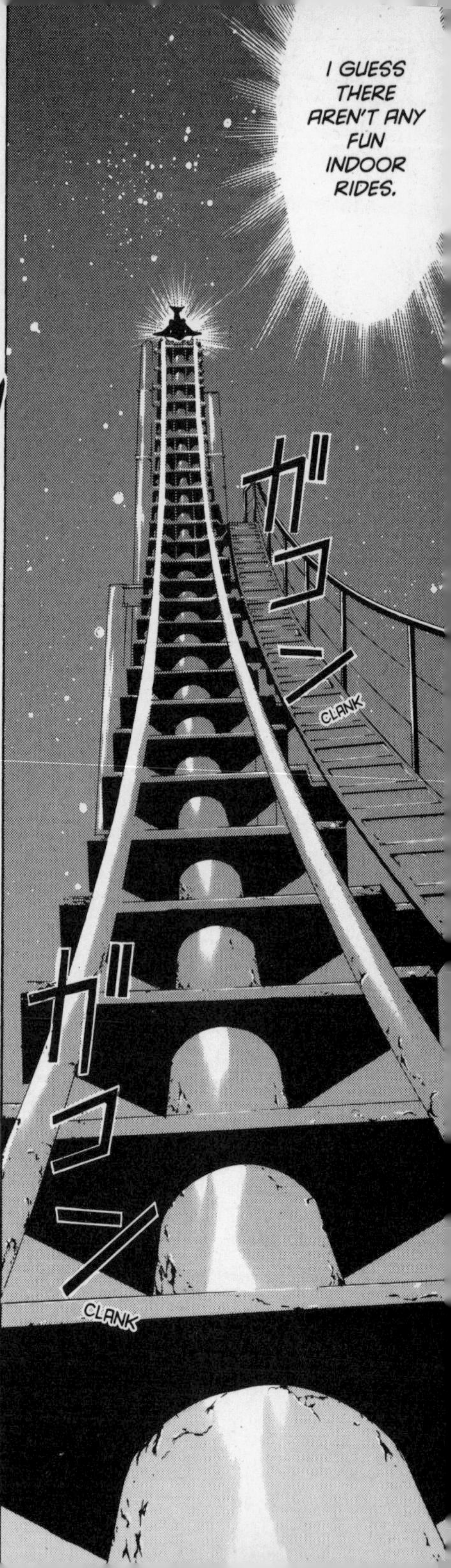
I GUESS THERE AREN'T ANY FUN INDOOR RIDES.
CLANK
CLANK

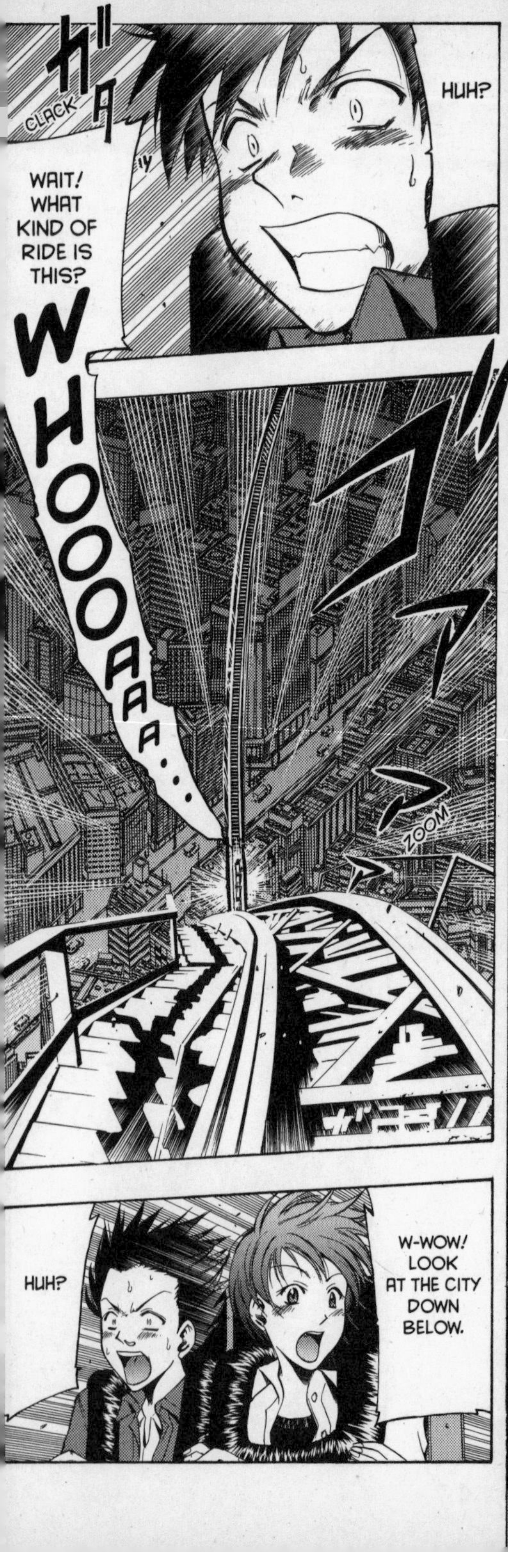
CLACK
HUH?
WAIT! WHAT KIND OF RIDE IS THIS?
WHOOOAAAA...
ZOOM
W-WOW! LOOK AT THE CITY DOWN BELOW.
HUH?

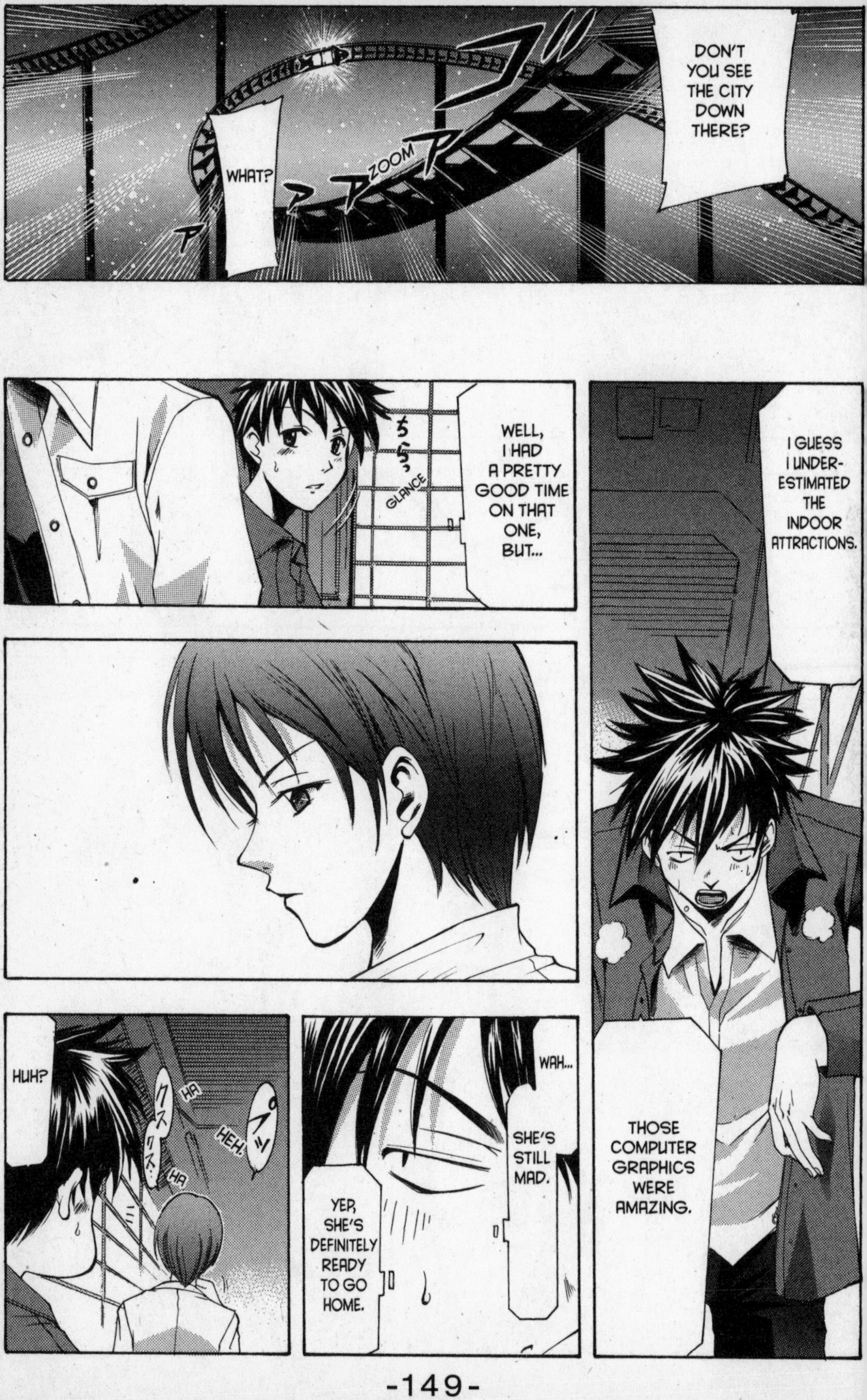
DON'T YOU SEE THE CITY DOWN THERE?
ZOOM
WHAT?
I GUESS I UNDER-ESTIMATED THE INDOOR ATTRACTIONS.
THOSE COMPUTER GRAPHICS WERE AMAZING.
WELL, I HAD A PRETTY GOOD TIME ON THAT ONE, BUT...
GLANCE
WAH...
SHE'S STILL MAD.
YEP, SHE'S DEFINITELY READY TO GO HOME.
HA
HEH
HA
HUH?

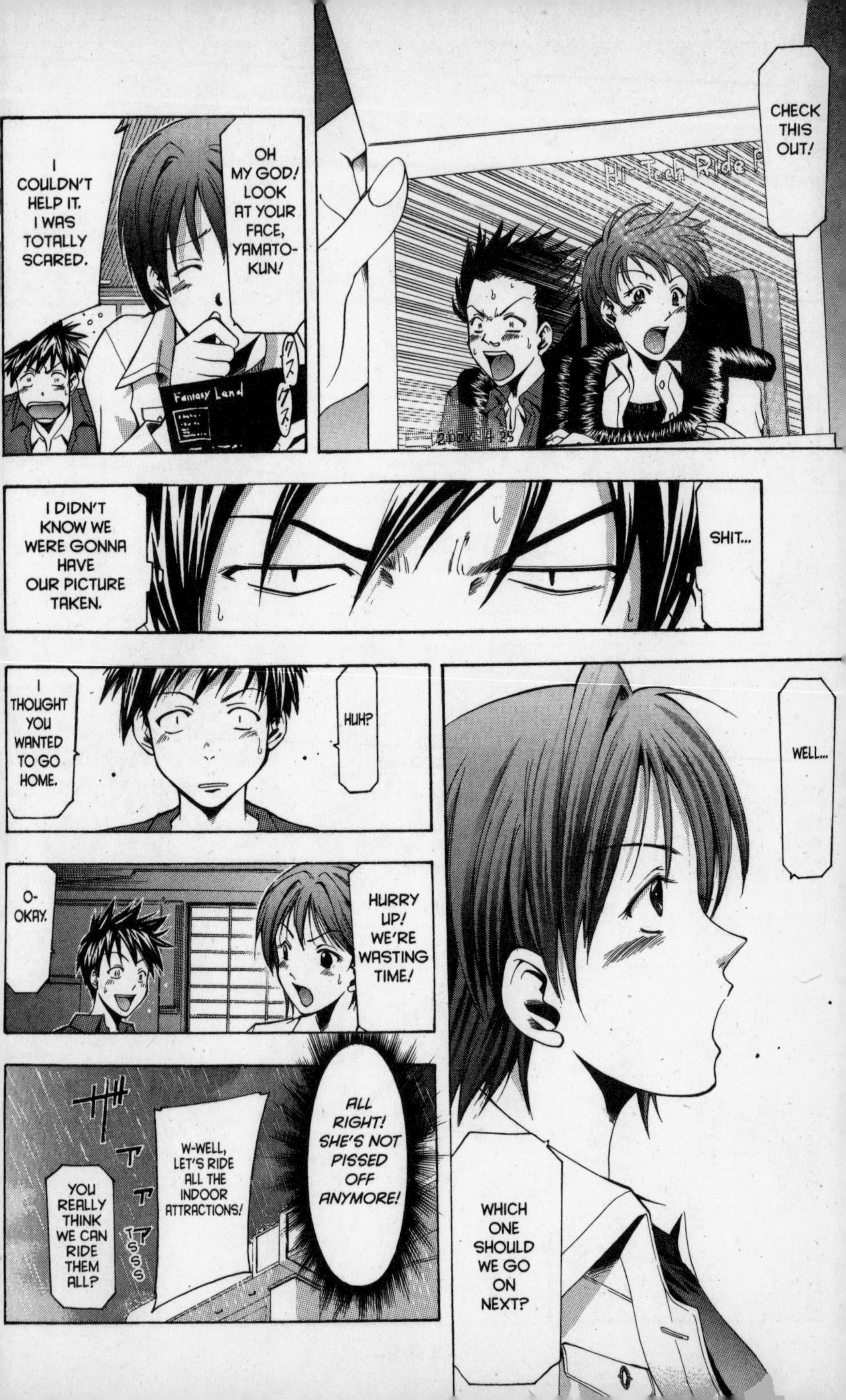
CHECK THIS OUT!
Fantasy Land
OH MY GOD! LOOK AT YOUR FACE, YAMATO-KUN!
I COULDN'T HELP IT. I WAS TOTALLY SCARED.
SHIT...
I DIDN'T KNOW WE WERE GONNA HAVE OUR PICTURE TAKEN.
WELL...
WHICH ONE SHOULD WE GO ON NEXT?
HUH?
I THOUGHT YOU WANTED TO GO HOME.
HURRY UP! WE'RE WASTING TIME!
O-OKAY.
ALL RIGHT! SHE'S NOT PISSED OFF ANYMORE!
W-WELL, LET'S RIDE ALL THE INDOOR ATTRACTIONS!
TSSS
YOU REALLY THINK WE CAN RIDE THEM ALL?

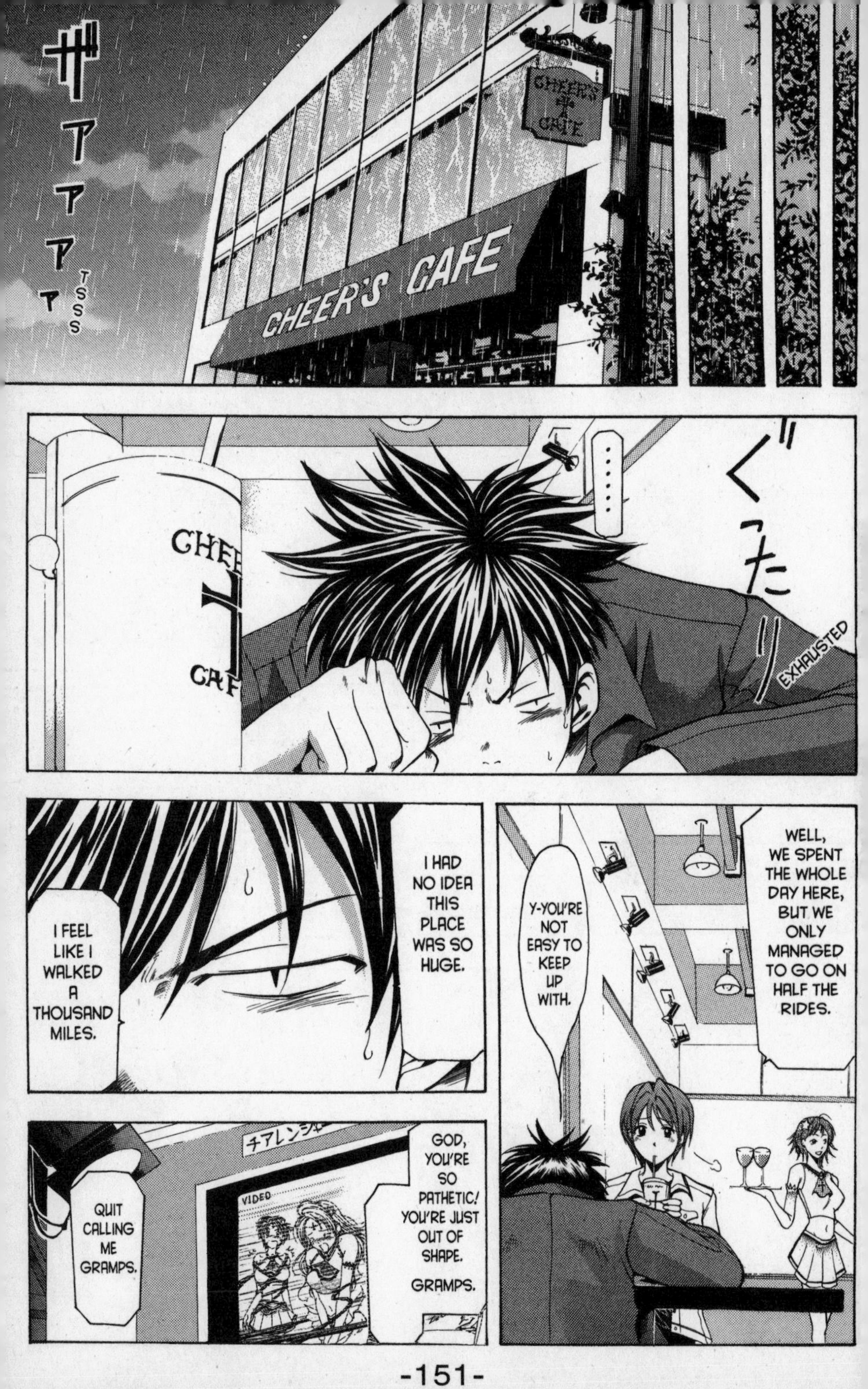
ザアアアア
TSSS
CHEER'S CAFE
CHEER'S CAFE
......
ぐったり
EXHAUSTED
WELL, WE SPENT THE WHOLE DAY HERE, BUT WE ONLY MANAGED TO GO ON HALF THE RIDES.
Y-YOU'RE NOT EASY TO KEEP UP WITH.
I HAD NO IDEA THIS PLACE WAS SO HUGE.
I FEEL LIKE I WALKED A THOUSAND MILES.
GOD, YOU'RE SO PATHETIC! YOU'RE JUST OUT OF SHAPE.
GRAMPS.
QUIT CALLING ME GRAMPS.
VIDEO

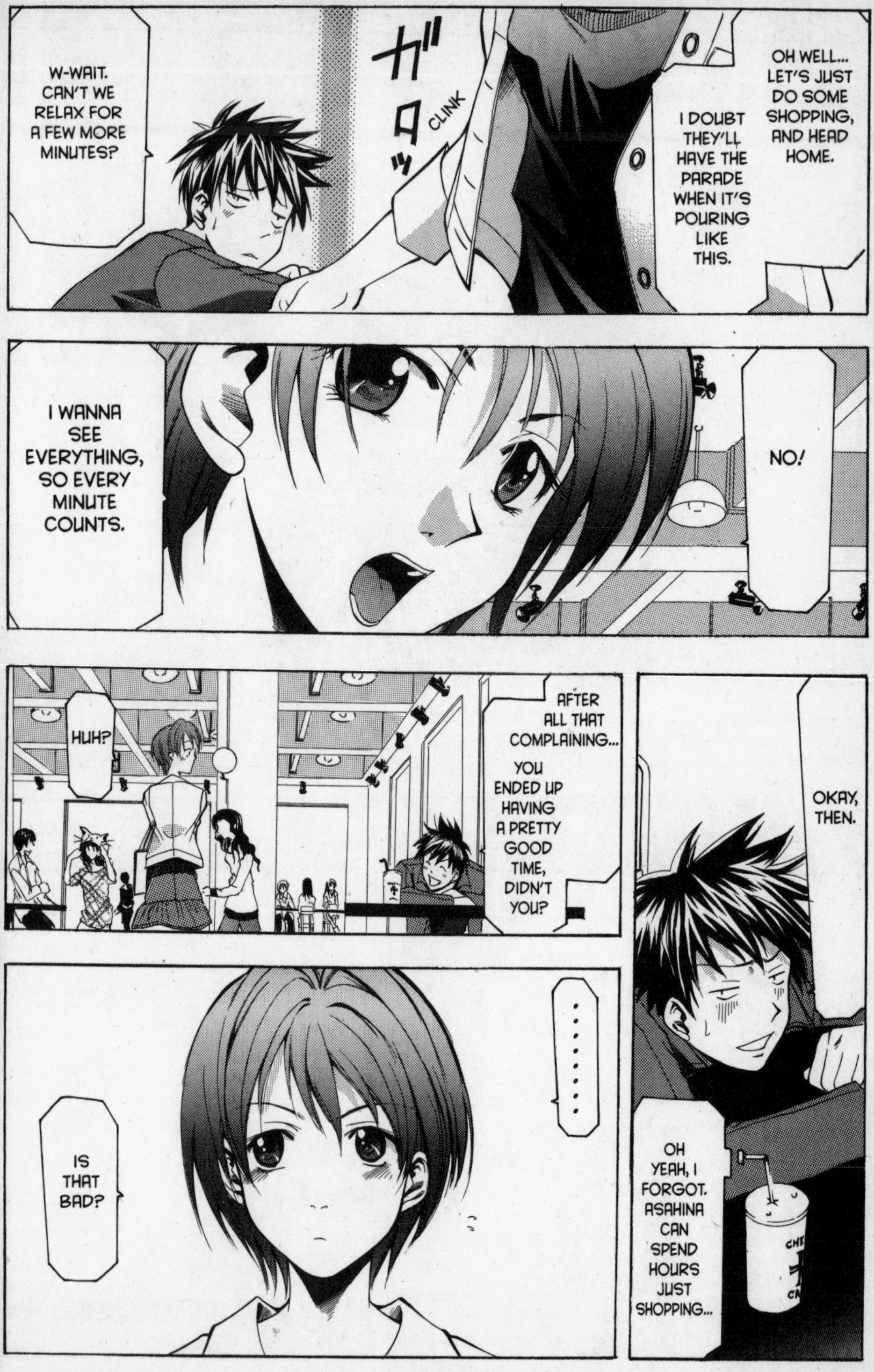
OH WELL... LET'S JUST DO SOME SHOPPING, AND HEAD HOME.
I DOUBT THEY'LL HAVE THE PARADE WHEN IT'S POURING LIKE THIS.
ガタッ
CLINK
W-WAIT. CAN'T WE RELAX FOR A FEW MORE MINUTES?
NO!
I WANNA SEE EVERYTHING, SO EVERY MINUTE COUNTS.
OKAY, THEN.
OH YEAH, I FORGOT. ASAHINA CAN SPEND HOURS JUST SHOPPING...
AFTER ALL THAT COMPLAINING...
YOU ENDED UP HAVING A PRETTY GOOD TIME, DIDN'T YOU?
HUH?
....
IS THAT BAD?

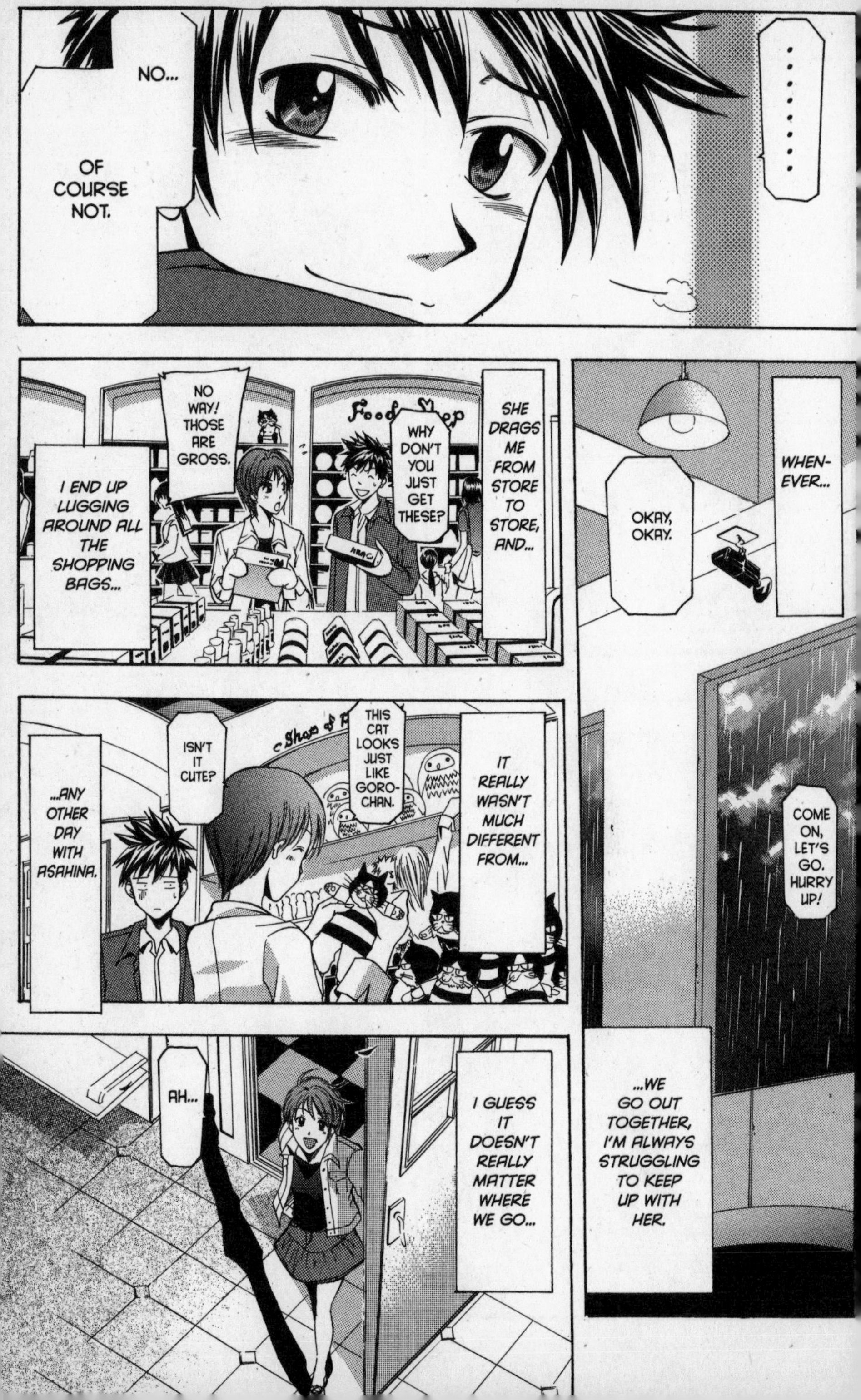
......
NO...
OF COURSE NOT.
WHEN-EVER...
OKAY, OKAY.
COME ON, LET'S GO. HURRY UP!
...WE GO OUT TOGETHER, I'M ALWAYS STRUGGLING TO KEEP UP WITH HER.
SHE DRAGS ME FROM STORE TO STORE, AND...
WHY DON'T YOU JUST GET THESE?
NO WAY! THOSE ARE GROSS.
I END UP LUGGING AROUND ALL THE SHOPPING BAGS...
Food Shop
IT REALLY WASN'T MUCH DIFFERENT FROM...
THIS CAT LOOKS JUST LIKE GORO-CHAN.
ISN'T IT CUTE?
...ANY OTHER DAY WITH ASAHINA.
I GUESS IT DOESN'T REALLY MATTER WHERE WE GO...
AH...

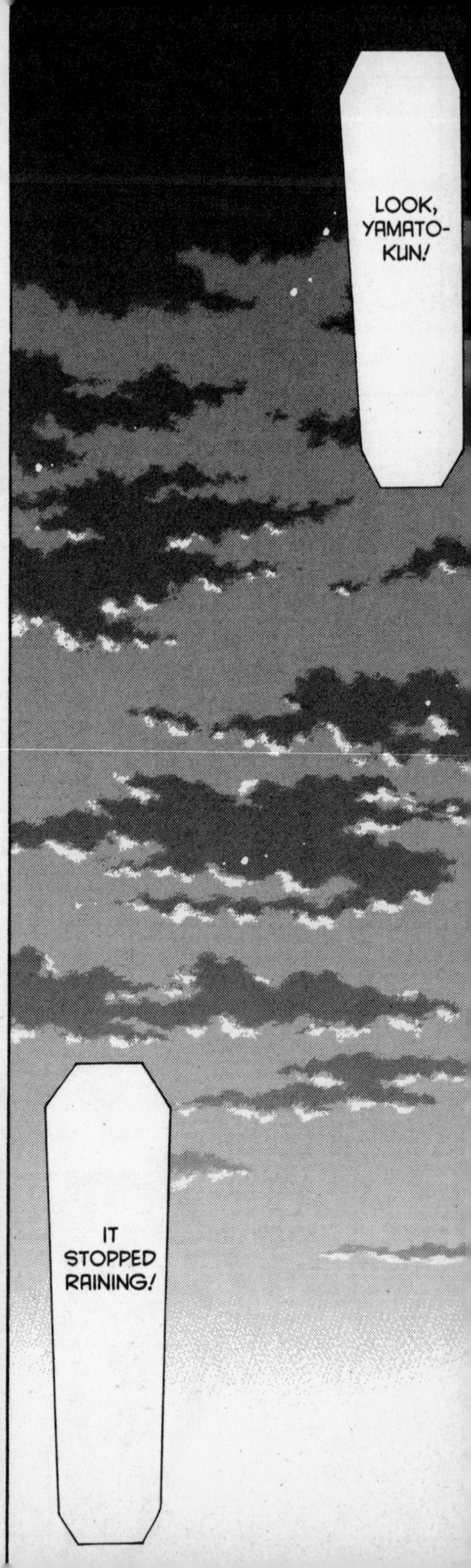
LOOK, YAMATO-KUN!
IT STOPPED RAINING!

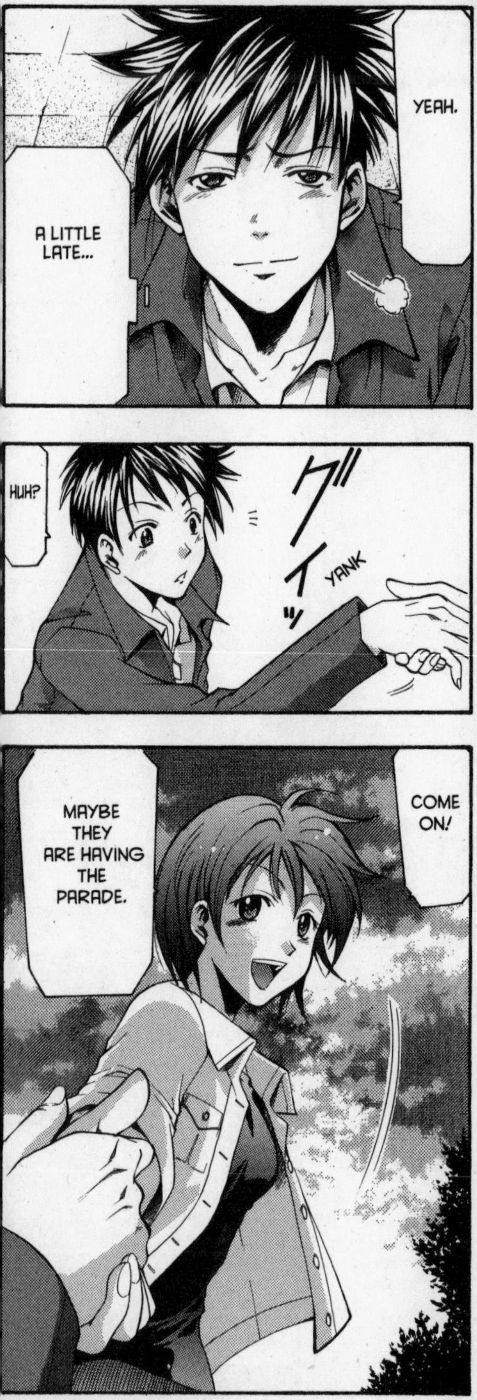
YEAH.
A LITTLE LATE...
YANK
HUH?
COME ON!
MAYBE THEY ARE HAVING THE PARADE.

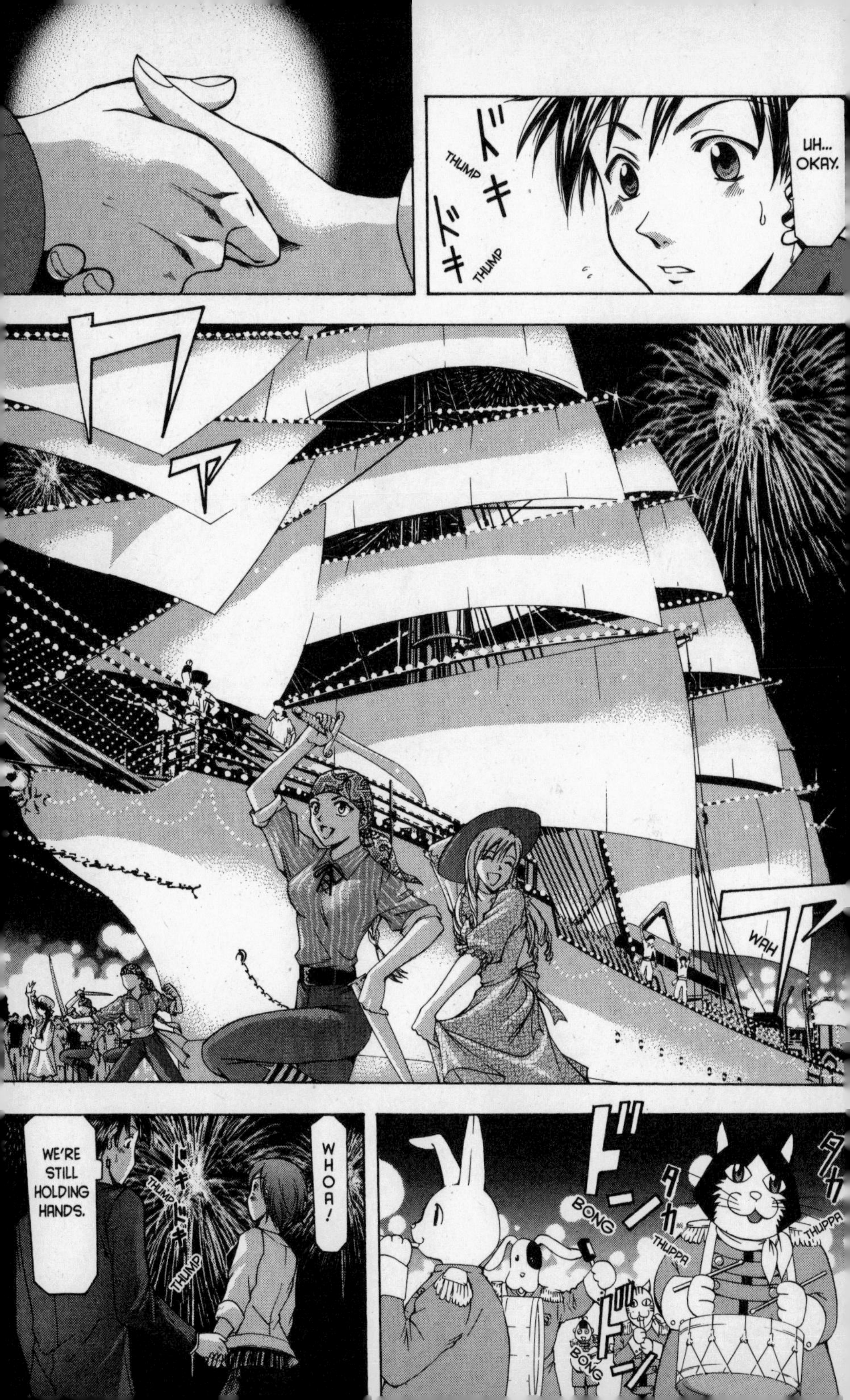
UH... OKAY.
THUMP
THUMP
WAH
BONG
THUPPA
THUPPA
BONG
WHOA!
WE'RE STILL HOLDING HANDS.
THUMP
THUMP

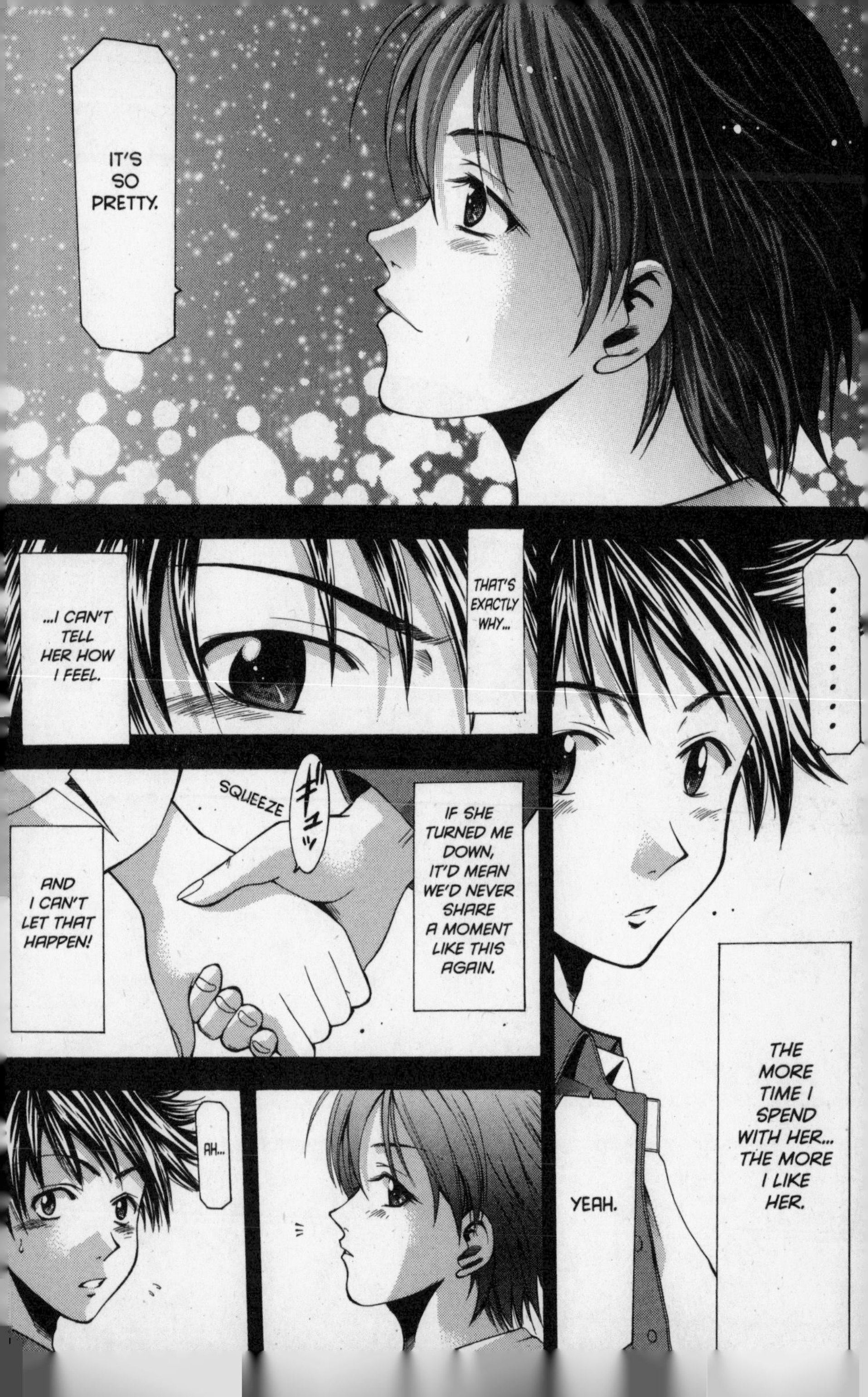
IT'S SO PRETTY.
......
THAT'S EXACTLY WHY...
...I CAN'T TELL HER HOW I FEEL.
IF SHE TURNED ME DOWN, IT'D MEAN WE'D NEVER SHARE A MOMENT LIKE THIS AGAIN.
ギュッ
SQUEEZE
AND I CAN'T LET THAT HAPPEN!
THE MORE TIME I SPEND WITH HER... THE MORE I LIKE HER.
YEAH.
AH...

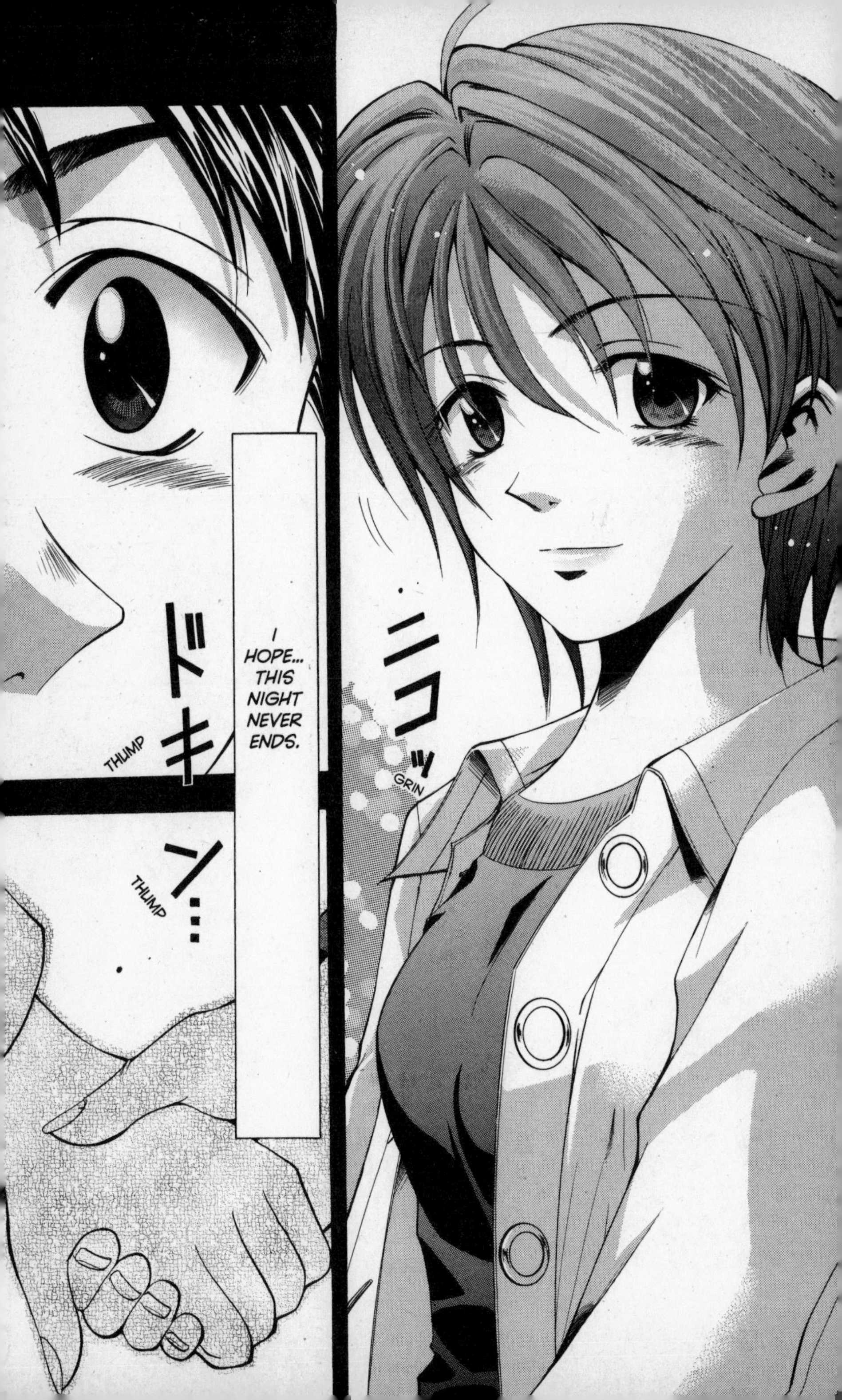
ニコッ
GRIN
I HOPE... THIS NIGHT NEVER ENDS.
ドキン…
THUMP
THUMP

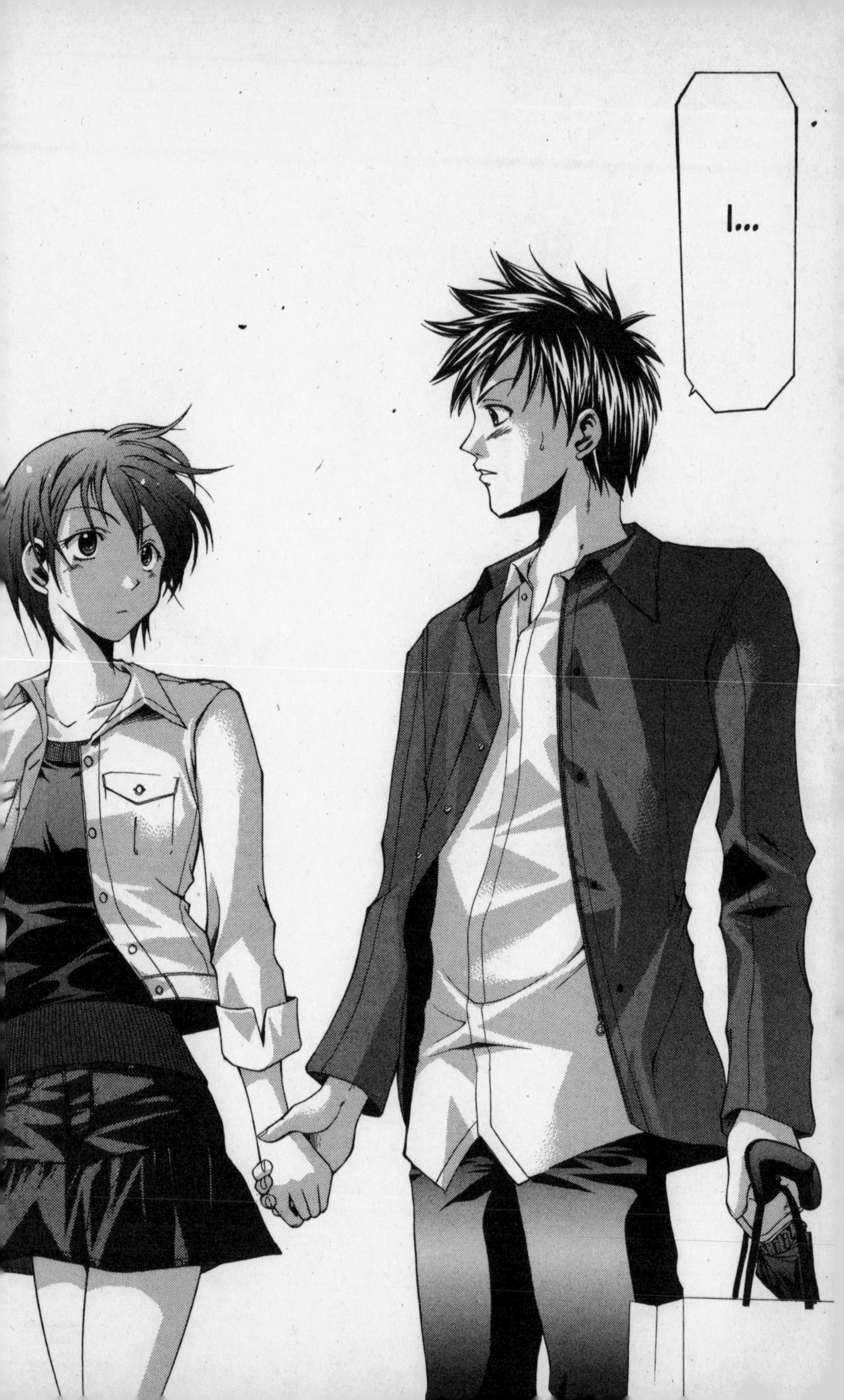
I...

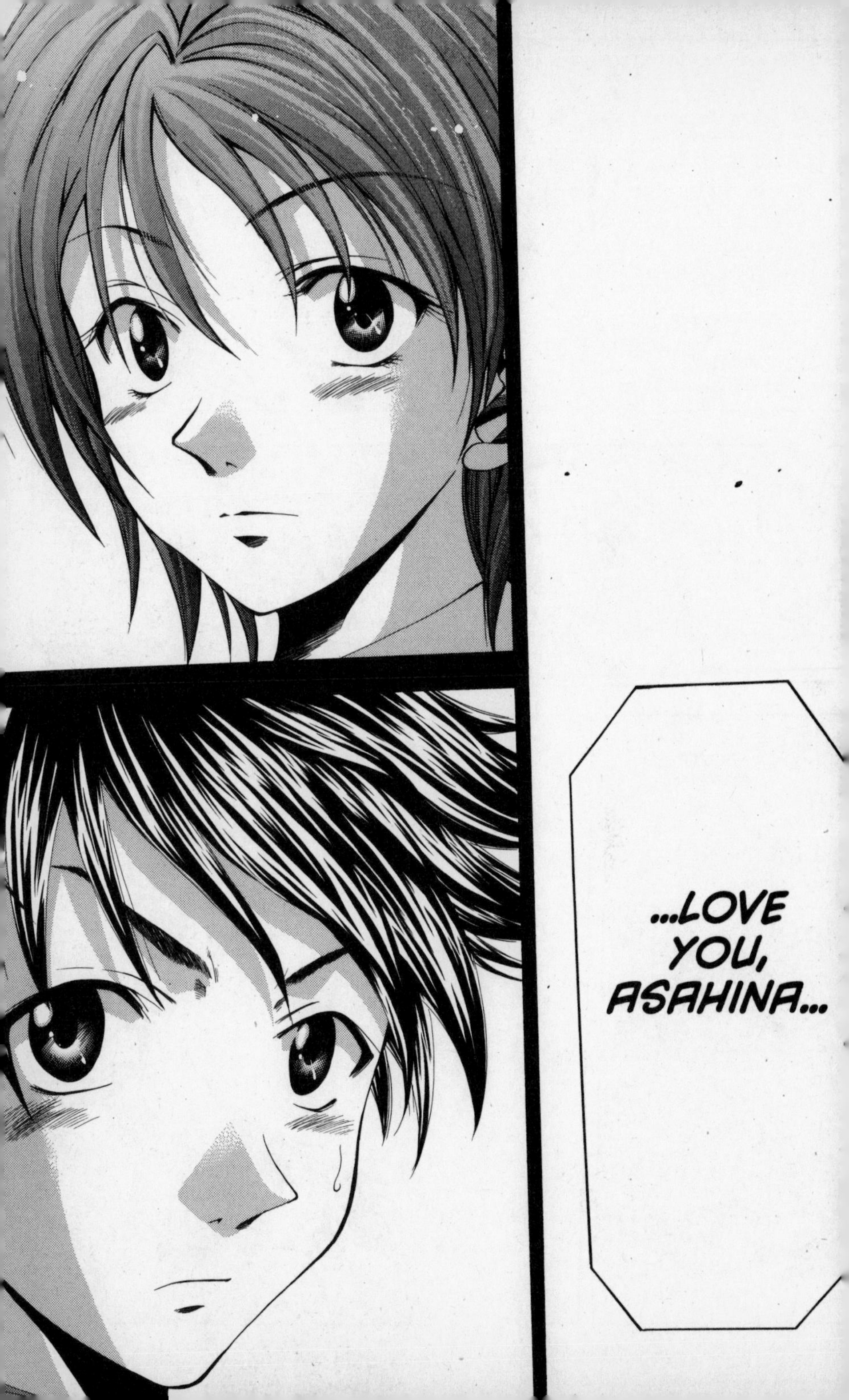
...LOVE YOU, ASAHINA...

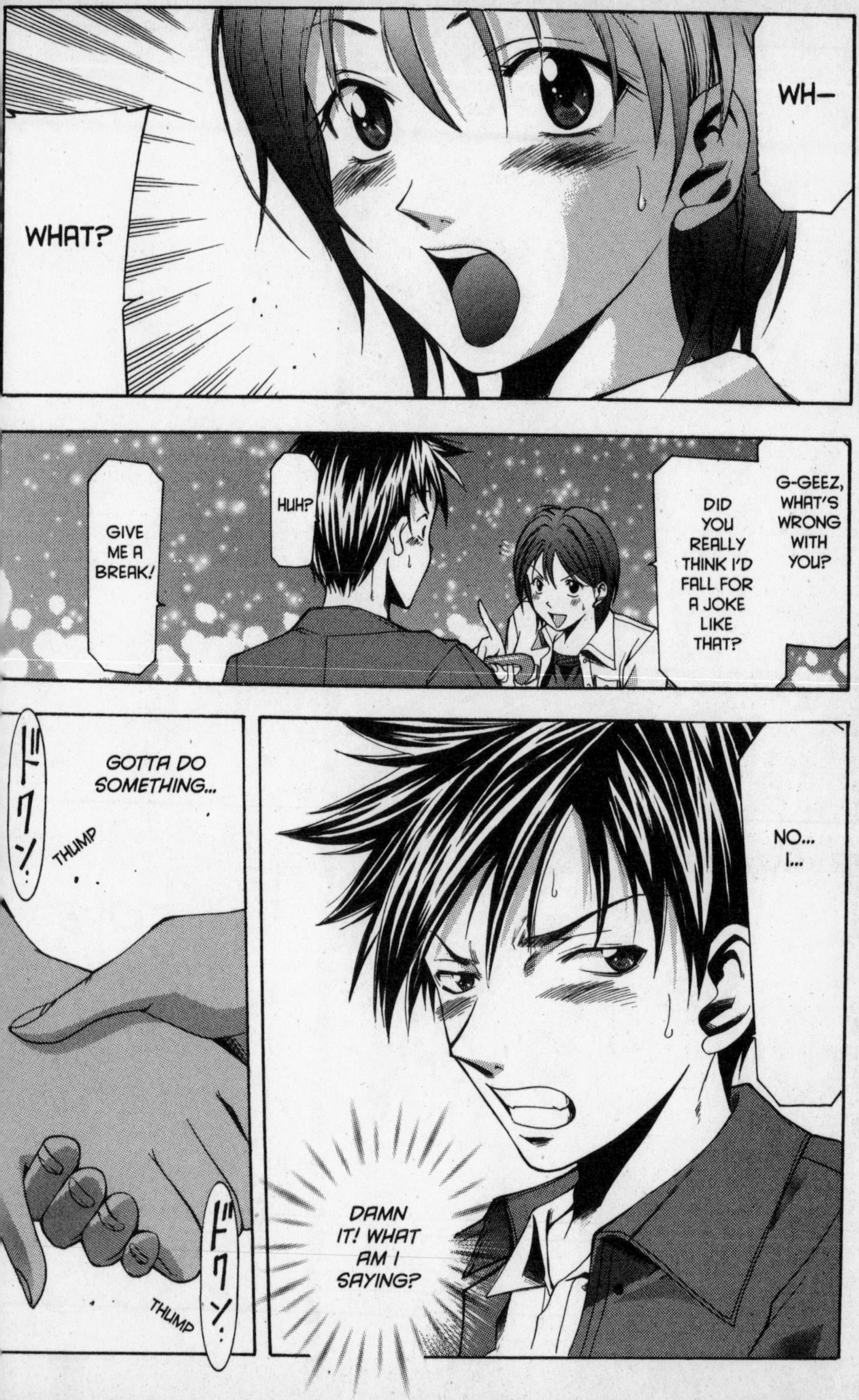
WH–
WHAT?
G-GEEZ, WHAT'S WRONG WITH YOU?
DID YOU REALLY THINK I'D FALL FOR A JOKE LIKE THAT?
HUH?
GIVE ME A BREAK!
NO... I...
DAMN IT! WHAT AM I SAYING?
GOTTA DO SOMETHING...
ドクン
THUMP
ドクン
THUMP

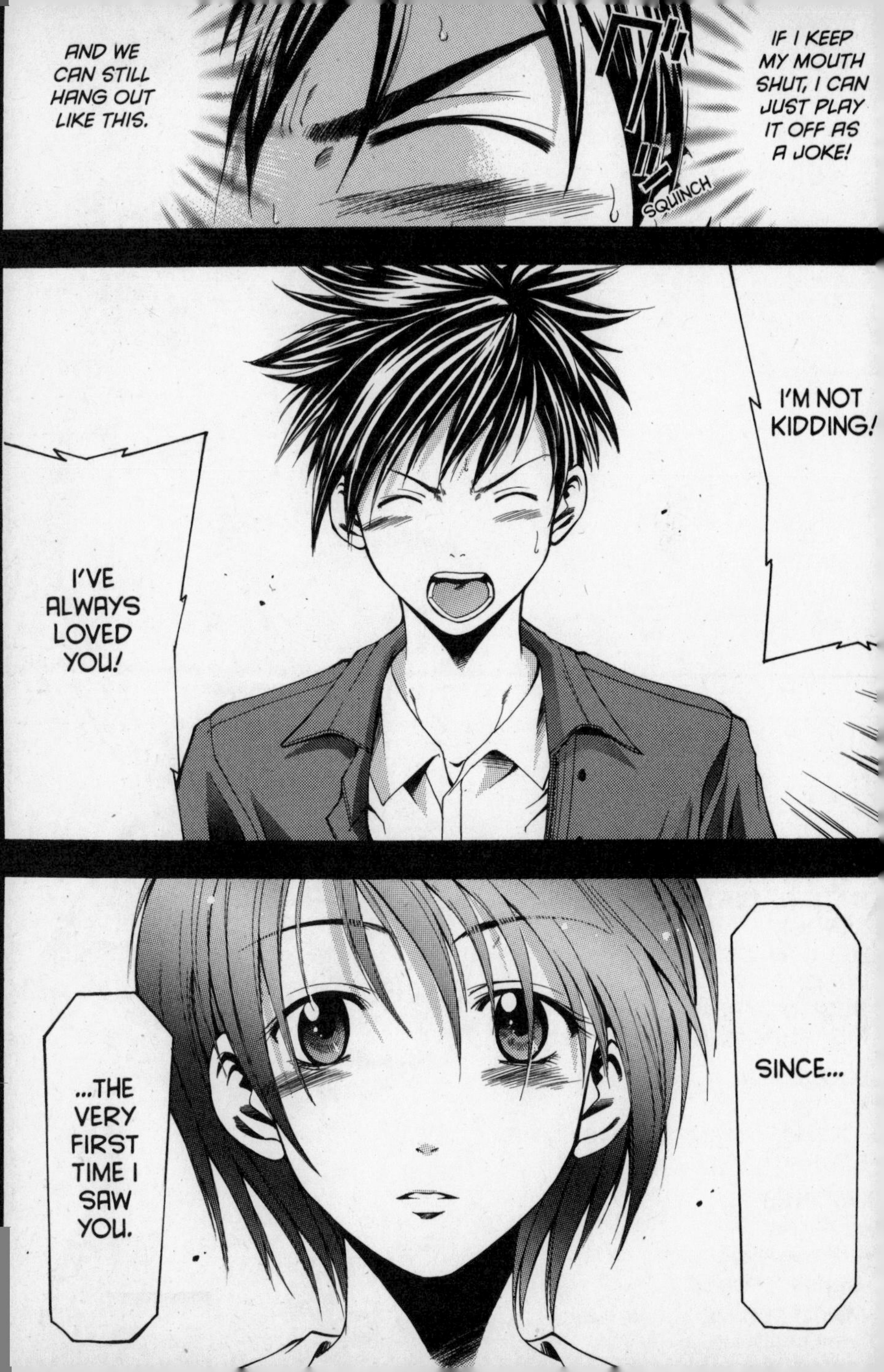
IF I KEEP MY MOUTH SHUT, I CAN JUST PLAY IT OFF AS A JOKE!
SQUINCH
AND WE CAN STILL HANG OUT LIKE THIS.
I'M NOT KIDDING!
I'VE ALWAYS LOVED YOU!
SINCE...
...THE VERY FIRST TIME I SAW YOU.

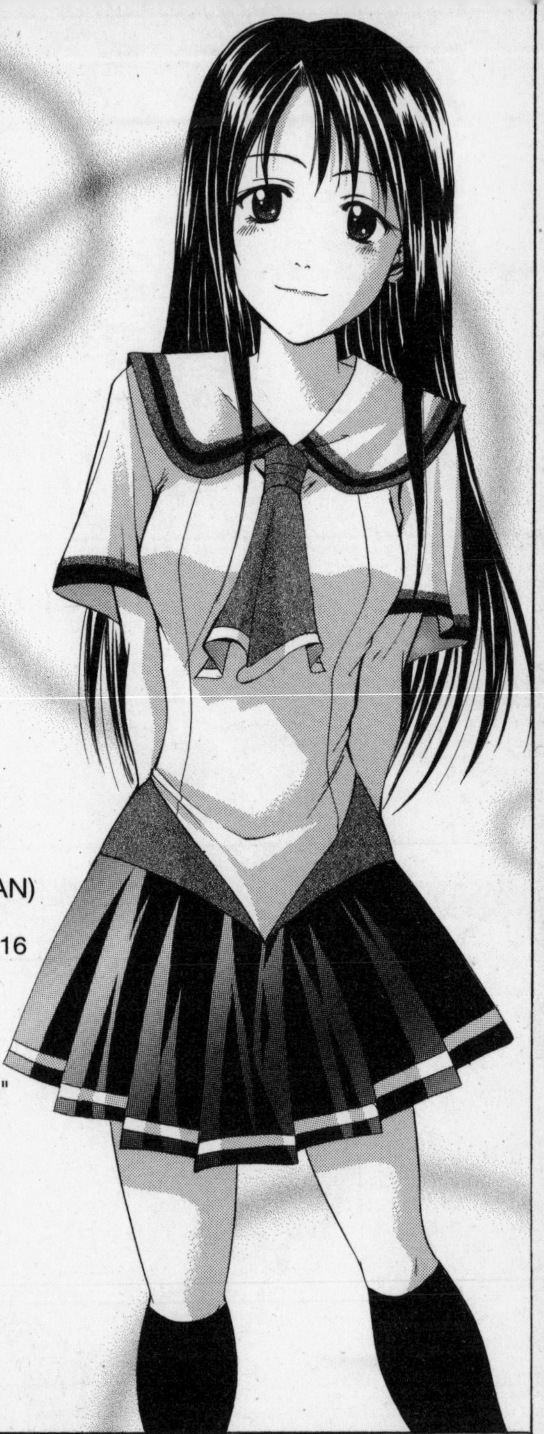

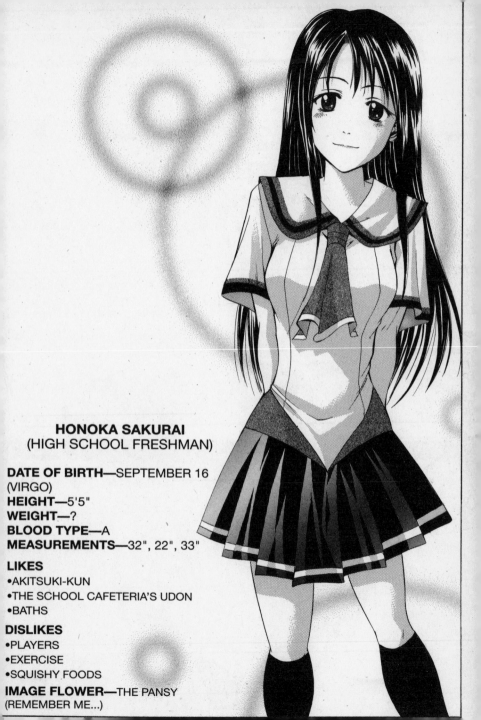

HONOKA SAKURAI
(HIGH SCHOOL FRESHMAN)

DATE OF BIRTH—SEPTEMBER 16 (VIRGO)
HEIGHT—5'5"
WEIGHT—?
BLOOD TYPE—A
MEASUREMENTS—32", 22", 33"

LIKES
- AKITSUKI-KUN
- THE SCHOOL CAFETERIA'S UDON
- BATHS

DISLIKES
- PLAYERS
- EXERCISE
- SQUISHY FOODS

IMAGE FLOWER—THE PANSY (REMEMBER ME...)

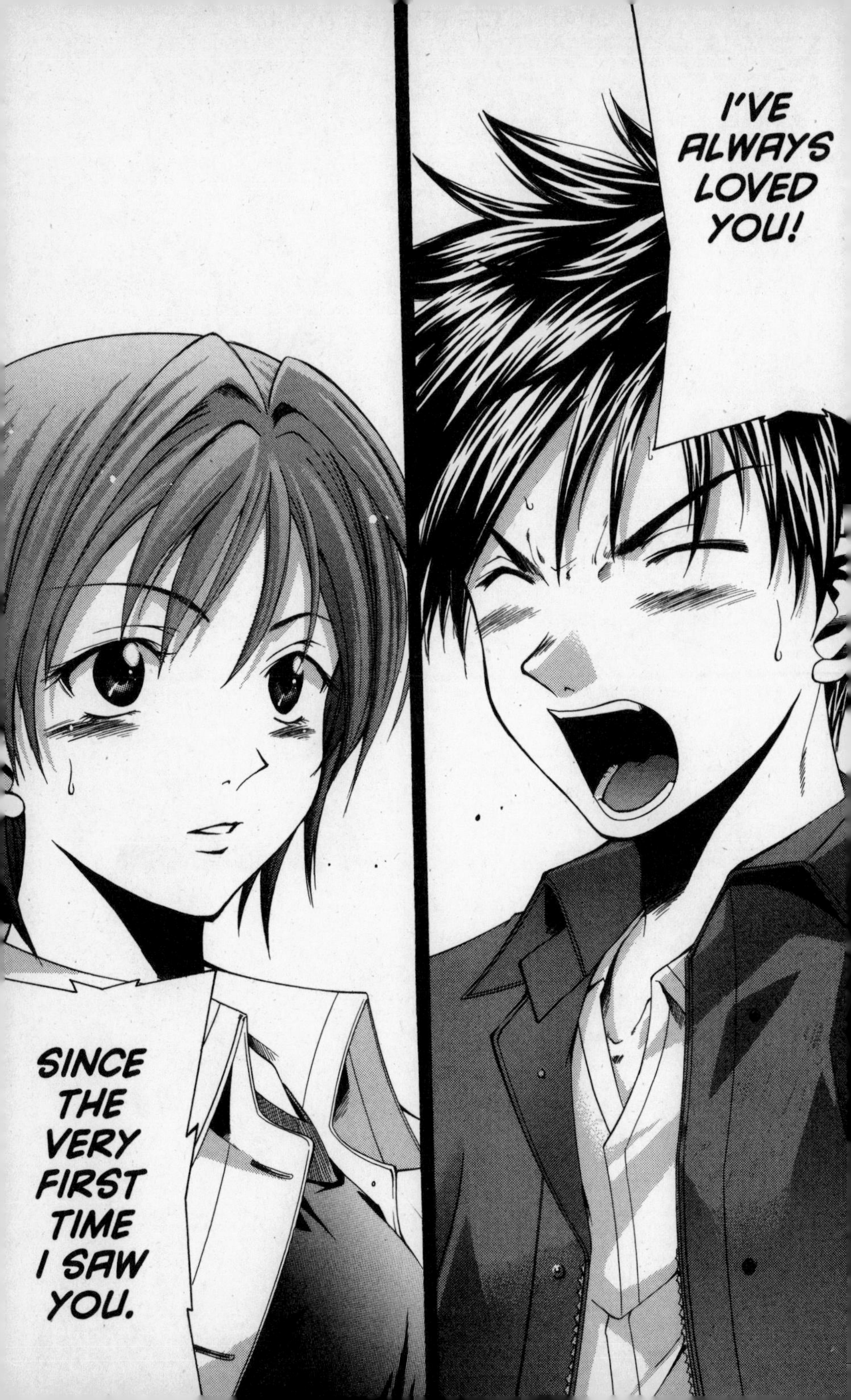
I'VE ALWAYS LOVED YOU!
SINCE THE VERY FIRST TIME I SAW YOU.

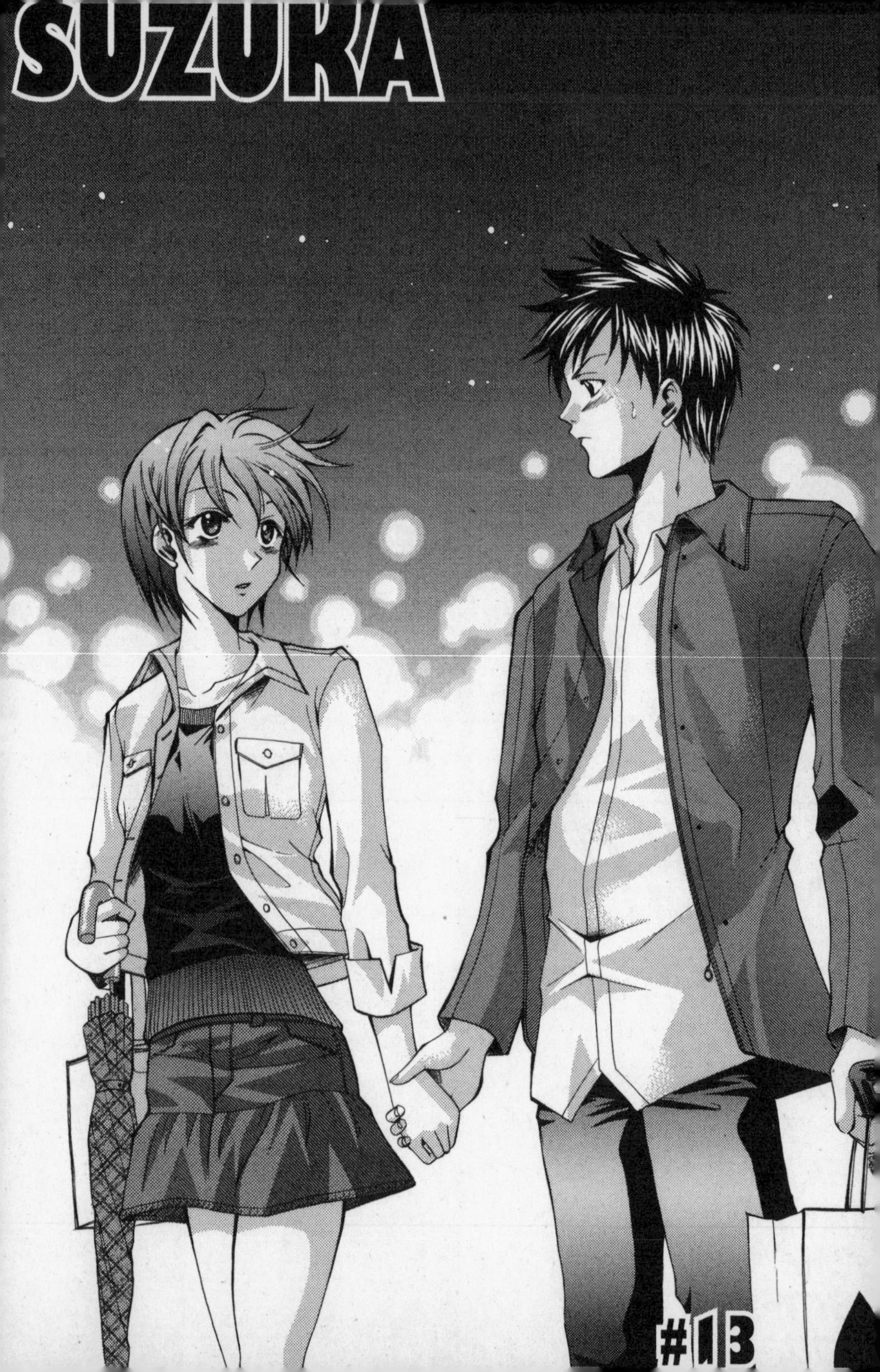
SUZUKA
#13

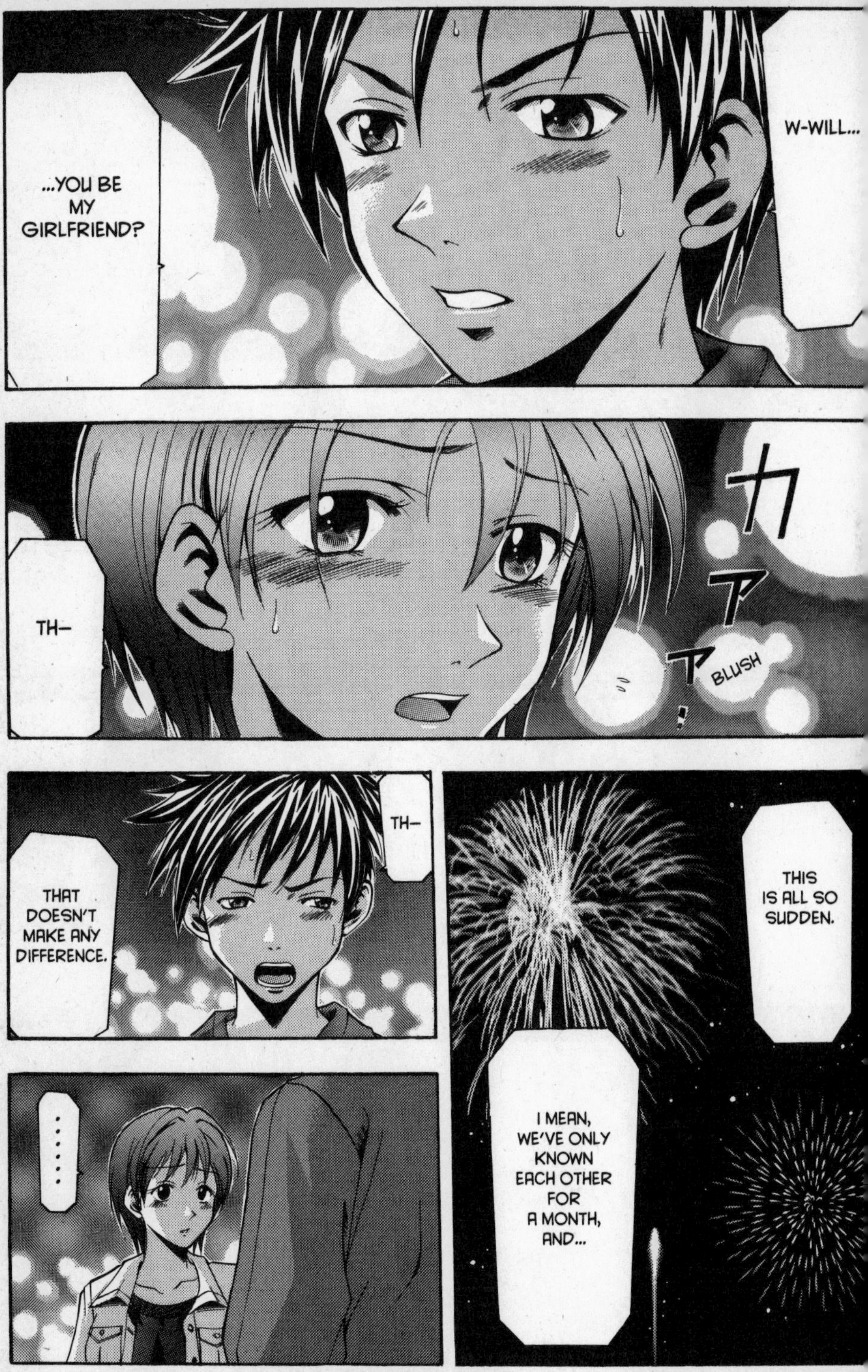
W-WILL...
...YOU BE MY GIRLFRIEND?
カァァ
BLUSH
TH–
THIS IS ALL SO SUDDEN.
I MEAN, WE'VE ONLY KNOWN EACH OTHER FOR A MONTH, AND...
TH–
THAT DOESN'T MAKE ANY DIFFERENCE.
......

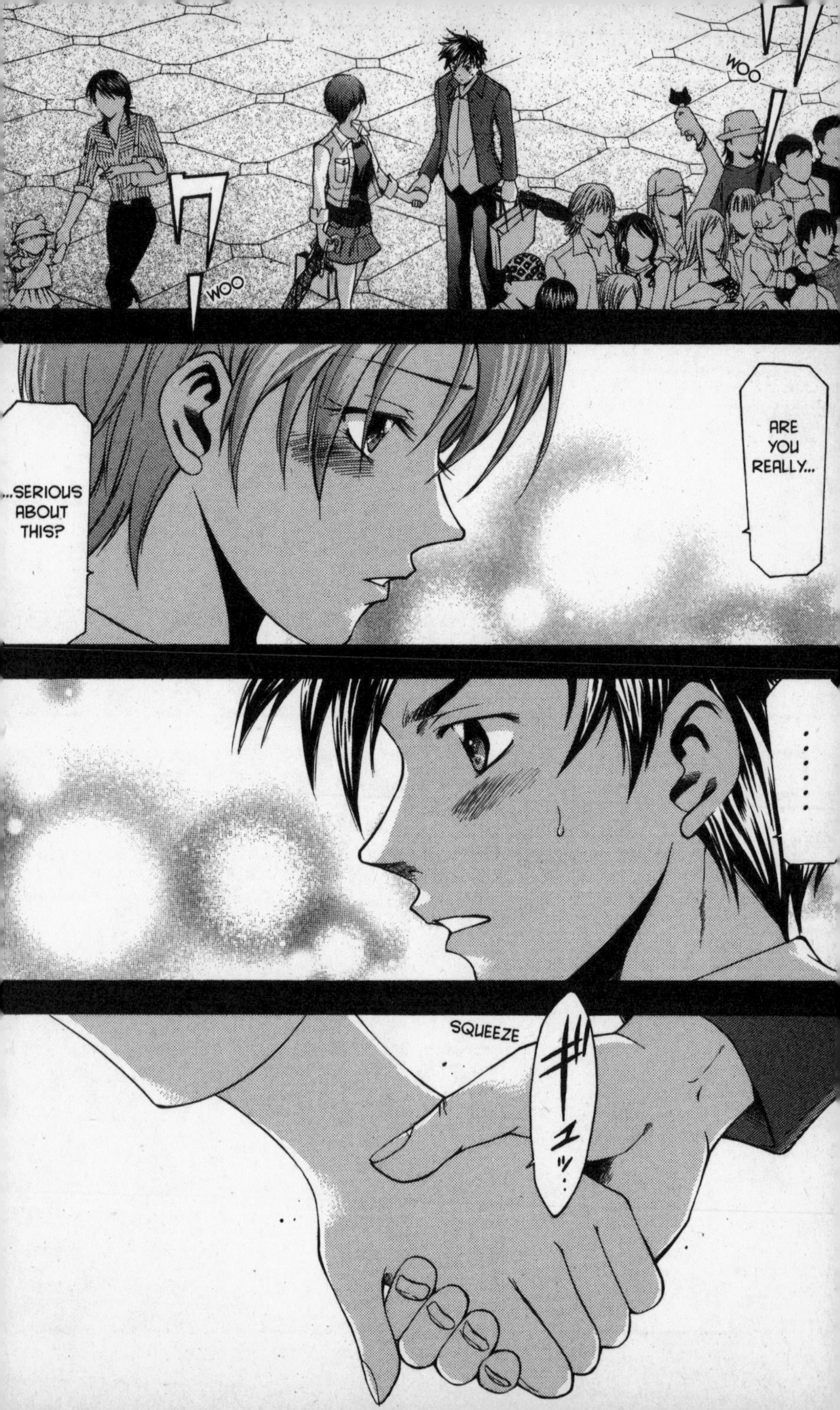
WOO
WOO
ARE YOU REALLY...
...SERIOUS ABOUT THIS?
......
SQUEEZE
ギュッ…

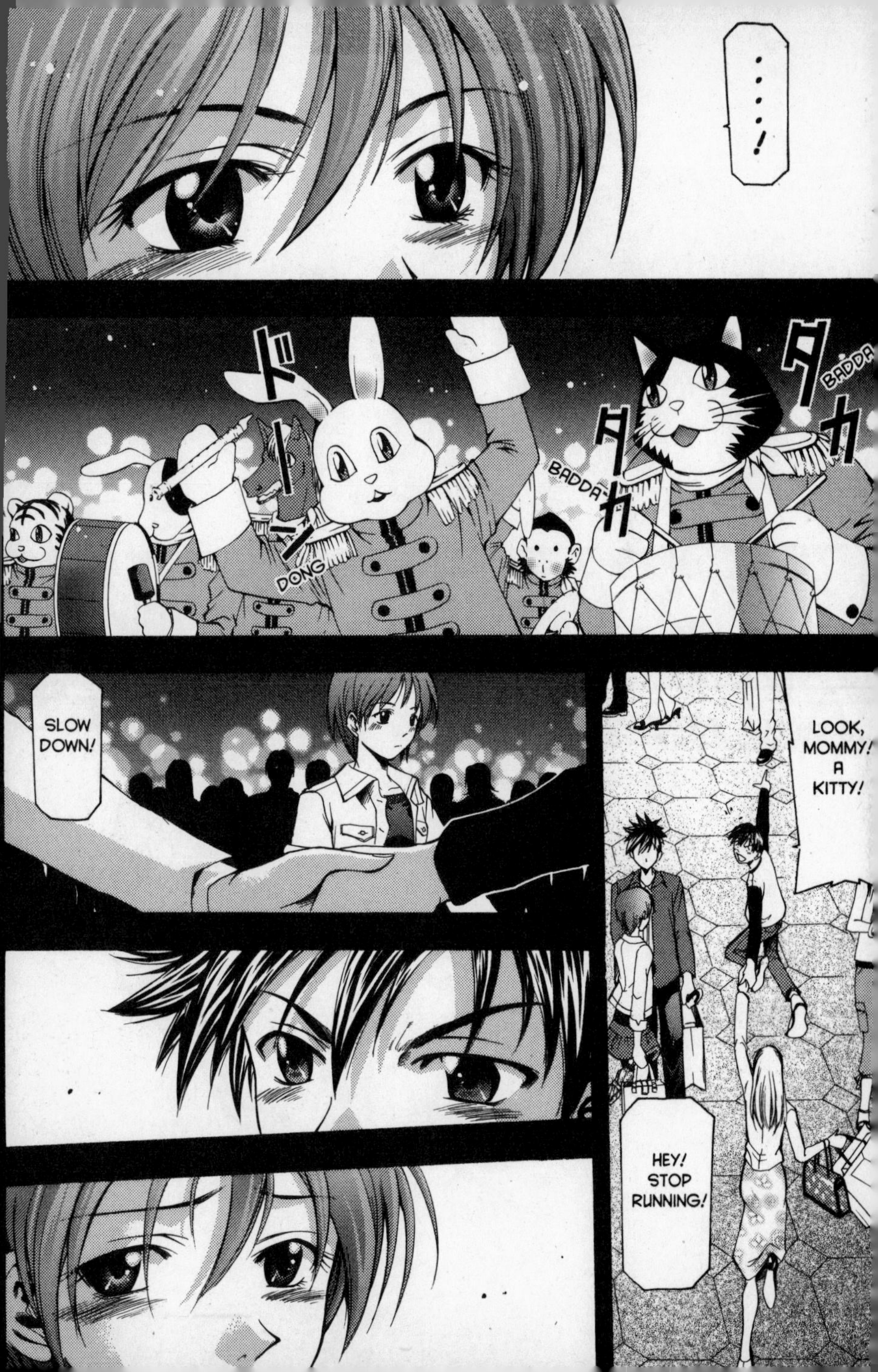
....!
タカ
BADDA
タカ
BADDA
ドーン
DONG
LOOK, MOMMY! A KITTY!
HEY! STOP RUNNING!
SLOW DOWN!

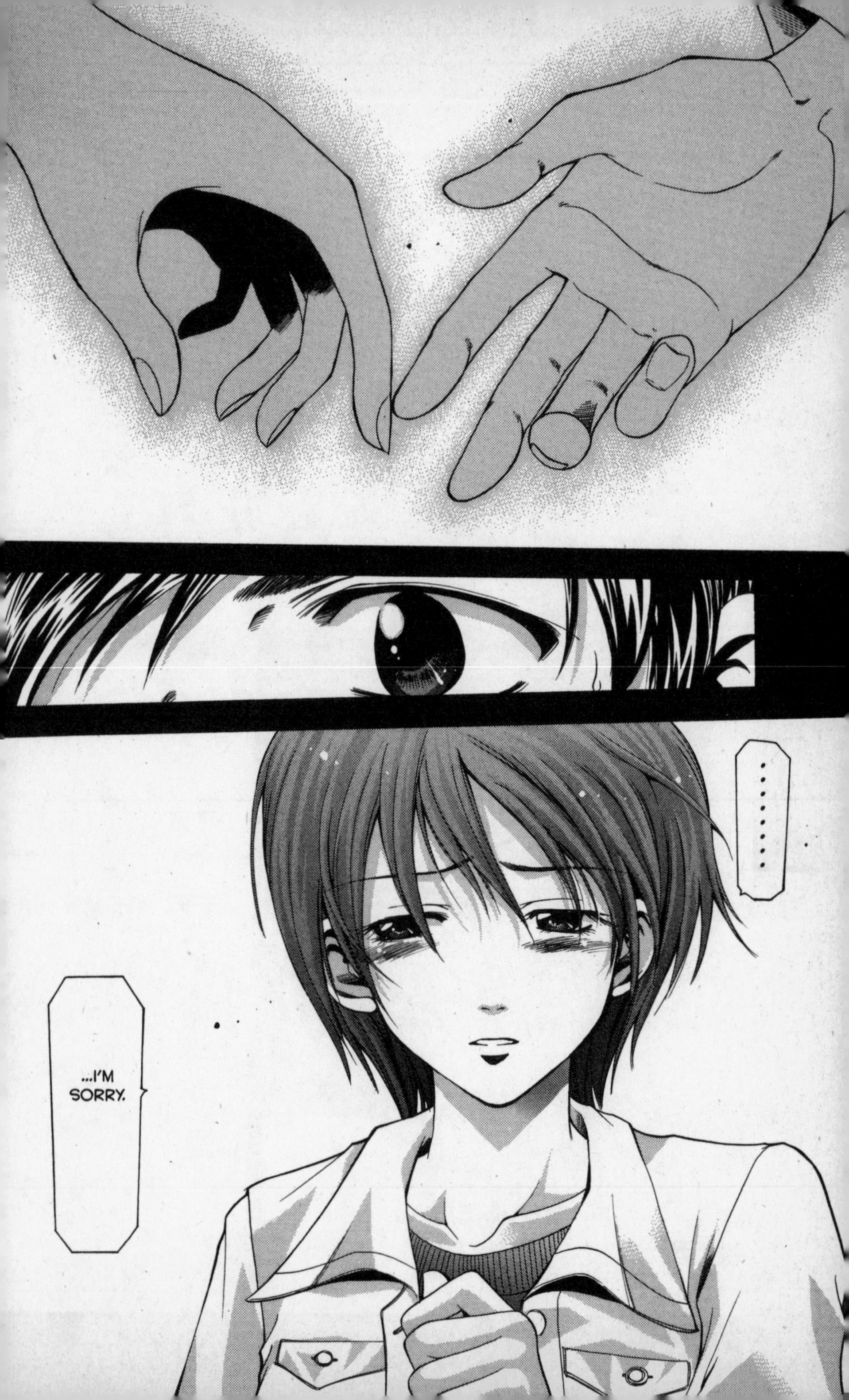
....
...I'M SORRY.

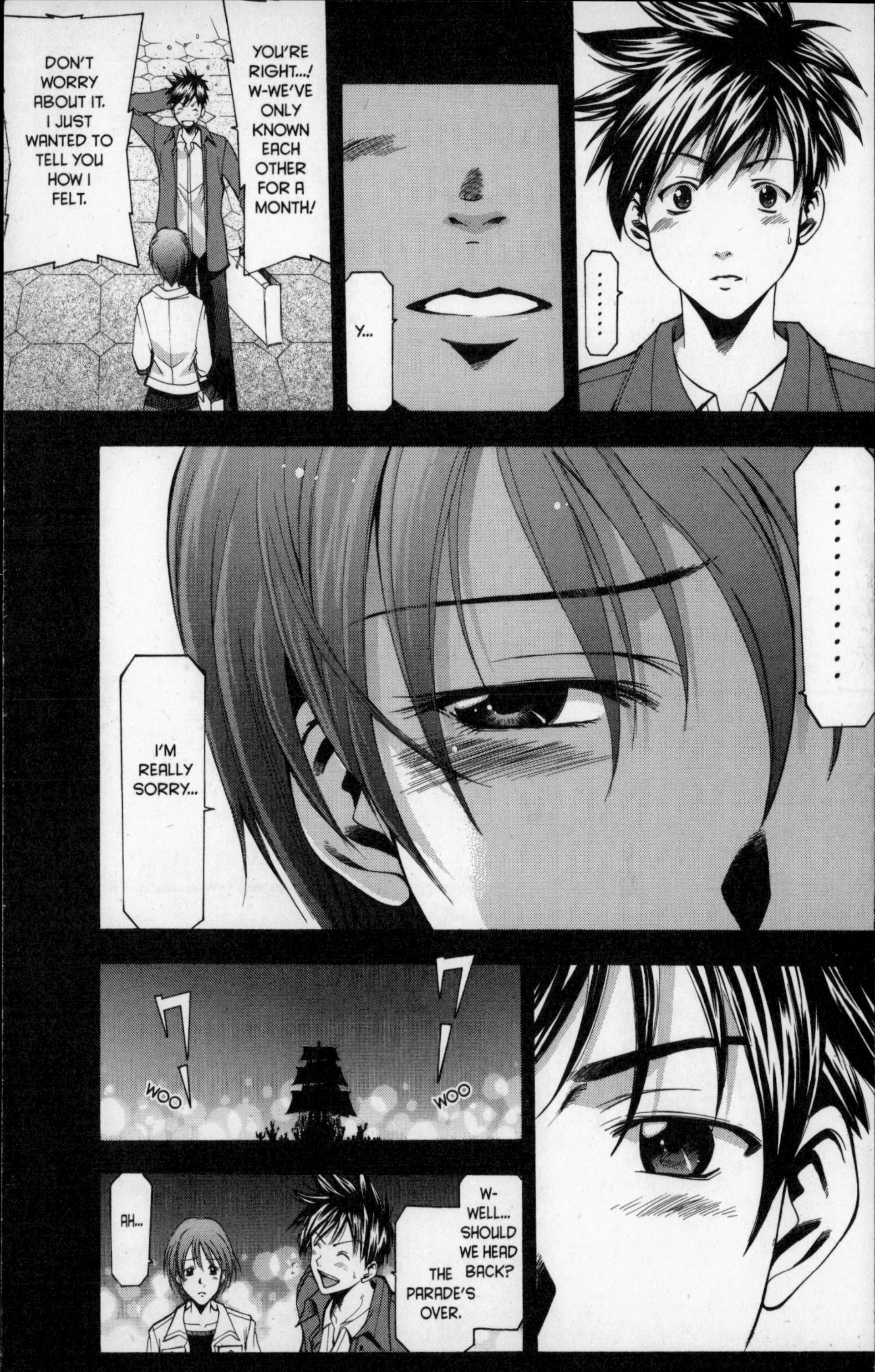
......
Y...
YOU'RE RIGHT...! W-WE'VE ONLY KNOWN EACH OTHER FOR A MONTH!
DON'T WORRY ABOUT IT. I JUST WANTED TO TELL YOU HOW I FELT.
......
I'M REALLY SORRY...
WOO
WOO
W-WELL... SHOULD WE HEAD BACK? THE PARADE'S OVER.
AH...

I'LL... CARRY THE BAG...

HUH?

IT'S NOT THAT HEAVY.

TH-THAT'S OKAY.

YEAH, BUT...

...YOU SHOULDN'T HAVE TO CARRY IT.

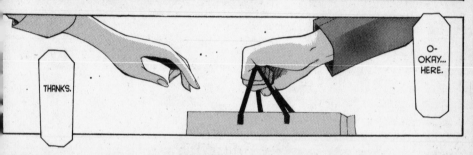

THANKS.

O-OKAY... HERE.

STEP

STEP

ASAHIYU BATHS

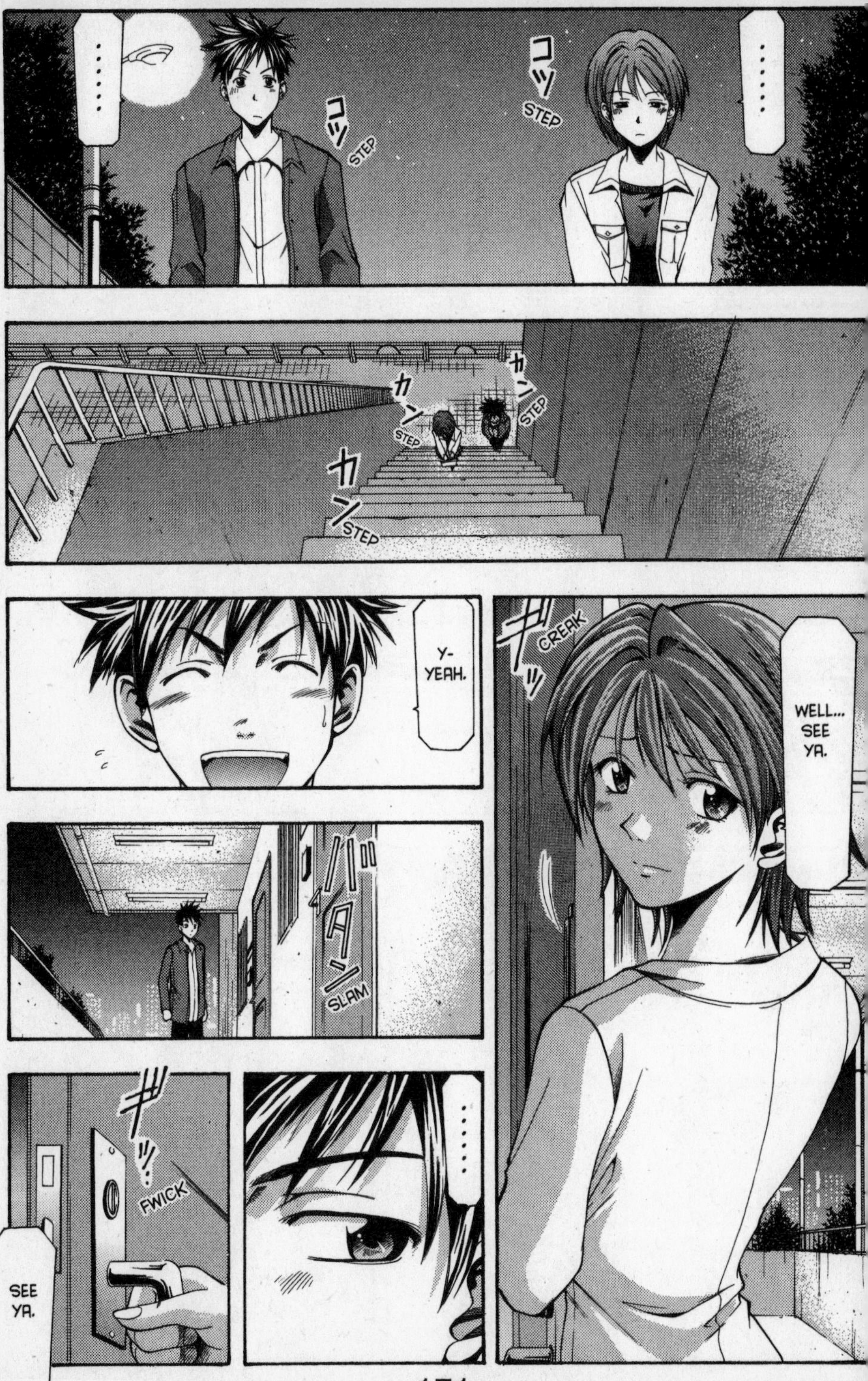
......
コツ
STEP
コツ
STEP
......
カン
STEP
カン
STEP
カン
STEP
ギッ
CREAK
WELL... SEE YA.
Y-YEAH.
バタン
SLAM
......
ギッ
FWICK
SEE YA.

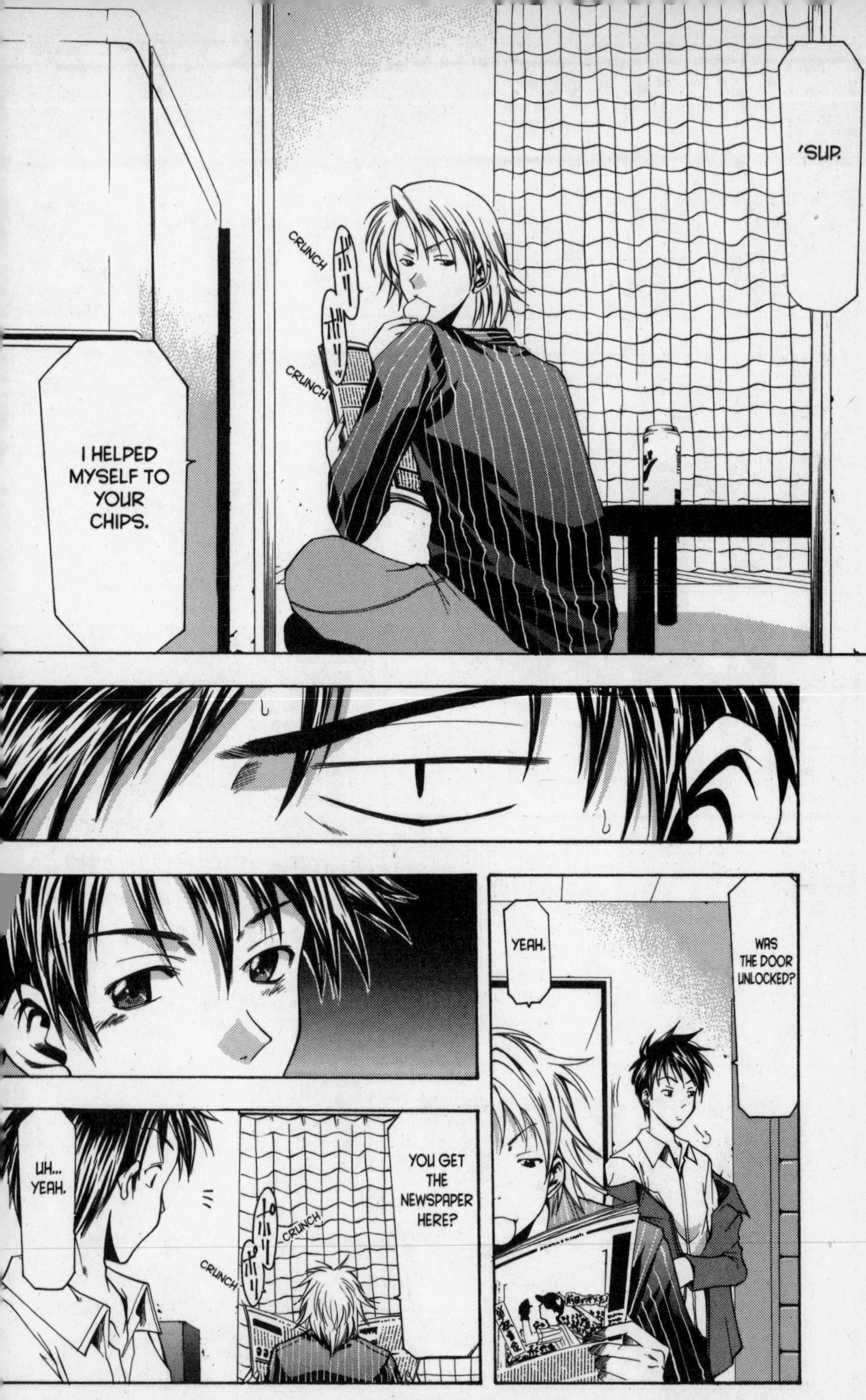
'SUP.
ポリ ポリッ
CRUNCH
CRUNCH
I HELPED MYSELF TO YOUR CHIPS.
WAS THE DOOR UNLOCKED?
YEAH.
YOU GET THE NEWSPAPER HERE?
ポリ ポリ
CRUNCH
CRUNCH
UH... YEAH.

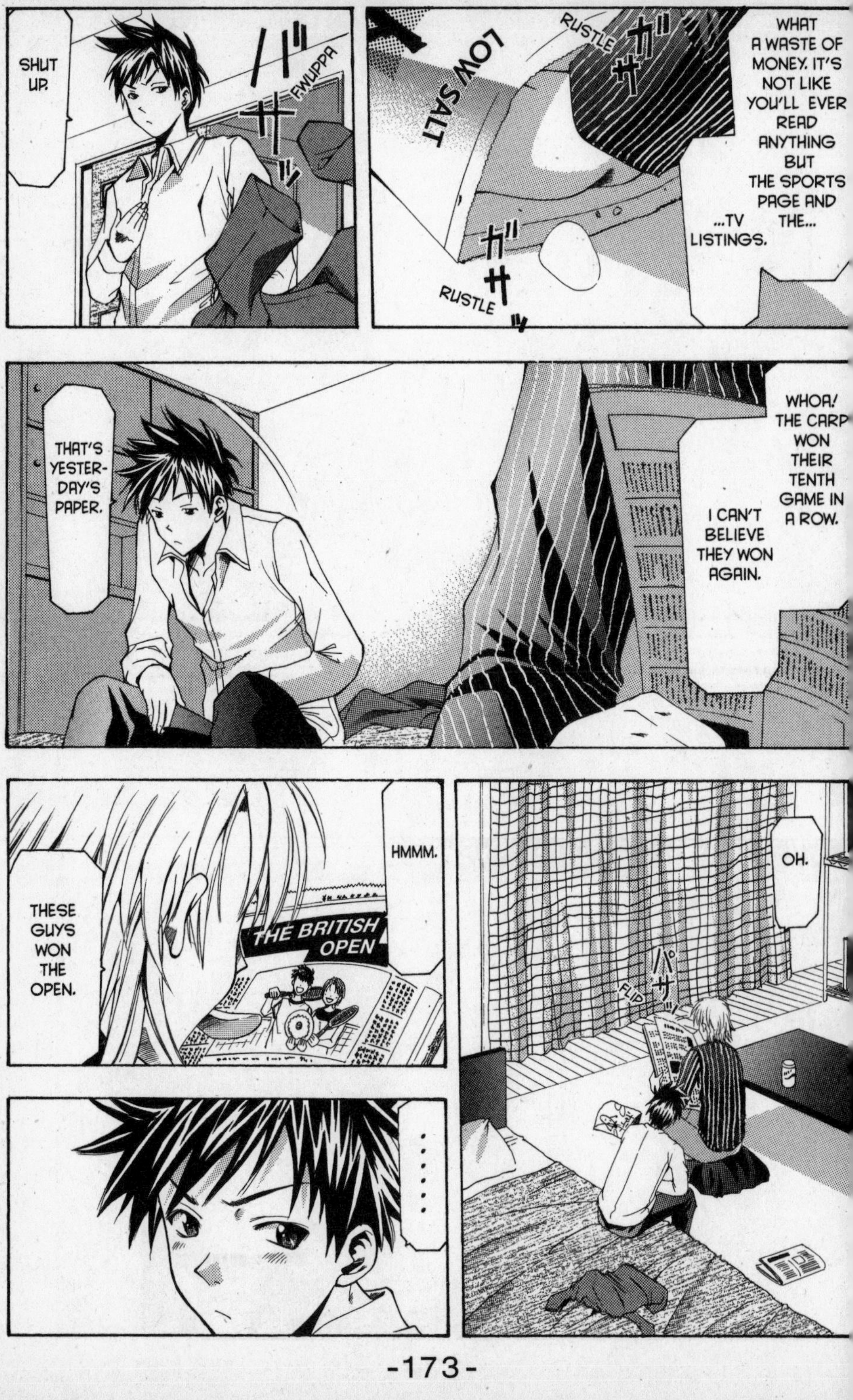
RUSTLE
LOW SALT
WHAT A WASTE OF MONEY. IT'S NOT LIKE YOU'LL EVER READ ANYTHING BUT THE SPORTS PAGE AND THE...
...TV LISTINGS.
RUSTLE
SHUT UP.
FWUPPA
WHOA! THE CARP WON THEIR TENTH GAME IN A ROW.
I CAN'T BELIEVE THEY WON AGAIN.
THAT'S YESTER-DAY'S PAPER.
OH.
FLIP
HMMM.
THESE GUYS WON THE OPEN.
THE BRITISH OPEN
......

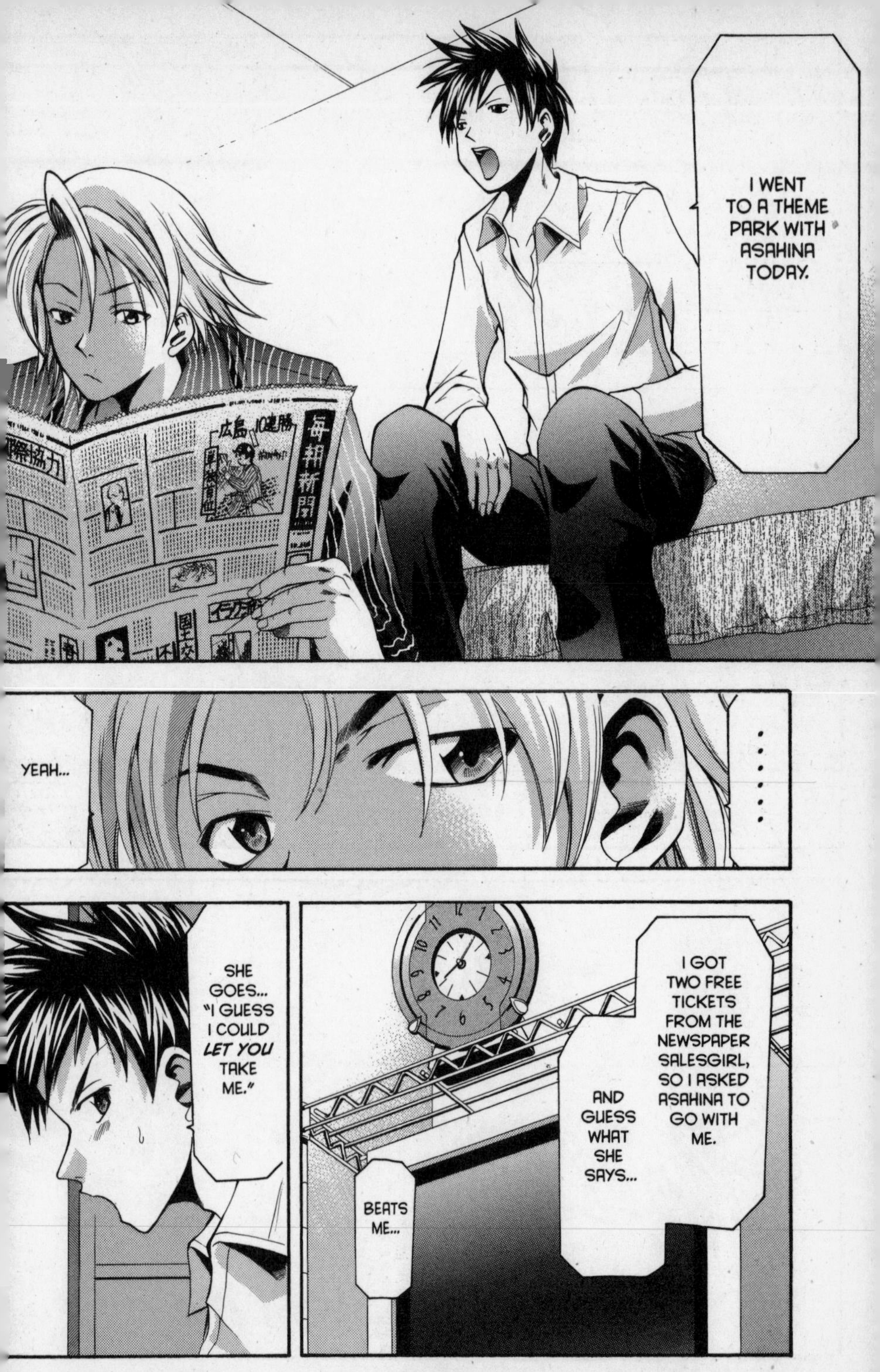
I WENT TO A THEME PARK WITH ASAHINA TODAY.
毎朝新聞
......
YEAH...
I GOT TWO FREE TICKETS FROM THE NEWSPAPER SALESGIRL, SO I ASKED ASAHINA TO GO WITH ME.
AND GUESS WHAT SHE SAYS...
BEATS ME...
SHE GOES... "I GUESS I COULD *LET YOU* TAKE ME."

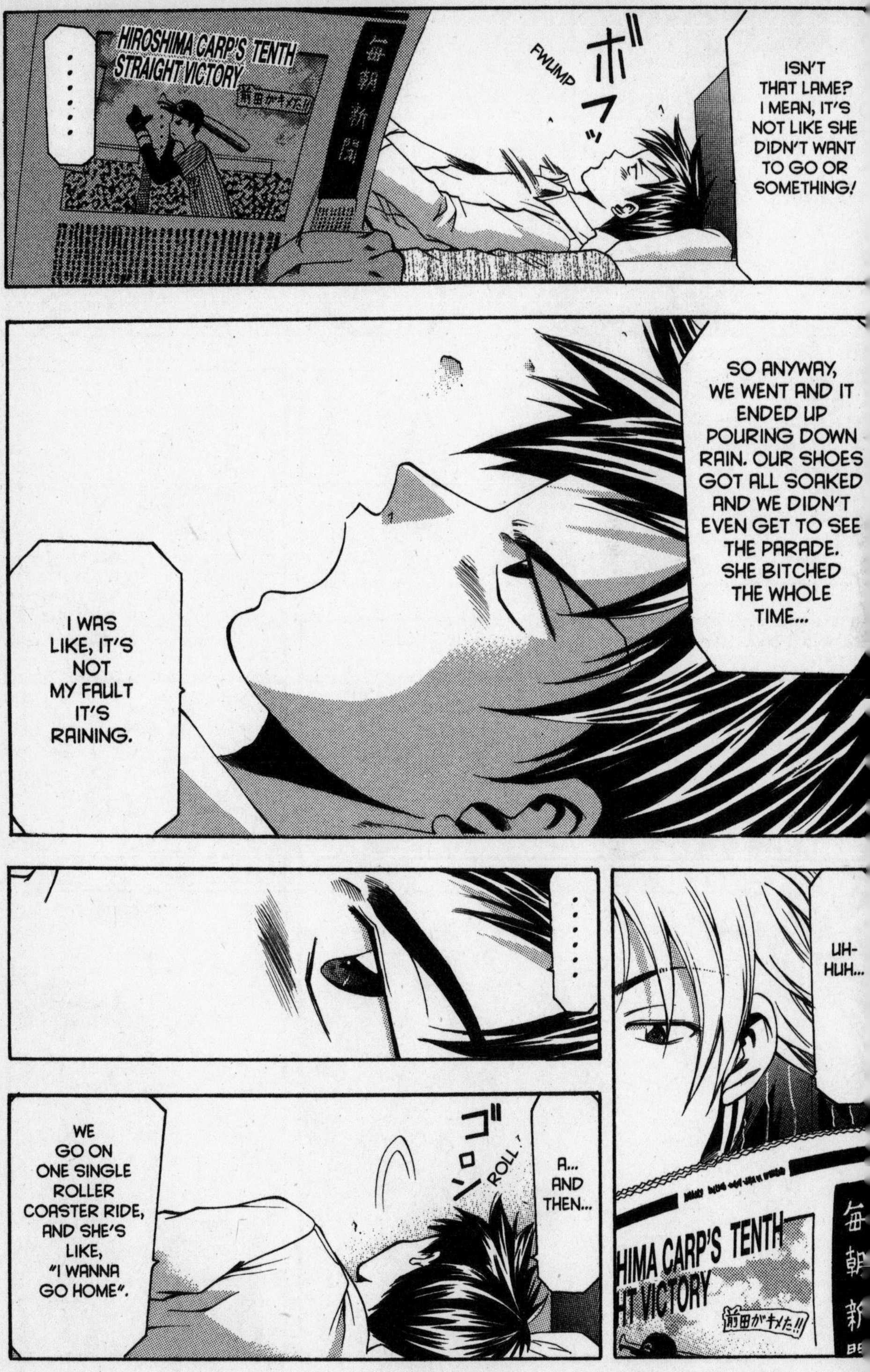
ISN'T THAT LAME? I MEAN, IT'S NOT LIKE SHE DIDN'T WANT TO GO OR SOMETHING!
ボフッ
FWUMP
毎朝新聞
HIROSHIMA CARP'S TENTH STRAIGHT VICTORY
前田がキメた!!
......
SO ANYWAY, WE WENT AND IT ENDED UP POURING DOWN RAIN. OUR SHOES GOT ALL SOAKED AND WE DIDN'T EVEN GET TO SEE THE PARADE. SHE BITCHED THE WHOLE TIME...
I WAS LIKE, IT'S NOT MY FAULT IT'S RAINING.
UH-HUH...
毎朝新
HIMA CARP'S TENTH
HT VICTORY
前田がキメた!!
......
A... AND THEN...
ゴロン
ROLL
WE GO ON ONE SINGLE ROLLER COASTER RIDE, AND SHE'S LIKE, "I WANNA GO HOME".

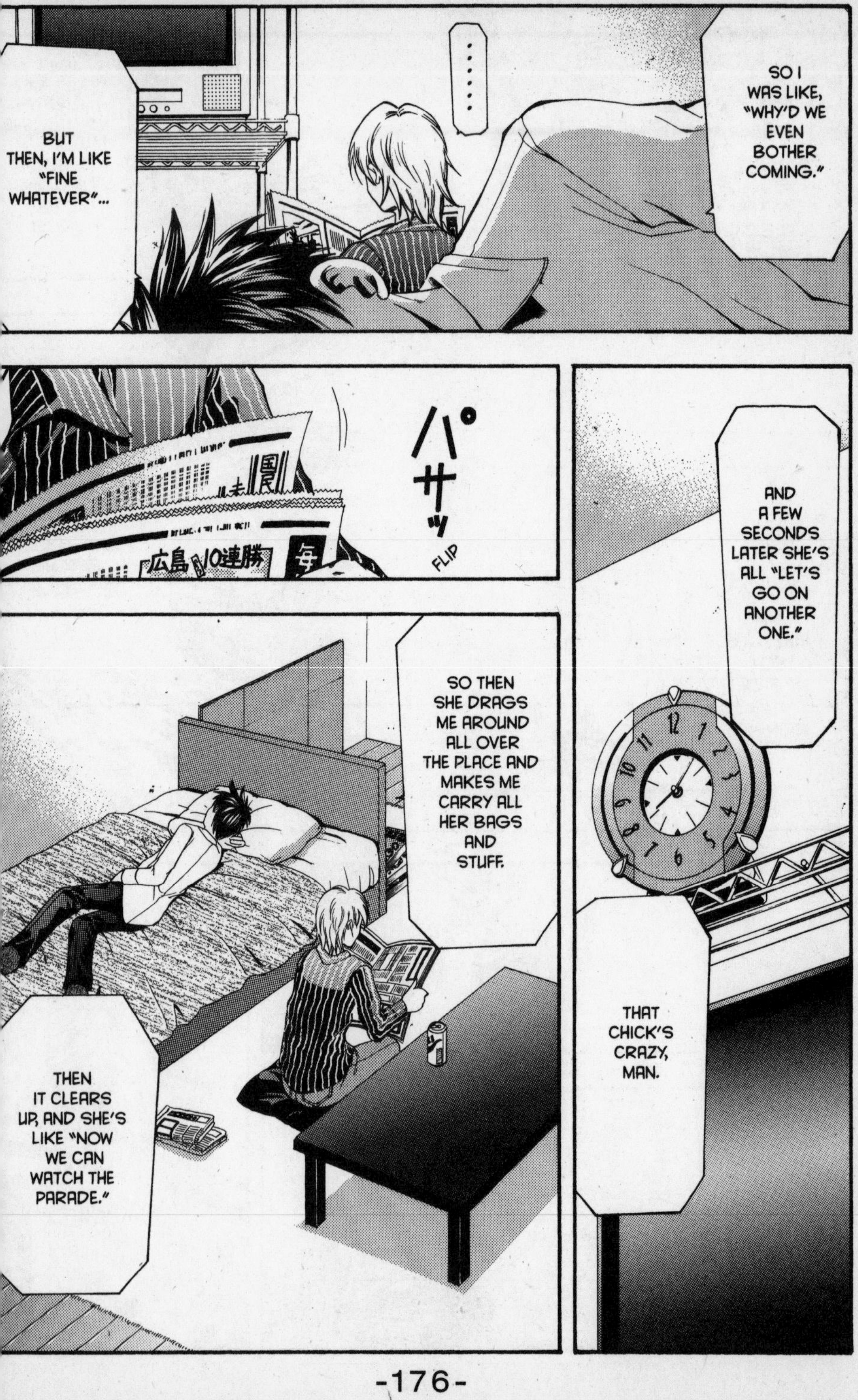
SO I WAS LIKE, "WHY'D WE EVEN BOTHER COMING."
......
BUT THEN, I'M LIKE "FINE WHATEVER"...
AND A FEW SECONDS LATER SHE'S ALL "LET'S GO ON ANOTHER ONE."
THAT CHICK'S CRAZY, MAN.
パサッ
FLIP
広島 10連勝
SO THEN SHE DRAGS ME AROUND ALL OVER THE PLACE AND MAKES ME CARRY ALL HER BAGS AND STUFF.
THEN IT CLEARS UP, AND SHE'S LIKE "NOW WE CAN WATCH THE PARADE."

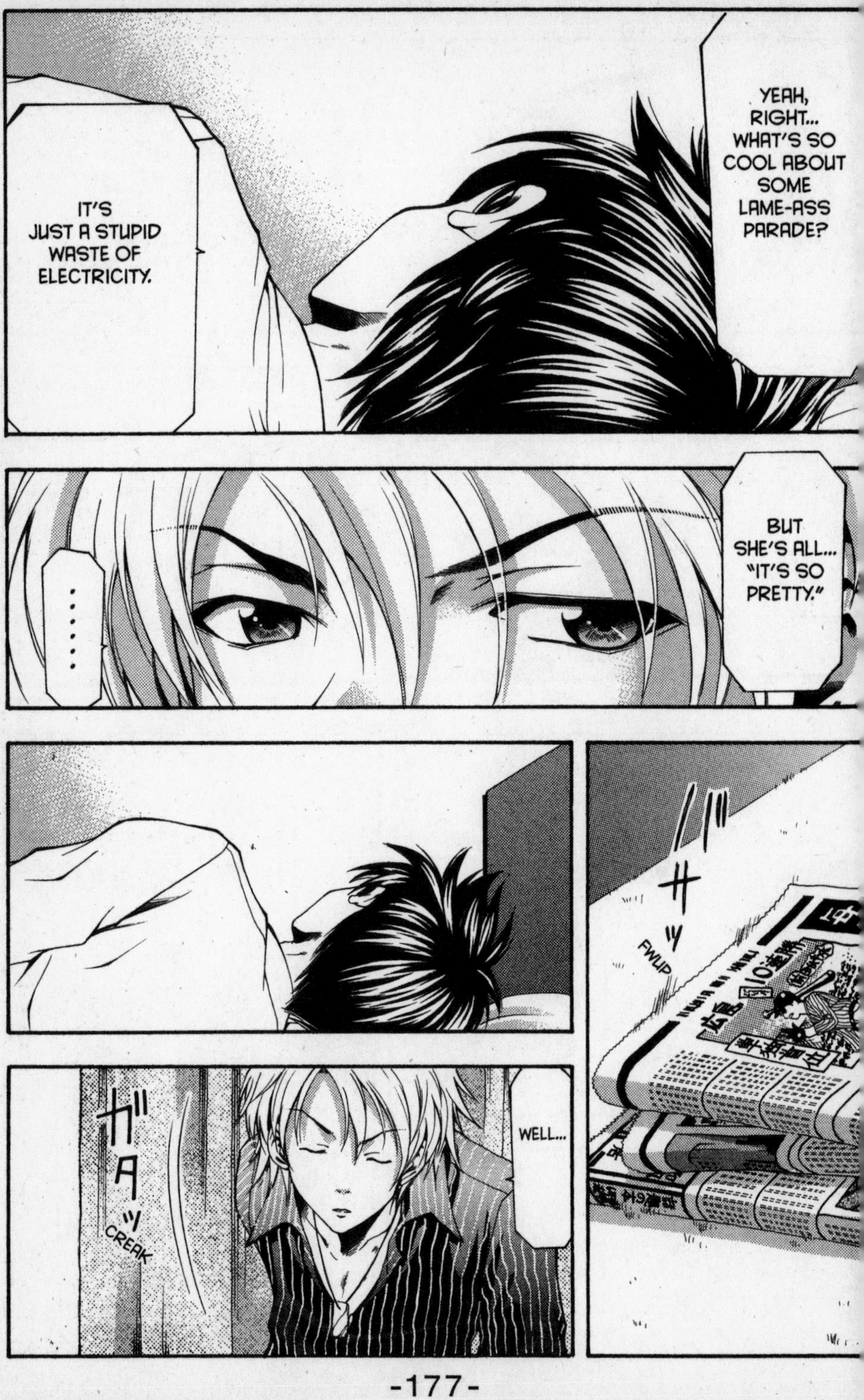
YEAH, RIGHT... WHAT'S SO COOL ABOUT SOME LAME-ASS PARADE?
IT'S JUST A STUPID WASTE OF ELECTRICITY.
BUT SHE'S ALL... "IT'S SO PRETTY."
......
バサッ
FWUP
WELL...
ガタッ
CREAK

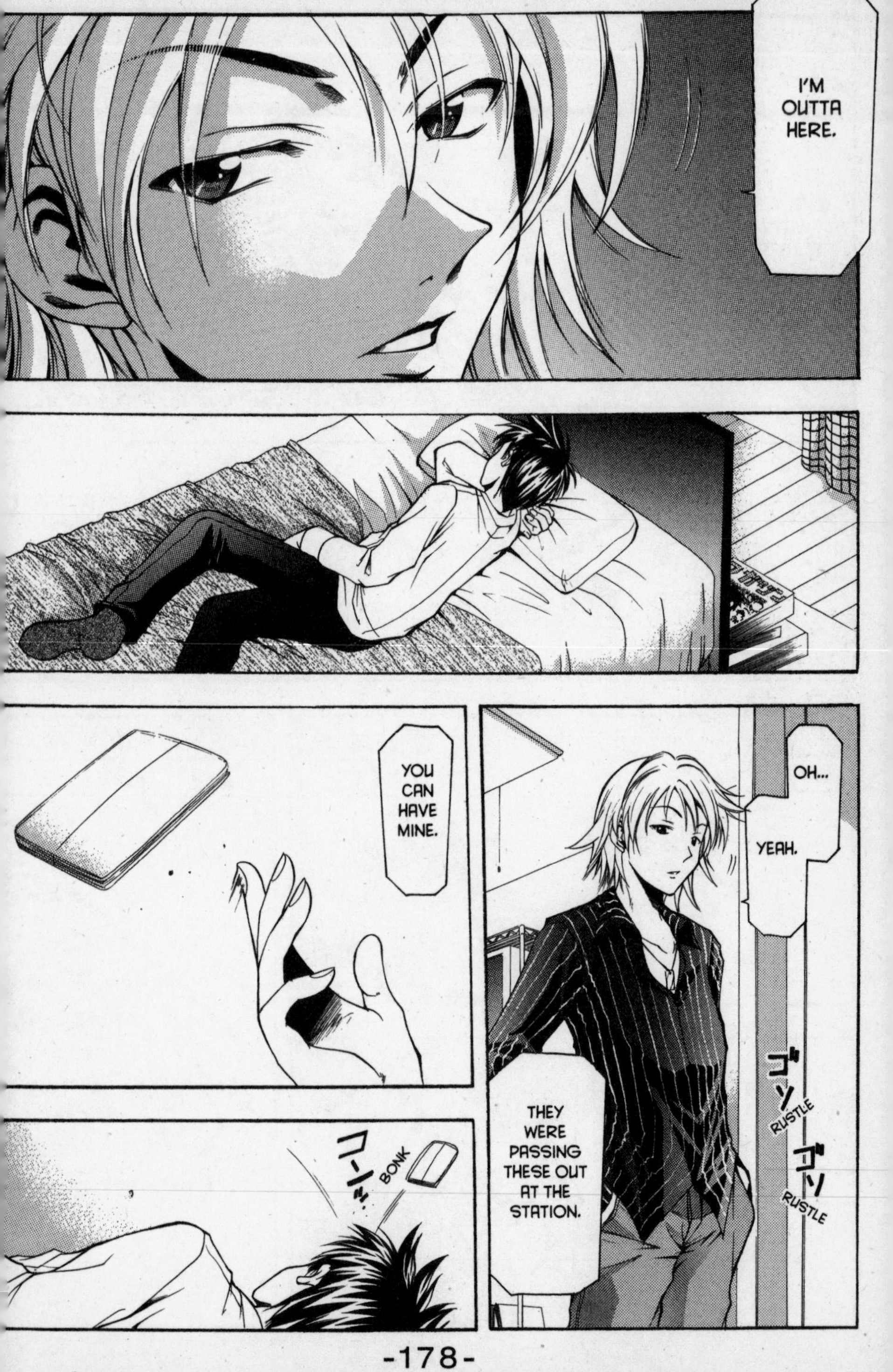
I'M OUTTA HERE.
OH...
YEAH.
ゴソ
RUSTLE
ゴソ
RUSTLE
THEY WERE PASSING THESE OUT AT THE STATION.
YOU CAN HAVE MINE.
コーン
BONK

LATER.
CREAK
DON'T FORGET TO LOCK THE DOOR.
SLAM
STEP
STEP
STEP
TRY AIBURU!
GIVE US A CALL. WOOF.
03-3XXX-00XX
042-5XX-52XX
TCH...
WHAT DO I NEED WITH YOUR STUPID TISSUES?
SCHWIK

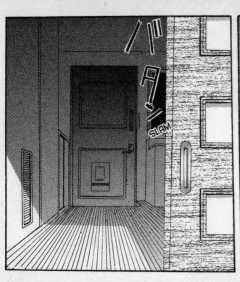

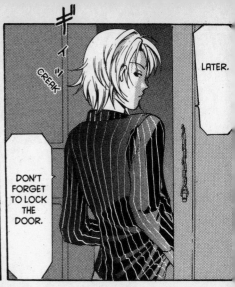

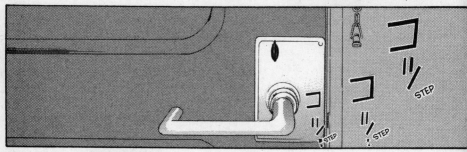

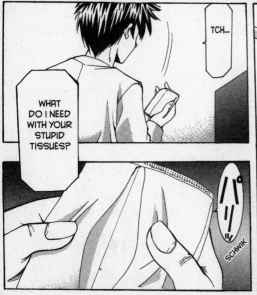

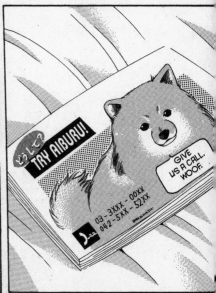

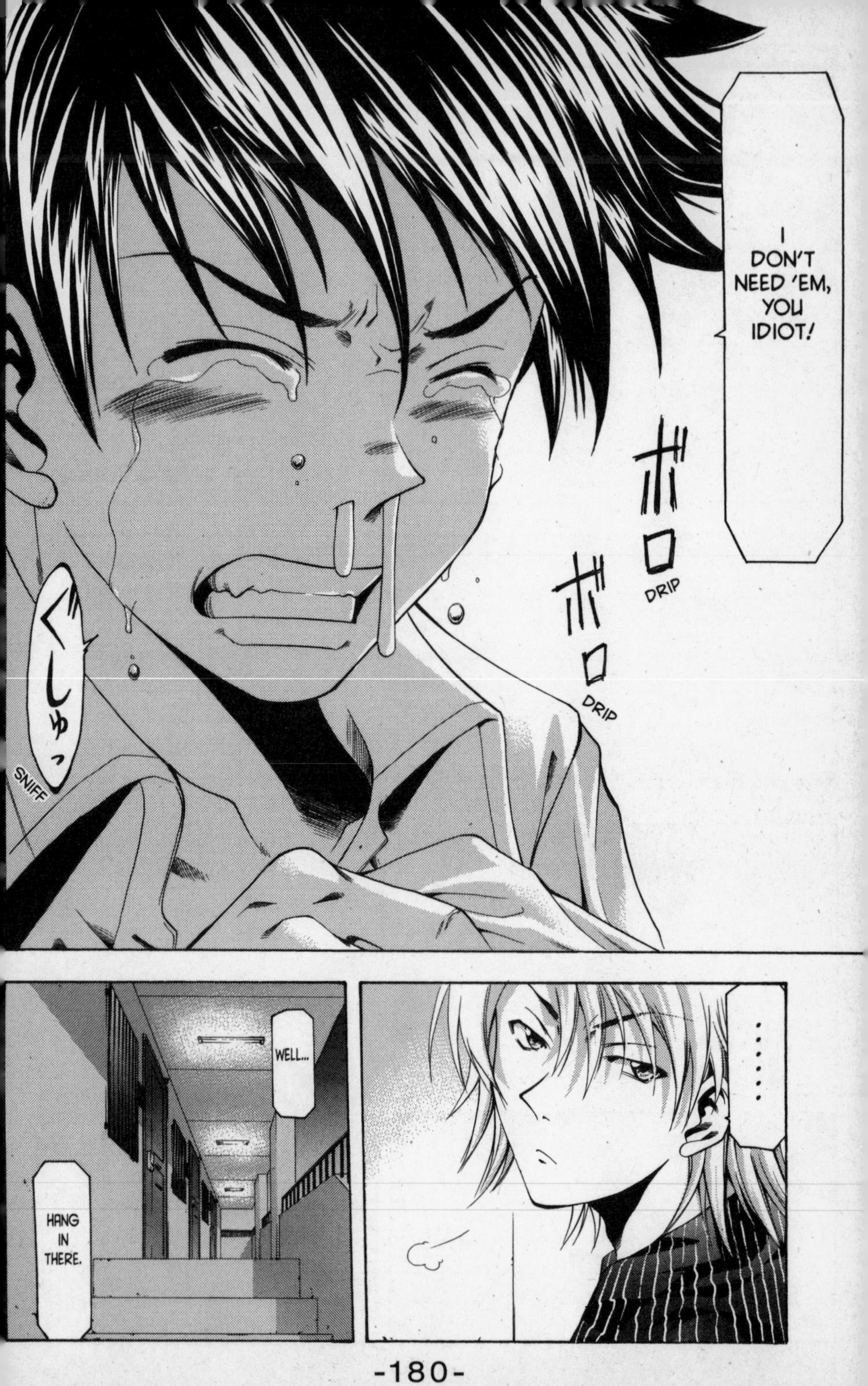
I DON'T NEED 'EM, YOU IDIOT!
ボロ
DRIP
ボロ
DRIP
ぐしゅっ
SNIFF
......
WELL...
HANG IN THERE.

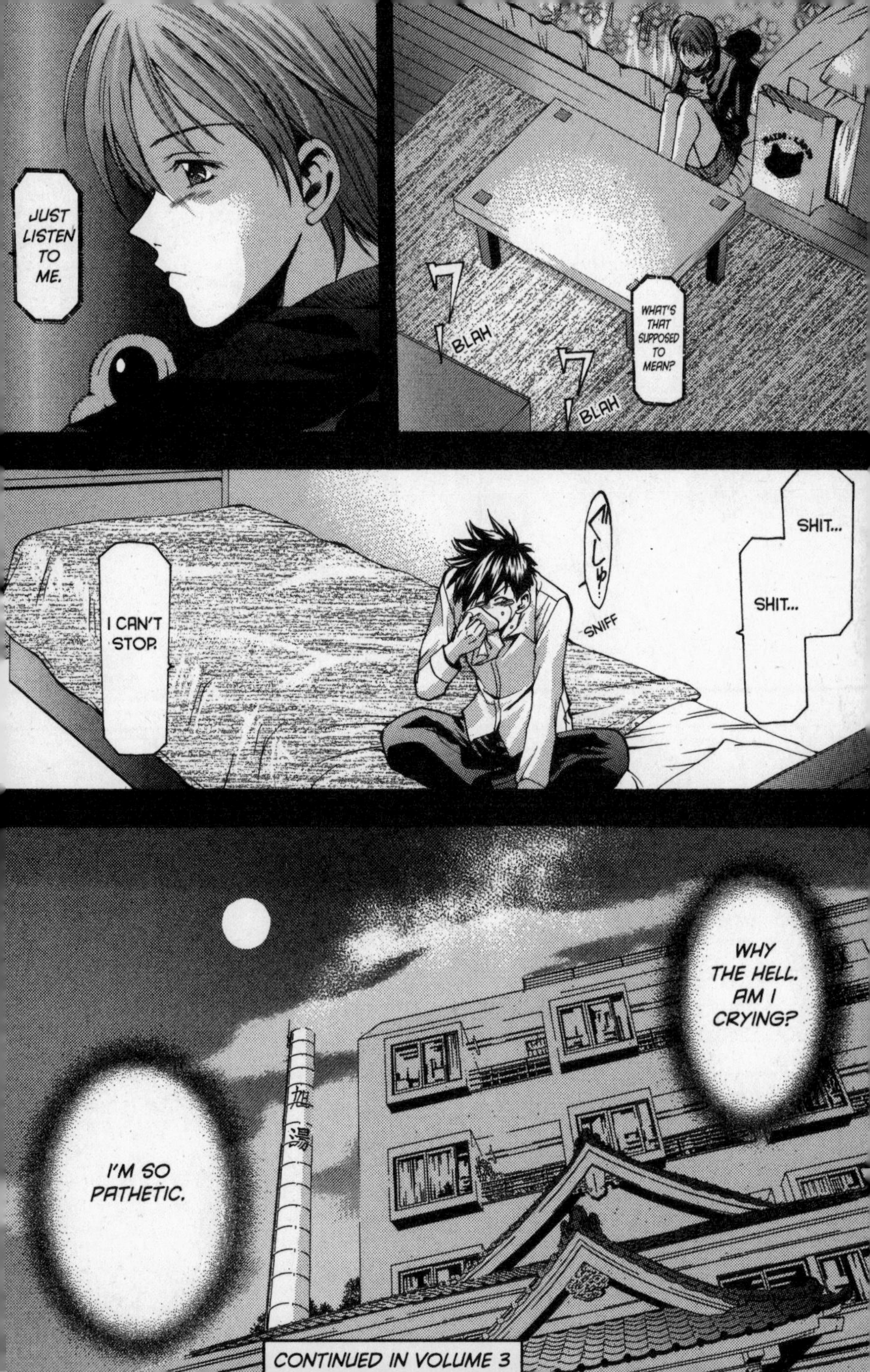
WHAT'S THAT SUPPOSED TO MEAN?
BLAH
BLAH
JUST LISTEN TO ME.
SHIT...
SHIT...
SNIFF
I CAN'T STOP.
WHY THE HELL. AM I CRYING?
I'M SO PATHETIC.
CONTINUED IN VOLUME 3

BONUS MANGA—A WEEK IN THE LIFE OF KOUJI SEO

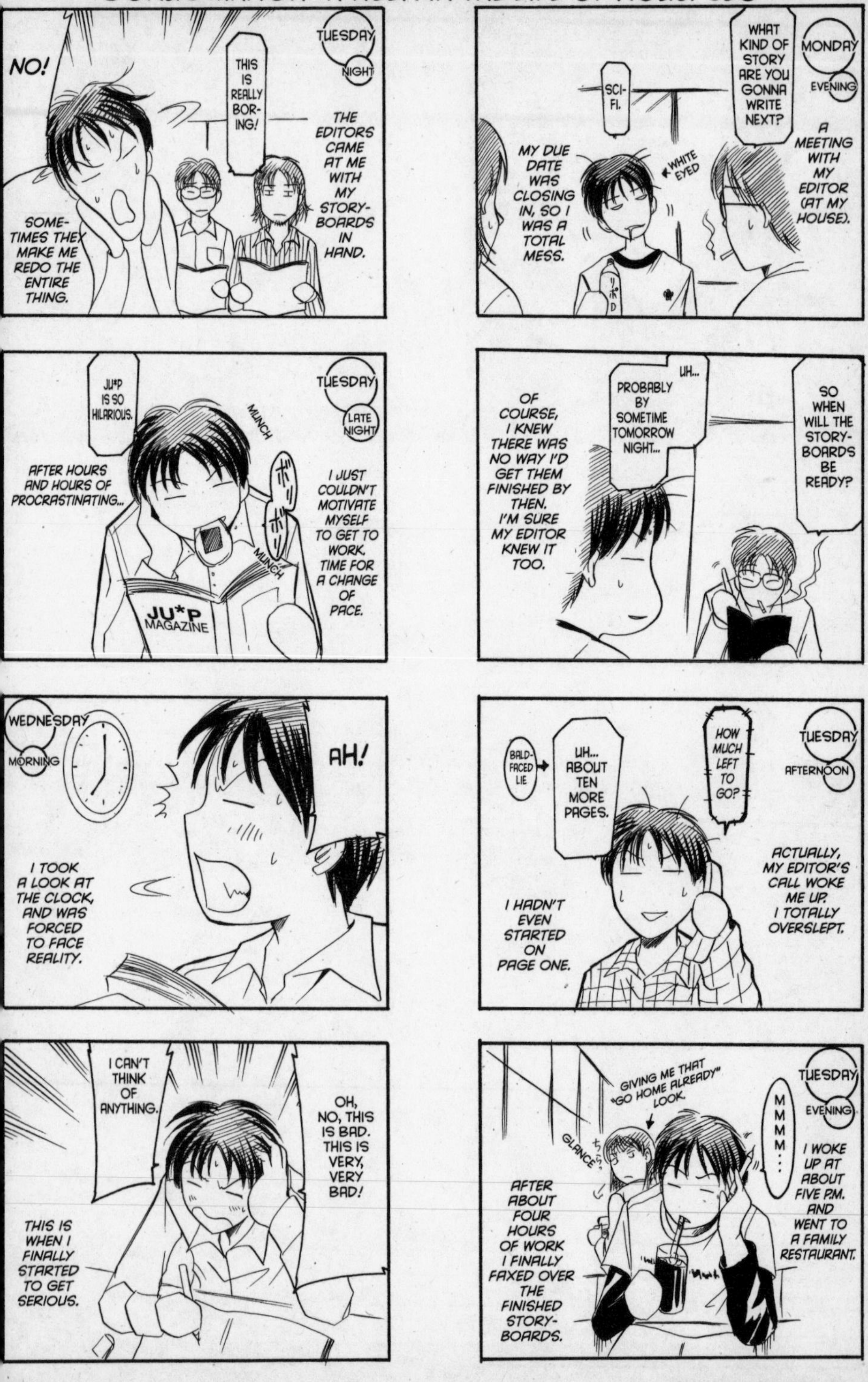
MONDAY
EVENING
A MEETING WITH MY EDITOR (AT MY HOUSE).
WHAT KIND OF STORY ARE YOU GONNA WRITE NEXT?
SCI-FI.
MY DUE DATE WAS CLOSING IN, SO I WAS A TOTAL MESS.
WHITE EYED
SO WHEN WILL THE STORY-BOARDS BE READY?
UH...
PROBABLY BY SOMETIME TOMORROW NIGHT...
OF COURSE, I KNEW THERE WAS NO WAY I'D GET THEM FINISHED BY THEN. I'M SURE MY EDITOR KNEW IT TOO.
TUESDAY
AFTERNOON
ACTUALLY, MY EDITOR'S CALL WOKE ME UP. I TOTALLY OVERSLEPT.
HOW MUCH LEFT TO GO?
UH... ABOUT TEN MORE PAGES.
BALD-FACED LIE
I HADN'T EVEN STARTED ON PAGE ONE.
TUESDAY
EVENING
I WOKE UP AT ABOUT FIVE P.M. AND WENT TO A FAMILY RESTAURANT.
MMMM...
GIVING ME THAT "GO HOME ALREADY" LOOK.
GLANCE
AFTER ABOUT FOUR HOURS OF WORK I FINALLY FAXED OVER THE FINISHED STORY-BOARDS.
TUESDAY
NIGHT
THE EDITORS CAME AT ME WITH MY STORY-BOARDS IN HAND.
THIS IS REALLY BOR-ING!
NO!
SOME-TIMES THEY MAKE ME REDO THE ENTIRE THING.
TUESDAY
LATE NIGHT
I JUST COULDN'T MOTIVATE MYSELF TO GET TO WORK. TIME FOR A CHANGE OF PACE.
MUNCH
JU*P IS SO HILARIOUS.
MUNCH
AFTER HOURS AND HOURS OF PROCRASTINATING...
JU*P MAGAZINE
WEDNESDAY
MORNING
AH!
I TOOK A LOOK AT THE CLOCK, AND WAS FORCED TO FACE REALITY.
OH, NO, THIS IS BAD. THIS IS VERY, VERY BAD!
I CAN'T THINK OF ANYTHING.
THIS IS WHEN I FINALLY STARTED TO GET SERIOUS.

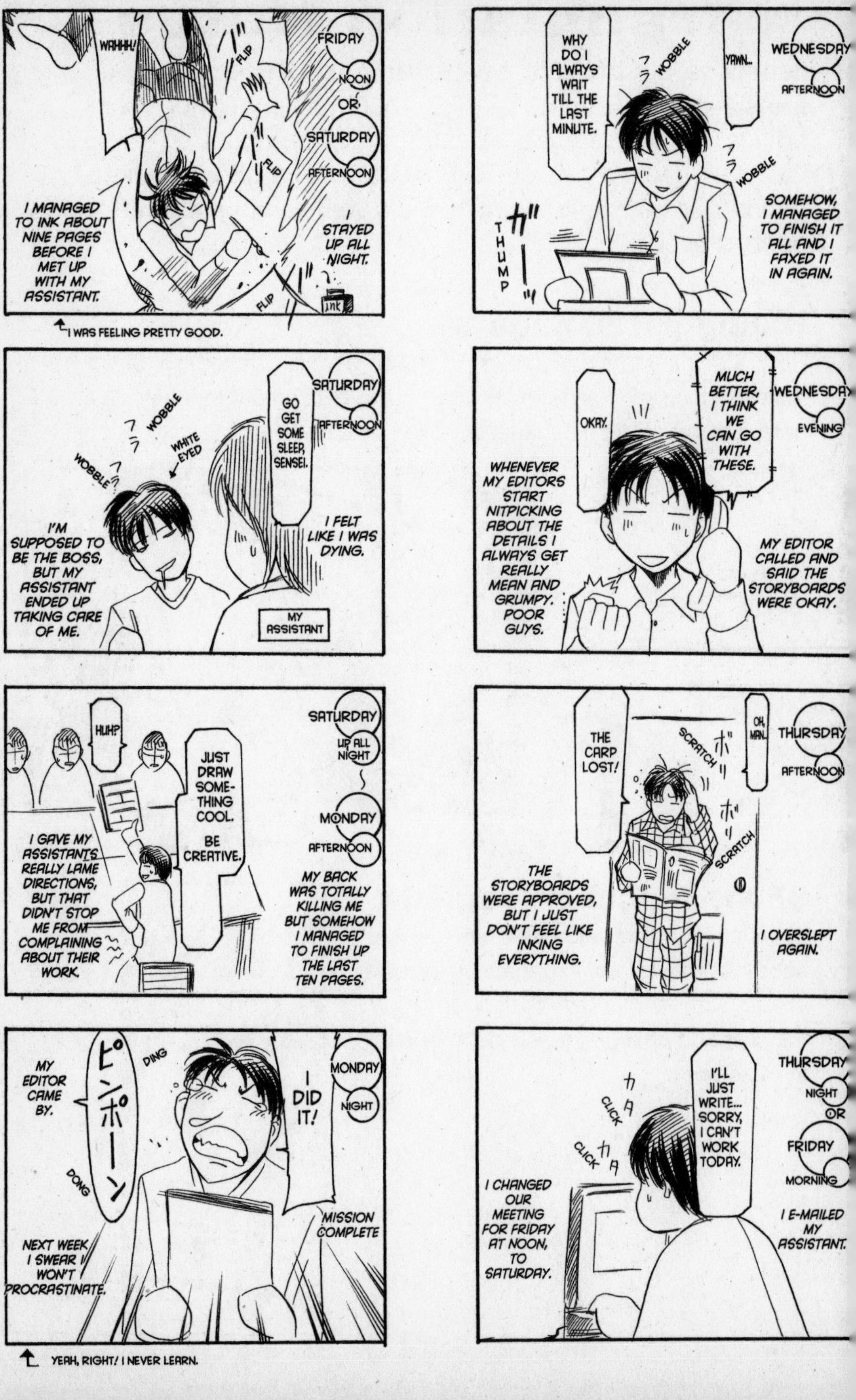
WEDNESDAY
AFTERNOON
YAWN...
SOMEHOW, I MANAGED TO FINISH IT ALL AND I FAXED IT IN AGAIN.
フラ WOBBLE
WHY DO I ALWAYS WAIT TILL THE LAST MINUTE.
フラ WOBBLE
ガー THUMP
WEDNESDAY
EVENING
MUCH BETTER, I THINK WE CAN GO WITH THESE.
MY EDITOR CALLED AND SAID THE STORYBOARDS WERE OKAY.
OKAY.
WHENEVER MY EDITORS START NITPICKING ABOUT THE DETAILS I ALWAYS GET REALLY MEAN AND GRUMPY. POOR GUYS.
THURSDAY
AFTERNOON
OH, MAN.
I OVERSLEPT AGAIN.
ボリ SCRATCH
ボリ SCRATCH
THE CARP LOST!
THE STORYBOARDS WERE APPROVED, BUT I JUST DON'T FEEL LIKE INKING EVERYTHING.
THURSDAY
NIGHT
OR
FRIDAY
MORNING
I E-MAILED MY ASSISTANT.
I'LL JUST WRITE... SORRY, I CAN'T WORK TODAY.
カタ CLICK
カタ CLICK
I CHANGED OUR MEETING FOR FRIDAY AT NOON, TO SATURDAY.
FRIDAY
NOON
OR
SATURDAY
AFTERNOON
I STAYED UP ALL NIGHT.
FLIP
FLIP
WAHHH!
FLIP
I MANAGED TO INK ABOUT NINE PAGES BEFORE I MET UP WITH MY ASSISTANT.
ink
I WAS FEELING PRETTY GOOD.
SATURDAY
AFTERNOON
GO GET SOME SLEEP, SENSEI.
I FELT LIKE I WAS DYING.
MY ASSISTANT
WHITE EYED
フラ WOBBLE
フラ WOBBLE
I'M SUPPOSED TO BE THE BOSS, BUT MY ASSISTANT ENDED UP TAKING CARE OF ME.
SATURDAY
UP ALL NIGHT
MONDAY
AFTERNOON
MY BACK WAS TOTALLY KILLING ME BUT SOMEHOW I MANAGED TO FINISH UP THE LAST TEN PAGES.
JUST DRAW SOMETHING COOL.
BE CREATIVE.
HUH?
I GAVE MY ASSISTANTS REALLY LAME DIRECTIONS, BUT THAT DIDN'T STOP ME FROM COMPLAINING ABOUT THEIR WORK.
MONDAY
NIGHT
I DID IT!
MISSION COMPLETE
ピンポーン
DING
DONG
MY EDITOR CAME BY.
NEXT WEEK I SWEAR I WON'T PROCRASTINATE.
YEAH, RIGHT! I NEVER LEARN.

Translation Notes

Japanese is a tricky language for most Westerners, and translation is often more an art than a science. For your edification and reading pleasure, here are notes on some of the places where we could have gone in a different direction in our translation or where a Japanese cultural reference is used.

Dating party, page 31

Hattori is going to a dating party or *gokon.* This is a Japanese dating ritual in which an even number of guys and girls go out together on a date. It's sort of like a Japanese version of speed dating.

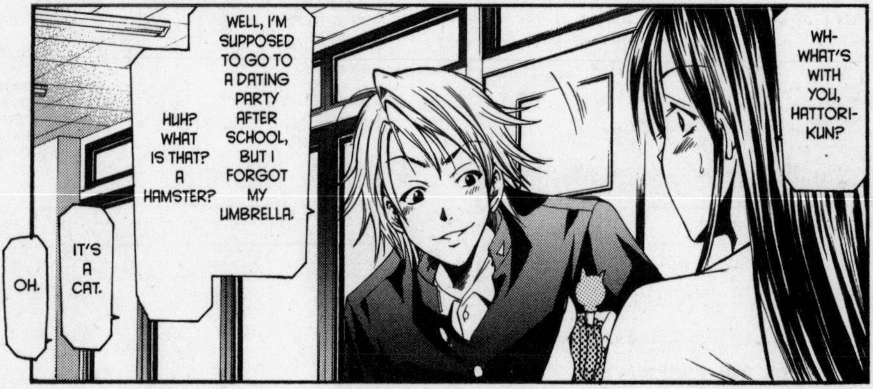
WH-WHAT'S WITH YOU, HATTORI-KUN?
WELL, I'M SUPPOSED TO GO TO A DATING PARTY AFTER SCHOOL, BUT I FORGOT MY UMBRELLA.
HUH? WHAT IS THAT? A HAMSTER?
IT'S A CAT.
OH.

Shoes in locker, page 34

In Japan, people customarily remove their shoes when indoors. In Japanese schools, students generally place their shoes in a locker and change into slippers for use in classrooms.

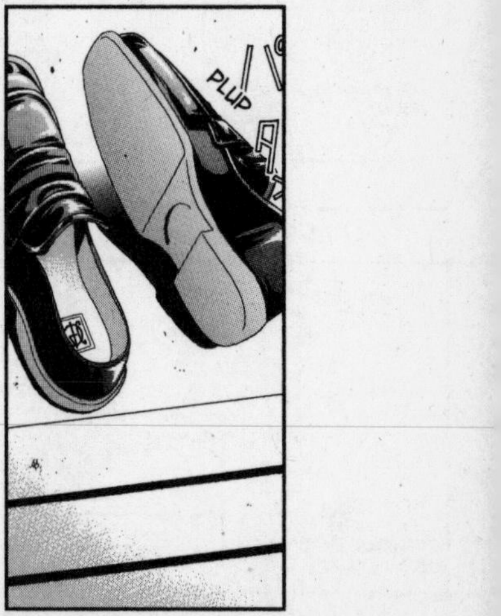
PLUP

Tamagozake, page 57

Tamagozake is a traditional home remedy for colds consisting of raw eggs and sake.

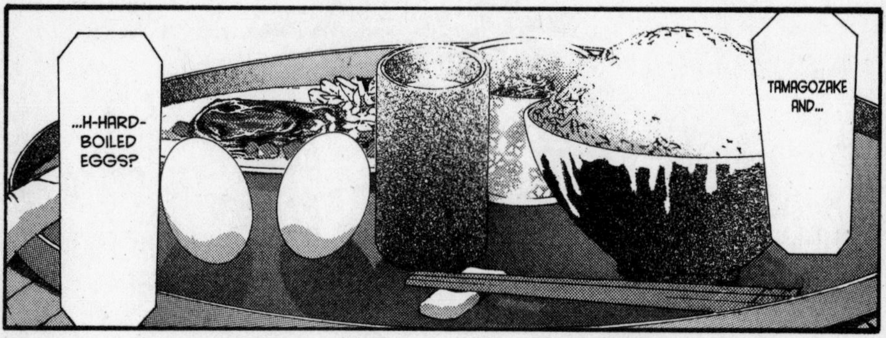
TAMAGOZAKE AND...
...H-HARD-BOILED EGGS?

Exploding hard-boiled eggs, page 61

In *Suzuka,* Volume 1, Asahina made “exploding” hard-boiled eggs and clumpy *tamagozake* for Yamato.

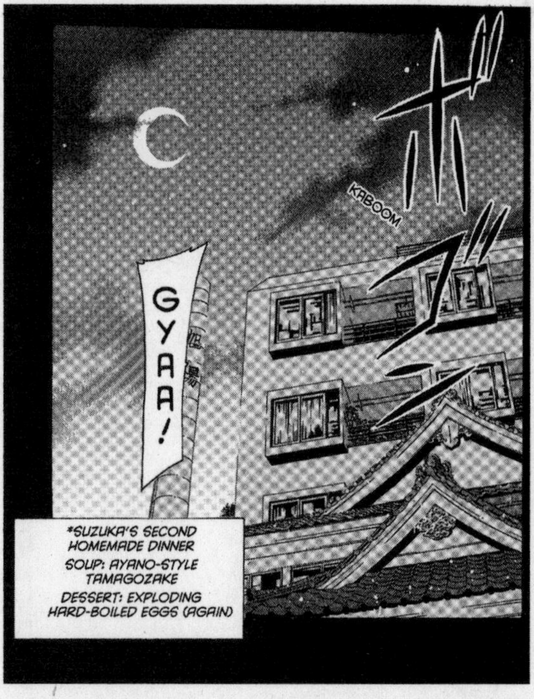
KABOOM
GYAAA!
*SUZUKA'S SECOND HOMEMADE DINNER
SOUP: AYANO-STYLE TAMAGOZAKE
DESSERT: EXPLODING HARD-BOILED EGGS (AGAIN)

The Hiroshima Carp, page 70

The Hiroshima Carp are a Japanese baseball team.

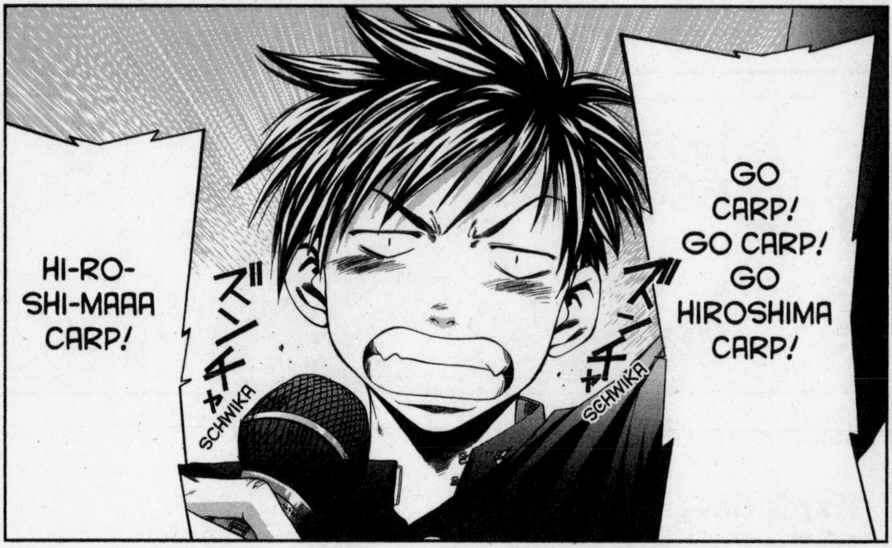
GO CARP! GO CARP! GO HIROSHIMA CARP!
SCHWIKA
HI-RO-SHI-MAAA CARP!
SCHWIKA

Karaoke box, page 70

Yamato and the gang are in a karaoke box. Karaoke boxes are private karaoke rooms rented by the hour. You get your own karaoke machine, and you can order drinks and snacks. This is the most popular type of karaoke in Japan.

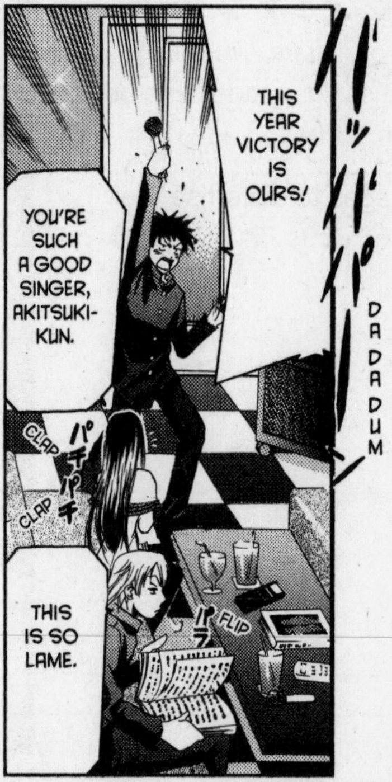
THIS YEAR VICTORY IS OURS!
DA DA DA DUM
YOU'RE SUCH A GOOD SINGER, AKITSUKI-KUN.
CLAP
CLAP
FLIP
THIS IS SO LAME.

Yakisoba and *udon*, page 109

Yakisoba is a popular fried noodle dish. *Udon* is a thicker noodle that's often eaten in soup.

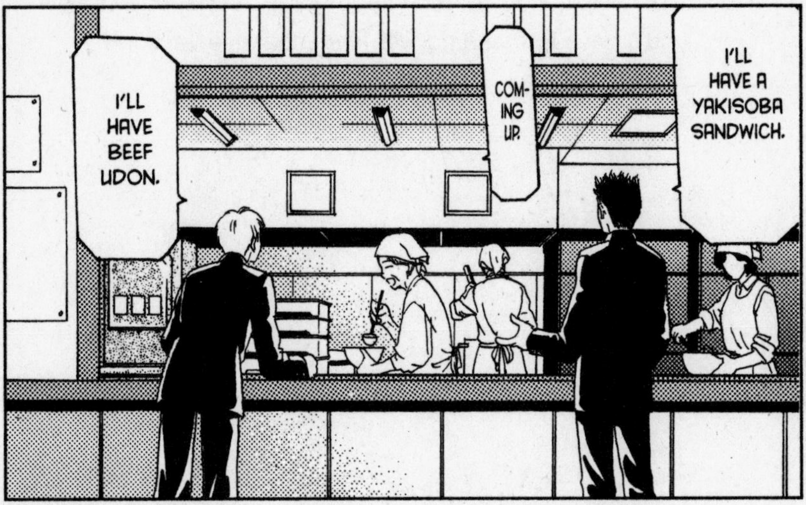
I'LL HAVE A YAKISOBA SANDWICH.
COM-ING UP.
I'LL HAVE BEEF UDON.

Try Aiburu! page 179

Japanese companies often use tissue packages to advertise their services. The fictional company Aiburu is probably a takeoff on the Japanese money-lending company Aifuru.

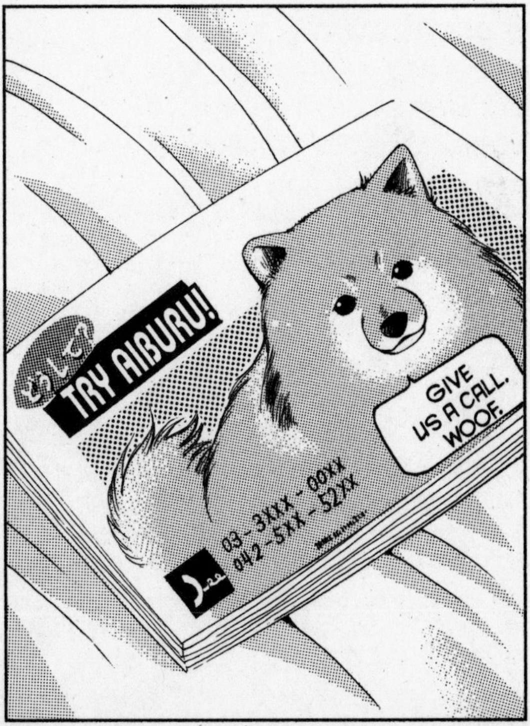
TRY AIBURU!
GIVE US A CALL. WOOF.
03-3XXX-00XX
042-5XX-52XX

Preview of Volume 3

We are pleased to present you with a preview of *Suzuka,* Volume 3.
It will be available in English on February 27, 2007, but for now
you'll have to make do with the Japanese version!

おー
待ってたぞ秋月!!
体力測定の時は
すごかったなー!!

いやーっ!!

ウチの小早川に
勝ったんだって!?

・・・・・

短距離特待生
小早川健二くん

秋月
キミは何の種目を
選ぶつもりだ？

えっと・・・・
一応100mを

うん・・・・
それがいいと思います
キャプテン

彼は短距離選手
向きです

任せてください!!

オレ
頑張ります!!

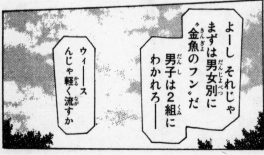

よーし それじゃ
まずは男女別に
男子は2組に
わかれろー

"金魚のフン"だ

ウィース
んじゃ軽く流すか

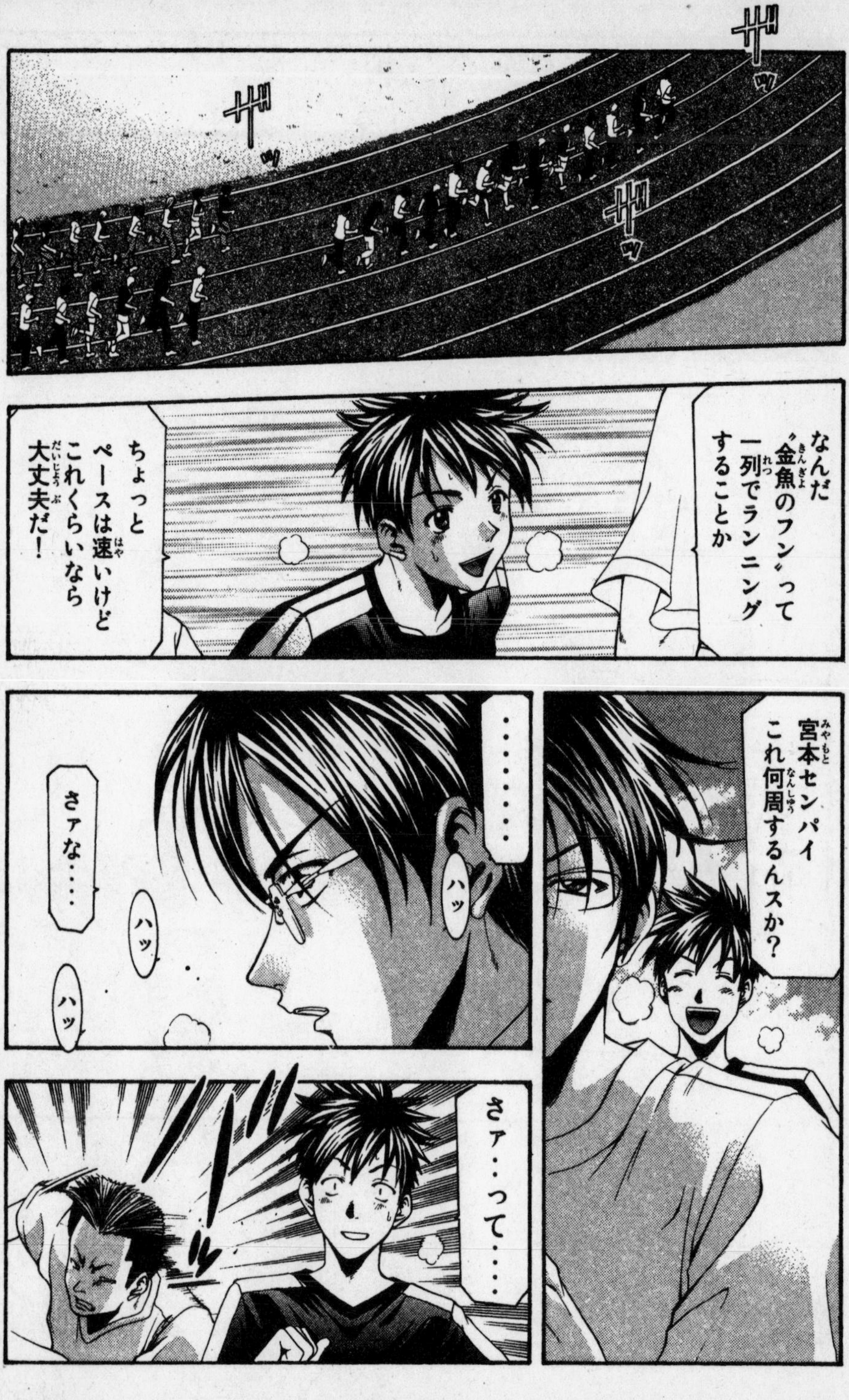
ザッ
ザッ
ザッ
なんだ“金魚のフン”って一列でランニングすることか
ちょっとペースは速いけどこれくらいなら大丈夫だ！
宮本センパイこれ何周するんスか？
………
ハッ
ハッ
ハッ
さァな……
さァ…って……

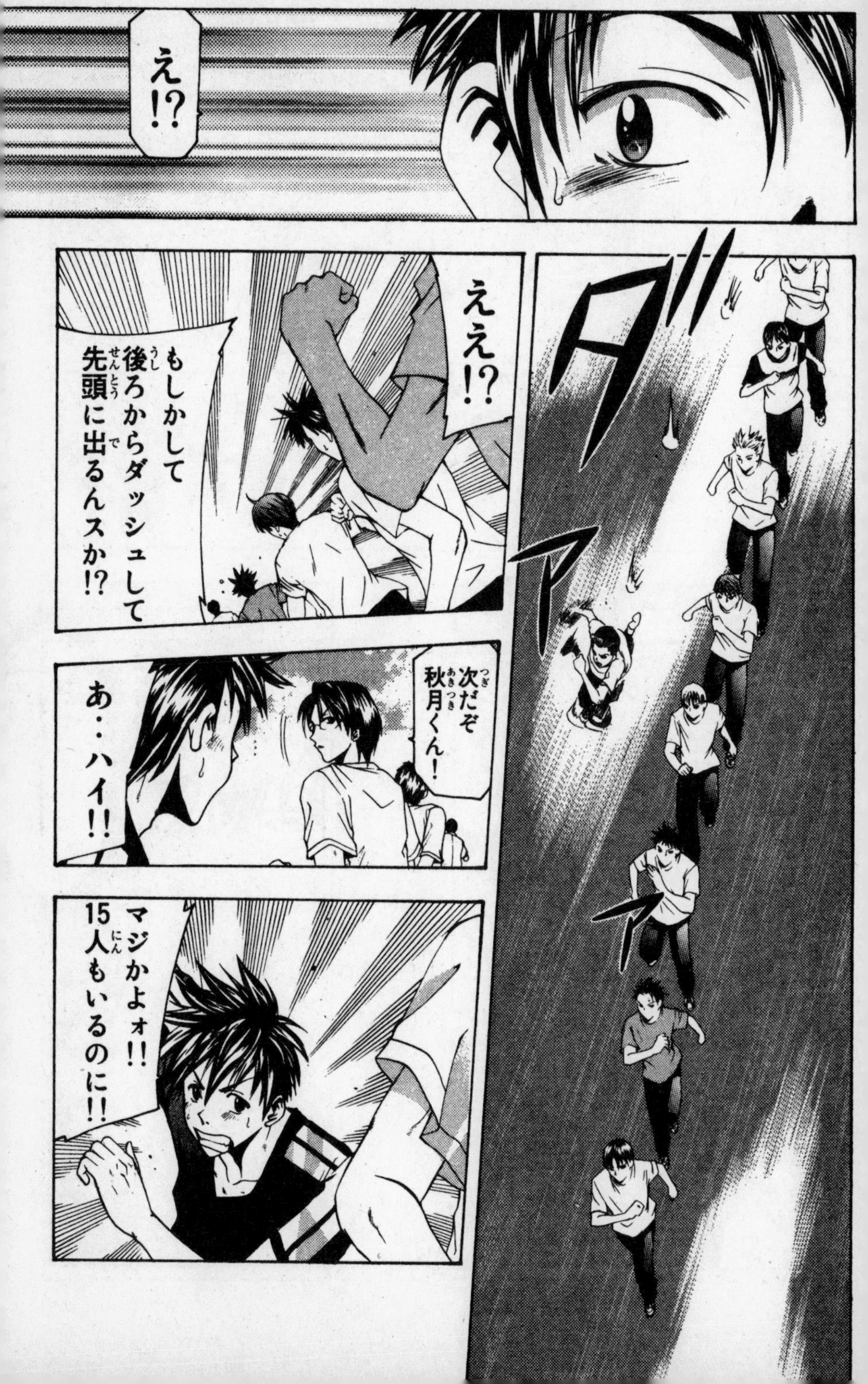
え!?
ダァァ
ええ!?
もしかして後ろからダッシュして先頭に出るんスか!?
次だぞ秋月くん!
あ・・ハイ!!
マジかよォ!!
15人もいるのに!!

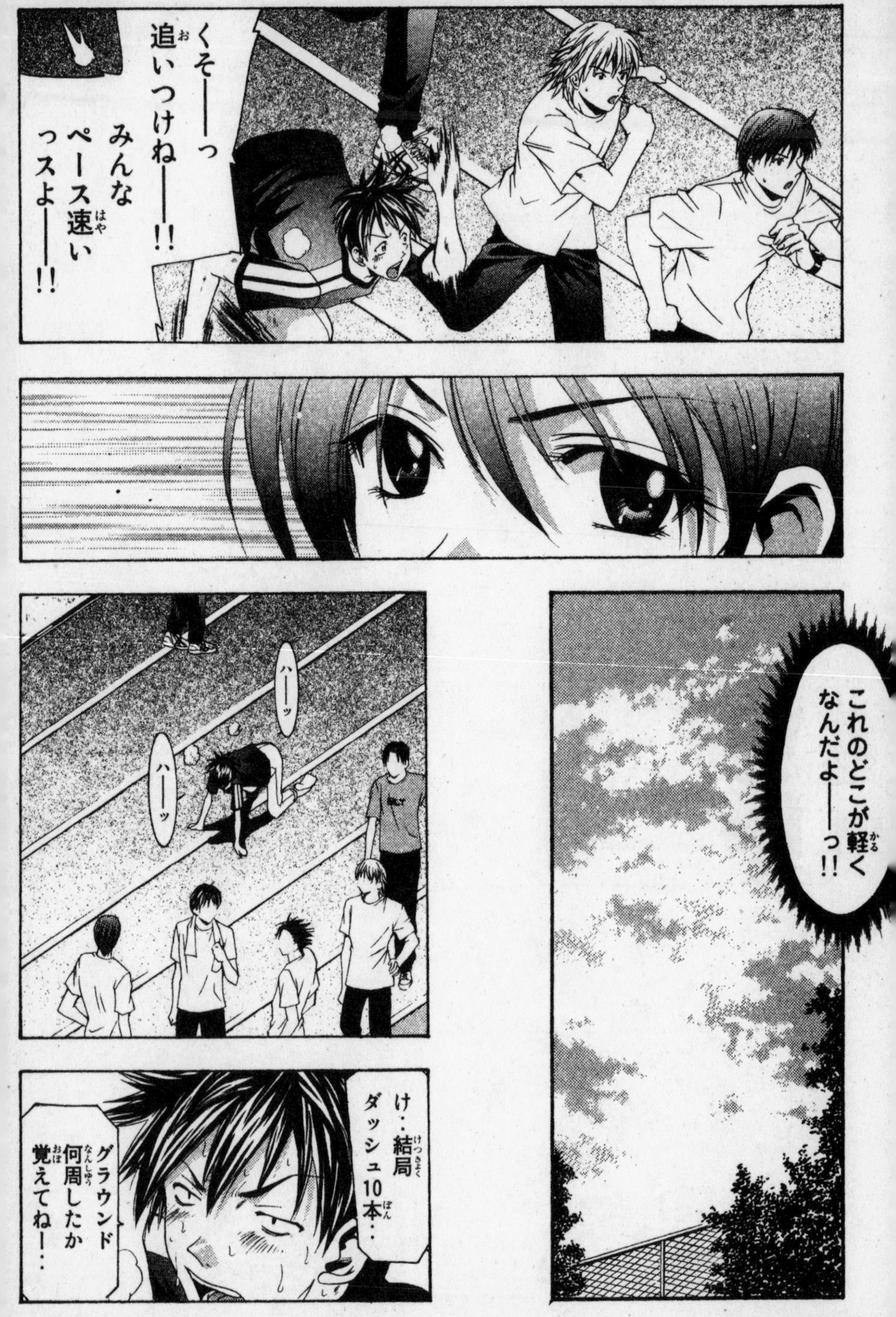
くそ――っ追いつけね――!!
みんなペース速いっスよ――!!
これのどこが軽くなんだよ――っ!!
ハ――ッ
ハ――ッ
け・・結局ダッシュ10本・・
グラウンド何周したか覚えてねー・・

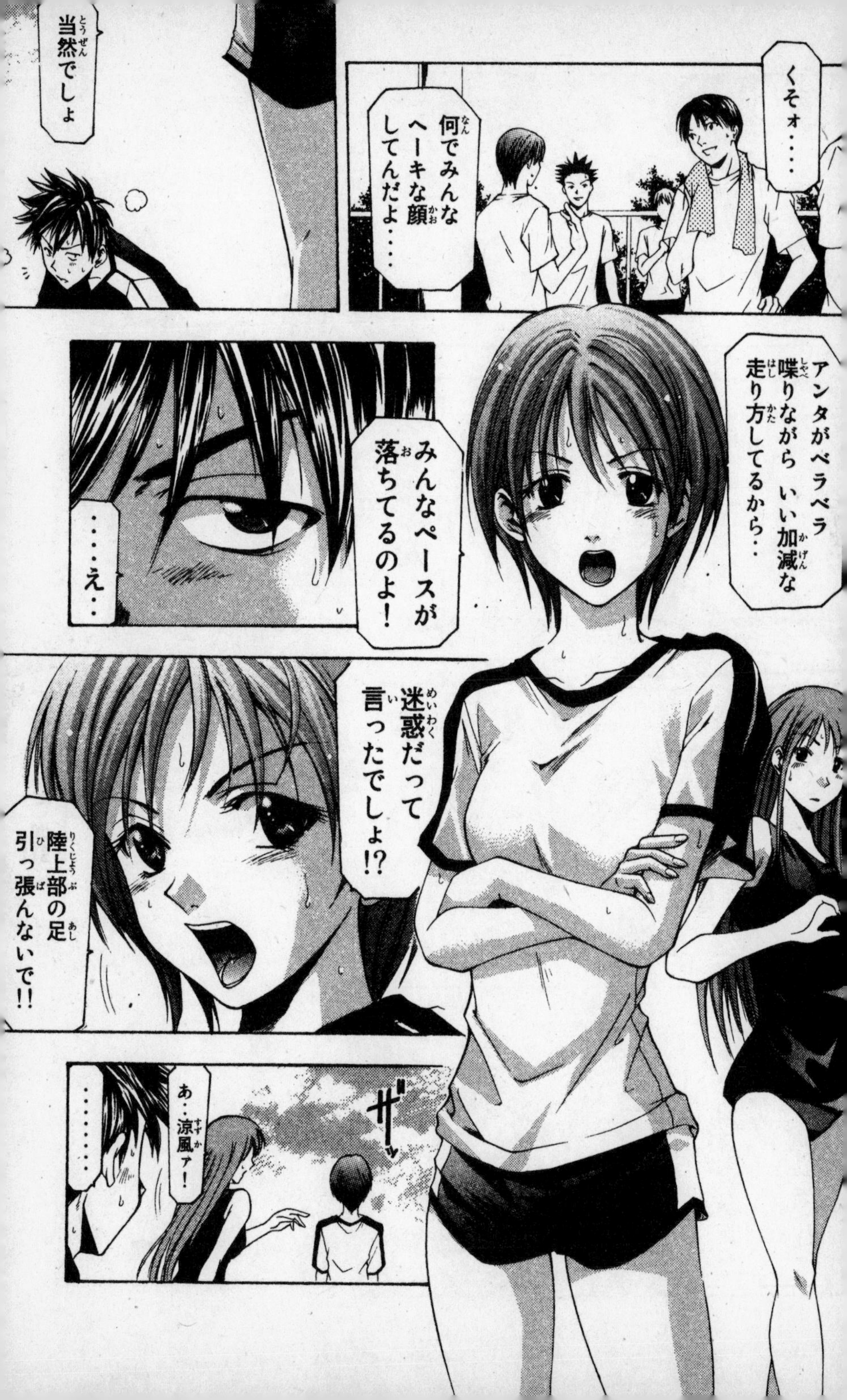
くそォ・・・・
何でみんなヘーキな顔してんだよ・・・・
当然でしょ
アンタがベラベラ喋りながら いい加減な走り方してるから・・
みんなペースが落ちてるのよ！
・・・・え・・
迷惑だって言ったでしょ!?
陸上部の足引っ張んないで!!
ザーッ
あ・・涼風ァ！
・・・・・・・・

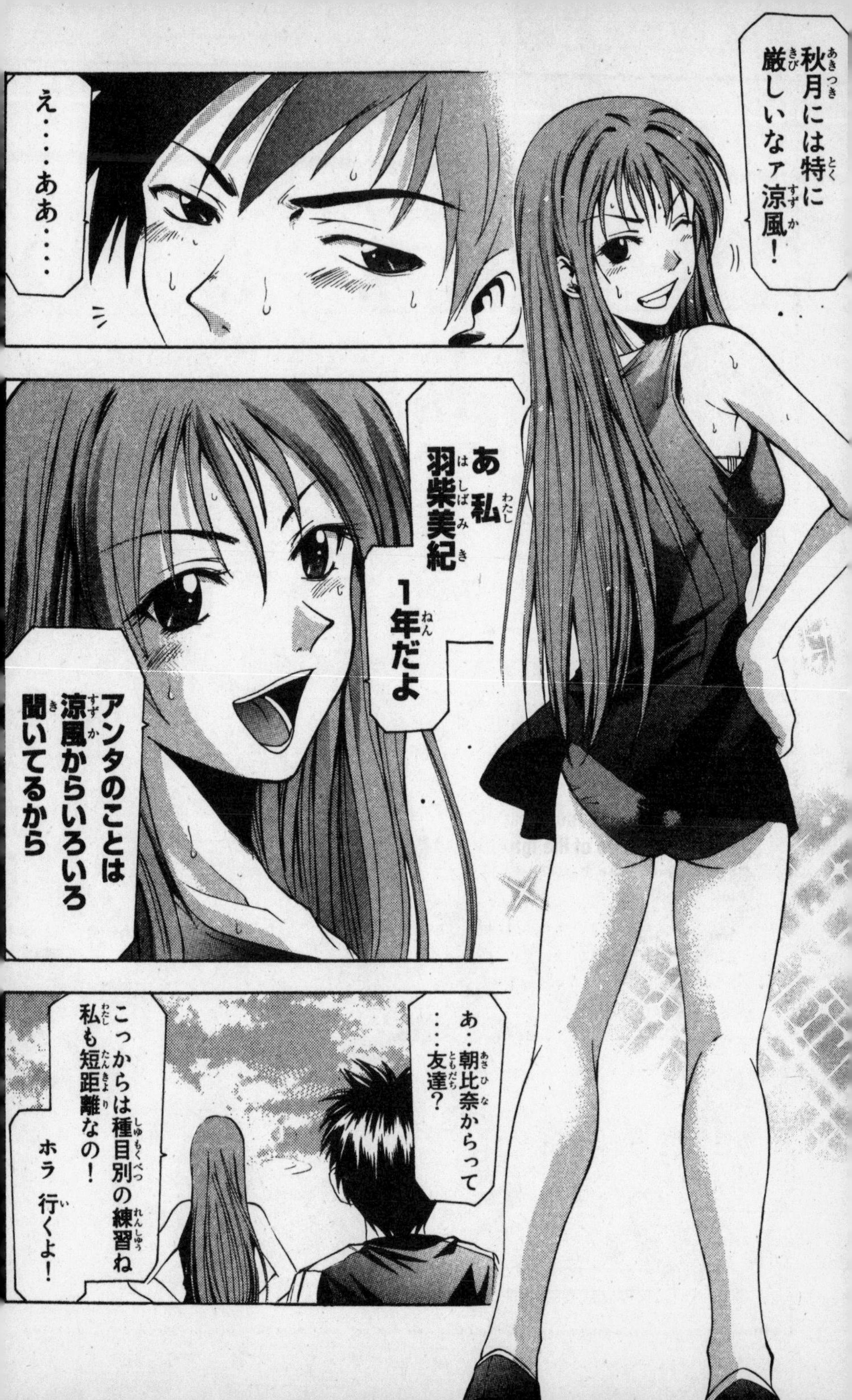
秋月には特に厳しいなァ涼風!
え・・・・ああ・・・・
あ 私 羽柴美紀 1年だよ
アンタのことは涼風からいろいろ聞いてるから
あ・・朝比奈からって・・・・友達?
こっからは種目別の練習ね 私も短距離なの!
ホラ 行くよ!

Basilisk

ORIGINAL STORY BY FŪTARO YAMADA
MANGA BY MASAKI SEGAWA

THE BATTLE BEGINS

The Iga clan and the Kouga clan have been sworn enemies for more than four hundred years. Only the Hanzo Hattori truce has kept the two families from all-out war. Now, under the order of Shogun Ieyasu Tokugawa, the truce has been dissolved. Ten ninja from each clan must fight to the death in order to determine who will be the next Tokugawa Shogun. The surviving clan will rule for the next thousand years.

But not all the clan members are in agreement. Oboro of the Iga clan and Gennosuke of the Kouga clan have fallen deeply in love. Now these star-crossed lovers have been pitted against each other. Can their romance conquer a centuries-old rivalry? Or is their love destined to end in death?

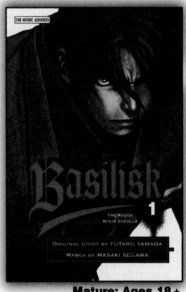

Mature: Ages 18 +

Special extras in each volume! Read them all!

VISIT WWW.DELREYMANGA.COM TO:
• Read sample pages
• View release date calendars for upcoming volumes
• Sign up for Del Rey's free manga e-newsletter
• Find out the latest about new Del Rey Manga series

BY OH!GREAT

Itsuki Minami needs no introduction—everybody's heard of the "Babyface" of the Eastside. He's the strongest kid at Higashi Junior High School, easy on the eyes but dangerously tough when he needs to be. Plus, Itsuki lives with the mysterious and sexy Noyamano sisters. Life's never dull, but it becomes downright dangerous when Itsuki leads his school to victory over vindictive Westside punks with gangster connections. Now he stands to lose his school, his friends, and everything he cares about. But in his darkest hour, the Noyamano girls give him an amazing gift, one that just might help him save his school: a pair of Air Trecks. These high-tech skates are more than just supercool. They'll enable Itsuki to execute the wildest, most aggressive moves ever seen—and introduce him to a thrilling and terrifying new world.

Ages: 16 +

Special extras in each volume! Read them all!

BY JIN KOBAYASHI

SUBTLETY IS FOR WIMPS!

She . . . is a second-year high school student with a single all-consuming question: Will the boy she likes ever really notice her?

He . . . is the school's most notorious juvenile delinquent, and he's suddenly come to a shocking realization: He's got a huge crush, and now he must tell her how he feels.

Life-changing obsessions, colossal foul-ups, grand schemes, deep-seated anxieties, and raging hormones—School Rumble portrays high school as it really is: over-the-top comedy!

Ages: 16 +

Special extras in each volume! Read them all!

BY KEN AKAMATSU

Negi Springfield is a ten-year-old wizard teaching English at an all-girls Japanese school. He dreams of becoming a master wizard like his legendary father, the Thousand Master. At first his biggest concern was concealing his magic powers, because if he's ever caught using them publicly, he thinks he'll be turned into an ermine! But in a world that gets stranger every day, it turns out that the strangest people of all are Negi's students! From a librarian with a magic book to a centuries-old vampire, from a robot to a ninja, Negi will risk his own life to protect the girls in his care!

Ages: 16 +

Special extras in each volume! Read them all!

VISIT WWW.DELREYMANGA.COM TO:
- View release date calendars for upcoming volumes
- Sign up for Del Rey's free manga e-newsletter
- Find out the latest about new Del Rey Manga series

GHOST HUNT

MANGA BY SHIHO INADA
STORY BY FUYUMI ONO

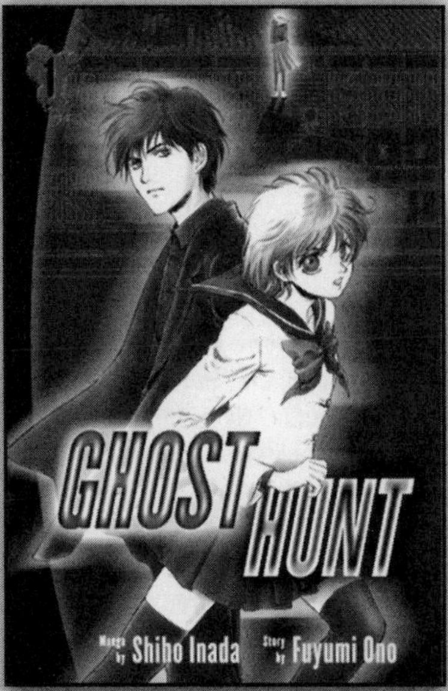
GHOST HUNT
Shiho Inada
Fuyumi Ono

Ages: 13+

The decrepit building was condemned long ago, but every time the owners try to tear it down, "accidents" start to happen—people get hurt, sometimes even killed. Mai Taniyama and her classmates have heard the rumors that the creepy old high school is haunted. So, one rainy day they gather to tell ghost stories, hoping to attract one of the suspected spirits. No ghosts materialize, but they do meet Kazuya Shibuya, the handsome young owner of Shibuya Psychic Research, hired to investigate paranormal activity at the school. Also brought to the scene are an exorcist, a Buddhist monk, a woman who can speak with the dead, and an outspoken Shinto priestess. Surely one of them will have the talents to solve this mystery. . . .

Special extras in each volume! Read them all!

VISIT WWW.DELREYMANGA.COM TO:
- Read sample pages
- View release date calendars for upcoming volumes
- Sign up for Del Rey's free manga e-newsletter
- Find out the latest about new Del Rey Manga series

KURO GANE

BY KEI TOUME

AN EERIE, HAUNTING SAMURAI ADVENTURE

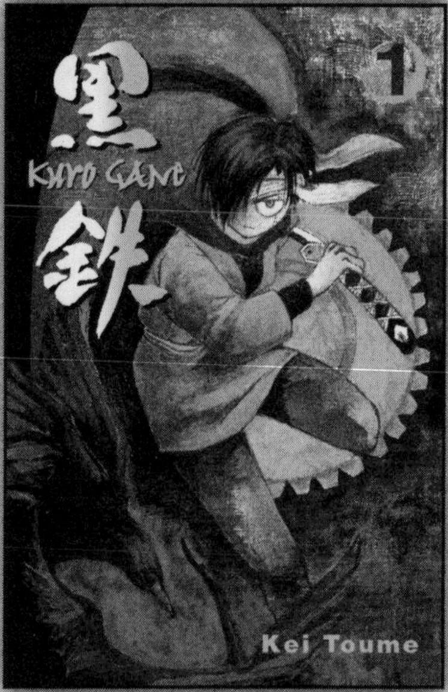
1
黒
KURO GANE
鉄
Kei Toume

Teen: Ages 13+

Avenging his father's murder is a matter of honor for the young samurai Jintetsu. But it turns out that the killer is a corrupt government official—and now the powers that be are determined to hunt Jintetsu down. There's only one problem: Jintetsu is already dead.

Torn to pieces by a pack of dogs, Jintetsu's ravaged body has been found by Genkichi, outcast and master inventor. Genkichi gives the dead boy a new, indestructible steel body and a talking sword—just what he'll need to face down the gang that's terrorizing his hometown and the mobster who ordered his father's hit. But what about Otsuki, the beautiful girl he left behind? Steel armor is defense against any sword, but it can't save Jintetsu from the pain in his heart.

Special extras in each volume! Read them all!

DEL REY

VISIT WWW.DELREYMANGA.COM TO:

- Read sample pages
- View release date calendars for upcoming volumes
- Sign up for Del Rey's free manga e-newsletter
- Find out the latest about new Del Rey Manga series

TOMARE!
[STOP!]

You are going the wrong way!

Manga is a completely different
type of reading experience.

To start at the *beginning,* go to the *end!*

That's right! Authentic manga is read the traditional Japanese
way—from right to left. Exactly the *opposite* of how American
books are read. It's easy to follow: Just go to the other end of
the book, and read each page—and each panel—from right side
to left side, starting at the top right. Now you're experiencing
manga as it was meant to be.